Michigan's
TOPFishing
Maps

Frank Amato
Publications

Michigan's

TOP Fishing
Maps

Keweenaw
(Isle Royale)

LAKE
SUPERIOR

UPPER   PENINSULA

LAKE
HURON

LAKE
MICHIGAN

NORTHERN
LOWER
PENINSULA

SOUTHERN
LOWER
PENINSULA

LAKE
ERIE

WARNING!
IMPORTANT NOTICES

Boating: This book is not meant for navigational purposes. Extreme caution is advised at all times, as is the use of Coast Guard-approved personal floatation devices (pfds).
Fishing Regulations: Fishing regulations often change. Check the Michigan Sport-Fishing Regulations before each season, and before fishing a new piece of water.

Frank Amato
Publications

FRANK AMATO PUBLICATIONS, INC.

All inquiries should be addressed to:

PO Box 82112 • Portland, Oregon 97282 • 503.653.8108 • www.amatobooks.com

Author: Chuck Lichon • **Book Design & Map Illustrations:** Esther Appel Design, 503-641-8079
Photography: Chuck Lichon, unless otherwise noted

ISBN-13: 978-1-57188-496-1 • ISBN-10: 1-57188-496-3 • UPC: 0-81127-00342-6
Printed in China

About the Author

Chuck Lichon has spent his entire life in Michigan, and currently resides along the cattail-lined shores of renowned hunter and angler paradise, Saginaw Bay. He began his writing career over 30 years ago starting as an outdoor columnist for the *Saginaw News*, thanks to well-known Michigan-based outdoor writer, Steve Smith. From there, Chuck started writing regularly for *Michigan Sportsman* magazine, and within a year he became Boats & Blinds Columnist for the first issue of nationally acclaimed *Wildfowl* magazine, which he continued doing for 20 consecutive years. He has also written articles on a variety of topics for numerous other well-known state, regional, and national outdoor publications.

Chuck has authored and self-published a book entitled *Waterfowling Boats, Blinds, & Related Gear*. His website is chucklichon.com. He has two children — Michelle and Jeff — both of Michigan.

This photo was taken on the famed Two Hearted River in Michigan's Upper Peninsula in early October 2012 where the author fished one of the most beautiful stretches of the river.

Introduction

Welcome to the newest Michigan fishing map book. This extensive book provides brief summaries of some of the most popular inland lakes, rivers, and various Great Lakes areas in the state. Updated information has been provided via many discussions with district fish biologists, bait & tackle shops, guides, and a lot of old-timers who know every rock and drop-off in the particular body of water that they frequent.

When it comes to fishing in Michigan, you could write a series of books. With over 11,000 lakes, 36,000 miles of streams and rivers, and hundreds of miles of Great Lakes shoreline, it is difficult at best choosing a handful of inland lakes and rivers to write about. But in reality, it is a good problem to have. We are truly blessed in Michigan having these resources available to us.

More than 20 percent of the world's fresh water supply flows through Michigan and there is no geographical point in the state that is more than six miles from a stream, river or lake. Forty-three percent of the Great Lakes are within Michigan's borders, making up approximately 8.3 percent of the world's fresh water.

Lake environments change, and fish populations change as well, due to a number of often uncontrollable circumstances. The author has made every effort to locate the most credible source of information so you, the reader, will have a grasp of the "who, what, when, why, and how" to fish each of these bodies of water. If I did not have the personal insight on a particular lake or river, I found those that did. I have fished Michigan waters all my life, but no one person can be an expert on all Michigan has to offer relative to fishing opportunities.

In essence, I did all the calling, talking, research and writing, so all you have to do is read it and head out fishing. It's all here in one neat package to get you going quickly with the insight to start fishing, without all the time-consuming "Joe and Me" stories. I added some historical bits of information I felt were of interest, and even some "fish biology" to help you understand the reasons for some of the changes in a particular body of water, whether they be beneficial or not. Many lakes have changed in a number of ways over the past 5-10 years, and some will continue to change as biologists work to improve our overall state fisheries.

The all-important maps can be used to give you a visual overview of the lake, boat landings, and locations where the best fishing can be found, depending on species, and contours on inland lakes.

Each description should place you in the ballpark of various species of fish, and allow you less time searching the prime areas. Remember, however, that even with the best available information, you always need to try different fishing methods and lure selection based on your success, or lack of, on any given day. As we all know, fish can be finicky and we need to adjust accordingly.

Every effort was made to search out and include local contact information on the Great Lakes, including bait & tackle shops, and contact information at or near the mapped locations in this book. I apologize to anyone I may have inadvertently missed.

Efforts were also made to add any special lures or baits used on a particular water, but often it is best to check with local bait and tackle shops for updated information. When no mention is made of lures/bait, generally the standard ones will work on that particular body of water.

I need to thank all the State of Michigan fish biologists that I communicated with many times in order to obtain much of the information included in this book, and for their unending dedication to the health of our valuable state fishing resource. They were all very willing, and frankly excited, to get the message out about the lakes, rivers, and Great Lakes waters in their "districts." I also need to thank the almost countless bait & tackle shops, convention & visitors bureaus, Chambers of Commerce, fishing guides, charter boat captains and all the knowledgeable anglers that assisted me with this publication.

A special thanks to DNR Photographer Dave Kenyon and many others for added photo support. The only charter captains and guides I included were the ones I had discussions with. It would be nearly impossible to include all of them. There are sites that list our qualified charter captains and fishing guides on the Internet, or via the area convention & visitors bureaus.

I hope you enjoy the content of this book, and as always, Keep a Tight Line!

Chuck Lichon
Linwood, MI

Michigan Sportfish

Pictured here are some of Michigan's more common gamefish species. Although not comprehensive of all our game fish, the chart will provide you with some identification of most species caught. For more information on our game fish, go to the Michigan DNR website: **www.michigan.gov/dnr**

Know Your Fish

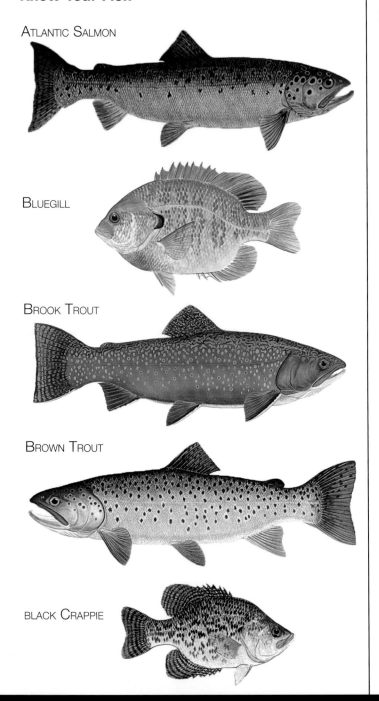

ATLANTIC SALMON

BLUEGILL

BROOK TROUT

BROWN TROUT

BLACK CRAPPIE

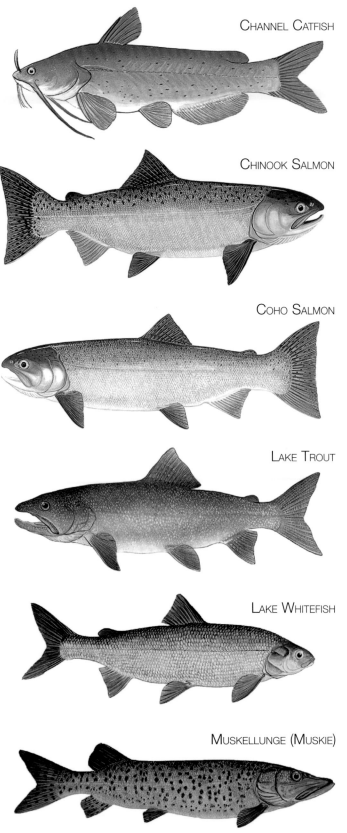

CHANNEL CATFISH

CHINOOK SALMON

COHO SALMON

LAKE TROUT

LAKE WHITEFISH

MUSKELLUNGE (MUSKIE)

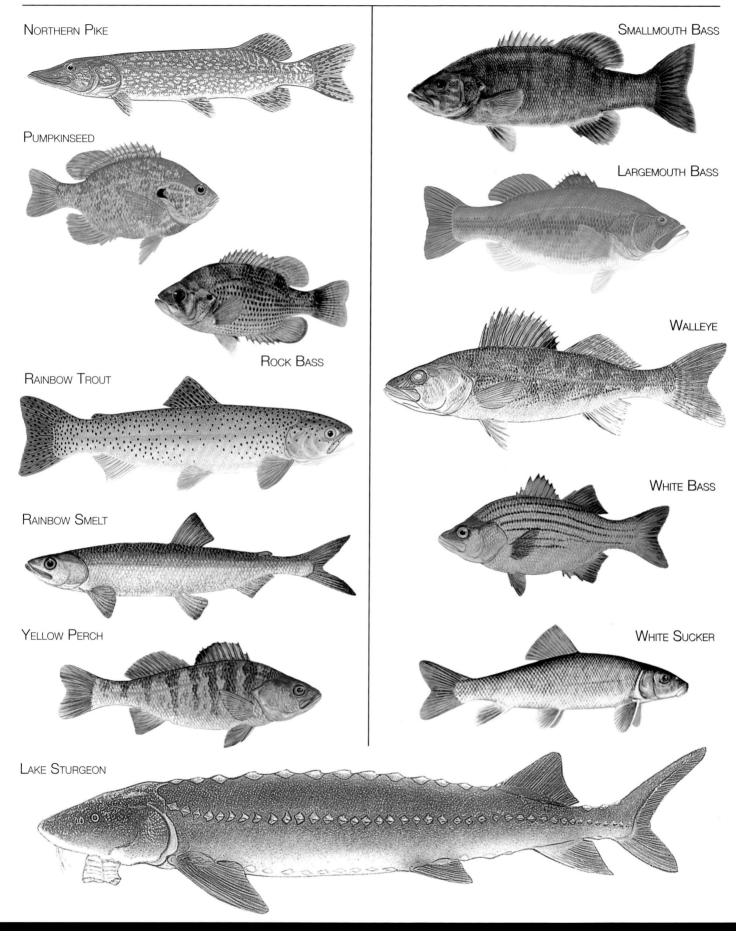

NORTHERN PIKE

PUMPKINSEED

ROCK BASS

RAINBOW TROUT

RAINBOW SMELT

YELLOW PERCH

LAKE STURGEON

SMALLMOUTH BASS

LARGEMOUTH BASS

WALLEYE

WHITE BASS

WHITE SUCKER

UPPER

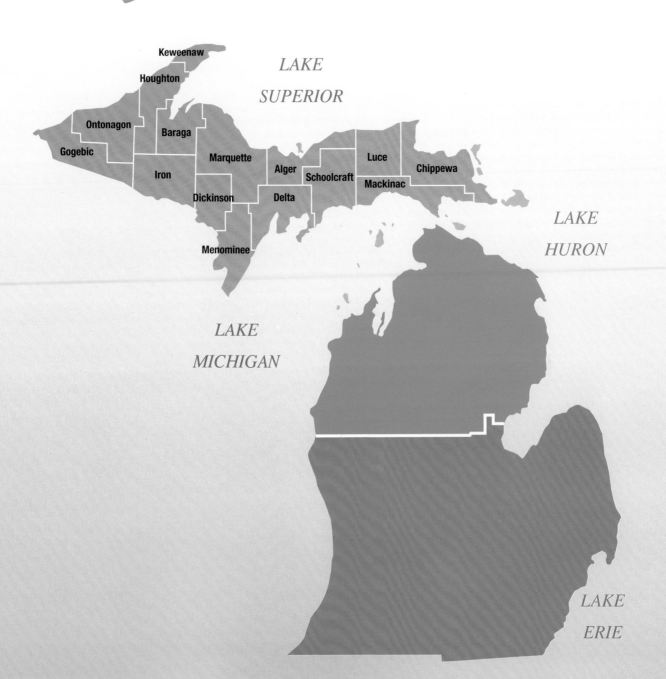

Keweenaw
(Isle Royale)

Keweenaw

Houghton

LAKE

SUPERIOR

Ontonagon

Baraga

Gogebic

Marquette

Luce

Iron

Alger

Chippewa

Schoolcraft

Dickinson

Delta

Mackinac

LAKE

HURON

Menominee

LAKE

MICHIGAN

LAKE

ERIE

PENINSULA

Beaver Lake Alger County

Sometimes, some anglers would just like to not only go fishing, but fish a lake that is unpopulated, and makes you feel like you are in the middle of a northern Canadian Province. As our population expands, such lakes become more rare, and, aside from the fly-in trips, or few mountain lakes out West, it is becoming difficult to find one that meets this definition.

Beaver Lake however is such a lake, and frankly, although a bit of a drive from the lower part of the state, it's doable.

Beaver is located in Alger County, in Michigan's Upper Peninsula, between Grand Marias and Munising, only a short walk from Lake Superior. No homes, no motors allowed (except electric), and a decent fishing lake. Don't look for Master Angler sized fish, but you can catch a meal to cook at the area campground.

As part of the Pictured Rocks National Park system, there are certain federal regulations that pertain to bodies of water that are within the

federal parks system. One, as mentioned above, is no motors allowed. A second, is that snowmobiles are not allowed on all areas, so always check with the local park office for updated information.

As for ice fishing this lake, it would be difficult at best since trekking in during the brutal winter months is not an easy task, and could even be dangerous if you are inexperienced. The other issue is that, as mentioned above, fish in this lake are far from world class, and you can do much better on easier, more accessible lakes.

But summer fishing is a different story.

Immediately adjacent Beaver Lake is Little Beaver Lake, a mere pond in the woods, that has a small campground. It is located 3 miles north of Alger County Road H-58 and 20 miles northeast of Munising. Little Beaver Lake Campground has 8 campsites with one campsite being disabled accessible. A small boat ramp is available here for launching boats.

Little Beaver also features the White Pine Trail, a 1.0-mile self-guiding

Kids love to fish, and the best way to get them involved in such a great outdoor activity is to start them young.

DNR Photo, David Kenyon

interpretive trail. A 1.5-mile trail leads to Lake Superior and connects with the North Country National Scenic Trail.

Single-unit vehicles in excess of 36 feet and vehicle/trailer combined units in excess of 42 feet are prohibited at Little Beaver because of the small campsites and narrow, twisting, hilly access road.

So back to fishing.

Walleye: According to Steve Scott, area fish biologist with the DNR, a natural population of walleye exists in Beaver, but there are not many and not sizable. A 24-inch walleye would be a rarity here. Anglers who do fish this lake in the summer months mostly target walleye. As for where to fish, it's a hit and miss proposition. Take your electronics along to locate drop-offs and any weed beds, although there is a very short growing season and weedbeds are few at best.

Bass: There are some smallmouth bass, upwards of 16 inches, yellow perch in the 7-9-inch range at best, and some pike, which may be the best bet on Beaver. Pike have been known to be in the 30-plus range, and the last DNR survey found that over 50% of the fish caught there were over the legal limit size.

At over a mile and a half long and three quarter mile wide this lake (765 acres) is only about 35 feet deep in the center, and drops off quickly in 5-10-foot increments from the shoreline out to the center.

With an electric motor at best, be aware of weather and wind storms that can cause problems if you get caught on this lake without the proper sized boat or lack of sufficient power to get you back to safe land.

You are basically on your own on this lake, and will need to do some decisive moves should the winds pick up.

If you want to get away, enjoy some camping in a frankly beautiful area of the upper peninsula, and catch and eat fresh fish on an open fire, maybe this lake is for you. But do your homework, bring water and storm safety gear, and enjoy.

At a Glance

What: Fishing on an unpopulated lake in Michigan's Upper Peninsula

Where: Northeast of Munising in Alger County only a short walk from Lake Superior

Why: Enjoy the serenity of a lake without homes lining the shoreline

Information/Guides: Munising Visitors Bureau, P.O. Box 421, Munising 49862, www.munising.org; **Alger County Chamber of Commerce**, (906) 387-2138

Landings: One small landing for small boats on the southwest side of connecting Little Beaver Lake just west of Beaver

Bait & Tackle: Madigan Ace Hardware, 202 Elm Avenue, Munising (906) 387-2033

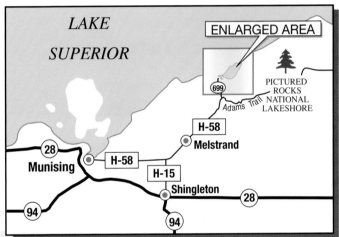

Beaver Lake

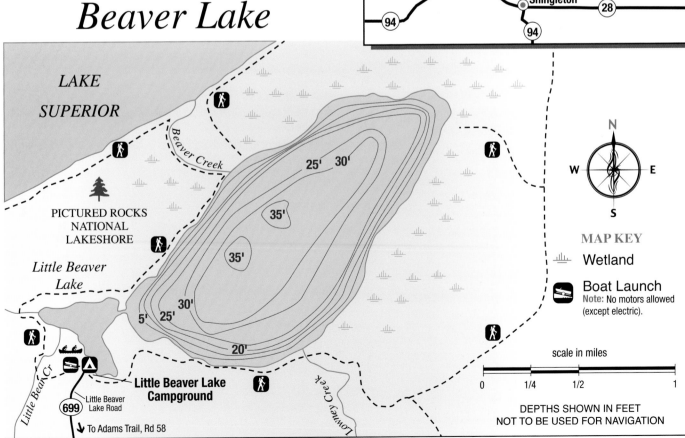

Big Manistique Lake
Mackinac County

Big Manistique Lake, with its over 10,000-acre size, ranks as one of Michigan's larger lakes. However its shallow depth (average 20') supports nice populations of pike, walleye, perch, bass, and a few muskie. Manistique is located in a very nice area of Michigan's Upper Peninsula, with Curtis being the nearest town. The length of this lake is approximately 6.5 miles long with a maximum width of just over 5 miles. The bottom of this lake is mostly sandy, with many flat rocks and some pulpy peat.

Curtis is surrounded by the largest lake complex in the Upper Peninsula! Visitors enjoy a variety of year-round recreational opportunities, great accommodations, water-filled activities, and plenty of wildlife to observe and photograph. Not to sound like a tourism board member, but this area offers a variety of activities, including of course fishing, but also hunting, mushrooming, canoeing, kayaking, boating, sailing, swimming, jet skiing, and ATV & ORV.

Game fish include walleyes, northern pike, rock bass, ciscoes, bluegills, sunfish, largemouth bass, few brook trout and smallmouth bass with a light population of sturgeon.

The few times I fished this lake, I often managed to hook many very nice pike over the sunken-island areas located in the area of Potter and Long Islands. However, according to Nick Petrie of JRs Sport Shop in the town of Curtis, pike are plentiful in many areas around the lake.

Pike:
Pike in the Big M used to be fairly common in the 40-plus size, but even though you can catch these monsters in that range, more of them run between 20-40-inch according to Petrie, with many 30-plus-inch size still common.

Try Cooks Bay at the southwest end of the lake where a convenient boat launch is located. Another place to try for pike is Portage Creek at the southeast end of the lake. Helmer Bay to the northeast, is shallow and weedy, ideal pike habitat. There are also two creeks that flow into this area.

Many anglers spear pike at the west end of the lake where the Manistique River empties into the lake. This is also a good area of ice fishing for perch. You would do well to also try the areas between the three islands on the west side of the lake. There exists a five-foot sunken island between these islands that can also be productive for pike and perch.

Muskie:
As for muskie, according to reports, there are not as many in the lake as there once was, however you can still hook a sizable one, often while fishing for pike, in some of the areas mentioned above.

Walleye:
Helmer Bay and Cooks Bay are good for walleye, especially in the fall according to Petrie. So are the islands productive for walleye and perch. Perch generally run 8-12 inches in the 12-18-foot water around the islands.

There are a few sandbars, Anderson and Home bars, on the east side of the lake by Burnt Island, that produce nice catches of walleye in the 16-18" size; not huge, but great eaters. Some six-plus-pounders are caught through the ice every winter.

Perch rig setup is a fairly simple process. Use a slip-bobber to locate a minnow a foot to a foot-and-a-half off bottom for the perch. Walleyes are taken with the same rig, in addition to using tip-ups and jigging.

A note of caution:
Be careful when boating around Burnt Island to the SE. As the story goes, a guy tried to build a road from the mainland to the island quite some time ago, never finishing it, but created a very shallow area for boat motors to get hung up. Travel around the west end of the island to be safe.

Some notes of interest regarding Big Manistique Lake:

• Big Manistique Lake is fed by Helmer Creek on the north and Portage Creek on the south.

• Portage Creek flows from South Manistique Lake into Big Manistique Lake and contains a small control structure designed to elevate the South Manistique Lake water level for summer recreation.

• The Portage Creek Dam allows fish passage in both directions during most flows. Helmer Creek, a designated trout stream, is the outlet of North Manistique Lake, and also has a lake-level control structure (Tressler Dam). Tressler Dam allows downstream fish passage, but upstream fish passage is likely difficult for many species due to the shallow depth below the dam. A dam on Black Creek is owned by MDNR Wildlife Division and creates the Black Creek Flooding.

• The Manistique River is an outlet on the west side of Big Manistique Lake and drains to Lake Michigan. The Manistique Lake Dam is approximately four miles downstream of the lake, and immediately downstream of the confluence with the Fox River. The dam blocks upstream fish passage to Big Manistique Lake through the Manistique River, though fish can move between Fox River and Big Manistique Lake.

• The shoreline of Big Manistique Lake is largely developed with private and

At a Glance

What: Pike fishing on the Big Manistique

Where: Mackinac County, Curtis, MI

Why: Catch some very sizeable pike, and other species as well

Techniques: Slip-bobbers to locate minnows a foot to a foot-and-a-half off bottom for the perch and walleye

Launch: East side off H-33, on the north side off CR-98, on the southwest corner off Curtis Road or H-42. You can get on the ice on the east side off H-33, on the north side off CR-98, on the southwest corner off Curtis Road or H-42, and in Cooks Bay

Information: Curtis Michigan Chamber of Commerce, P.O. Box 477, Curtis 49820, (906) 586-3700 www.curtismi.com

Bait & Tackle: Helmer Grocery & Bait Shop, 2936 County Road 377, McMillan, (crawlers only during the summer), 906-586-6353; **JR's Sport Shop**, Main Street on top of the hill, Curtis, (906) 586-6040 (Very good resource for fishing this lake); **Fish & Hunt Shop**, 17148 Main, Curtis, (906) 586-9531, Toll Free: (877) 586-9531

commercial residences; the only public frontage can be found at the four boat access sites.

• Fish stocking in Big Manistique Lake has involved a variety of species, ages, and sizes dating to 1935. Walleye fry were stocked in 1935, and stocking of this species did not resume until 1970, when either fry or fingerlings were annually stocked through 1980. Stocking ceased until recently, when both walleye fry and fall fingerlings were stocked in 2005. Lake sturgeon were stocked in Big Manistique Lake in 1983, 1984, 1988, 1990, and 1993, and smallmouth bass were stocked in 1998.

• There have been three State of Michigan Master Angler award fish taken from Big Manistique Lake during 1994–2005, including northern pike, rock bass, and smallmouth bass.

Pike are popular with anglers in this sizable U.P. lake.

Big Manistique Lake

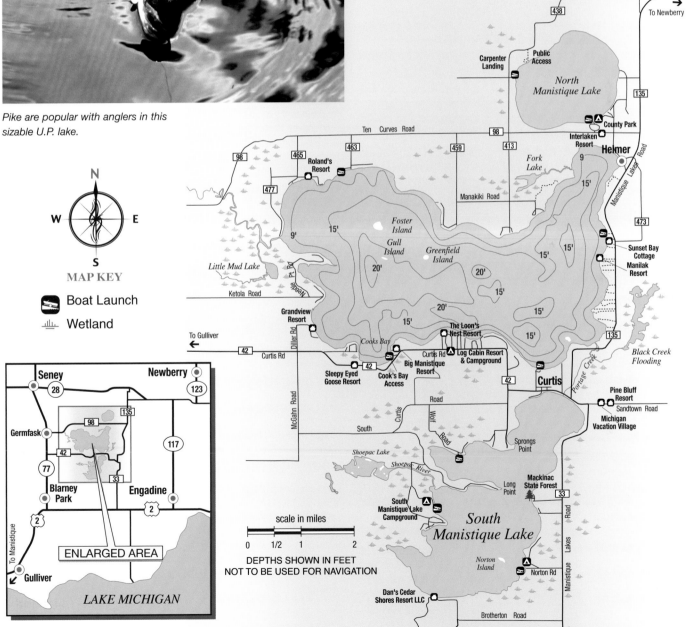

MAP KEY

Boat Launch

Wetland

ENLARGED AREA

scale in miles

0   1/2   1   2

DEPTHS SHOWN IN FEET
NOT TO BE USED FOR NAVIGATION

Lac Vieux Desert Lake
Gogebic County (MI) & Vilas County (WI)

If having the numbers 3 & 4 world-record tiger muskie hanging on the wall of a local bait and tackle shop means anything, then maybe also having the number 1 means something about the local fishery. If you go to the Minnow Bucket in Phelps, WI, not far from the MI/WI boarder, you will be able to view these mounts, all taken from Lac Vieux Desert Lake (pronounced *"La View Deser"* as well as other pronunciations), which rests in both Michigan & Wisconsin boundaries.

Lac Vieux Desert is a lake that exists in two adjoining counties, Gogebic County, Michigan, and Vilas County, Wisconsin. Fed primarily by springs in the surrounding swamps, it is the source of the Wisconsin River, which flows out of its southwest corner. The lake contains a number of small islands, especially in its northeastern lobe, including Draper Island in Michigan and Duck Island, in Wisconsin.

Lac Vieux Desert has a sizeable surface area of 4,260 acres, of which, approximately double the lake size is in Wisconsin (2853 acres) versus in Michigan (1407 acres). The maximum depth is 42 feet, however the average depth is only in the 12-foot range.

The name was given by French fur trappers, who were some of the first Euro-Americans in the region, and who literally translated the name from the Anishinaabe language, Gete-gitigaani-zaaga'igan, meaning *"Lake of the Old Clearing"* or *"Old Garden."*

The Michigan shore of Lac Vieux Desert is the only part of the Upper Peninsula of Michigan that is part of the drainage area for the headwaters of the Mississippi River.

This vast Wisconsin-Michigan border lake has a reputation for producing big fish in its fertile waters. Many large muskies are caught here annually, with even world-record-class muskies being produced to its credit.

The prominent fish species are muskie and walleye, but many anglers also pursue abundant perch and crappies. A northern pike can also be had in these waters.

Matt Ebert, a local guide, says that this lake is, "one of the premier lakes and largest in the area." The main game species according to Matt are muskie (mostly northern now), pike, walleye, panfish (gills, crappie, perch, sunfish) largemouth bass which has made a comeback recently, and a few smallies.

Muskie:
This is a summer fishery only, since it is closed during the winter months in WI, so it is closed for the entire lake. The lake is very shallow and weedy, says Matt, with the deepest hole at 38 feet located near the south shore. The entire south end of the lake has a bar along the shoreline, and this is a good area to fish for muskie. There is plenty of structure here. Any depth of 13 feet or shallower will contain muskie, says Ebert.

The average-size muskie taken in this lake range from 38-43 inches. You may also try fishing the west shore, just south of the northwest point that extends out into the lake. "Muskie," says Ebert, "are actually everywhere in the lake." Another good area is back in Rice Bay, along the south shore, east of Draper Island. June, July, and August are the best months to fish for them. Cast with bucktails and jerkbaits, but since it is weedy, crankbaits do not work well here.

The Wisconsin Muskie Tour website indicates that early season muskies on Lac Vieux Desert are attracted to smaller number 5 blade bucktails and safety-pin style spinners. Silver blades dressed with natural color hair work well early in the clearer waters of spring. Later in the season when the lake becomes murkier, fluorescent orange and chartreuse become more effective, along with copper blades.

Jerkbaits work well all season long, especially in black and perch colors. Again, smaller baits of 6-7-inch lengths work well in the first few weeks of the season, progressing to 8-12-inch baits later in the season.

Prop baits, creepers and walk-the-dog style topwater lures work well in low light conditions, especially on Lac Vieux Desert's vast weed beds. Large amounts of muskies congregate here, including some of the larger fish. The weeds are so vast that muskie fishing on the flats can be like finding the proverbial needle in the haystack. Fishing for muskies here becomes a numbers game, the more casts you make, the better your odds in contacting active fish.

Crankbaits have picked up in popularity in the area, twitched along and within the weeds and over the many rock humps (most of these rock humps are known only to the locals or anglers who have put their time on this water). Along with concentrating your fishing efforts on the weed flats, points and rock humps, the saddles between the chain of islands and their points will also provide some hot action.

Fall fishing on Lac Vieux Desert can produce the largest muskies of the year. Large suckers on quick strike rigs and big jerkbaits are the weapons of choice.

Walleye:
Walleye in the smaller 15-20-inch size can be found almost anywhere along a weed edge, such as in the south end of the lake. Rice Bay, according to Ebert, has not been good in recent years. The bigger fish are generally caught during the winter ice fishing season, where upwards of 25-inch fish can be expected. Fish the same areas during both summer and winter, i.e., the weed beds using tip ups or your favorite jig in 1/8-ounce size, tipped with a fathead minnow for spring walleye. In the summer, slip-bobbers with medium leeches on the deep weed edges are your best bet.

Pike:
Once again, you can find the pike, like most lakes, in weedbed areas. Pike are decent size and worth searching for, but being a muskie lake, most anglers are in search of the larger of these two major predators. Pike average around the 20-24-inch size. Use artificial spinners over the weed tops, or live chubs suspended with a bobber.

At a Glance

What: Major muskie lake existing in both MI & neighboring WI

Why: Trophy muskie

Regs: Being a boundary lake, Michigan & Wisconsin fishing licenses are both legal on Lac Vieux Desert regardless of where you fish. Muskie fishing closed during the winter months

Information/Guides: Land O' Lakes Chamber-Commerce, 6484 State Road 45, Land O' Lakes, WI, (715) 547-3432, www.landolakes-wi.org; Matt Ebert, guide, (715) 891-3927, mebertmotorsports@gmail.com

Landings: Boat landings exist on the west (3) and southeast side of the lake. In Misery Bay, there is good access and parking; in Thunder Bay, same story; West Shore, shallow water, poor access; Indian Village, for ice fishing only

Bait & Tackle: Minnow Bucket, 6104 County Hwy E, Phelps, WI (715) 547-3979

Lac Vieux Desert Lake

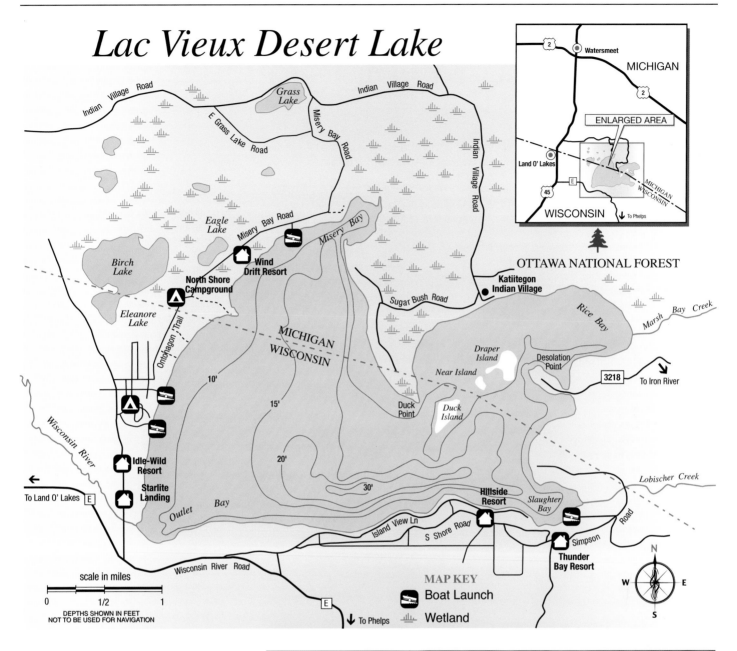

Panfish: Panfish are generally found anywhere in Rice Bay in 6-8 feet of water. Perch can be caught in the 7-9-inch size according to Ebert. Bluegills are handsize, and crappie in the 10-12-inch range. Crappie minnows work best, and worms or small leeches work well for the perch or gills in the weed pockets.

Bass: Largemouth bass in the 14-18-inch length are found along the shoreline or in Indian and Rice bays where the bulrush exist. It's best to use a weedless lure in these areas.

Notes: The weed edge forms at around the 13-foot depth. For ice fishing, medium golden shiners and tip-ups are used for walleye. Large golden shiners and tip-ups for pike.

Fishing on a relatively deserted lake can be relaxing and very enjoyable, regardless of the final results.

Lake Gogebic Gogebic County

Lake Gogebic is an unmistakable long narrow lake in the rural and beautiful western upper peninsula encompassing almost 13,000 total surface acres. Anglers in this part of the country all know how good the fishing is, and many who have never fished it have a desire to make the trek up to this paradise area of the state and country. At 14 miles long and over 2 miles wide, with an average depth of 17 feet and maximum of 37 feet, it has a habitat sufficient to provide an excellent fishery for many species of fish, including walleye, perch, crappy, smallmouth bass, lake herring, and northern pike. The center of Gogebic, called the mud flats, is 24 feet deep and runs the full length of the lake. There are some 30-35-foot holes, however the bays are generally 4-10 feet deep.

In this particular lake there are two species well-informed anglers take on, and both are worth mentioning.

Walleye: Walleye are the number one target fish by anglers in this magnificent fishing lake. The average size caught is around 17-21 inches says Russ Hewitt, of Russell's Bait & Tackle in Bergland at the north end of Gogebic. "The walleye fishing," says Hewitt, "has improved from some years back," he says, "mostly due to added feed for the walleye; i.e., more smaller perch and lots of minnows added to the lake." There have been several local projects to assist with providing food for the walleye. There are no fish plantings by DNR in Gogebic, in fact Gogebic is like a hatchery in itself whereby some walleye are removed to plant other lakes.

Hewitt says early in the ice fishing season anglers hit the north Bergland Bay in 4-10 feet of water. After around January, the fish seem to move to the western portion of the bay, and to the Porcupine Point area on the east side around the first bend from the north bay to the long straight shot south on Gogebic. The area off Ontonagon County Park on the west side of the lake is also good this time of year.

Most anglers use tip-ups with a sucker minnow, or jig with a fathead minnow. A lot of ice fishermen will set up a tip-up and then jig in the area of the tip-up.

For spring walleye, once again head up to the north end to Bergland Bay. Troll with Rapalas, or drift with crawler harnesses. If there is a brisk northwest or west wind, troll the east shore or drift with the wind using crawler harnesses bouncing on the bottom. Sometimes anglers even limit-out walleye fishing in water as shallow as 2-4 feet deep using this method. You can also try the area about three-quarters of the way south on the lake in front of Gogebic Lodge, on the west shore about a mile or more south of the Lake Gogebic State Park. Same techniques as used above.

Another take on walleye here is from Tim Long, of Timber's Resort on Gogebic. Once again he says that walleye are the number one target fish here, especially during the winter months. Tim, once a tournament angler both in this area as well as in his native Wisconsin on Lake Winnebago, states that "many times subtle jigging is better and that first ice is the best time for walleye because the bite tends to slow down as winter progresses." The fish become lethargic as winter progresses, so you need to look for any green weed growth that supplies oxygen in the water, such as in north end. As the O_2 is produced, minnows are drawn in and the walleye quickly follow.

As for time of day, Tim states that "early morning and later in evening is best." Sometimes jigging techniques work better than tip ups, which is a very popular method of fishing for walleye, here as well as on most inland walleye lakes.

Long says that the southern end of the lake can also produce walleye, but look for rock structure and weed beds.

As for summer walleye, Tim states that typically any lake in the Midwest in June is the best month to fish, period. Fish are in late-spring patterns and schooled-up and by June most anglers have generally figured out where they are and what the best techniques are to catch them. Once again, work the shallow water, weed beds, and shallow rock areas. There are "105 ways" to fish for walleye, and jigging presentations, trolling rigging presentations, etc all play a role in your success or lack of when it comes to walleye fishing. Target shallow water in Gogebic, that is, 10 feet or less early in the season, then after June you need to head out to deeper water since the heavy weed growth at the surface makes it difficult to fish. Troll the trough that exists in the center of the lake.

Perch: As the walleye ice fishing starts to slow down later in February, anglers target its cousin, the perch, but not just small perch, jumbo perch. March is prime time for the yellow bellies on Gogebic. The hotspots, according to Hewitt,

At a Glance

What: Great walleye and perch fishing

Where: Over much of the lake shoreline and especially in the north end

Regs: Starting in 2012 spring fishing season, perch limits went from the standard statewide 50 per day, to 25; also you can only keep five (5) perch over 12 inches per day

Special Note: Recognize that there is a time-zone change about halfway down the lake, from eastern time to central

Information/Guides: Tim Long at eyes-guy.com, or thetimbersresort.com

Landings: In Bergland south off M-28 at the end of Ash Street is a small park and beach with picnic tables, a vault toilet and a single cement boat ramp. The water is shallow in Bergland bay with rocks close to the ramp so be careful headed out; Ontonagon County Park located on the west side of the lake off Highway 64. The facility includes a concrete boat launch with loading dock, paved parking, restrooms, phones, picnic and swim area; There is a new DNR-operated launch site about 1 mile south of Montgomery Creek off E. Shore Of Lake Gogebic Road with two concrete ramps, a dock, and plenty of parking; Lake Gogebic State Park, located on the west side of the lake off Highway 64 has two concrete ramps and dock with camping area; The Gogebic County Park, located on the southwest corner of the lake off Highway 64 in Ice House Bay at the Slate River, also has two concrete ramps with a dock and restrooms

Contacts: Western U.P. Convention & Visitor Bureau, P.O. Box 706, Ironwood 49938, (906)-932-4850 or 800-522-5657, www.explorewesternup.com

Bait & Tackle: Gogebic Grocery, N946 Hwy. M-64, Marenisco 49947, (906) 842-3322; **Russell's Bait & Tackle,** Russ Hewitt, 203 Elm Street, Bergland 49910, (906) 365-5505; **West Shore Resort,** Ron Searles, N10960 State Hwy M-64, Marenisco 49947, (906)-842-3336; **Bear's Nine Pines Resort,** N9426 Hwy. M-64, Marenisco 49947, (906) 842-3361

are off Porcupine Point at the northeast end of the lake, and south of there all along that eastern shore toward Eight Mile Bay and beyond. There is deeper water through that stretch and perch tend to congregate there; nice size perch upwards of 12-14 inches and larger.

Summer perch fishing is often considered not as productive as ice fishing. But if you head to the northern region in the bay, the weed beds can be promising. Use a slip bobber in weeds in 10-12 feet of water; also head out in front and just north of Ontonagon Park on the west shore. Weed beds in this area hold some nice perch.

Long's take on perch, is that most anglers use a slip-bobber rig, with Beaver tails (short crawlers), or just cut a crawler in half or thirds; you can also try leeches and fish the same areas as you would for ice fishing, meaning Bergland Bay. Just south of the boat landing on the east shore is good also. Perch work the mud areas on the south end searching for wigglers, so you may find some good fishing along the south end as well.

In March, Long says, you can find perch in the deeper water, that is, the 22-30-foot depths. "You also need to be mobile," he says, "in an attempt to find a roaming school of perch." Try the eastern shore, but frankly both sides of the lake are worth working. The only problem with the western shore is there is usually more snowmobile activity which can spook the fish.

Bass: Regardless of the excellent reputation Gogebic has for walleye and perch, smallmouth bass are a worthwhile consideration here as well. "There is a good supply of smallies," says Hewitt, "and early season is a good time to search them out in the weed beds along the east shore which is somewhat rocky. Casting with most any bass lures in this area might produce a very respectable 20-inch smallmouth."

Long states that smallmouth are known to be "trophy" size in Gogebic Lake. It is not uncommon to catch 20-inch smallies here; larger sizes are not uncommon either. The rocky shoreline on both sides of the lake are considered good places to work your lures for these monsters. This is commonly where bass make their beds. Work the shoreline right down to southern end of lake

Crappie: If you should limit-out on walleye and perch, you can always try the relatively hard-to-find crappies on Gogebic. There are many smaller lakes in this region where crappie fishing is frankly easier so not too many anglers look for them on Gogebic. But you can try the east end of the north bay area where there are submerged pilings. Hewitt states that it is not all that uncommon to hook some 8-14-inch fish if you can find them. Most are caught in the summer months while perch fishing.

Pike: Pike are generally caught when fishing for walleye using tip-ups, and some are in the 25-35-inch range. You can work the edge of the weedbeds all along the shorelines using crawler harnesses.

Note: A local chapter of Walleyes For Tomorrow works to improve the habitat in this lake alongside the DNR. Money goes, for instance, to create rock reefs, crayfish, minnow and snail habitat to provide food for the game fish, especially walleye. They also provide shiners as a forage base for walleye and help increase perch numbers. Walleyes For Tomorrow was started here by Long as a spin off to the one he was involved with in Wisconsin. Tim heard lots of fishing rumors when he arrived on Gogebic, which he found were mostly not true. So he became proactive to work on a more productive lake, even though it was a very productive lake at the time, but like most lakes, some improvements were in order. There are probably more walleye per acre in Gogebic than most lakes in the Midwest, but a lot of them die in the winter, as many as 50% in some estimates, due to lack of fat tissue going in to the winter months. So forage fish are an important ingredient in the life of fish like walleye.

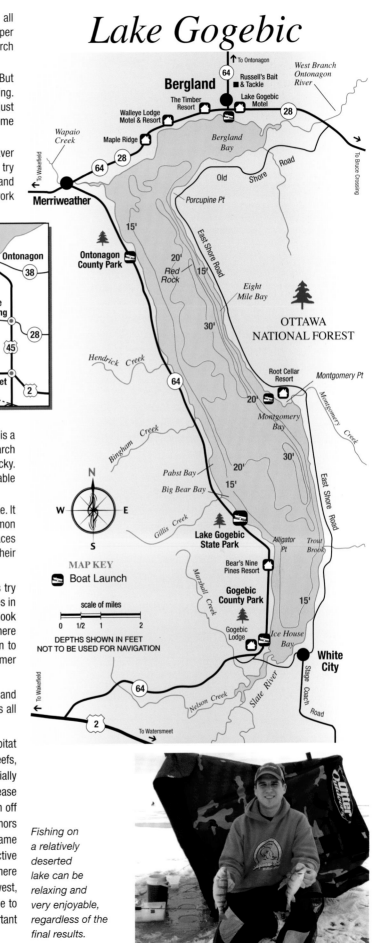

Fishing on a relatively deserted lake can be relaxing and very enjoyable, regardless of the final results.

Otter Lake Houghton County

Otter Lake is 3 miles long, 1.5 miles wide and 30 feet deep. The lake has northern pike, walleye, small- and largemouth bass, crappie and perch, albeit on the stunted side. Spring and fall are the ideal times for walleye fishing here. In the Otter River Watershed there are numerous rivers and streams with rainbow and brook trout. The majority of the lake is surrounded by wetlands, woods and steep hills preventing the heavy developments that many lakes encounter.

History: It's hard to visit this area of Michigan without knowing some brief history about the area. The waters of Keweenaw Bay were once scattered with large, wooden masted ships hauling loads of timber, copper, and iron ore down the Great Lakes waterway. The town of L'Anse, nestled in the curve at the bottom of the bay, was a popular stop along the way, whether you needed safe harbor or just some overdue rest and recreation. The great old ships are mostly gone now, but the memories of bygone days remain alive in the heart of this lakeside town.

In 1968 it became home to Indian Country Sports, servicing mostly local hunting, fishing and outdoor enthusiasts. But when Steve and Anne Koski took over in 1977 it became much more. Their homegrown knowledge of the area, easy-going manner and love of all things nautical have transformed Indian Country Sports into an area landmark.

In 1995, Steve's ultimate dream was realized with the completion of a 44-foot-tall, fully operational, Coast Guard-approved lighthouse. The lighthouse and store symbolize the recent revitalization of the beautiful L'Anse waterfront—an effort due, in no small part, to Indian Country Sports. Locals still stop by to visit and swap stories over a cup of coffee. Tales of fishing the Big Lake, hunting the elusive monster buck or exploring the rugged back trails are among the hottest topics. Displays of nautical, fishing and hunting antiques and memorabilia line the walls, recalling a history rich in local lore and adventure.

Harold Filpus, who resides on this lake and owns a couple of rental cabins here, said the main species of fish anglers go after are pike, walleye and crappie. Pike upwards of 20 pounds have been taken in Otter Lake according to Filpus. Most fish during the summer months since the winter fishery is spotty. Harold says he does not see anyone spearing for pike on this lake.

Pike: Harold states that there are "no real secret spots to fish in this lake, and it is easy to troll around even in a smaller boat." For pike, most anglers head to the north end, or north bay area trolling with crawler harnesses or most any other of your favorite pike lures. But you can work the shoreline weed areas as well most anywhere on the lake for pike.

Crappie: Good crappie lakes in the western U.P. are about as easy to find as a palm tree, but there are a few (crappie that is). Otter Lake happens to come to mind when you talk about big crappies however. According to local fish biologists, crappies are kind of cyclic and now the population in Otter Lake is on the high side. Summer crappie fishing is best along the shoreline, almost anywhere on the lake. You can find some 10-12-inch crappie according to Filpus. There are some artificial "cribs" at both the north and south ends of the lake (middle of bay in south end), as well as off the west side boat landing where the crappie tend to hang out in about 10 feet of water.

Perch: Although perch are available in Otter Lake, most are stunted and not pursued.

Walleye: Walleye fishing, according to Harold, is better in the fall months. Walleye have not been planted in Otter Lake since 2004, at which time there were plantings of 10,000 per year for the years 2000, 2002, and 2004. The average walleye here is in the 17-24-inch range. For fall walleye fishing, work the area on the south end of the lake, in the bay area.

Bass: Both large- and smallmouth bass can be found in and around the shoreline weedbed areas. Harold says bass in the 3-5-pound range are typical here.

Harold states that there are no secret methods to fishing this lake. Anglers use minnows for panfish, or crawlers, and both cast or troll for pike and walleye. Don't be surprised if you are trolling and hook a sturgeon in this lake. Harold has seen some 4-5-footers, but they are not legal to take from this lake.

Note: For the most part Otter Lake has a nice gradual bottom and is a quiet lake for those who want the serenity of fishing in the Upper Peninsula.

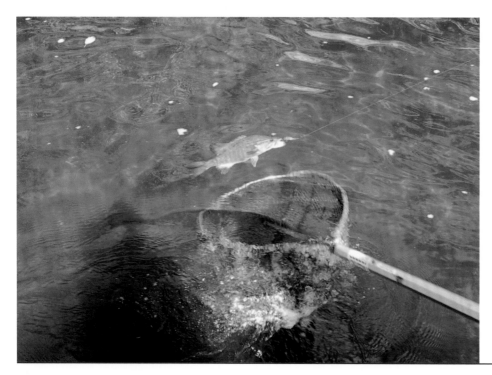

A good overall variety of game fish are found in Otter Lake, including some very nice bass.

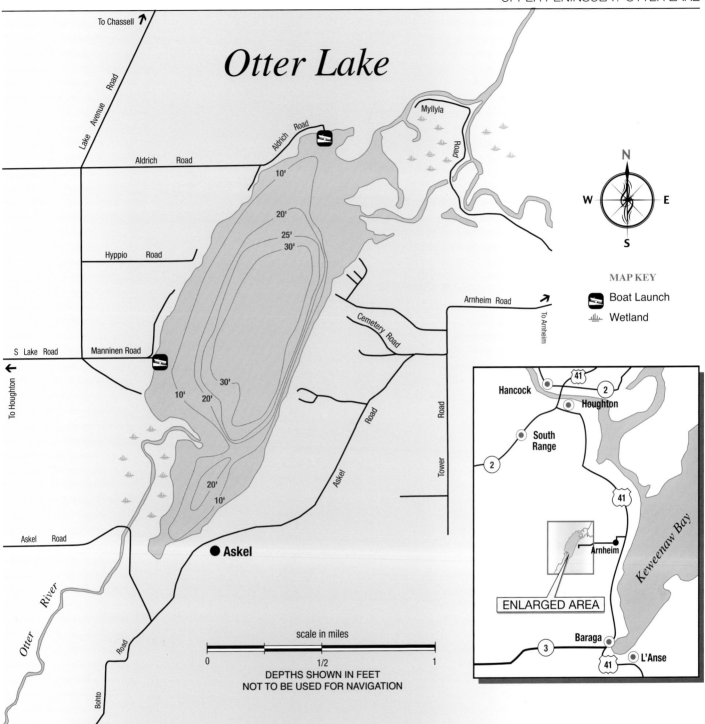

At a Glance

What: Walleye, pike, panfish

Where: A quiet, unpopulated lake in a very historic area of the Upper Peninsula

Information/Guides: Keweenew COC, 902 College Avenue, Houghton 49931-1821, (906) 482-5240; www.exploringthenorth.com/filpus/cabins.html; check out **Petersons Fish Market** (has been in several national magazines), 49813 Us Highway 41, Hancock 49930, (906) 482-2343; www.exploringthenorth.com/houghton/main.html

Landings: Northeast end (no dock) and west end of the lake off Manninen Road

Bait & Tackle: Chassell General Store, US 41, (906) 481-8030; **Indian Country Sports**, 17 S. Front Street, L'Anse 49946, (906) 524-6518, indiancountrysports.com

N O R T H E R N

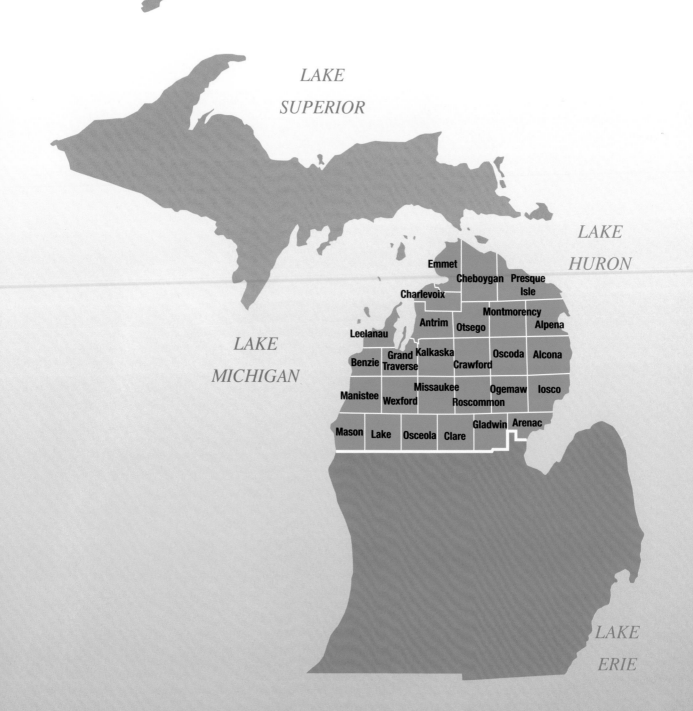

Keweenaw
(Isle Royale)

LAKE
SUPERIOR

LAKE
HURON

LAKE
MICHIGAN

Emmet

Cheboygan

Presque
Isle

Charlevoix

Montmorency

Antrim

Otsego

Alpena

Leelanau

Kalkaska

Oscoda

Alcona

Benzie

Grand
Traverse

Crawford

Manistee

Missaukee

Ogemaw

Iosco

Wexford

Roscommon

Mason

Lake

Osceola

Clare

Gladwin

Arenac

LAKE
ERIE

(LOWER)
PENINSULA

Arbutus Lake Grand Traverse County

Arbutus Lake is seemingly five lakes, all joined by a narrow "channel-like" opening between each section. In fact, the lakes are referred to as Sections, 1, 2, 3, 4, & 5, starting from the south (#1) and moving up to the north end (#5). And the unusual design does not end there. Each section supports numerous bays and points that jut out into the main part of each area. Anglers can find perch, bluegills, crappies, bass, and pike in Arbutus, but the mainstay fish are gills and bass.

There are so many bass in Arbutus the size limit is 10 inches and up, rather than the normal legal state size of 14 inches.

The average depth of this lake is 20 feet, but there are some 40-foot holes in many of the sections. Combined, this entire lake system is just under 400 acres.

Bluegill:
Most anglers who ice fish for bluegill fish the north section (#5), according to Josh Hentschel from Roy's General Store. There is also a convenient fishing deck in this area for those people who don't own a boat. It makes a nice spot for kids especially, with a nice state-run campground nearby on the lake.

Use wax worms and a tear drop, and fish the areas close to shore in the 10-20-foot range. Bluegills can also be found in sections 3 & 4. Look for them near or in the numerous bays.

For summer fishing, gills can be found in the same areas.

Pike:
Pike can be found in many areas of this lake, but most are in the 20-foot depths. Most pike here are on the smaller size, under 30 inches, but there are plenty to give anglers lots of action when ice fishing using tip-ups baited with grays or blue minnows.

Perch:
Ice fishing, or summer fishing for that matter, tasty perch are found mostly in section 3, as well as in 5. Fish the areas around the island. There are several humps and drops in this section and generally they will support schools of fish. Don't expect limits of jumbo perch in Arbutus, most are smaller and few in number.

Bass:
Summer bass fishing is very popular in the numerous weedbeds found in most all the coves. Typical bass lures (spinners, top-water lures) can net some excellent action here.

Crappie:
Crappie are numerous here, but you need to find the right spot, which means moving around. Usually, according to Josh, the best time to fish for crappie here is an hour after dark. They will start biting and provide action for an hour or so before shutting down. Try the deeper holes first, then move up from there because they are often suspended. There are some nice-size crappie in Arbutus, around the 8-10-inch-plus size, so when you find them you will be well rewarded.

Josh states that summer crappie fishing here is moderate at best.

My recent, limited experience on this lake started out with a nice 18-inch largemouth in area 4 fishing from shore by the campground. There were also some nice-sized bluegills in the spawning beds, but it was June and the action was light at best. Most of the gills were in the 8-9-inch size, but quite a few were smaller as well. What seemed to work well that day was dropper rigs with leaf worms, with the dropper a couple of feet above the weight. We fished in the 15-25-foot depths along the drop-offs.

At the time I visited this lake, there was a neat old-time general store at the edge of town, called Roy's that looks like it could have been there in the early 1900s or earlier. It's on the way to Arbutus Lake from Traverse City at the corner of Three Mile and Hammond. They carry a good selection of live bait, not to mention items for your cooler.

Tasty bluegills are a bonus when fishing for these scrappers.

Arbutus Lake

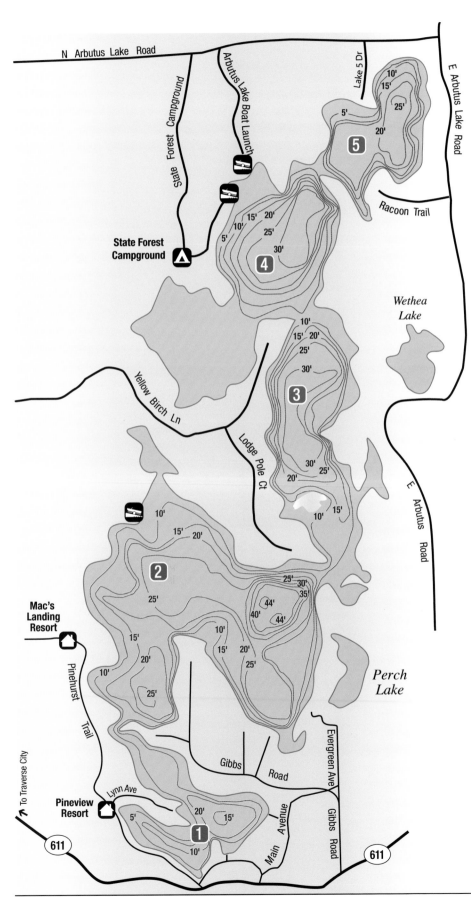

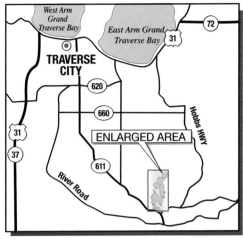

At a Glance

What: Fishing for bass, pike, and panfish

Where: Not far from Traverse City

Why: A very unique lake with several "lakes" joined by channels

Landings: Northwest side of the lake off N. Arbutus Road.

Special Regulations: Bass are legal at 10" rather than 14"

Contacts: Traverse City Convention & Visitors Bureau, 101 W. Grandview Parkway, Traverse City, 49684, Toll Free: (800) 940-1120, (231) 947-1120

Bait & Tackle: Roy's General Store, 963 Hammond Road East (corner of Three Mile), Traverse City, (231) 946-5633, www.royscorner.com

MAP KEY

🚤 Boat Launch

scale in feet

0   125   250   500

DEPTHS SHOWN IN FEET
NOT TO BE USED FOR NAVIGATION

Avalon Lake Montmorency County

Avalon Lake, a small, 75-foot deep and very clear 372-acre lake in Montmorency County, has one fish that you don't often see in many lakes, splake. And good numbers of them. Lack of aquatic vegetation in this lake provides good fishing opportunity, but in a somewhat different manner. Much of this lake is over 40 feet in depth, but fish have no place to hide, allowing predator fish such as splake, smallmouth bass, and the few pike that exist here to feed on perch and other smaller fish.

A 2010 DNR survey indicates that Avalon Lake is low in natural productivity due to these conditions, and therefore has a low diversity in fish populations.

Splake: If you enjoy fishing for splake this is the lake. Virtually every year from 2000 on to 2010 (last available figures) has been stocked with 20,000 or more splake. And they can be reasonably sizable in this lake, ranging from 7-17 inches in size.

Gill Potter, who lives on this lake and is very familiar with it, says "splake is the #1 fish anglers seek out here." Plantings started about 50 years ago or more, and have been a mainstay ever since. "One local angler caught," according to Potter, "apparently what could have been a world record at the time for an inland lake." But even that record fish size would have been broken several times since.

Potter states that there is a lot of ice fishing for splake, but, he adds, "you need to know what and how to catch splake during both the winter and summer season. You need to fish very deep (60-70 feet) in this sandy and very clear lake," he says. It's easy to see 25 feet down or more in this spring-feed lake. "The fish are wide open with no significant weed growth," he says.

During summer, this highly developed lake is full of summer boating activities, therefore early morning or late evening are the best times to fish.

Locals can be found trolling for splake in the deep areas on the edges of the drop-offs, often with an old, traditional Andy Reeker spoon tipped with small minnow, or the more current Swedish Pimple. In winter, fish the shallows (4-6 feet) along the shoreline.

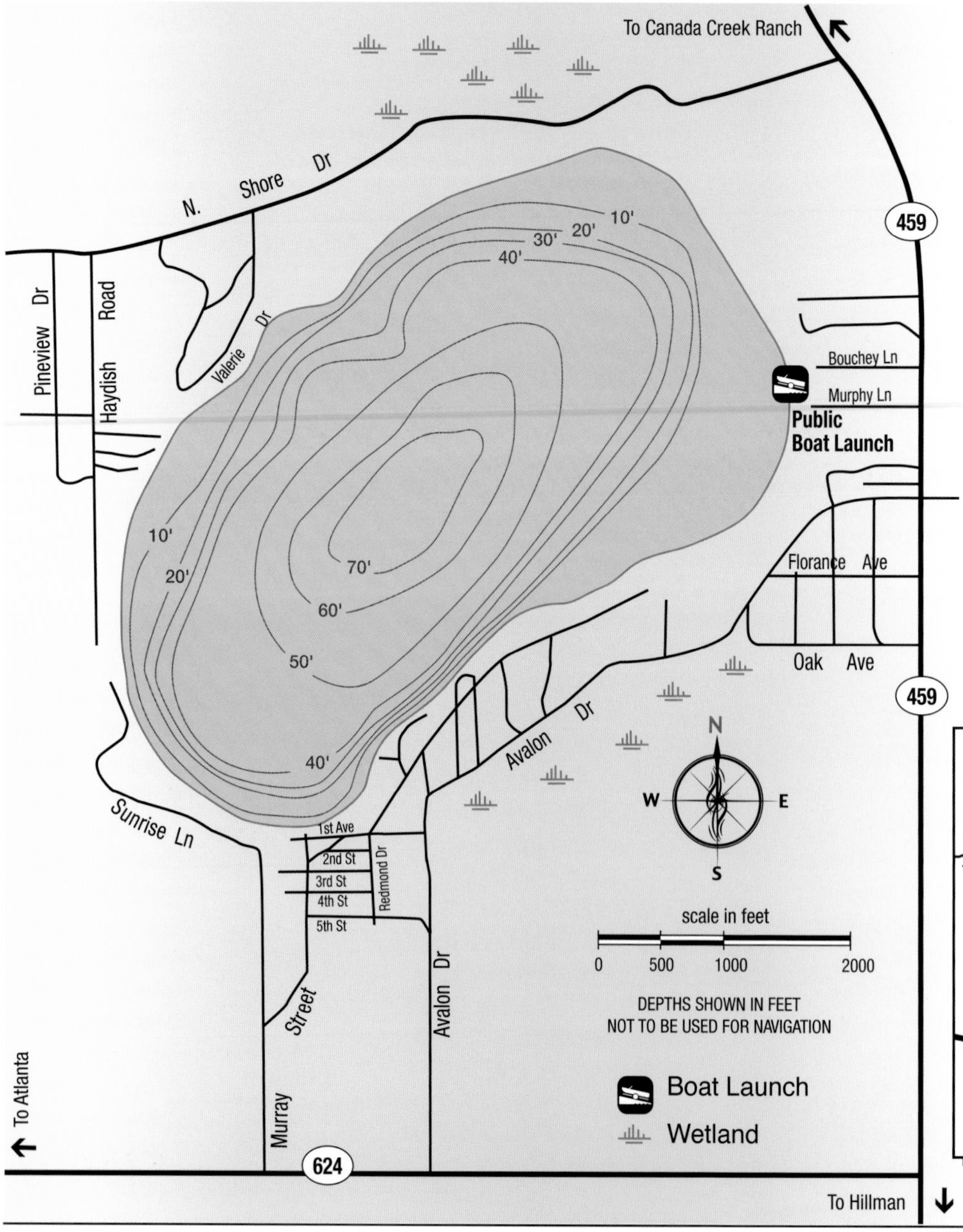

Avalon Lake

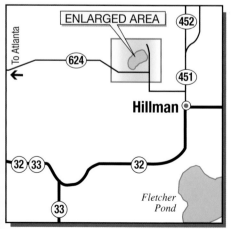

Map labels

To Canada Creek Ranch

N. Shore Dr

Pineview Dr
Haydish Road
Valerie Dr

459

Bouchey Ln
Murphy Ln
Public Boat Launch

Florance Ave
Oak Ave

459

10' 20' 30' 40'

70' 60' 50' 40'

10' 20'

Sunrise Ln

1st Ave
2nd St
3rd St
4th St
5th St
Redmond Dr

Murray Street

Avalon Dr

Avalon Dr

To Atlanta

624

N
W   E
S

scale in feet
0   500   1000   2000

DEPTHS SHOWN IN FEET
NOT TO BE USED FOR NAVIGATION

Boat Launch
Wetland

To Hillman

ENLARGED AREA
452
To Atlanta
624
451
Hillman
32 33   32
33
Fletcher Pond

Potter says an average splake can be in the 12-14-inch size in Avalon, but he has seen them up to 30 inches. For shallow-water ice fishing, go to northeast corner of the lake, just north of boat landing and work the 8-10 feet of water along the drop-off. Try using a small treble hook with minnow on it or a Swedish Pimple.

Currently, it is believed that the splake fishery is almost entirely relegated as a winter fishery.

Smallmouth Bass:
Warm- and cool-water predators in Avalon Lake include smallmouth bass, largemouth bass, and northern pike, but the smallies are king here. During the 2010 DNR survey, highly prolific smallmouth were caught in the 2-18-inch size. DNR reports indicate a decent growth range in Avalon Lake for smallmouth, and there were significant numbers of fish in the 14-inch size. But a lot of legal size were also part of this survey catch, and most were age 6 at the time of the survey.

Gill Potter says that he has caught smallmouth up to 6 pounds (22 inches) on a bare crawler in 22-23' of water. Potter says his average catch is in the 12-17-inch range. He states that he would fish both the northeast and southwest side of the lake for bass. As stated previously, evenings and mornings are best due to the heavy boating traffic midday. There are no rocks or weedbeds for spawning, so the bass will spawn in 10-12 feet of water wherever they can. Just follow the shoreline early in the season for these fighters, but keep in mind that it is always advisable during spring spawning to return the females back to the water to keep the population healthy for future years. Most any spinner lure seems to work well for bass.

One note to mention, bass in this lake, due to the overall habitat, are not considered good eaters, so catch and release is often the rule of thumb.

Lake Trout:
A total of 190 adult lake trout were stocked in Avalon Lake in fall 2009. These fish were large broodstock from the federal hatchery system in the Upper Peninsula. They averaged 28 inches at stocking. This effort was done to add species and catch diversity to Avalon Lake, but mostly, to simply give these "retired" broodstock lake trout a new habitat outside of the federal hatchery system. Most of these fish are caught in the deeper waters as incidental catches since there are so few of them.

Pike:
Northern pike were also found to be in very low numbers during nearly every survey of Avalon Lake and the latest survey found a similar pattern. Three legal-size (24 inches and larger) pike were caught, including a large 40-inch specimen. Food is abundant for this species here, yet spawning habitat is naturally limiting causing a low population. Once again, pike fishing here is very sparse and it is hit and miss.

Gil states that pike seem to catch the imagination of anglers, since even though they are few in numbers, there are some big ones, like the 34-pounder speared many years ago. A pike state record was once caught here and is mounted in the Highway Inn in Hillman.

Panfish:
Three species of panfish were collected during the recent survey. Yellow perch are the most abundant and popular fish but are relatively small and not targeted by anglers. Few may reach beyond the 8-inch size. Most are forage fish for the predators in this lake.

Suckers:
White suckers were collected in good numbers and sizes in Avalon, but once again not highly pursued by anglers, so little information on fishing for them is available. It is apparent that suckers grow well in this lake and compete for food resources.

Overall, the current fish community in this lake is considered to be fairly unproductive. In general it has a panfish community with very limited diversity and dominated by small yellow perch, a limited predator population not dependent on stocking and dominated by smallmouth bass. It has a cold-water species community dominated by stocked splake which appear to survive fairly well.

Bass are generally easy targets for anglers.

At a Glance

What: Splake and smallmouth fishing

Where: Avalon Lake

Why: One of the better splake fisheries on a small, very clear lake

Landings: East end of the lake has one landing that is a fair sized public boat launch. The ramp is hard-surfaced and provides parking for 25 boat trailers.

Contacts: Hillman Area Chamber of Commerce, PO Box 506, Hillman, 49746, (989) 742-3739, www.hillmanchamber.com.

Bait & Tackle: A1 Woods & Waters, 141 N. State St., Hillman, (989) 742-3878; **A-Frame Party & Pizzeria,** 17984 N County Road 459 (on the lake), Hillman, 49746, (989) 742-3220; **Wild Bills Bait & Tackle,** 19485 M 32 W, Hillman, 49746, (989) 742-4874

Black Lake

Cheboygan / Presque Isle Counties

Black Lake is one of Michigan's only premier muskie lakes. There is a small yet stable population of very large muskies in the lake. Fifty-inch-plus fish are consistently taken every year. As good as that might sound, Black is also the mother of sturgeon inland lakes in Michigan. There are very few elsewhere. Otsego, for instance, has a few stocked fish, but no natural population.

Black is also one of the largest and most strikingly beautiful lakes in the Tip of the Mitt Watershed Council service area. In fact, in terms of surface area, Black Lake, at over 10,000 acres, is the 9th largest inland lake in the state of Michigan. It is located in the northeast corner of the Lower Peninsula; in both Cheboygan and Presque Isle Counties. The lake's shoreline measures approximately 19 miles and depth maps show the deepest point, about 50 feet, in the southwest section of the lake. The northwest end of the lake is characterized by extensive shallow areas that deepen gradually while the southeast end is much deeper and wider and has a more pronounced drop-off, particularly on the western side.

Muskie: "Everything in Black Lake, except sturgeon and walleye, are wild strains," states Tim Cwalinski, District Fish Biologist, and someone who has spent considerable time surveying and studying this popular lake. "We basically take a hands-off approach with regard to muskies in Black, Burt and Mullet lakes," said Cwalinski. "We know that there is a population of muskies in those lakes and they are sustained mostly by natural reproduction. There's enough peripheral habitat for spawning to sustain the fishery."

"There are concerns by anglers that the statewide regulations are not appropriate for muskie here," he says. Furthermore "there will probably be some changes in next few years." Muskie are still popular here, but if you look at the season opener in April, when spawning takes place along the lower river in May, this places the spawning females at a disadvantage. Half the pressure on muskie is from winter spearing, and you obviously don't get catch and release with spearing.

Fish the north side of the lake, close to river outlet where there are some humps and where the vegetation is predominant. The majority of the muskies, though, are caught in the lower reaches of the Black and Cheboygan rivers in late spring.

Method: Trolling with giant crankbaits, casting big bucktails or soaking oversized suckers all take the occasional monster that will top 50 inches and 30 pounds.

Where to Fish: Trolling is most popular since you are covering a rather large area for limited fish, but some cast as well.

Sturgeon: There was a reduced harvest of two fish in 2012, based on the population of adults in Black Lake, but this limit does not change much from year to year. There is a 50/50 agreement between the area tribe and the state, whereby after a quota decision is reached, the tribe receives half the limit and the state the other half.

The two fish taken in 2012 were both between 50-60 inches. There are a fair number of adult sturgeon, estimated somewhere between 1100-1200, and a good number of young fish as well. However it takes twenty-plus years for a young sturgeon to reach adult status. Most of the young are stocked, and at this point it looks like the population should move upward in future years.

Sturgeon are a "specialty fish" that few anglers pursue. The winter spearing season is very short and limits overall are slim, making this type of fishery not very popular.

Walleye: The walleye is the biggest story in recent years in Black Lake. A 2005 population survey indicated only a fair density, but most were 17-20-inch fish. Few were under legal size. Black Lake was always a good wild-production lake, but DNR officials are not sure why it has diminished, so state stocking has taken place along with the lake association. Between the two stocking programs, anglers are now starting to catch young walleye, which is good for future populations. But it is still a mystery why the walleye eggs and fry are not surviving. However there are still enough walleye to keep anglers busy, even an occasional ten-pounder or so, and a fair number of 5-7-pound fish.

Where to Fish: Fish the weed beds in north area for walleye, the south end by the state park in fall, and the river mouth. Actually there is no one good location, being a relatively uniform lake with lots of 20-foot water depths.

Methods: I know of a stick sinker rig that seems to work well with leeches when drifting slowly through the weeds for walleye, or a crawler harness slowly drifted through the weeds as it gets toward evening.

Perch: Black Lake perch were never high on the list of fishing here; very few 10-12-inchers like other lakes, and bluegills are very limited. Big lakes like Black are not conducive to most panfish with the sandy areas along the shoreline, making it a poor habitat for spawning.

Smallmouth bass fishing is fair at best.

At a Glance

What: Pike, Sturgeon, Muskie, Panfish

Where: Black Lake

Why: A premier muskie lake that also offers good walleye fishing

Regulations: Special regulations on sturgeon; check annually with DNR for the latest updates. Anglers can call the Gaylord Field Office at (989) 732-3541 for more details

Landings: Onaway State Park is located on the southeast shore of Black Lake, just a few miles north of Onaway on 211. Modern bathrooms, showers, water, pumping station, and electric hook-up are all perks of Onaway State Park. A picnic area with indoor pavilion and swim area are also here, along with a boat launch, dock and plenty of parking

On the northwest end of Black Lake the channel entrance to Black River is marked by a series of buoys. This area is shallow so maintain a zone between the buoys and keep your prop raised a bit. Black Lake Marina is on the left as you enter Black River and maintains a concrete ramp, parking, fuel, guest docks and bait

Bait & Tackle: Parrott's Outpost, 20628 State St., Onaway, (989) 733-2472, info@parrottsoutpost.com

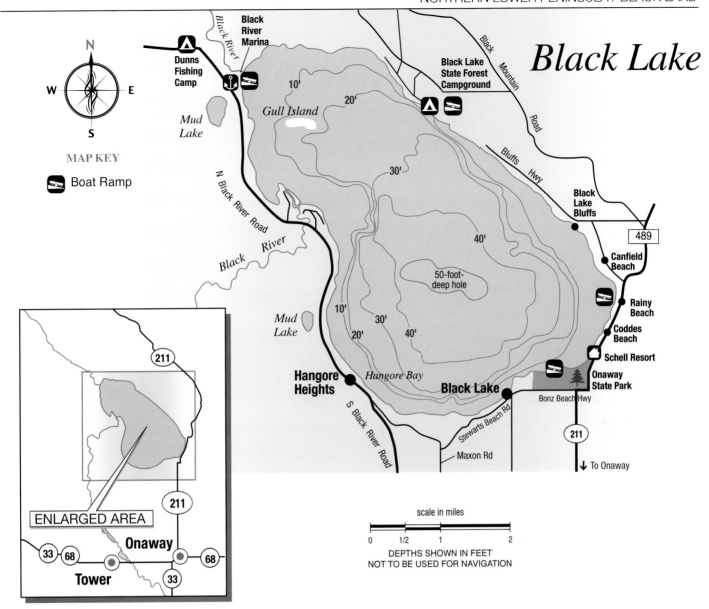

Black Lake

N
W   E
S

MAP KEY

Boat Ramp

Black River Marina

Dunns Fishing Camp

Mud Lake

Gull Island

10'

20'

30'

Black Lake State Forest Campground

Black Mountain Road

Bluffs Hwy

Black Lake Bluffs

489

Canfield Beach

40'

50-foot-deep hole

Rainy Beach

Coddes Beach

Schell Resort

Onaway State Park

N Black River Road

Black River

Mud Lake

10'

20'

30'

40'

Hangore Heights

Hangore Bay

Black Lake

Bonz Beach Hwy

211

S Black River Road

Stewarts Beach Rd

Maxon Rd

To Onaway

211

ENLARGED AREA

Onaway

33 68

Tower

33

68

scale in miles

0   1/2   1   2

DEPTHS SHOWN IN FEET
NOT TO BE USED FOR NAVIGATION

Pike: Black Lake is undoubtedly the best pike lake between its neighboring Mullet and Burt lakes. Slightly south of Five Mile Point is the Pine Grove Beach area. Pike and walleye hold along the steep banks throughout the summer.

Methods: I like to work crankbaits and spinners along the outside points and over the weed beds at around 10-15 feet. Come in shallow at night with floating cranks over the shallow weed beds for walleye action in early summer. Later in the season try moving out into the 30-foot range for suspended fish.

General Discussion: The waters in front of Onaway State Park hold walleye, bass and pike year round. Work the 10- to 15-foot drop line in the early morning and evening hours for some good walleye action.

BLACK LAKE WALLEYE STOCKING NUMBERS

State Stocking efforts, June, Muskegon Strain, Southern Lake Huron reared, VHS tested

2010: 192,000 spring fingerlings, not marked

2011: 119,983 spring fingerlings, marked

Black Lake Association Stocking efforts (St Mary's River strain most years)

2008: 2,950 fall fingerlings, average length 8 inches

2009: 10,000 fall fingerlings, average length 6 inches

2011: 10,160 fall fingerlings, average length 6 inches

Patience pays off when muskie fishing.

Big Star Lake Lake County

This 912-acre inland lake west of Baldwin is surrounded by hundreds of tiny cabins and trailers located on multiple private roads. Star Lake Drive is the main public road—a loop drive that encircles the lake off of 76th St. There is one public-access point on the south corner (south end of the south arm). This is the largest lake in Lake County.

Big Star is also a somewhat odd-shaped lake in that it is made up of three distinct arms, or bays, running from southwest to northeast. For ease of description, I will define them as the south, middle, and north arms, the south arm being where the only boat landing exists. You could actually use west end, middle, and east end because the lake runs diagonal. The north end is the furthest end from the boat access.

Crappie: George Tharp, who works at Ed's Sport Shop in Baldwin, and an avid angler on Big Star, states that you can catch some lunker crappie in the 17-18-inch size here. Ice fishermen work the north end of the lake, just off the campground at the east end of the north arm (off Star Lake Drive). This is also the area to hit during spring and summer, where good weed beds develop. The middle arm is also good for crappie, especially from the area around the opening and inward. The north arm is fished in about 14-16-foot depth.

Bluegills: Tharp states that 10-11- bluegills are also abundant in the north arm, but typically are around the 7-9-inch size. During ice fishing season, the area just east of the boat landing at the south arm is usually good. Fish closer to the middle arm along the east side of the lake. In spring, the area by the boat landing and the narrow bay can be good for tasty gills. You may also want to try fly-fishing along the shoreline in spring when bluegills are on their beds. This area can be very weedy in the summer months, but fish tend to hang out here.

Largemouth Bass: Largemouth bass fishing is popular in this lake along the edges of the middle arm. In mid-summer try the weed beds in front of the campground at the north end of the lake using your favorite bass offerings.

Muskie/Pike: Although muskie and pike are in this lake, and there are some sizable ones, it has only been very recently where you can actually fish for them, and most anglers do not seek them out in Big Star. During summer, the lake traffic drives these larger fish to the bottom and they are hard to entice. There is very little winter effort to set out tip-ups or spear them, so at this early stage little information is available on these two species. Tharp says that there are definitely some pike in the 30-plus-inch size, and if you wish to try for them he suggests heading to the north arm off Star Lake Drive. In spring, try the south arm in the morning, then move to the middle arm where there's a drop-off.

At this age the size of the fish is not what counts, rather it's the focus on developing a lifelong healthy outdoor activity.

At a Glance

What: Nice crappie and decent bluegills

Where: North arm, but also catchable elsewhere

Landings: One landing along the south arm at the south end of this arm (or west end of the lake). The boat landing has a paved ramp with a dock in the center, turnaround space, and parking for a good number of vehicles with trailers

Contacts: Lake County Chamber of Commerce, 911 Michigan Avenue Box 130, Baldwin, 49304, (231) 745-4331, 1-800-245-3240, Email: info@lakecountymichigan.com; www.lakecountymichigan.com

Bait & Tackle: Ed's Sport Shop, 712 Michigan Ave, Baldwin, 49304, (231) 745-4974, edssportshop@yahoo.com

Walleye: Walleye in this lake are not hogs by any means. Mostly they are good eating size, under 20 inches. And few anglers pursue them during the winter, choosing to focus on panfish. In spring and summer, work the north arm along the east end and off both points that protrude out heading in the north end. The last DNR survey of this lake indicates that while this lake may not currently offer large numbers of walleye, many of the walleyes that are present are of decent size. Walleye plantings by the DNR include the following years and number of fingerlings planted: 2004, 10,000; 2005, 20,000; 2009, 28,000; 2009, 22,000.

Perch: Although perch are in this lake they are mostly small, in the 6-7-inch size. There are some 9-11-inchers, but they are few in number. Most anglers do not pursue them here.

Note: The most recent DNR survey of Big Star Lake indicates that this lake has no inlet and one intermittent outlet with a lake-level control structure. Water that flows out of Big Star Lake through the outlet flows through a series of wetlands into Jenks Creek, a tributary of Danaher Creek, which is a tributary of the Pere Marquette River.

The survey indicates that this lake has panfish populations that are generally healthy. Bluegill were very numerous in the 2004 survey of Big Star Lake, with some individuals reaching eight inches. Bluegill should provide good fishing opportunity, as well as being an excellent forage base for predators like walleye and largemouth bass. The black crappie population also appears healthy, although they are not as numerous as bluegill. Although yellow perch are numerous in Big Star Lake, most are small and exhibit poor growth. The largemouth bass population appears to be healthy, with a fair number of fish over the minimum legal size limit of 14 inches.

Big Star Lake

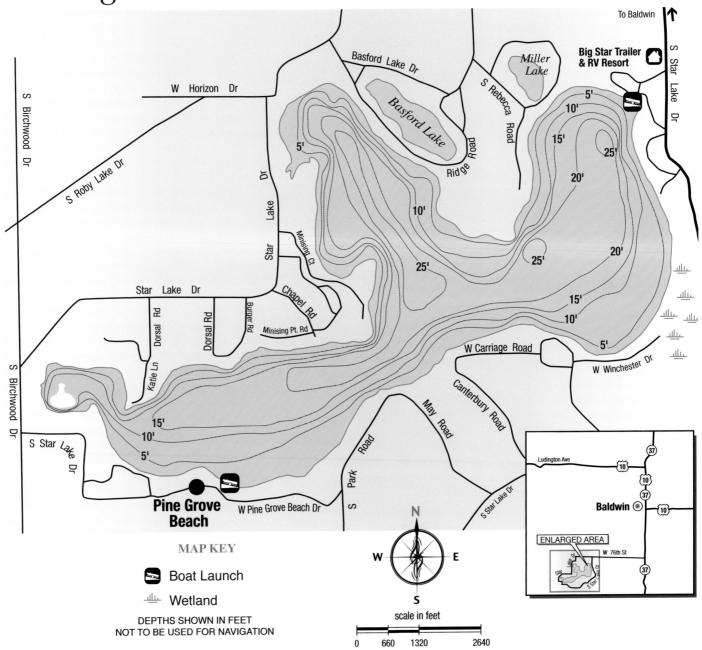

MAP KEY

Boat Launch

Wetland

DEPTHS SHOWN IN FEET
NOT TO BE USED FOR NAVIGATION

scale in feet

0   660   1320   2640

Budd Lake Clare County

Budd Lake is located in central Clare County in Harrison, Michigan. The lake is 175 acres and has no inlets or outlets. The lake drops off gradually on the east side, and more steeply on the west side. Budd Lake has a maximum depth of 34', and the width of the shoal varies from 50-300'. The east end of the lake has some emergent vegetation located near the boat launch and in the small lagoon area. This lake boasts great fishing in all seasons, with a large population of muskellunge, bass, panfish and walleye also inhabit the lake.

Perch: Nancy Buerkel-Rothfuss, who is active on the Budd Lake Association and very familiar with fishing on this lake, states that the north end of the lake is an active area both winter and summer for perch. "They are plentiful and sizable, many in the 9-12-inch size," she says. DNR survey figures on this lake indicated that yellow perch are quite numerous. And the captured perch ranged in size from 3-7 inches, however 1 out of 4 were over 7 inches.

Muskie: In particular, Budd Lake is known for muskies. Most are under 40 inches, though larger individuals are occasionally hooked with traditional muskie-sized bucktails, spinners and crankbaits. A forage base of shiners helps the lake produce good-sized predators. The south end of the lake is shallower, while the rest runs up to 30 feet deep. Drop-offs near the shoreline provide deep-water refuge.

Cold-weather muskie fishing can produce some nice fish.

"Budd Lake has been a steady muskie producer for years," states Nancy. The lake has a good population of lake chubs and suckers that make for perfect muskie forage fish. Regular plants help sustain muskie populations in the lake. Because of the lake's size, finding muskies in Budd Lake isn't difficult; however, catching them can be. The best tactic is to cover the water by trolling at a fairly good clip while pulling big Bombers, Rapalas and Believers in frog, shad and perch finishes. Fish come from both the north and south ends in 10 to 25 feet of water. There is a ban on spearing on this lake.

Once again, DNR muskie survey revealed a good size spread between19-44 inches. These muskies represented 7 different year-classes, and survival has been very good in this lake. Muskie are not easy to catch, but the numbers in this lake provide a good chance for anglers who wish to pursue them.

Walleye: The 30-foot-plus deeper zones are down the center of the lake north and south of the island that exists on the north-central area of the lake. This is a popular area for fishing walleye, both summer and winter. Like most lakes and river systems, tip-ups and jigging are popular methods in the winter, and summer trolling with the typical walleye lures works on this lake. Another local hotspot is on the southwestern corner of the lake in the submerged vegetation. Another good bet is in the cove along the eastern shoreline toward the north end of the lake. Approximately 13,000 walleye were planted in 2009 and should be sizable by the time this book goes to print.

During the same DNR survey, walleye ranging from 8 to 27 inches were caught. Apparently walleye had survived from past stocking as the species was represented by 8 year classes. The walleye were growing at 2.1 inches above state average.

Bass: The association has stocked largemouth bass in this lake, but now has future plans to stock smallmouth. In the DNR survey, largemouth bass were caught ranging from 4 to 19 inches. Only 12% of the largemouth collected were of legal size, which indicates a small part of the fishery in this lake.

Sunfish: Budd Lake also appears to have a good population of large sunfish. They can be caught throughout the lake, especially in the shallows.

Note: Pike exist in this lake, but are generally not a target species due to their size and low numbers.

At a Glance

What: Muskie

Where: Budd Lake, one of the better muskie lakes in Michigan

Regs: No spearing allowed

Information/Guides: Wilson State Park is located on the southwest end of the lake

Landings: Budd Lake has an access site and boat ramp owned and maintained by the City of Harrison located off Grant Road on the southeast end of the lake. There is also a fishing platform located along the western shoreline, and shore access within Wilson State Park on the northwest end of the lake. Also has a handicapped restroom

Contacts: Harrison Chamber of Commerce, 809 North First Street, P.O. Box 682, Harrison, 48625, (989) 539-6011, (877) 539-6011, Email: harrisonchamber@sbcglobal.net

Bait & Tackle: Ken's Landing, North First St., Harrison, (989) 539-3700 www.kensbaitandtackle.com; **Jay's Sporting Goods,** 8800 South Clare Avenue, Clare, (989) 386-3475, www.jayssportinggoods.com; **Trestain's Long Lake Store,** 8036 North Clare Avenue, Harrison, (989) 539-9617; **Dave's Lake 13 Party Store,** 587 W Surrey Rd., Farwell, (989) 588-6744

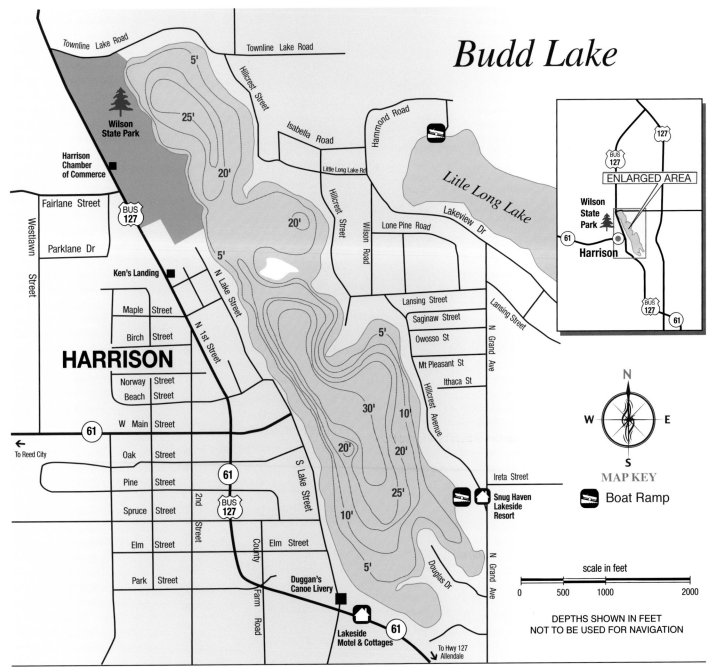

Budd Lake

MAP KEY

▥ Boat Ramp

scale in feet

0   500   1000   2000

DEPTHS SHOWN IN FEET
NOT TO BE USED FOR NAVIGATION

Burt Lake Cheboygan County

Burt Lake in Cheboygan County is a 17,000-acre lake on the northern tip of the lower peninsula at the town of Indian River. Among the state's largest inland lakes, Burt Lake is named after William A. Burt, who, together with John Mullett, made a federal survey of the area from 1840 to 1843. The average depth of this large body of water is approximately 73 feet, large and deep enough to support an array of fish species.

These include: Crappie, bluegill, brown and rainbow trout, largemouth and smallmouth bass, muskie, northern pike, steelhead, walleye, and perch. Walleye and perch, as with most lakes, are the popular species that anglers seek here.

When you scan the map of Burt Lake you will quickly see the various bays and points along the varied shoreline, with names like Sturgeon Bay, Walleye Alley, Cedar Bay, Colonial Point, and others. The popular inland waterway connects Lake Michigan with Lake Huron, travels through Burt Lake, via Indian River. This waterway is Michigan's longest chain of rivers and lakes. The Waterway, which is more than 40 miles long, also runs through Pickerel Lake, Crooked Lake, Crooked River, Indian River, Mullet Lake, Cheboygan River, and finally into Lake Huron. The Inland Waterway can handle boats up to 65 feet long (18-foot beam) with up to a 5-foot draft.

Burt Lake is a real gem for ice fishing. There are probably more anglers on Burt Lake on a Saturday in February than on any day in the summer. The lake has a wonderful population of walleye and pike and the perch are both large and plentiful. The walleyes fortunately reproduce naturally so you generally see nice numbers.

The lake also has an appealing population of both brown and rainbow trout, however these are seldom caught in the summer, since they remain at depths well below those that are normally fished for walleye or perch. In the fall they will move into the shallows as soon as the water cools sufficiently and are then often caught in the same 12- to-14-foot depths that you will find the walleye, pike and perch.

Burt Lake is largely composed of relatively shallow flats, with a great deal more fishable water than the other large but very deep lakes.

Anglers also enjoy two blue-ribbon trout streams which flow through the town of Indian River, the magnificent Sturgeon River—the fastest flowing river in the Northern Lower Peninsula—and the beautiful Pigeon River—a naturally protected river—each ending in Burt Lake and Mullett Lake respectively.

When discussing Burt Lake fishing locations, the easiest way to break it down is by the various bays and points versus species of fish. Larry Drozdzewski, who is very knowledgeable about this lake, from Pat & Gary's Bait and Tackle Shop, breaks down the fishing opportunities as follows:

Sturgeon Bay: The center area of Sturgeon Bay is rocky, resulting in good fishing opportunities for both smallmouth and walleye throughout the year. A narrow underwater point runs out from here and is considered one of the better spots on the lake for walleye in spring, early summer and for ice fishing. Perch are also good here, according to Larry, with 8-10" fairly common.

Colonial Point: Around this rocky point is a good place to fish for smallmouth bass or walleye. Crawfish, a main dish, are abundant in the rocks and therefore provide a great area to find game fish. Troll large crankbaits spring and fall or drift through the point with bottom walkers and a crawler harness on summer evenings. Walleyes can be caught along the 10- to 20-foot contours off both Colonial and Kings points (just south of Scotty's Landing).

Scotty's Landing: (lower west side of lake) Scotty's Landing is a small bay just south of Kings Point and considered a decent walleye fishing area. Larry states that there is a sizable flat that comes up very slowly from 20 to 8 feet, starting from the NE and eventually entering the bay area. Troll deep for walleye in the daylight and stay in 10 feet or less at night, using side planers or you can also drift fish with a crawler harness. A gold wire #4 hook and a stick sinker is a good choice. Burt holds some nice walleye ranging 6-8 pounds, with a few over 8 pounds.

Walleye Alley: (lower SE area of lake) The area between Indian River and Sturgeon River to the south is known as Walleye Alley. Spring fishing for walleye at this location is considered some of the best on Burt Lake. Pike, trout, bass, panfish, and smallmouth bass are also abundant year round. Use the same tactics mentioned for walleye elsewhere in this section.

Maple Bay: (west side of lake) Within Maple Bay, an area somewhat protected from the wind, there is a large sand bar off the western point just south of Maple River that is recognized as a good fishery for walleye, perch and pike year round, with good brown and rainbow trout in spring and fall. Muskie are good here also, from midway up the river on the west side (from Colonial Point down). Some 50-plus-pound muskie have been taken in this area of the lake during the winter spear fishing season. The not-so-favorable news is this fishery for Muskie has decreased over the past ten years, and not many are speared during the ice fishing season. Although pike are to be found in this area, even here, the spawning habitat is limited, which of course limits good fish populations.

Ice fishing with jigs or using tip-ups are a popular ways to land a limit of walleye.

Cedar Bay/Point: When fishing Cedar Bay, locate the tower on shore south east of Colonial Point. At this point you are in the middle of Sturgeon Bay east Burt Lake. This area is very rocky and makes for good fishing for smallmouth and walleye year round. A narrow underwater point runs out from here and is one of the best spots on the lake for walleye in spring, early summer and ice fishing. Jigs tipped with minnows work great early in the season on Burt Lake. Crawler harnesses just off the bottom get results through summer. If you're fishing Burt Lake, try this area. Later in the season, try the irregular contours along the east side between Dagwell and Cedar points, and off Greenman Point at the northeast end.

Poverty Bay: Crooked River, flowing from the west, empties into Poverty Lake. The water averages 5 to 7 feet throughout the flats that cover this bay and off the main channel on either side. It's a popular location to find some perch in the early season, as well as pike in the weedy areas on the north side of the channel. Jigging a large minnow across the weedy bottom with a steel leader, of course, could land you a nice fish. Walleye, pike, perch and even smallmouth bass are worth trying here as well. Burt Lake is a good lake for nice size bass, but generally speaking, they don't have the large numbers of its sister lake across I-75 (Mullet). Try spinnerbaits near the sunken logs during the summer for smallmouth bass, while fall angling requires crankbaits.

Larry said that the DNR has not planted many walleyes in Burt Lake in recent years, but did plant in 2011. The lake is basically self-sustaining. Northern pike were also found to be fairly common, with some pushing the 40-inch size, although the average fish is generally between 18 and 25 inches.

Perch can also be sought after during midwinter in the 30- to 50-foot depths in the center of the lake. Schools of perch roam the deeper water, and if an angler works at it, you can take a bucketful from 8 to 10 inches and larger, some 14+ inches in the deeper water areas. Wigglers fished below a slip-bobber is a proven tactic. Minnows work as well, according to Larry.

Burt Lake also features an untapped winter fishery for steelhead and brown trout. It receives regular plants of both species. The steelhead run up Sturgeon and Maple rivers in spring and fall, but few anglers pursue them in the winter.

Burt Lake

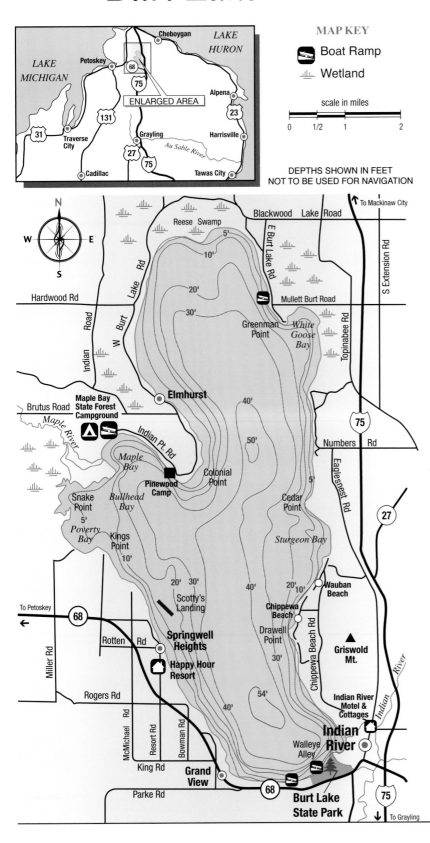

MAP KEY

🛥 Boat Ramp

🌿 Wetland

scale in miles

0   1/2   1   2

DEPTHS SHOWN IN FEET
NOT TO BE USED FOR NAVIGATION

At a Glance

What: Walleye and perch

Where: Many of the shallow flats

Why: Excellent variety of fish, and nice size walleye and perch

How: Jigging, perch rigs, and even spearing of pike

Information: Indian River Chamber of Commerce, P.O. Box 57, Indian River, 49749, (231) 238-9325, dbodnar@irchamber.com or www.irchamber.com

Landings: Burt Lake State park is located at the SE end of Burt Lake in Indian River. Campground has modern camp sites, bath and showers, a beach house, playground, picnic area, general store and a boat ramp with parking. Also you can find a boat landing by Mullett and Burt Rd., one by Maple Bay, Kings Pt., and Chippewa Beach

Bait & Tackle: Pat & Gary's Party Store, 3758 South Straights Hwy., Indian River (Off I-75), (231) 238-6776

Crystal Lake Benzie County

When I head for Crystal Lake in the northwest side of the lower peninsula, almost a "stone's throw" from Lake Michigan, my mind always wanders toward all the quaint little towns like Beulah, Frankfort, Benzonia, and the famed Betsie River just to the south. Crystal is about as clear a lake as you can find, with very steep drop-offs in increments of 10-20 and 90-140 feet to a final depth of 160 feet. Certainly this almost 10,000-acre lake with that type of depth and clarity makes for a big-water fishery. It's a great lake to fish, but a magnificent lake to be on.

Overall, Crystal has good populations of smallmouth bass, rainbows, salmon, browns, lakers, perch, whitefish and smelt. It is stocked with rainbows and lakers approximately every other year, but other species such as coho and brown trout are not since they seem to reproduce naturally. This lake regularly produces Master Angler Awards in lake trout, rock bass, and smelt.

Smelt: Crystal is one of the best smelt lakes in the state. It is mostly a winter fishery. Anglers work the areas off Lobb Road (County Hwy 687 off M-115 on the south end of the lake) or in the bay areas. Popular baits are red spikes (maggots) for smelt or grubs. Anglers usually work between 40-100 feet down. Smelt were first stocked in Crystal Lake in 1912 and have thrived ever since. The smelt in Crystal can range upwards of 8-10 inches.

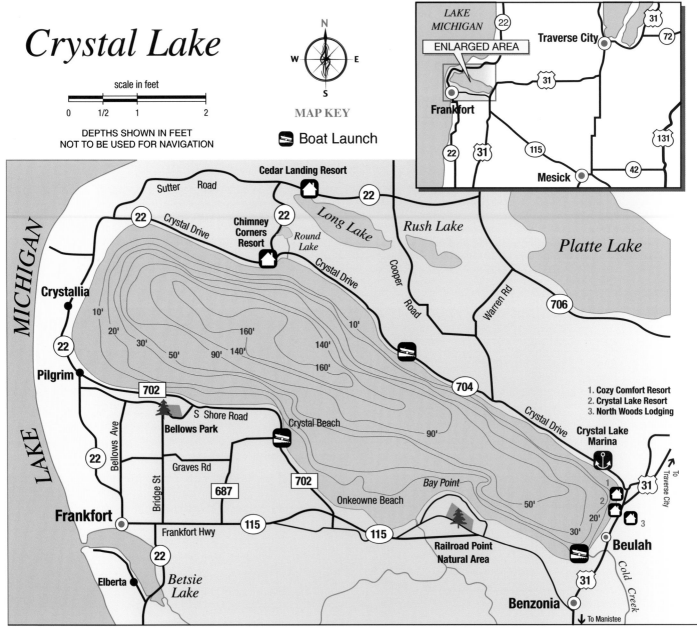

Lake Trout: Probably the number one fish species for anglers on Crystal is lake trout. In winter they jig in 160 feet of water and in summer they troll. Lake trout can be caught trolling with several different baits like spoons, flashers, cowbells, and minnows. It's best to send the line deep. Basically a lot of the same rigs you would use on Lake Michigan work on Crystal. Try the west end of Crystal in the deeper waters, or north and west end where there are some nice drop-offs in the 80-160-foot depths. During the ice fishing months, anglers jig with white or silver Swedish Pimples or Sandkicker jigs, which have a hook on both ends. Tip these with a gray or blue minnow and you will have what it takes to hook the popular lake trout.

Rainbows are probably the next most popular fish that anglers pursue on Crystal. Most are caught in the spring or fall, usually surf fishing off Beulah (village) Beach. Rainbow trout are imported from the Pacific Northwest. They're best caught during spawning runs from October to May, and you'll need spawn (loose eggs in bags), spinners, plugs, or crankbaits to catch them. They are also caught shortly after ice-out trolling in these same areas. Rainbows in the 15-18-inch size are not uncommon.

In deep lakes such as Crystal, it pays to have a fish locator for finding fish schools before setting up your gear.

Brown Trout: Although brown trout are not as plentiful in this lake, some anglers seek them out along the east shore where Cold Creek runs into Crystal Lake. This area is where the browns go to spawn. Anglers use tip-ups in this area of the lake.

Cohos are caught in spring and fall by shore fishermen. Summertime anglers catch them by trolling for lakers when often a coho will hit. They are caught in the ice fishing months by anglers fishing for whitefish. Cohos in the 18-21-inch size are not uncommon. Because of the water quality of this lake, the cohos are very pretty silver fish, and excellent eaters. If you're seeking salmon, you'll need crankbaits and artificial minnows.

Whitefish are actually popular here as well. The north shore from the marina in the northeast corner down to Buttercup Shores is the area anglers work during May and June especially, but these tasty fish can be caught all summer. Ice fishing these same areas, silver and white Swedish Pimples are the lures of choice.

Perch: You can catch perch in Crystal year around in the 8-60 feet water depths. They are plentiful all around the lake and it is not uncommon to catch them in the 14-15-inch size, although the average is more like 8-10 inches. Use minnows, waxworms and spikes. The Hali jig is popular and can be used all year, but especially in the winter.

Smallmouth Bass: Can grow to monstrous proportions in Crystal. There are some bass tournaments on this lake thanks to a growing exposure to the current bass population. You can find bass virtually all around the lake where drop-offs are located, and you do not have to go deep to find them. Fish shallow in June, then as the summer progresses try a bit deeper by slow trolling and casting. Use every typical bass lure, live bait to hardware. It is not uncommon to catch 5-6-pound bass here. Fish around boat docks along shore in the early morning for best success.

Rock Bass: There are "tons" of big rock bass in Crystal Lake, many in the 11-13-inch range. They can be found all around the lake and many anglers catch them when perch fishing. Rock and smallmouth bass can be caught with many different artificial lures, including bottom-bumpers and diving plugs.

Note: If you decide to ice fish Crystal Lake, try to pull off an ice-fishing marathon. Go for perch during the day and then set up for tasty smelt at night. Lakers might also be part of your catch. Access on the south side of the lake where you will only be a short walk out on the lake.

At a Glance

What: Lake trout, rock bass, smallmouth bass, perch, various other trout species

Where: One of the prettiest lakes in the state

Regulations: There are sturgeon here, but currently not allowed to be fished

Why: Enjoy fishing and enjoy the surroundings

Landings: A new state boat landing with four launch sites was completed in late 2011 on the south shore, off M-115 (Frankfort Hwy) on Mollineaux Road

Contacts: Benzie County Visitors Bureau, (800) 882-5801, Benzonia

Bait & Tackle: Five Corners, 284 S. Benzie Blvd., Beulah, 49617, (231) 882-5202

Deer Lake Charlevoix County

A lone early fall angler takes advantage of the glass-like waters and colorful reflections from nature's best on Deer Lake.

Deer Lake, located between Boyne Falls and Boyne City in Charlevoix County, is considered to be one of the small gem lakes by many people in this area, at only 443 surface acres in size. And that says a lot, considering that lakes like Charlevoix, Walloon, and many others exist here that dwarf Deer Lake in size. This lake is situated in one of the most popular summer resort areas of the state, such towns as Boyne City, Charlevoix, Petoskey, Harbor Springs are in this vicinity. If the hubby enjoys fishing, you can always drop your spouse or girlfriend off in one of the quaint little towns listed above and they can shop all day while you fish.

There are no DNR plantings in this lake, but rather all the fish thrive here via natural reproduction methods.

Tom Dureki, of Tom's Bait & Tackle, says that Deer Lake has, "lots of weed beds, with no significant drop-offs, aside from the one on the south end of the lake not far out from the boat landing." The south end of the lake has a contoured area that "steps down" from 5 feet to close to 20 feet in five-foot increments.

This lake is known for its bass, walleye, pike, bluegills, and more recently crappie. The perch population has unfortunately dwindled significantly over the years for unknown reasons, although Dureki thinks the cormorants had a lot to do with the demise of perch here.

Pike: Although not often large, pike can be occasionally found in these waters summer or winter. Many are undersized according to Dureki, but either spearing or using sucker minnows can land you a nice one.

Pike/Walleye Methods: Tip-ups are used for both pike and walleye during the ice-fishing season. Try the area off the boat landing in about 9 feet of water, and also in the north end of the lake. During summer, a crawler harness is most popular for walleye, and also larger size Rebels in blue and silver. Try the center of the lake, as well as the weed areas to the north and near the boat landing.

"Walleye are abundant here, and many are in the 18-22-inch size," says Dureki. Anglers fish for them summer and winter.

Bluegills/Crappies: Slab crappies in Deer Lake go on a feeding frenzy in May. Check out around the weed areas and stumps that occupy heavily in the lake. Crappies up to 14 inches are common. During summer, both of these popular and tasty panfish can often be found in 8-12 feet of water using waxworms and tear drops with a small bobber. In spring, both fish species are along the shallows where their beds are located. Since this lake has a gradual contour in most areas, try working most any of the shoreline shallows.

Bass: Bass, both large- and smallmouth, are considered excellent in Deer Lake. "It's not uncommon to land them in the 17-20-inch range," says Dureki. Casting around the weed beds at the north end of the lake, and also at the south end off the boat landing, are often productive. Also work the weed beds in the center of the lake. Top-water lures are popular on this lake, as are typical bass fishing methods.

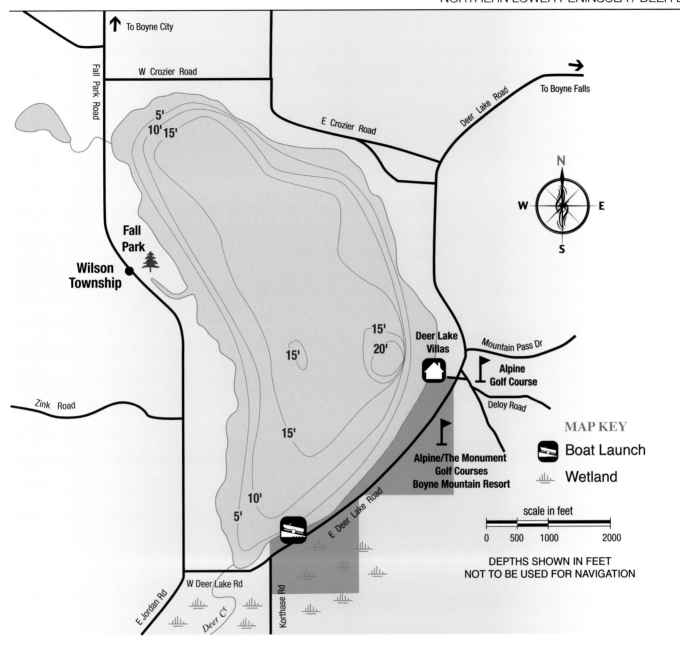

Deer Lake

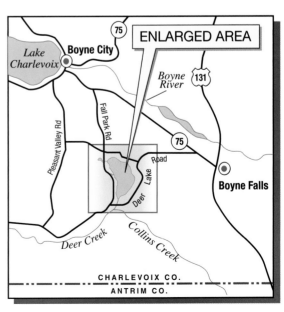

At a Glance

What: Deer Lake

Where: Near Boyne City and Charlevoix

Why: Great small lake for walleye and bass

Landings: One landing at the SE end of the lake

Bait & Tackle: Tom's Bait & Tackle, 801 Water St. East Jordan, 49727 (231) 536-3521

Eight Point Lake Clare County

Eight Point Lake is aptly named since the lake, as you might guess, has eight points extending from the water inland, some much more pronounced than others. Located about 15 miles west of Clare, this 387-acre lake has no real inlets and outlets, with the exception for a small drainage area that drains to a wetland.

Much of this lake is shallow, with a maximum depth of 25 feet. A lake association was established in 1946 and has taken a role in managing the lake. Over the years, the association has tackled such issues as water safety, fish stocking and violations, road and signage improvements, aquatic nuisance control, and swimmer's itch. The State acquired property on Eight Point Lake in 2008 and opened a public boating access site in September 2009.

Overall, in a 2010 DNR Survey of this lake, it was noted that bluegill remain the most abundant species. One species, pumpkinseed sunfish, seems to be increasing in abundance and size structure and age distribution appear very good, offering anglers another panfish to target. Walleye, smallmouth bass, largemouth bass, northern pike, rock bass and black crappie occur in lesser abundance but provide additional angling opportunities.

Bluegill: *"Bluegill are typically the most abundant fish species present in many lakes in this region,"* says Kathryn Schneider, Fish Biologist from the Bay City District office, *"and play a key role in community structure and overall sportfishing quality,"* she adds.

One species that should be highlighted in this lake is the pumpkinseed sunfish. These sunfish exhibit excellent growth, according to the DNR Survey, and attain very desirable sizes. Their success is probably tied to the large population of snails in Eight Point Lake. These, together with the bluegill, offer anglers great opportunities for fishing.

Rock bass catch rate and size structure in 2010 appears satisfactory and improved from 1995 and there is ample opportunity for anglers to catch them.

Very few black crappie were netted in 2010. Despite the low number caught, data suggests that crappie are growing well and reach larger sizes offering anglers opportunities to catch harvestable fish.

Largemouth Bass and Smallmouth Bass: Two of the primary predator fish in Eight Point Lake. Numbers of largemouth bass appear high but size structure shows them stacking up from 9 to 13 inches, and few larger ones were present. Growth is also slow. Very few largemouth bass were legal size in the netted population. There appear to be adequate older fish up to age 8 but very few are attaining larger sizes due to slow growth. Not enough smallmouth bass were caught to assess the population but they did appear larger than the largemouth.

Bluegills range from 7-9 inches according to Jim Darland, Eight Point Lake Association President, but he adds that, like a lot of the fish in this lake, they are not easy to pursue. The lake has no real structure, no major fish habitat, and therefore the fish are generally not concentrated, making fishing here a hit-and-miss proposition.

As for ice fishing, Jim says it seems like the fish are spread out, but like any body of water you always "look for the bodies" on the ice when you arrive if you are not familiar with the lake.

Walleye: Jim says that they are not wall hangers, but rather in the 17-19-inch average size. Once again, he states there is no one hotspot or structured area to look for them.

The catch rate, size structure, and growth of walleye, according to the DNR Survey, indicate a fairly stable population. Captured walleye ranged from 12 to 27 inches. Ninety-four percent were legal size, or 15 inches or greater. There were 9 year classes represented suggesting survival of stocked fish and survival of naturally reproduced fish. Walleye growth is excellent. There are large walleyes available for anglers to catch. The reason for this survival may be that the larger fall fingerlings stocked in the past exhibited superior survival.

Perch: The survey indicates appreciable numbers, but their size structure and age distribution was relatively poor. Few yellow perch appear to survive beyond age 3 and grow large enough to recruit into the harvestable fishery. At best, the current fishery only offers an opportunity

DNR Photo, David Kenyon

Float tubing and fly-fishing for gills on the beds is a great way to spend a spring day on the lake.

for incidental catch of yellow perch of harvestable size.

A new fisheries DNR management prescription for Eight Point Lake is currently being drafted and it recommends stocking walleye to help maintain the population. The Lake Association has started stocking walleye and there is evidence that the population was also present historically. With the added pressure and the new access site it may be important to supplement the stocking. This prescription recommends stocking up to 20,000 walleyes every other year. DNR stocks spring fingerlings that average 2 inches in length, in contrast to the fall fingerlings stocked by the Association which are often 6 inches or larger.

The northern pike population was found to be abundant and slow growing with very few or none reaching legal size. Recommendations would be to thin the stunted population and allow the fewer remaining northern pike to experience better growth. Unfortunately, according to the 2010 DNR Survey notes, at the present time no changes can be made to the northern pike regulations.

Note: The more recent private-party fish planting of this lake includes some sizable fish, including 7-inch crappie in 2007, a thousand 6-7-inch walleye in 2008 and 2010, along with 30,000 DNR-planted walleye in 2011.

At a Glance

What: Bluegill, walleye, sunfish

Where: An overall shallow lake, with no real hotspots

Information/Guides: Clare County Convention & Visitors Bureau, 429 North McEwan Street, Clare, (989) 386-6400

Landings: A newly constructed (as of this writing) DNR landing at the south end of the lake along the arm that runs south

Bait & Tackle: Bev's Eight Point Lake Store, 10585 South Shore Drive, Lake, (989) 544-3340 (dockside fuel also)

Eight Point Lake

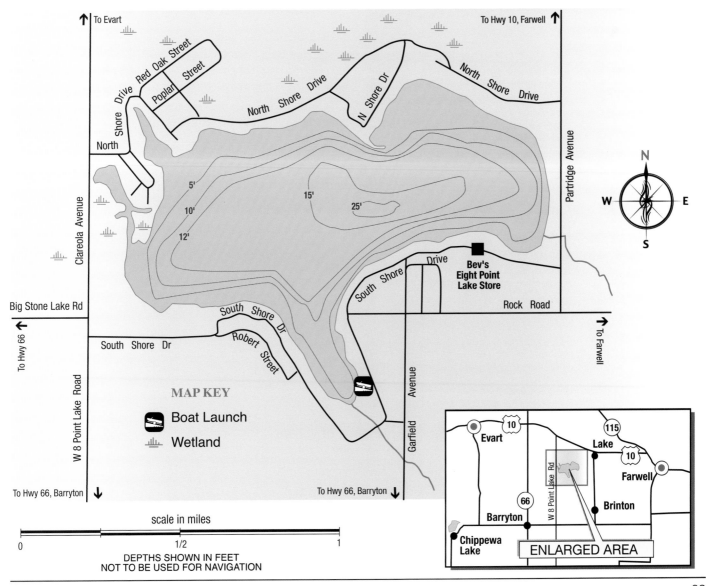

MAP KEY
- Boat Launch
- Wetland

scale in miles

0   1/2   1

DEPTHS SHOWN IN FEET
NOT TO BE USED FOR NAVIGATION

ENLARGED AREA

Fletcher Pond Alpena County

Fletcher Pond always holds a special place in my hunting and fishing experiences. It has the habitat for great pike fishing, and the "flooded woods" type environment conducive to some quality duck hunting. I was first introduced to Fletchers when I used to go turkey hunting up in that area. After a morning hunt, we would head out to Fletcher's to fish for hammer handle pike.

The term "pond" is sort of a misnomer since the surface are of Fletcher is almost 9,000 acres, with a shoreline of 25 miles. It's a shallow body of water, only averaging 5-7 feet with a maximum depth of around 11 feet. Fletcher is actually a 9,000-acre flooding, created by damming the South Branch of Thunder Bay River for hydro-electric power generation. Prior to its being flooded in the 1930s, this area was a sizable cedar swamp, providing wintering habitat for thousands of deer annually.

Being shallow, and the fact that it was previously a wooded habitat, Fletcher contains many dead heads and snags. There are extensive areas of cattails in the shallow shoreline areas, especially in the southern portions of the lake, making for good waterfowl and fish habitat. No Lake Huron beaches here. But a sportsman's paradise nonetheless.

This very shallow body of water with its heavy cover supports a variety of game and fish, making it a great place for anglers. Six-pound largemouth bass are caught here every year, and 30-inch pike are common, although there are a lot of hammer handles as well.

The challenge at Fletcher Pond is to find a way to fish it without losing one's rigging in the heavy cover. The fishing season is summer and winter, with ice fishing nearly as popular as the summer season.

According to well-versed resident Dean Robinson from Jack's Landing in Hillman, largemouth bass are the biggest draw to anglers here, followed by pike and some excellent crappie and perch fishing. "Wait for three contiguous warm days in the spring when there is an ice meltdown, then the fishing kicks in with full force" says Dean. Ice meltdown will do two positive things: runoff causes oxygen levels to increase and water temps to rise, both producing increased fish activity.

Robinson also stated that the pike caught in Fletcher are larger in bulk, that is, a 30-inch pike caught in ABC Lake is not as heavy as a pike caught in Fletcher. Although not a scientific study, with 9000 acres of excellent fish habitat, this could very well be the case.

Winter pike can be found almost anywhere in Fletcher, but check out the high weed trough in front of Jack's Landing; an area about a mile long and quarter mile wide running in an east/west direction. During winter this zone has the most water after the fall/winter draw-down when most of the lake becomes almost fishless. More than half the lake is less than three-foot deep, and after the two-foot drawdown, the fish concentrate in the deeper areas, the area near Jack's.

Largemouth bass are caught more than smallmouth on about a 9 to 1 ratio. One note of caution: when bass are caught off their spawning beds, it pays dividends to release them back into the body of water they were taken from so that spawning continues and future generations of fish are produced. Catch and keep does not take place until the last Saturday in May on Fletcher.

Methods: For early season bass, topwater lures work best. Bass will explode out of the water and grab your offering. For pike, the word is big and flashy. I've also caught pike on spinnerbaits and crankbaits in chartreuse, bright orange and white. Also try Magnum Shad Raps in a fire or perch finish.

The most common method of pike fishing is to head up wind, shut off your boat motor, and drift fish. You will eventually be taken over active fish. Don't forget to use a strong line and heavy rod for pike, along with a tight drag. Bass are more sensitive to line choice, but, once again, a good balance between line and drag is important. When the bluegills are up in the shallows, green pumpkin and other natural colors would be a good bet.

I also enjoy fly-fishing along the shoreline for bluegills and crappies using a simple Foam Spider to entice them. Weedless spoons and swim baits have also proven themselves to be effective, as well as soft plastics twitched along the submerged timber for bass or pike. A Texas rig and rubber is another way to work the area without snagging up.

At a Glance

What: Fishing a very shallow and unique body of water

Where: Hillman in NE part of the lower peninsula

Why: Great pike fishing, along with significant bass and panfish

Regs: No pike spearing here

Techniques: Lots of topwater lures to help avoid snags

Landings: North side of the lake off Emil's Landing Road and Tennis

Bait & Tackle/Information: Jack's Landing, 20836 Tennis Rd., Hillman, 49746, Email: jackslanding@gmail.com, (989) 742-4370; **Fletcher's Landing Fishing Resort,** 5614 Emils Landing Road, Hillman, 49746, (989) 742-4166; **Lyons Landing & Travel Trailer,** 24553 Landing Rd., Hillman, 49746, www.lyonslanding.net/, E-mail: lyons_landing@hotmail.com, (989) 742-4756; **Anglers Hideaway,** Miller Rd., Hillman, 49746, info@anglershideaway.net, (989) 742-4565

Tube fishing can be a very relaxing and rewarding method of fishing.

Fletcher Pond

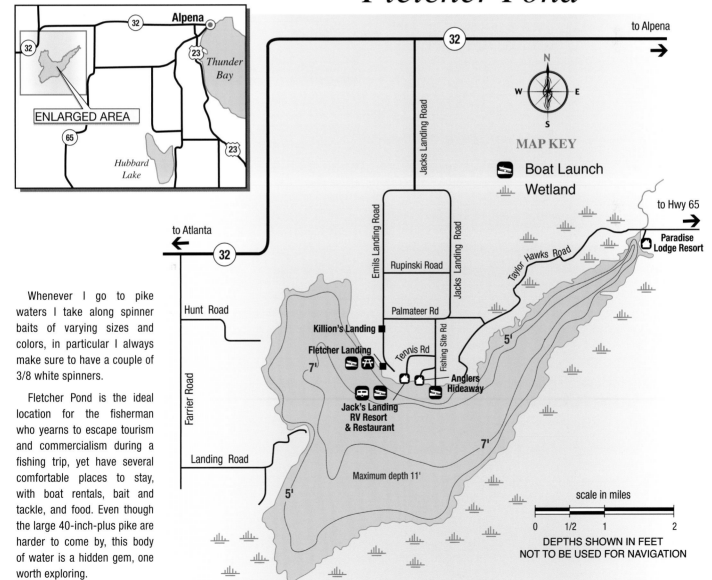

Whenever I go to pike waters I take along spinner baits of varying sizes and colors, in particular I always make sure to have a couple of 3/8 white spinners.

Fletcher Pond is the ideal location for the fisherman who yearns to escape tourism and commercialism during a fishing trip, yet have several comfortable places to stay, with boat rentals, bait and tackle, and food. Even though the large 40-inch-plus pike are harder to come by, this body of water is a hidden gem, one worth exploring.

Grand Lake Presque Isle County

Grand Lake is a substantial-sized lake of 5,660 acres located in Presque Isle County. It is approximately 7 miles in length and up to 1.5 miles in width. The lake lies on the landward side of a prominent promontory (i.e., peninsula) in the county that juts out into Lake Huron, thereby making the promontory almost an island and indirectly giving the promontory and county their name of "Presque Isle."

Lori Vanschoten of the Fireside Inn on the lake is very familiar with fishing on Grand. She says that there are four main fish that anglers pursue here: walleye, pike, smallmouth bass, and perch. One note is that this lake has the luxury of having many islands, allowing anglers a spot to fish even when it is windy, utilizing the leeward side of an island if the winds pick up.

Smallmouth: Lori says that bass can be found on almost any island point or rock formation, and there are 18 islands existing on Grand Lake. There is a very favorable rocky bottom with a limestone base in this lake bottom, and lots of outcroppings that bass prefer hanging around. The bass are average in size, according to Lori, but in the respectable 3-5-pound range. The shoreline is about 6-8 feet deep.

Walleye: Trolling around the group of smaller islands east of Grand Island is a good starting point for summer walleye; also try off Whiskey Point to the south, and in the bay at the north end of the lake. In the winter months, ice fishing is popular in the north bay area with walleye averaging in the small, but good eating size of 15-18 inches.

Terry McConnell, Lori's husband and the organizer for the summer and winter pike festival, states that although the average pike size in this lake is in the 28-32-inch range, it is not uncommon to catch 30-plus- or even 40 plus inch pike.

The areas popular for both winter and summer pike are Black Bass Bay early in the season, off the islands such as Three Sister's Island, south end of Grand Island, by Warren Creek on the southwest end of the lake, and the shoreline along M-23. Walleye and bass also compete for these same areas.

You can try trolling from the south end of Grand Island and move along

A lazy day in a canoe casting for bass or pike.

DNR Photo, David Kenyon

to about three quarter miles to the south toward Warren Creek, then back again. Popular lures are Shad Rap in the Perch color, crawler harnesses, and the Broken Back Rapala. With its slight exaggeration of the Rapala's unique baitfish-in-distress behavior, the Jointed gets the undivided attention of otherwise uninterested gamefish. This articulated, or "broken back," bait can be fished like the Original Floating, top to bottom. It's a good choice after a cold front, when fish are traditionally finicky and in a negative feeding mood.

A live sucker minnow hanging about three feet below the water surface from a large bobber floated over a weed bed is also a good method to catch pike. Winter time is for the common tip-up method with sucker minnows.

Terry also says the bluegills and perch are coming back due to the cormorant control placed in this area over the past several years. In June, check the beds

At a Glance

What: Walleye, bass, pike, gar pike, perch

Where: Fish the many bays and islands located on this lake

Regs: No pike spearing

Information: www.presqueislemi.org; Presque Isle County - Visitor Information Service, 151 East Huron, Rogers City, 49779, (989) 734-8446

Landings: There are three public boat launches on the west side of Grand Lake, accessible via State Hwy 23

Bait & Tackle: Buck's Bait & Tackle, 8501 U.S. 23 North, Alpena, 49707, (989) 595-2121, budd@bucksbait.com; **Adrian's Sport Shop,** 335 North Bradley Hwy., Rogers City, 49779, (989) 734-2053

along the shoreline for bluegills, using poppers or a crappie rig. Terry states that it is not uncommon to bring home some nice-eating 9-11-inch perch. Try the south end of the lake along the shoreline for bluegills.

McConnell also stated that there are a lot of gar pike in this lake if you are interested. They are all over the lake and the best bet is to work the shoreline.

Panfish: Perch in the 9-11-inch size are not uncommon in Grand Lake, says McConnell. Even perch in the 12-14-inch range are often caught here. You can find perch anglers all over the lake, South Bay, Grand Island, North Bay, etc. The panfish have "exploded" according to Terry, since the cormorant control program went into effect.

Notes: Black Bass Bay is very shallow, less than a few feet deep, and much of it has a mucky bottom. Back in 2000, the DNR planted 7000 northern pike in Grand Lake.

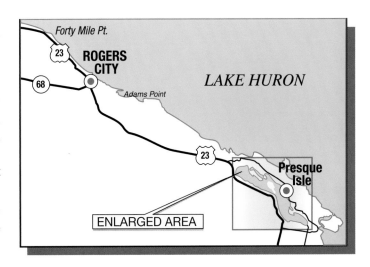

Grand Lake

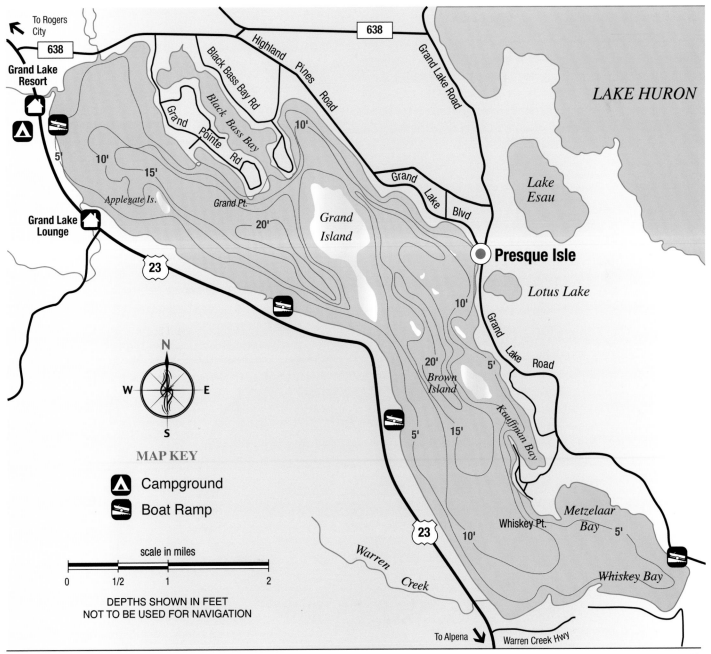

MAP KEY

▲ Campground

🚤 Boat Ramp

scale in miles

0   1/2   1   2

DEPTHS SHOWN IN FEET
NOT TO BE USED FOR NAVIGATION

Hamlin Lake Mason County

Hamlin Lake, another one of the many high-quality lakes within the shadows of Lake Michigan, is located 4 miles north of Ludington. It is more than 12 miles long and 5,000 acres in size, providing ample space for boaters and anglers alike. A terrific catch of fish is promising both in the summer and winter when tip-ups and shanties dot the ice.

Whether you work the bayous or head for deeper waters, Hamlin offers a nice variety of fish. Muskie, northern pike, large- and smallmouth bass, perch, crappie, bluegill and over 150,000 walleye and 12,000 northern muskie were planted in 2011 alone, providing great fishing opportunities.

Hamlin Lake has had a reputation for producing big bluegills and other panfish for ice-anglers, and the last few winters have been fantastic.

This lake has changed according to Dave Mahannah of Hamlin Sports Center located on the lake. Dave states that there was a flood a few years prior to this writing that moved some of the deep water areas around. One area in the center of the lake was over 100 feet deep, and now is around 96 feet due to the sand filling in the lake. This filled area now extends an incredible mile and a half long and a quarter mile wide. There are no accurate topo maps for this lake due to these changes. There are lots of 25-50-foot areas of water, but the bayous are mostly under 10 feet deep.

Northern Pike:
Pike can be taken on the edge of the shallow-water weed lines and on the edge of the shallow-water drop-offs. Fishing pike usually means using minnows (shiners, suckers) either with a hook or a jig. You can catch them with rod and reel or with a tip-up. If you like to spear, pike can be taken by spear in the same locations. Either live suckers or decoys can be used as bait.

Recommended artificial baits include large Jigging Rapalas, lead-head jigs, Swedish Pimples, Hopkins Spoons, and live bait would be your standard shiners and suckers.

Walleye:
Jigs worked on the drop-offs seem to work best. I recommend tipping your jigs with shiner minnows.

A small to medium size Walleye Flyer Jig by System Tackle has been a very good jig for Dave. He usually tips them with a shiner minnow, but you can use them minus the shiner as well. A small to medium size Rapala Jigging Minnow also works well. Both the perch and the natural (silver) minnow colors are popular.

Use Hopkins Spoons or Swedish Pimples, Walleye Flyer, Fuzz-e-Grub type jigs, and live bait use shiners, or creek minnows.

Large- & Smallmouth Bass:
Generally, bass can be found in the shallow-water weed beds or on the edge of the shallow-water drop-offs. You can catch them on minnows or large wax worms, but jigging with artificial baits usually works better.

Try Jigging Rapalas, and small-dressed jigs tipped with a minnow, or use medium size shiner minnows.

Bluegill:
The most common method used to catch bluegill through the ice is a small ice-fishing jig tipped with a wax worm, corn bore or spike. You can either tight-line them or use a small float or spring bobber. Usually in 4 to 10 feet of water around weed beds is best. At first ice, the mouth of Indian Pete Bayou on Upper Hamlin Lake is a popular spot. Other popular spots are the South Bayou and the center of the mouth to North Bayou. From mid January on, the most popular spots are in the middle of Upper Hamlin Lake just north and east of Wilson Hill Park and in the South Bayou on Lower Hamlin Lake. Try fishing for both suspended and bottom-feeding fish.

For gills use small ice-fishing jigs, or wax worms and spikes.

Crappie:
You can catch crappie in the same bluegill areas fishing with wax worms, corn bores and spikes during the early part of the ice-fishing season. Usually right at dawn and again right at dusk is best. I prefer waiting until February and fishing 18 to 24 feet of water on the north-side drop-off in Upper Hamlin Lake at night. There, I would use a small treble hook (size 12 to 16) tipped with a small shiner minnow beneath a small slip bobber.

Use small ice-fishing jigs, small jigs with spinners. Live bait includes wax worms, spikes, corn bores, and smaller shiner minnows.

Perch:
During early ice, perch can be caught at both the edge of the shallow-water weed beds (6 to 12 feet) and on the edges of the steep drop-offs. I find that typically after the first couple of weeks of ice, the bigger perch seem to school-up in the deeper water (16 to 45 feet) of the steep banks. Some spots to try are straight off the Middle Bayou in about 30 to 45 feet of water and off the North Bayou in 12 to 30 feet of water. I like to fish small jigs tipped with minnows, but plain hooks and minnows will also work.

Use 1/32- or 1/16-ounce jigs, small Rapala jigging lures, small Swedish Pimples, small Hopkins Spoons, shiner minnows, or wax worms.

Ice-Fishing Note:
The fish are usually pretty sluggish when the water gets cold. A general tip is work your baits very slowly and be patient. Also, the water is cold, switch to minnows. Either a plain hook tipped with a minnow or a jig tipped with a minnow. A shanty or wind screen is almost a must on Hamlin Lake on most winter days. Being so close to Lake Michigan, and being such a large lake with many wide open areas, the wind is usually very chilling.

Tens of thousands of walleye plantings provide results like this.

At a Glance

What: Good panfishing

Where: A unique lake near Lake Michigan

Regs: Recent no-size-limit regulations for pike in Hamlin Lake seem to be paying big dividends

Information/Guides: www.hamlinlake.com; for more detailed information on fishing Hamlin, go to: www.nbayou.com

Landings: There are boat landings in the north end in upper Hamlin, or you can launch at the state park on the west side north of the dam. There is also a landing in the south bayou which is free, but you must travel through a tunnel and under a bridge. A larger boat or pontoon will not fit. Something in the 18-foot size or smaller should be able to fit. Hamlin Resort has one but being a private area there is a fee involved

Contacts: Ludington Area Convention & Visitors Bureau, VisitLudington.com, 800-542-4600 or online at www.ludingtoncvb.com, pureludington.com.

Bait & Tackle: Hamlin Grocery (carries tackle and limited live bait), 3611 N. Jebavy Rd., (231) 843-2058; **Dave Mahannah Hamlin Sport Center,** 5760 W. Dewey, (231) 845-0001(tackle and repairs), **North Bayou Resort & Marina** (live bait and tackle on the east side of the lake), 4849 N. Lakeshore Drive, Ludington, 49431, (231) 845-5820

Hamlin Lake

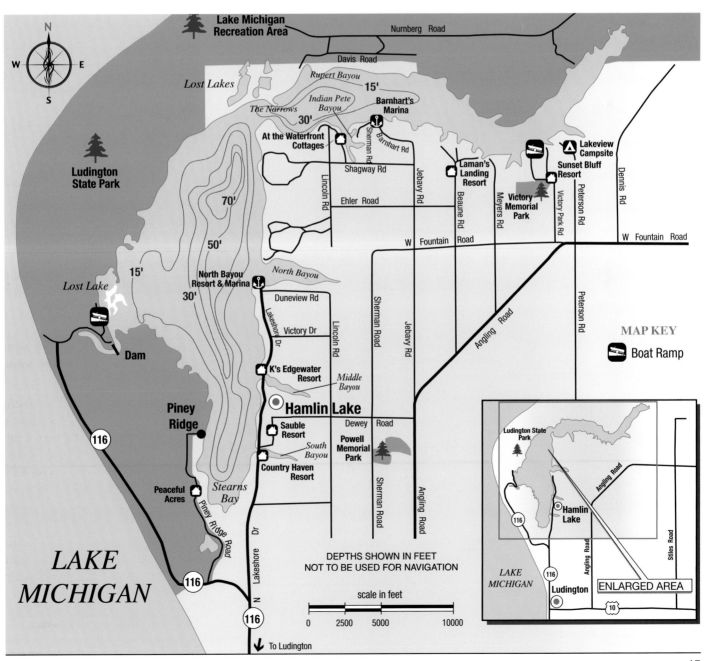

DEPTHS SHOWN IN FEET
NOT TO BE USED FOR NAVIGATION

scale in feet

0   2500   5000   10000

Higgins Lake Roscommon County

Higgins Lake is, rightfully so, considered one of the most beautiful lakes anywhere. How can it not be? Approximately 10,000 acres of crystal-clear Caribbean colored water, with a maximum depth of 136 feet. Scuba divers enjoy the shallow shoreline that eventually drops off like the Grand Canyon.

Centuries before European settlers came to North America, the Chippewa Indians called the lake Majinabeesh, which means "sparkling water". A well-earned distinction.

Ice Fishing: Higgins is normally a cold lake due to its depth and many springs that add cold (approx 50-degree) water on a constant basis. The clarity of the water allows ice anglers in a shanty to view fish swimming tens of feet below the surface. Ice-fishing on Higgins means a variety of trout species and of course the highly prized yellow perch. Be aware, however, that Higgins is deep and therefore slow to freeze, therefore safe ice-fishing often does not take place until later in the ice-fishing season.

Once considered safe, this lake produces some of the best and most consistent ice-angling in the state. You should also be aware of the springs and currents that can cause weak ice on the lake. Also check the ice every so often as you move around to be sure you are venturing onto solid ice.

Higgins Lake

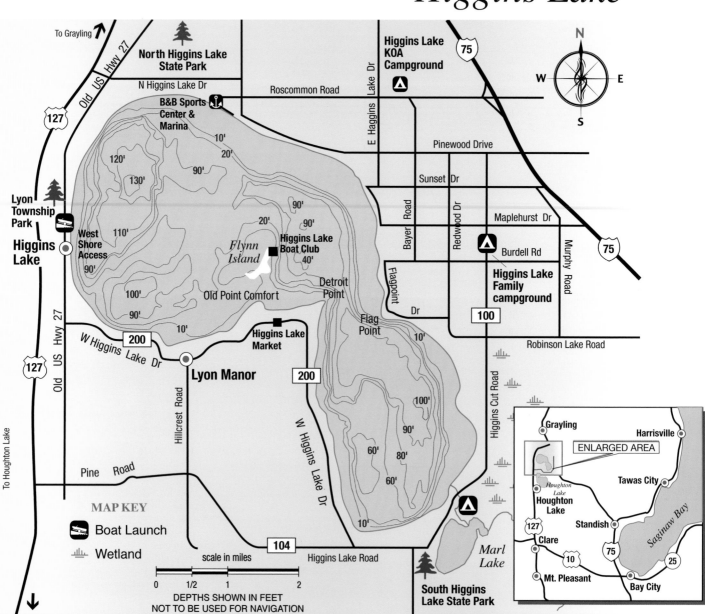

MAP KEY
🚤 Boat Launch
🌿 Wetland

scale in miles
0   1/2   1   2

DEPTHS SHOWN IN FEET
NOT TO BE USED FOR NAVIGATION

At a Glance

What: Trout, pike, perch, smelt

Where: Higgins Lake south of Grayling

Why: One of Michigan's most beautiful lakes, with plenty of fishing action.

Landing: The best boat access is the North and South State Park areas. Both have camping facilities as well, but check with the DNR for reservations, (michigan.gov/dnr)

Information: Higgins Lake/Roscommon Chamber of Commerce at (989) 275-8760, www.hlrcc.com

Bait & Tackle: B&B Sports & Marina, 431 Clare Blvd., Roscommon, 48653, (989) 821-6549; **Evergreen Party Store,** 9961 N. Higgins Lake Dr., Roscommon, 48653, (989) 821-5425; **Higgins Lake Sport & Party Store,** 10028 West Shore Dr., Roscommon, 48653, (989) 821-9517; **Phoenix Party Store,** 9374 W. Higgins Lake Dr., Higgins Lake, 48627, (989) 821-7220; **Sports Barn,** 9475 N. Cut Rd. Roscommon, 48653, (989) 821-9511

Perch: Dozens upon dozens of ice shanties can be seen on Higgins, especially on the weekends, most seeking 8-10-inch perch. Not huge perch by any means, but tasty nonetheless.

Early season perch fishing activity occurs on both the north and south shores of Higgins in 20 to 40 feet of water, using a typical two-hook perch rig baited with spikes or wax worms. Minnows and wigglers can be very effective as well. The sunken islands are also good places to seek out perch, and it's not uncommon to take your limit in these areas.

Smelt: For smelt or perch, try the W. Higgins Lake Road boat launch, just south of the Phoenix Party Store. Eric Carlson, owner of the store, which also sells bait and tackle, can assist you with information. The smelt are fairly active, but there was a die-off a couple of years ago, which apparently is normal, and cycles with the perch. When the smelt are low in numbers, the perch size seems to increase.

Lake Trout: Lakers hang out and feed in the deeper zones on Higgins, usually greater than 70 to 100 feet of water. I start in the shallow depths early in the day and gradually moving to the deeper holes using a slip sinker rig. Lake trout averaging 5-8 pounds, with a few in the 15-20-pound-plus range, can be caught on any given day. Anglers often use slammers or tip-ups baited with live smelt, blue or gray shiners, dropping them on the bottom. Jigging with spoons can be highly effective, too.

Rainbows/Browns: Although there is a reasonably good population of rainbows and browns (but not as many as years ago, possibly attributed to fewer plantings of trout and the lake levels near stream mouths), less attention is paid to them for whatever reason. They are usually taken in the top 20 feet of water. Use a light line, outfitted with bobbers and wigglers, spawn or minnows for hooking these species. Swedish Pimples also work well. The west-shore public access is active for rainbows and browns. Then later in the season, anglers seek out rainbows in water as shallow as 3 feet where some creeks enter the lake along the west shore.

Pike: Pike spearing through the ice is very popular on Higgins. If you wish to try your hand at this, the set-up is quite "simple." An ice shanty, suitable in size to be able to use a spear, a pike-spearing decoy, and bait. Forty-inch-plus pike are not uncommon in Higgins. Try the area off Lincoln Rd, on the southwest corner of the South Arm of the lake. Also the east side can be productive about mid way up off Kelly Beach. Most spear in 20-30 feet of water, meaning just off the drop-off. While sitting in the shanty waiting for that monster pike to swim through your hole, you may want to place a tip-up close to your shanty, baited with a gray or smelt in hopes of hooking a nice pike or trout. You can always set-up and spear for pike anytime of the day.

Note on Spearing: Most spear-anglers use a wooden or plastic decoy to attract fish to their holes. The decoys usually imitate a pike or perhaps a sucker and may be as large as 12 to 15 inches in length. The spear is suspended above the hole with the end of the handle attached to a long rope. The rope is often secured to the inside of the top of the shanty. The spear is designed to be dropped, rather than thrown and the design permits it to sort of glide through the water rather than angling off to one side or the other.

Warm-Weather Fishing: In spring and summer, anglers enjoy the beauty of Higgins even more, as the water takes on its brilliant blue/green color.

Bass: This is the time of the year when smallmouth bass in the 5-pound range are popular targets for anglers. May is a good month along the shallows near the island and the drop-offs. When off their beds, try casting with various lures along shore where docks are located, or under some of the boats anchored in the shallows. One note however, it pays in the long run to release the bass back into the water. Most anglers are not fond of eating bass, so releasing them will assure good fishing opportunities in the future.

Perch: Perch are also abundant in the weed areas, north of North Point, as well as off Treasure Island in 30-40 feet of water. Also try the south end of the lake on both the east side as well as the southwest corner. Maintain the approximately 40' depth no matter where you fish for perch during the summer months.

Lakers: For lakers, meander the areas along the drop-offs which are readily noticeable due to the color changes along the entire shoreline. Try various hardware, such as Rapala's or cowbells, trolled along the drop-offs. In late summer, downriggers in deeper water can be productive.

If you have young kids and wish to introduce them to fishing, try rock bass around the sunken island. Perch rigs, crawlers, spoons, Diamond Kings, and Stingers will provide hours of almost non-stop action; a great way to get your young kids interested in the sport of fishing.

Patience will pay off for this angler on Higgins.

Houghton Lake
Roscommon County

Houghton Lake is one of the state's premier highly fished lakes; not because you can catch Master Angler sized fish, but rather because it is a complete 20,000-acre, shallow-water fishery that provides thousands of hours of fishing opportunities for Michigan anglers of all ages. It is Michigan's largest inland lake, with a maximum depth of 22 feet and average depth of only 8 feet. Due to its shallow depth, during most years, there is plenty of ice by Christmas, and anglers are often still on the ice in early April. Houghton Lake is sometimes referred to as "Michigan's other Great Lake."

"There are no known guides on this large lake," says Chip McCullough, a local resident and knowledgeable angler on this lake. The reason, he states, "is because it is such a humbling lake, one that does not always allow you to find a definitive fishing pattern. Just when you think you have it figured out, it changes," he says. "But it is a fun lake and a complete fishery," Chip says.

McCullough states that "finding the weed edges is key to finding fish during first ice." Panfish tend to go on a feeding frenzy during this early season ice on Houghton.

Species fished in Houghton Lake include walleye, pike, bluegills, perch, crappie, and both large- and smallmouth bass.

Walleye:
Walleye fishing at Houghton Lake will not provide you with the monster walleye you can find in the Saginaw Bay or elsewhere. The average size in this lake will be more like legal size up to around 18-19 inches. Good eating size. It is rare, according to Chip McCullough, to catch a walleye in the mid to upper 20-inch size. You will catch multiple year class, i.e, 12-14 inches and up.

For both summer and winter fishing, all species in Houghton relate to the extensive weed areas that you find where there is the transition from 8-12 feet of water. It is where the weed lines exist in the 2-4-foot depth, or the 100 acre middle grounds in the north central area of this large lake, and it is where the sand bars exist that finds the water depths dropping off from 8-12 foot. In other words, Houghton has an extensive weed bed growth all around not only the shoreline, but in the middle as well. Chip states that the walleye fishing is best early and late in the day. Early in the season, the walleyes will be fairly shallow in 6 to 8 feet of water. As the season progresses, the walleyes move from the shallow areas to deeper waters, in the 12- to 14-foot depths, and fishing can become a bit more of a challenge.

DNR stocking records indicate over 100,000 fingerlings were stocked in 2011, but that was to make up for the lack of stocking for several previous years due to the contagious VHS fish virus problem. Those fish should be at catchable size late 2013.

Tip-ups and jigging with walleye minnows work best here as they do on other walleye lakes. Swedish Pimples are a popular lure for walleye.

Pike:
Pike are often caught while fishing for walleye, using the same tip-ups tipped with golden shiners or sucker minnows and jigging. Winter is the best time to fish for pike here. There is no spearing allowed on this lake. Fish the same areas as you do for walleye, i.e., weed beds along shore or out in the middle. Pike are predators and look for areas to ambush their meal.

A 40-inch pike is rare, according to McCullough, but pike in the 30-inch range are not uncommon. During summer, anglers troll using live bait along the weed line edges.

Bass:
Bass, both largemouth and smallmouth, are significantly under fished in Houghton Lake. There are good numbers of bass in this lake, and a few 20- inch smallmouth available. But overall there are many other better bass fishing lakes in Michigan and in this area of the state, that Houghton has not gained a strong reputation as a bass fishing lake. The forage-fish population is not high here either, making smaller perch, bluegills, and other small fish food for the predators.

For bass fishing locations, there are significant areas of weed growth all along the shoreline drop-offs, as well as the middle grounds in the north-central area of the lake. All are potential bass hangouts. With the weed growth,

At a Glance

What: Panfish and walleye fishing

Where: During first ice panfish can often be found in the south-shore weed beds. Crappies can be found at this time in 6 to 8 feet of water. Panfish can be found from top to bottom of the water column.

Why: Some great fishing opportunities all packed into one magnificent lake.

Regs: No pike spearing here

Techniques: In general, chartreuse and gold teardrops for panfish

Landings: West Shore Landing: Located on the west side of the lake a half mile north of the intersection of M55 and Highway 27. This is one of the better boat ramps on the lake with lots of parking and restroom facilities. The ramp has six launch lanes; **South Shore Boat Landing:** This ramp is located half way between Prudenville and Hwy 27 in downtown Houghton Lake. The South Shore boat ramp is a DNR ramp and one of the better launch facilities on the lake with lots of parking and restroom facilities; **East Shore Boat Ramp:** This landing is located on East Houghton Lake Drive between Hwy 18 and the Roscommon Airport. It is a DNR ramp that has one dock and restroom facilities. The ramp is pretty much out in the open lake and can pose some challenges on a windy day. There are also many private boat-access facilities spotted around the lake.

Contacts: Houghton Lake Area Tourist & Convention Bureau, (800) 676-5330, www.visithoughtonlake.com, www.roscommoncounty.com

Bait & Tackle: Edgewater Beach Marina, 8320 W. Houghton Lake Dr., Houghton Lake, 48629, (989) 422-4221; **Heights Marina,** 900 Shoreline Dr., Houghton Lake, 48629, (989) 422-5712; **Korbinski's Marine & Bait Shop,** 365 W. Houghton Lake Dr., Prudenville, 48655, (989) 366-5306; **Lyman's on the Lake,** 6560 W. Houghton Lake Dr., Houghton Lake, 48629, (989) 422-3231, www.HoughtonLakeFishing.com; **Zager's Sportsman Bait & Tackle,** 228 Rapson Ave., Houghton Lake, 48629, (989) 366-5471.

you will need plenty of weedless lures, or try a crawler harness along the edge of the weed beds.

Bluegills:
Back in 2002, a weed treatment program took place here as well as on many inland lakes in Michigan due to milfoil and other invasive weeds. After the treatment, and prior to more weeds developing, the existing bluegill populations would school-up under pontoon boats seeking some refuge, however they were heavily predated by larger fish and were easily over-harvested by anglers. It has taken many years for them to rebound, but as of this writing, the gill population is again at healthy levels due to emergent weed growth. Such weed growth in many of our inland lakes can act as a two-edged sword. They are beneficial on one hand, but can be a problem for boaters trying to access good fishing locations.

For both winter and summer fishing once again look for weedbed areas, mostly in the 8-foot weed flats. Most anglers use small minnows and tear drops. You will find 8-10-inch gills here with some larger catches possible. Houghton Lake has no rock structure or buried log structures so, once again, everything here relates to weed beds. Try the beds along the shoreline in spring and weed-line edges in the deeper water at the north-central part of the lake for best success.

Chartreuse and gold teardrops are popular for panfish, with the jigs tipped with wax worms or spikes.

Crappie:
Crappie are often an incidental catch in Houghton Lake, as anglers target walleye or other fish species. There are some sizable crappie in this lake, and a 12-inch fish is not uncommon. In spring, the many channels can be hot for crappie and gills. But after that, you just need to be in the right place at the right time to catch these appetizing fish. Use live bait, small minnows, for catching them.

Perch:
Perch are fairly small in this lake, most commonly in the 7-8-inch size. A rare one is in the 10-inch-plus size. You will probably work hard to get a limit of harvestable-size perch says McCullough, but try the same weed areas as you would for bluegills and other panfish.

Michigan's largest inland lake is always popular for walleye.

Houghton Lake

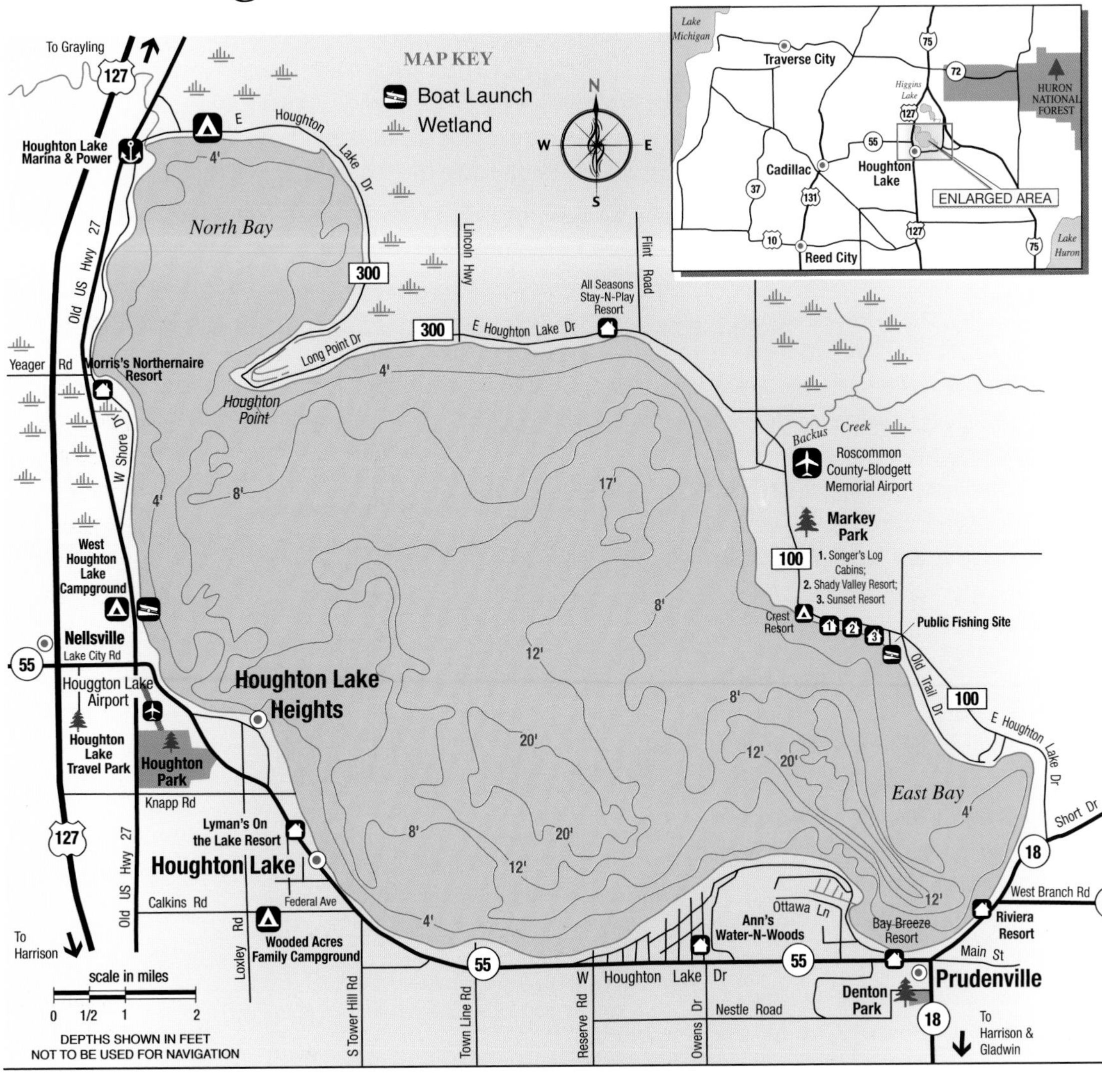

MAP KEY

🛥 Boat Launch

🌾 Wetland

Note: Get a contour map of this lake, take your electronics along, and look for the drop-offs along the shoreline, or head out to the middle grounds. You will find a weed bed on the south end of the middle grounds, then a 17-foot channel, then another weed bed. They are sizable and you should not have much of a problem locating them. You could spend the entire summer fishing just the middle grounds since it holds a plethora of fish species.

Houghton Lake DNR Note:
Just prior to the publication of this book, it was learned that after nearly 75 years, the spearfishing prohibition on Houghton Lake in Roscommon County has been removed. The order also allows for crossbows to be added to the list of acceptable spearing gear for anglers spearfishing in Michigan. Both opportunities went into immediate effect on October 11, 2012.

Map labels

To Grayling
127
E
Houghton Lake Marina & Power
Houghton Lake Dr
North Bay
4'
300
300
Lincoln Hwy
Flint Road
All Seasons Stay-N-Play Resort
E Houghton Lake Dr
Yeager Rd
Morris's Northernaire Resort
Long Point Dr
Houghton Point
Houghton Point
4'
W Shore Dr
Old US Hwy 27
8'
8'
17'
Backus Creek
Roscommon County-Blodgett Memorial Airport
Markey Park
100
1. Songer's Log Cabins;
2. Shady Valley Resort;
3. Sunset Resort
West Houghton Lake Campground
4'
8'
1 2 3
Crest Resort
Public Fishing Site
Nellsville
Lake City Rd
55
Houggton Lake Airport
12'
100
Houghton Lake Heights
E Houghton Lake Dr
Houghton Lake Travel Park
Houghton Park
Knapp Rd
20'
8'
12'
8'
East Bay
4'
Short Dr
127
Lyman's On the Lake Resort
8'
20'
18
Houghton Lake
Calkins Rd
Federal Ave
12'
12'
West Branch Rd
55
4'
Loxley Rd
Wooded Acres Family Campground
Ottawa Ln
Ann's Water-N-Woods
Bay Breeze Resort
Riviera Resort
Main St
Prudenville
To Harrison
scale in miles
S Tower Hill Rd
Town Line Rd
Reserve Rd
Owens Dr
55
W Houghton Lake Dr
55
Nestle Road
Denton Park
18
To Harrison & Gladwin
0 1/2 1 2
DEPTHS SHOWN IN FEET
NOT TO BE USED FOR NAVIGATION

Inset map labels
Lake Michigan
Traverse City
75
72
Higgins Lake
HURON NATIONAL FOREST
127
55
Cadillac
Houghton Lake
37
131
ENLARGED AREA
10
Lake Huron
Reed City
75

Hubbard Lake   Alcona County

Hubbard Lake may be the tenth largest lake in Michigan at over 8800 acres, but it is in my top five for great fishing lakes. It is fairly deep in spots at 87 feet, but averages 33 feet. It is seven miles long from the south to the north end, and two miles wide at its widest point.

An interesting fact about Hubbard is that permanent white settlers did not begin to arrive in the area until the 1830s and 40s, at which time it was known as the "Bottomless Lake". In 1867, it was named "Hubbard Lake" in honor of Dr. Bela Hubbard, who was a prominent geologist in the State of Michigan.

Many of the top fishing pros often visit this lake for walleye and smallmouth bass. It can be a challenge for walleye, but there are plenty of them in this large body of water. It takes persistence and time, so don't think you can arrive and go home early with a limit. "Smallmouth bass fishing is probably some of the best in this area of the state," says Len Barraco, a well-known angler from Side Door Bait & Tackle.

According to Barraco, early in the season, anglers can do well around Churchill Point and Doctor's Point. In theseareas, folks will want to pitch jigs tipped with minnows or half a crawler.

Ice-Fishing Walleye:
Barraco states that good walleye locations are Hardwood Point off the west shore, South Bay, Churchhill Point, Doctor's Point in the northwest arm area, and Mud Bay in 20-40 feet of water. Tip-ups with minnows or jigging with a rattling type jig and minnow are the best methods. These fish often will suspend at various depths, so start near the bottom then raise up at 4-5-foot increments until you get hits.

Summer Walleye:
The same suspending method mentioned above is used in the summer months. Also you can troll with crankbaits such as Hot 'N Tots, using planer boards or Dipsey Divers to get the lure down deep. Average walleye size in Hubbard is around 18-21 inches. When the wind picks up and blows into the points around the lake, slip-bobber presentations with leeches can really activate the walleye. Walleyes slip deep into the water because of the clarity of the lake. You'll need to really get down there at times to reach the larger ones. Hubbard Lake was a "test ground" back when the DNR wanted to first develop a program for walleye in Michigan, and they found positive results, after which walleye became a mainstay fish in Michigan. Overall, trolling for walleye is one of the best methods in the summer.

One time when I fished this lake, the larger fish were on the bottom in almost 40 feet of water off Churchill Point. Walleyes tend to feed on crawfish and are often aggressive. Slow-troll spinners and crawlers behind bottom-bouncers when you locate them.

Caution:
As for the North Bay region, walleye and perch can be found here in the winter, however the ice is not as thick so you need to be cautious when venturing out. Also be careful around the Shafer Creek discharge area, south of Comstock Bay, on the east side, and off the high banks on the northeast side where there are springs, often making the ice thinner than the rest of the lake.

Perch:
Perch are spotty in Hubbard, but you can often catch them in the 12-16-inch size or bigger, which makes up for the lack of numbers. They can also act "fidgety," that is, they will be in 15 feet of water one day and 25 the next. So be willing to adjust accordingly. There are a fair number of Master Angler perch caught in Hubbard, so the trip here is often worthwhile if you are looking for size.

Perch Tip:
When deer hunting, some hunters like to stalk the deer, moving from area to area slowly; others like to sit and wait for deer to come to them. As with perch fishing on Hubbard, Barraco says the best way to fish for them is to sit in one spot and wait for the school to come by. Fish the shallow-water areas.

Spring Pike:
Spring is good pike fishing season in the shallow waters off East Bay, as well as the south end of the lake, according to Barraco. Fish in the shallow bays, in 4-foot depths, using sucker minnows and a large bobber. A neat trick is that when the bobber is set, use your other rod to cast a spoon, such as a Johnson Weedless Gold Spoon, bringing it past the sucker minnow and bobber. You will often see a pike following the spoon, then when it sees the sucker minnow, it's time for action.

In summer, go to the South Bay near the West Branch River. Work this area along the shoreline up to Hardwood Point.

Ice-Fishing Pike:
You will find very little spearing on Hubbard Lake for whatever reason. The most common winter method is to use tip-ups; but here is the kicker: place the offering just below the ice, around the 2-3-foot water depth. That is where the pike often cruise in search of prey.

Try the southeast corner of the lake, near where Sucker Creek empties into the lake. Once again, watch for unsafe ice.

Bass:
Smallmouths are plentiful in Hubbard. Areas to search them out are the west shore from Hardwood Point south, as well as Churchill Point that juts out between the northwest and northeast bays. The area where Sucker Creek

These two anglers on Hubbard Lake hope to bring home a meal of tasty perch.

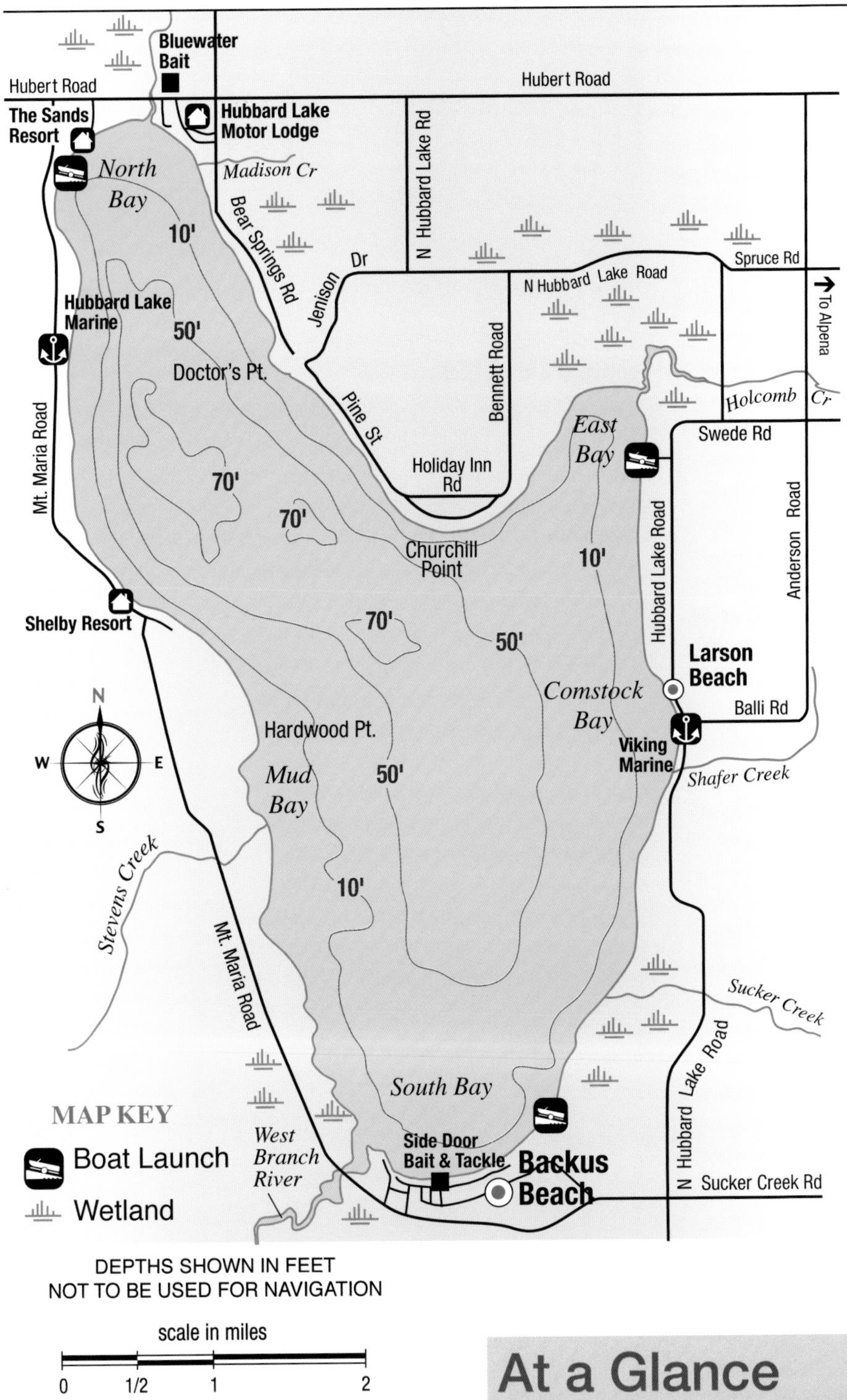

Hubbard Lake

Map

Bluewater Bait

Hubert Road

Hubert Road

The Sands Resort

Hubbard Lake Motor Lodge

N Hubbard Lake Rd

Madison Cr

Spruce Rd

North Bay

10'

Bear Springs Rd

Jenison Dr

N Hubbard Lake Road

To Alpena

Hubbard Lake Marine

50'

Bennett Road

Holcomb Cr

Doctor's Pt.

Pine St

Swede Rd

East Bay

70'

Holiday Inn Rd

Churchill Point

Hubbard Lake Road

Anderson Road

70'

10'

50'

Shelby Resort

70'

Larson Beach

Comstock Bay

Balli Rd

Hardwood Pt.

50'

Viking Marine

Shafer Creek

Mt. Maria Road

Mud Bay

N

W E

S

10'

Stevens Creek

Mt. Maria Road

Sucker Creek

South Bay

N Hubbard Lake Road

MAP KEY

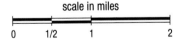

Boat Launch

West Branch River

Side Door Bait & Tackle

Backus Beach

Wetland

N Sucker Creek Rd

DEPTHS SHOWN IN FEET
NOT TO BE USED FOR NAVIGATION

scale in miles

0   1/2   1   2

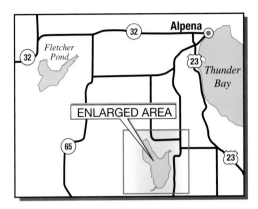

Alpena

32

Fletcher Pond

32

23

Thunder Bay

ENLARGED AREA

65

23

Public Landings: South Bay near the West Branch River and off Hubbard Lake Road. For fishing information, contact the folks at Side Door Bait and Tackle at (989) 736-6418. The Chamber of Commerce can be reached for lodging information at (989) 736-6418.

A nice pike landed while ice fishing is sometimes a bonus while walleye fishing.

discharges is also worth trying. Fish in 5-10 feet of water. The average size smallmouth runs around 17-18 inches.

Whitefish: One fish species that is generally untapped in Hubbard is whitefish. Anglers spear whitefish in fall, when the October 15 season opens. Night spearing consists of two people in a boat, traveling very very slowly with an underwater light. The person in the bow will look for whitefish along the shoreline in 3-7 feet of water most anywhere around the lake. This is a popular method for taking these tasty fish, and anglers often come home with a nice dinner.

At a Glance

What: Great overall fishing for many fish species

Where: Hubbard Lake SW of Alpena

Why: Some of the best bass, walleye and perch fishing in the area

How: Night spearing for whitefish

Landings: There are three main landings on Hubbard: one at the south end, near the West Branch River; one on the east bay side just north of Shafer Creek; Caledonia Township Boat Landing, half block west of Bluewater Bait (1595 Hubert Rd); recently renovated township boat landing.

Contacts: **Alpena Convention & Visitors Bureau** (CVB), 235 W. Chisholm St., Alpena, 49707, 1-800-4-ALPENA, (989) 354-4181

Bait & Tackle: Side Door Bait & Tackle, 3585 Woodlawn Dr, Spruce, MI 48762 (989) 736-6418; **Bluewater Bait,** 1575 Hubert Rd, Hubbard Lake, 49747 at north end; also carries propane for refueling; restaurant next door. (989) 727-2700

Intermediate Lake
Antrim County

Intermediate Lake in Antrim County is one of the main lakes in the Elk River Chain of Lakes which include Beals, Scotts, Six Mile, St. Clair, Ellsworth, Wilson, Benway, Hanley, Intermediate, Bellaire, Clam, Torch, Skegemog, and Elk lakes. Intermediate Lake was formed when the Intermediate River was dammed in 1900 to provide hydroelectric power for the small town of Bellaire at the south end of the lake. Fishing Intermediate Lake you will find a variety of game fish such as trout, walleye, bass, pike, perch and many more.

The lake is sizable at almost 1600 acres and has a maximum depth of around 75 feet. It is approximately 6 miles long and averages 2000 feet wide.

It can be a challenging lake to fish due to its long narrow configuration. There are several sunken islands at the south end of the lake. At one time decades ago, it was a tremendous muskie and more recently a walleye lake. But due to development, it has a lot of watersport activities on it that present an issue for fishing.

DNR stocked this lake with over 75,000 walleye fingerlings back in 2011, which, at the time of this writing, will soon becoming close to keeper size.

Bill Truscott not only fishes this lake on a regular basis, he grew up here and is very knowledgeable about the lake. Actually he swims with the fishes, having scuba-dived this lake, allowing him to become familiar with the bottom structure. Much of this dammed lake has logs lying on the bottom from the logging days, many stumps, and other structure that allow fish to thrive. Bill states that, "a lot of Master Angler fish come from this lake due to the great habitat for fish production."

Many bass tournaments are held annually on this lake, versus biennially as happens with most bass tournaments. Bill says that although muskie have been limited in the past ten or so years, they seem to be making a comeback. He recently saw a 42-inch muskie taken from a dock with a Mepps spinner topped with a crawdad. Some muskie groups fish Intermediate Lake each year, giving some indication of a rebound and an overall improving muskie fishery.

Bass: Truscott says that smallmouth bass fishing in this lake is excellent. Although mainly smallmouth, with a few largemouth, and some good rock bass, the smallies are generally found in the 3-5-pound range. And you can catch them almost anywhere on the lake due to the massive structure. The bigger fish are found in the central part of the lake, and also at the south end, where the water is more shallow. There are several islands in the south end, and some weed growth, but not overly thick. Once again, look for structure along the shoreline and at the south end. Where you find structure, you will most generally find fish.

Walleye: Ninety percent of winter walleye fishing takes place in the central part of this lake, the mid 75 percent of the lake area located between the two boat landings, although a few anglers will work the very south end of the lake. Truscott says that walleye range between 16-24 inches. For summer fishing, Bill says you can go just about anywhere on Intermediate Lake for walleye. Some anglers jig, but most troll the drop-offs along the edges of the lake. There are two submerged islands about eight feet deep in the south-central area of the lake where minnows tend to gather. Walleye feed on the minnows later in the afternoon and early evening. Also check out the numerous feeder creeks that dump into this lake. Once again, there are generally a lot of minnows in these

Intermediate Lake is a beautiful lake no matter the season, but is especially so during the colorful fall periods.

At a Glance

What: Smallmouth bass and walleye fishing

Where: In much of Intermediate Lake

Why: Nice size smallmouth, upwards of 3-5 pounds, and walleye in the 16-24-inch range

Information/Guides: Bellaire Chamber of Commerce, 308 East Cayuga Street, Bellaire, 49615, (231) 533-6023, www.bellairechamber.org.

Landings: Two improved landings on the west side of the lake

Bait & Tackle: Corner Store-Lakeside, 2410 Rushton Road, Central Lake, 49622, (231) 544-6121

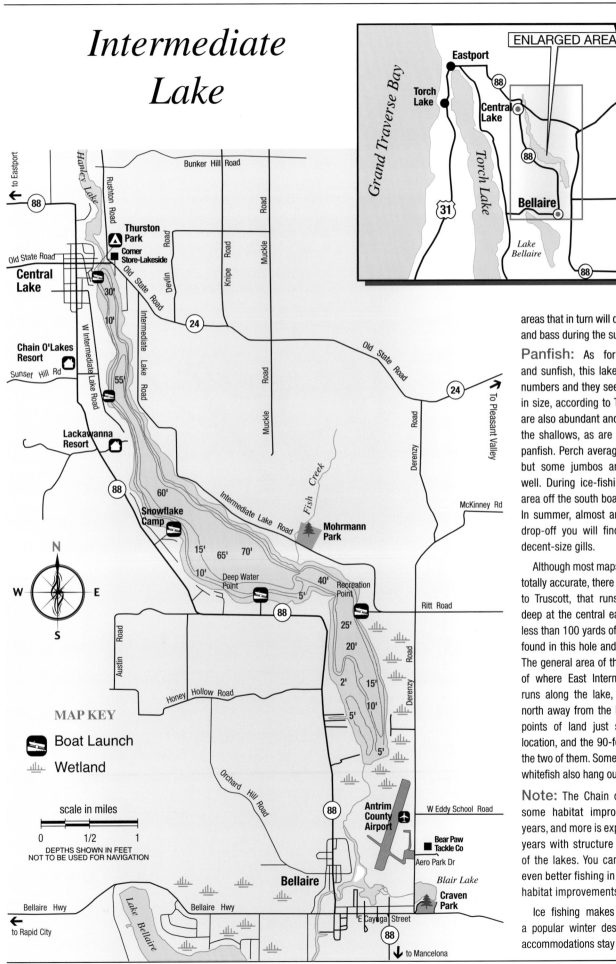

areas that in turn will draw in both walleye and bass during the summer.

Panfish: As for perch, bluegills, and sunfish, this lake has them in good numbers and they seem to be increasing in size, according to Truscott. Rock bass are also abundant and often fished along the shallows, as are most of the spring panfish. Perch average around 8 inches, but some jumbos are caught here as well. During ice-fishing season, try the area off the south boat landing for perch. In summer, almost anywhere there is a drop-off you will find perch and some decent-size gills.

Although most maps of this lake are not totally accurate, there is a hole, according to Truscott, that runs down to 90 feet deep at the central east end of the lake, less than 100 yards off shore. Fish can be found in this hole and it pays to locate it. The general area of the hole is just south of where East Intermediate Lake Road runs along the lake, then turns directly north away from the lake. There are two points of land just south of this road location, and the 90-foot hole is between the two of them. Some indications are that whitefish also hang out here.

Note: The Chain of Lakes has seen some habitat improvements over the years, and more is expected in upcoming years with structure being added in all of the lakes. You can expect more and even better fishing in future years as the habitat improvements are made.

Ice fishing makes Intermediate Lake a popular winter destination, and many accommodations stay open year round.

K.P. Lake Crawford County

K.P. Lake is located 12 miles from Grayling, and just west of Lovells. It has been some years since I actually fished K.P. Lake, but one thing you remember here is the tranquility this lake has to offer, being a no-gas-motor restricted lake, and not many summer homes along its banks. Overall it's a beautiful lake that you will not be disappointed visiting. And if you enjoy either fly-fishing for bluegills along the shallows as I did, or you're after a bass or two, you will enjoy being here. Just writing about K.P. makes me want to revisit this lake, and I most assuredly will sometime soon.

Fish species are few, and stocking of this lake does not take place, either by the DNR or the locals. Therefore writing about this lake is as simple as fishing it.

Tom Lampane, who is an area guide and occasionally fishes K.P. Lake, says that there are a number of sizable bluegills in this lake, along with some largemouth bass, a few pike, but not many larger fish, mostly panfish. There are some sunfish and perch as well, but not worth the effort. Most are caught while fishing for the gills.

Bluegills: K.P. is not much of a winter fishery. Most anglers fish it in the spring and summer. Being a motorless (other than electric) lake, it is serene.

In spring, fish the shallow shorelines and points for bluegills, especially along the north end, or 'north bay' as the locals call it. You may easily latch in to some 16-18-inch largemouth bass along the shorelines as well, and an occasional sunfish.

Another local who fishes this lake more frequently, Gary Boyd, confirms that bluegill fishing here is not very successful. He says that the lake does not drop off quickly and he often pulls in gills in the 3-5-foot water depths along the shoreline. You can find bluegills at either end of the lake, but once again, he suggests you head to the larger bay to the north, especially the northeast end. He regularly pulls in 9-10-inch gills. During mid or late summer, bluegills head to deeper water at the north end, in 14-15 feet of water. Jigging, or straight lining, with a slip bobber works well.

Largemouth Bass: Bass fishing on K.P. is most popular in the north bay, along the west side where habitat is conducive to bass populations. There is weed growth along much of the shoreline, so casting your favorite bass lure along the shallows is often productive.

As the sign indicates, no motors are allowed on this small, serene lake near Grayling.

At a Glance

What: Bluegill fishing

Where: A long beautiful lake near Grayling

Why: Sizeable bluegills on a serene lake

Regs: Motorless (gas) lake

Information: Fuller's, T.E. Guide Service, LLC & Fly Shop, 6122 East County Road 612, (Lovells) Grayling, 49738, (989) 348-7951; **Northern Exposure Guide Service,** 10045 Portage Heights Ave., Grayling, 49738, (989) 348-1875, **Tom Lampane** (616) 334-1483

Landings: One landing at the very south end of the lake

Contacts: Grayling Visitors Bureau, P.O. Box 217, Grayling 49738, (989)348-4945, (800) 937-8837 Email: visitor@grayling-mi.com

Bait & Tackle: Skip's Sport Shop, 5765 M-72 West, Grayling 49738, (989)348-7111

K.P. Lake

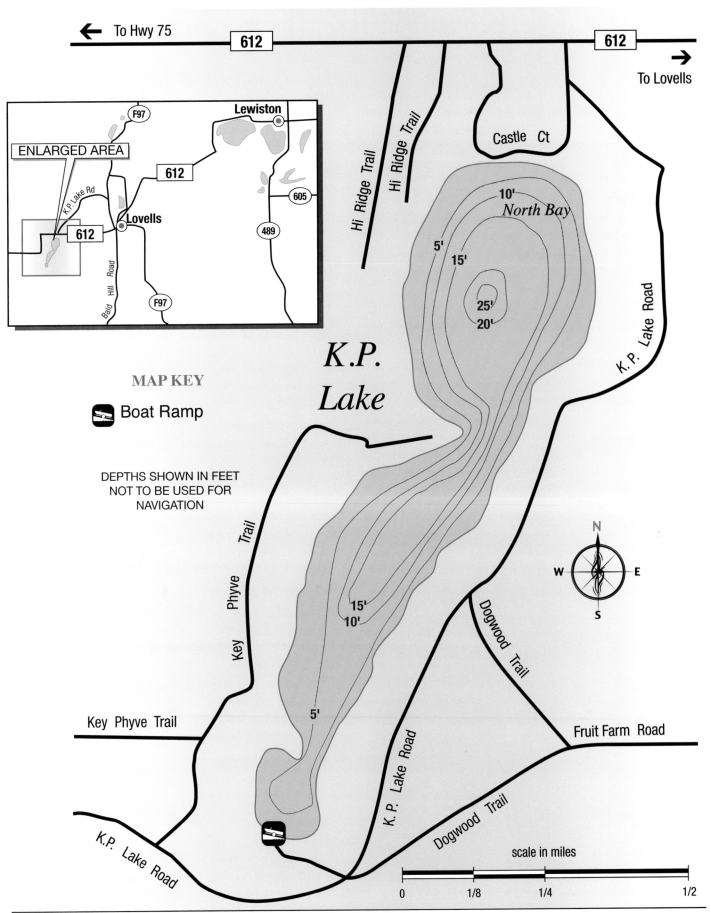

← To Hwy 75

612

612

To Lovells →

ENLARGED AREA

F97

Lewiston

612

605

K.P. Lake Rd

Lovells

489

612

Bald Hill Road

F97

Hi Ridge Trail

Hi Ridge Trail

Castle Ct

North Bay

10'

5'

15'

25'

20'

K.P. Lake Road

K.P.
Lake

MAP KEY

Boat Ramp

DEPTHS SHOWN IN FEET
NOT TO BE USED FOR
NAVIGATION

Key Phyve Trail

Key Phyve Trail

Dogwood Trail

15'
10'

5'

N
W   E
S

K.P. Lake Road

Fruit Farm Road

K.P. Lake Road

Dogwood Trail

scale in miles

0   1/8   1/4   1/2

Lake Bellaire Antrim County

Four-mile-long Lake Bellaire is part of the Chain O' Lakes in Antrim County, and is connected to Clam Lake to the south via the Grass River, and north to Intermediate River. There is a nice variety of fish in Lake Bellaire, including walleye, smallmouth bass, pike, perch, splake, and more recently the smelt seem to be returning. Lake Bellaire is a small, but deep lake with a maximum depth of 107 feet and an average depth of around 43 feet.

Although I am not positive, I would not be surprised if you could catch every fish found in all the waters in northern Michigan in these Chain O' Lakes, because each lake offers a different species of fish that is unique to the lake. Elk, Skegemog, Torch, Clam, Bellaire, and Intermediate lakes form the chain that has some of the best water in the world.

Lake Bellaire angler Larry Roote, who owns Mancelona Sports and sells bait and tackle, states that, "walleye is probably the number one fish on this lake, followed by perch, bass and pike. There are lots of perch and smallmouth bass, and a fair number of pike," he says. And once-popular smelt are starting a comeback in Bellaire.

Walleye:
For ice fishing walleye, Larry suggests heading out in front of Intermediate River on the east end of the lake for walleye. Intermediate River empties into Lake Bellaire off Highway M-88 approximately in the center of the lake. The north arm is also good ice fishing for both walleye and perch. Another good spot is where the lake empties into the Grass River on the southeast end of the lake. Winter walleye in the 17-24-inch size can be caught on a regular basis and Larry has seen some in the upper 20-inch size. Tip ups and jigging is a common method to catch them as is popular on most Michigan ice fishing lakes. The water in this area ranges in the 40-60-foot depth where it drops off. The drop off comes relatively quickly off shore.

For summer walleye, most anglers troll along the west side of the lake, parallel to Cottage Drive and just to the north, as well as in the North Arm. Long lining with floating Rapalas in the late evening near the boat launch can also be productive. The northeast side can also produce some nice fish as well, trolling parallel to the shoreline.

In 2011, DNR records indicate over 77,000 walleye fingerlings were stocked in this lake, making them legal size within a few short years, although there are many variables that can and do affect growth.

Perch:
During the ice-fishing season, perch can be found in the North Arm. Perch as large as 13-14 inches can be caught in Bellaire, however the more common 7-10 inches is the norm. There are plenty of small perch in this lake, but a meal of good eaters can often be found here. You may also try for perch in front of the Intermediate River, along M-88 on the east side of the lake, and near the Grass River which is an outlet for this lake.

Some years ago a seven pounder was caught here, and it is not difficult to hook some 4-6-pounders on this lake. Anglers often use sucker minnows in the spring, letting them swim around on a hook and bobber along the shore. There is a lot of soft, mucky bottom land in this lake, so be careful if you decide to wade.

Pike:
Pike spearing near the Grass River outlet is popular during winter. "Pike," according to Larry, "can range up to 40-plus inches." Tip-ups are often used as well for pike. For summer fishing, Larry stated that not many anglers go after pike on this lake during the summer months.

Splake:
Not too many years ago, an angler caught a splake in Lake Bellaire that was only 4 ounces short of a state record, and if he had taken it in for weighing shortly after he caught it, it may possibly have beat the record. But since most people fish for other species here, there is sketchy information on splake.

Bass:
There are plenty of smallmouth bass here if that is your thing. The usual bass lures, both live and artificial, are popular along the shoreline. And if you wish, try crayfish at the end of your line. Work the shorelines along the south end of the lake, or the northeast end.

Muskie:
According to anglers that fish this lake, the muskie population is fair, and some anglers will spear one on occasion while spearing for pike. Muskie are not easy to locate here.

Note:
The North Arm is deep, and as you head south out of it toward the larger area of the lake, you will find a sunken island, approximately 4-5 feet below the surface of the water. The water drops off quickly down to about 70 feet at the edge of this island. Some good angling can be had around this island both summer and winter. So it may be worth exploring.

The girls' day out on the ice, landing some nice perch for dinner.

At a Glance

What: Walleye and splake fishing

Where: One of the Chain of Lakes

Why: One of the unique series of connected lakes that you can travel to by boat

Information/Guides: Chamber of Commerce, P.O. Box 205 308 E. Cayuga St., Bellaire 49615, (231) 533-6023; **Village of Bellaire,** 202 N. Bridge St., P.O. Box 557, Bellaire 49615, (231) 533-8213

Landings: A state boat landing is located on the east shore off M-88 (along Fisherman's Paradise Road). The other landings on this lake are only for small boats or canoes

Bait & Tackle: Mancelona Sports, 311 N. Williams, Mancelona 49656, (231) 587-9421; **Butch's Tackle & Marina,** 6235 Cystal Spring Rd., Bellaire 49615, (231) 377-6787

Lake Bellaire

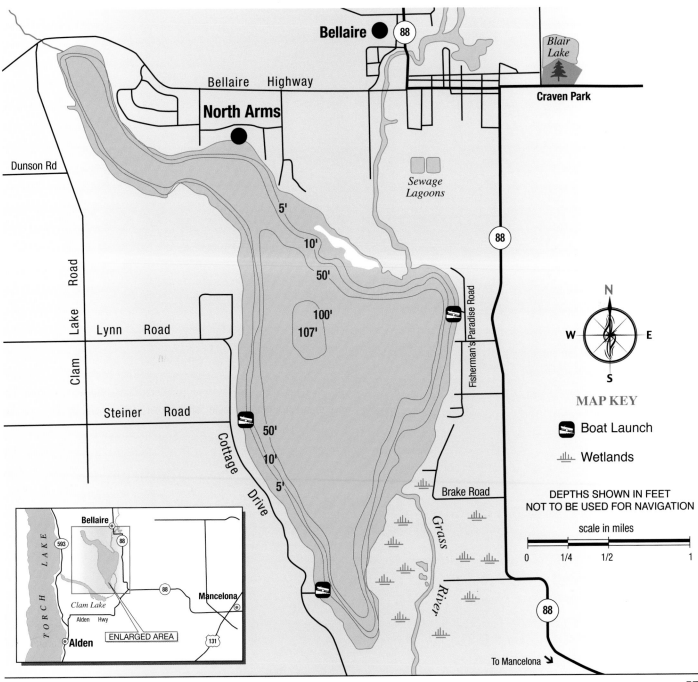

Lake Cadillac Wexford County

The principal fish species in Lake Cadillac are walleye, pike, perch, crappies and bluegills. This lake is fished hard for walleye, but is very popular for winter pike, especially those who like to spear pike, and it's also a well-known lake for crappie. Smallmouth fishing has improved dramatically according to area fish biologist, Mark Tonello, and has been especially good the past 10-15 years. Lots of tournament anglers visit this lake.

Tonello, states that, "it is hard to talk about Lake Cadillac without mentioning its sister lake to the west, Lake Mitchell." Tonello says that, "they are both quite similar except Mitchell is obviously much larger (2500 acres versus 1100 acres for Cadillac), and has more shallow areas; but both are popular with anglers, both locally and visitors from downstate and out of state."

The two lakes are connected by a canal built during the long and interesting northern Michigan logging era. The canal was originally built so lumbermen could float timber from the shores of Lake Mitchell to waiting sawmills on Lake Cadillac. Today the canal serves as a convenient link between two of Michigan's most popular fishing lakes.

Here however, we will focus just on Lake Cadillac (note: see Lake Mitchell on page 64).

Lake Cadillac features over 400 acres of prime fish-holding weed habitat, and good habitat makes for prime fishing. Approximately half the lake is 15 feet deep or less.

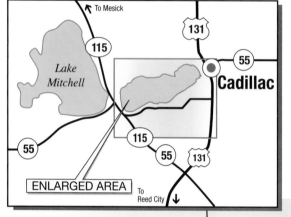

Lake Cadillac

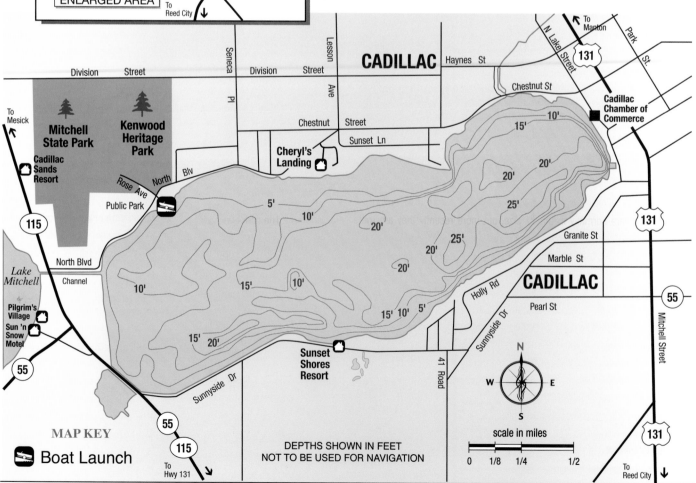

MAP KEY

Boat Launch

DEPTHS SHOWN IN FEET
NOT TO BE USED FOR NAVIGATION

scale in miles

0   1/8   1/4   1/2

Crappie: Steve Knaisal, owner of Pilgrim Village Bait Shop, says that, "crappie can be caught right off the causeway area by M-115, and in town in the deeper water by the city library where there are significant piles of slabwood which the crappie like as habitat." The submerged slabwood is from the old logging days of the 1800s. The east end of lake by the pilings across from high school on northeast side is also good for crappie, states Knaisal. There is a gradual drop off in this area which goes from 5 feet to 10-12 feet.

Anglers generally use small minnows for crappie, or even wax worms in winter. But their favorite food is minnows. In summer, use a slip bobber along the east end. Most crappie at this time are suspended in 18-20 feet of water. On cloudy days or early morning, start 4-5 feet off the bottom and gradually work upward as the day progresses.

Pike: Pike, according to fish biologist Mark Tonello, can be found most anywhere in the lake, summer or winter. "Pike size in Lake Cadillac is slightly larger than Mitchell, but Mitchell probably has a great number of pike overall," says Tonello. You can harvest pike in excess of ten pounds easy in Lake Cadillac. Knaisal says that, "the area straight off Kenwood Park in about 12-14 feet of water is good for pike using tip-ups." Knaisal confirms what Mark Tonello states in that "pike upwards of 10 pounds and larger are common in the winter using tip-ups. Many are 40-plus inches (13-15-pound weight, much above average weight for the length of the fish), and it is very common to land pike in the 30-inch range.

Bass: For bass, try the steep drop-offs near downtown, and the weedbeds all along the perimeter of the lake. The middle areas can be productive as well around the edges of the heavy milfoil weed growths. For bass, spinner baits or most any typical bass lure will work.

Rock Bass: Rock bass can be caught at the east end of the lake. Many are Master Angler size, i.e., over a pound in weight. Although most anglers shun rock bass, they can be fun to catch, especially for kids.

Walleye: Walleye are found in the deeper waters near the city of Cadillac, and off Kenwood Park in the northwest area of the lake, where, once again, there are piles of slabwood on the bottom of the lake. Ice fishing in these same areas is productive. The majority of the pike and walleye caught on Cadillac are on tip-ups. However, many anglers will jig with one rod and set a tip-up or two. Jigging Rapalas is popular, and often the smaller sizes, #3 or #5's, in the glow colors have been effective. Also try jigging spoons, such as an 1/8-ounce Slender Spoon, which is thin and has more action and flash than some of the other jigging spoons. You may also try this lure on pike and crappie as well. Walleye lures were normally in the #7 size, but more recently they are more productive if smaller. Apparently that is why lures like the Slender Spoons are back in the tackle boxes of anglers on Lake Cadillac.

Note on Walleye: Walleye have not been stocked in this lake since the 1930s because they had very good natural reproduction. But in the early 2000s, anglers complained that walleye were not as common, especially the smaller ones. A 2003 survey revealed that in the late 1990s they quit reproducing for some reason. Therefore, since 2004 a stocking program was initiated and has taken place four times since then. Walleye fishing is not nearly as good as it was 10-15 years ago, due to the loss of natural reproduction, but at this point no definitive theory has been proven as to why this has happened.

Channel connecting Lakes Cadillac and Mitchell: Don't rule out the shallow (approximately three-four feet deep) channel between the lakes, especially for kids, since it can produce some nice catches of bass, pike, even some walleye during the summer months.

Lake Cadillac may not have the pike numbers that its sister lake, Lake Mitchell, has across the road, but the sizes are definitely larger here.

At a Glance

What: Walleye, crappie, pike, bass

Where: Lake Cadillac by the city of the same name

Why: Relatively small lake packed with lots of fish

Landings: The parks (including William Mitchell State Park, Kenwood Park, and Keith McKellop Lakefront Walkway) provide outstanding access to Lake Cadillac. Each has a boat launch with parking for a number of vehicles and trailers, although the William Mitchell State Park boat launch on Lake Cadillac is used primarily by campers at the park. There is a public dock and fishing pier located on the eastern end of the lake near the downtown business district. Another public fishing pier was installed on Lake Cadillac at William Mitchell State Park in summer of 2006

Contacts: Cadillac Area Visitors Bureau, 201 North Mitchell Street, Suite 102, Cadillac, MI 49601, Phone (231) 775-0657, Toll Free (800) 22-LAKES

Bait & Tackle: Pilgrim Village, 181 S. Lake Mitchell, Cadillac, 49601, 231-775-5412, www.pilgrimvillagefishing.com, located next to Mitchell State Park off M-115

Lake Leelanau (North)
Leelanau County

Leelanau is one of the most picturesque areas of Michigan, and this lake has both great fishing and splendid scenery.

One thing that can be said for certain, the Leelanau Lakes not only provide fantastic fishing, but are also located in one of the most attractive areas of Michigan. Leland is aptly known as *"Fishtown."* If you go to the Chamber website (lelandmi.com), you will find a vast listing of summer events that will enhance your overall experience while visiting this area.

As with lakes Cadillac and Mitchell, and Houghton and Higgins, when you discuss North Lake Leelanau, you must also mention its sister lake to the south, South Lake Leelanau.

Back in the late 1950's North Lake Leelanau offered trophy brown trout fishing, with specimens upwards of 20 pounds. While its southern neighbor held browns, it was to North Lake Leelanau that anglers congregated for prized browns.

Covering almost 3,000 acres with depths of over 120 feet, the bottom consists of sand, gravel and assorted rubble in the shoal areas while deep water sits over sand, clay, and marl. A thermocline forms every summer at about 35 feet and can be a key to locating fish from trout to perch.

Both of these deep-water lakes are well taken care of by the DNR with thousands of brown and lake trout planted over the years. South Lake Leelanau found itself dumped with over 5 million walleyes back in 2001, and many more since that time period. They travel freely between the two lakes. Almost 100,000 lake trout fingerlings were planted in North Lake Leelanau just during the period from 2008-2012. Walleyes were planted by the thousands during the early 1990's as well. Fish plantings over the past several years have counted 112,000 brown trout, 94,000 rainbows and over 27,000 whitefish.

The waterway between these lakes is fairly wide and easily motored. Water flows from the southern lake into its northern neighbor. The text below will give you some idea of where to fish this lake, from two different perspectives; one is simply the gathering of information from various locals, DNR, and other sources, the other is a guide who has fished and guided on this lake since 1995. For starters, we will notate the former source of information.

Two basins form North Lake Leelanau, the southern one being shallow, with a gently sloping bottom of sand and gravel. This is a prime area for walleyes and smallmouth bass. Fishing methods include drift fishing, using both crankbaits and live bait. At night, trolling along the shoreline, shallow foot contour lines often bring in fish that travel out of the deeper water up to the shoal areas in search of forage fish.

The northern basin harbors trout and some walleye. Summer trolling along the ledges where the thermocline and bottom meet at about the 35-foot depth, using some of the more common lures, including the silver/black Rapala, especially for an occasional rainbow.

The browns tend to run in the deeper areas of the lake, along with the popular lake trout.

Four points, Brady Point and Cemetery Point on the west shore of this deep section, and Warden's Point and Porter Point on the east shore, offer a steep pitch from the shore into deep water.

Smallmouths can be found in the 20-30-foot depths and move up to the shallows off the points in the evening searching for a meal of minnows. The action begins about an hour before sunset with smaller bass and lasts for an hour or more after full dark. The pre- and post-dawn hours, can also be productive. Aside from the standard bass fishing hardware and live bait, leeches are often used to land the larger fish. Being deep, with a bottom of sand and gravel, wading anglers are rewarded with catches of smallmouth bass. Using lighter tackle, especially a long, limber rod and 4-pound-test line, the willing angler will be rewarded with jumping bass as you wade near the edge of one of these lakes' many drop-offs.

Trout Fishing Note: While deep-water trolling is common during the warmer months in the northern lake, with trout being the main target, fishing the contours in the early morning and late evening using casting gear should not be ignored. Wardens and Brady's Points, opposite each other at what might be called North Lake Leelanau's waist are prime spots for bottom-bouncing steep contour lines.

Ed Peplinski grew up on South Leelanau and is very familiar with fishing both the north and south lakes. Although he fishes mostly walleye, his perspective on trout fishing and whitefish is outlined below.

Trout: Ed says there are a few browns on south lake, but the fishery overall is not the best. For lakers, it is good on north lake, but since the south lake is only 60 feet deep, you find fewer trout. Trout are almost exclusively fished during the winter months. And often a walleye angler will catch a trout incidentally.

Lake trout fishing during the winter has been good, with catches of some in the 9-10-pound range. Usually these can be found in the 100-foot water depths, similar to where you find them on Higgins Lake. Smelt are commonly used to entice them to bite on a tip up, or a large Swedish Pimple used while jigging, as with Higgins.

Ed says it is rare to hear of anyone catching steelhead, but in Leland there have been some good catches recently during the winter fishing season.

Lake Leelanau (North)

Summer trout on north lake can be a worthwhile pursuit, using body baits, but most anglers hook a trout, once again, while walleye fishing.

For what it's worth, Ed noted that there is some very good smallmouth fishing, upwards of 18-22-inch range, along the drop-offs on the north lake.

Whitefish: Ed has seen quite a few whitefish this past winter (2011-2012). It was a good fishing opportunity for those who knew what they were doing on the north lake. He has seen some common takes of 3-5-pounders. Most anglers fish the drop offs along the banks at 60 feet. "This is one 'secret' on north lake that has not really got out yet," he says. Generally it has been a winter fishery.

Walleye: North Lake Leelanau with its myriad of structure and islands contains many very nice walleye, but the lake is tough to fish because it is so clear. Anglers can target them in the deeper waters using finesse techniques during daylight hours or, as often many anglers do, wait until after dark when the walleyes move shallow. Vertical jigging using light line, small jigs and live bait will take walleyes during the day in water as deep as 60 feet. Trolling along the 30- to 50-foot contours with crawler harnesses or crankbaits can be productive too. At night, casting stickbaits on the shelves and drop offs surrounding Long, Fox and South islands can be very productive for some sizable walleye.

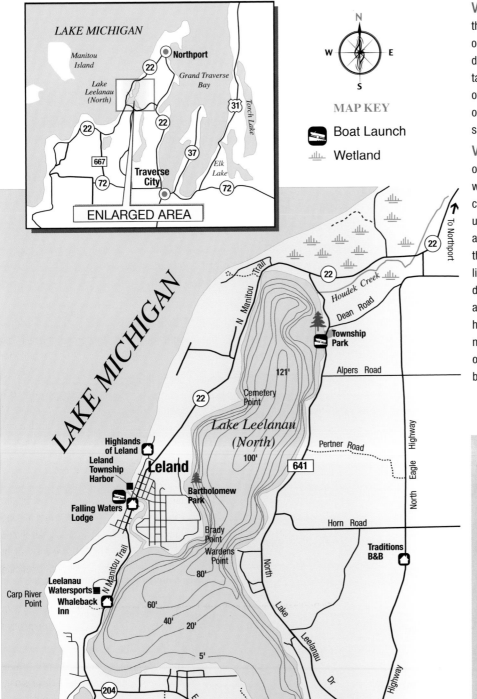

At a Glance

What: Fishing for walleye, and possibly an occasional trout

Where: One of the more beautiful lakes settled in a quaint part of the state

Why: Fishing is good, and other activities are also available while visiting this part of the state

Information/Guides: Leelanau County Chamber of Commerce at www.leelanauchamber.com or by calling (231) 271-9895. Cal Stier, cell 517-204-6680, office 989-224-2104, email: nofishnofee@hotmail.com, www.michigan.gov/documents/dnr/LakeLeelanau_184258_7.pdf (for maps)

Landings: There is a landing at the west end of the lake, just south of Brady Point, and one at the very south end, where the lake narrows.

Bait & Tackle: Narrows Passage Bait & Tackle, 102 St Mary's St., Lake Leelanau 49653 (231) 256-2547

Lake Margrethe

Crawford County

Lake Margrethe, formally known as Portage Lake, is a 1,922-acre lake in western Crawford County, three miles west of Grayling. It's the largest lake in Crawford County, and has Portage Creek as an outlet, which, in turn eventually empties into the Manistee River. The maximum depth of this lake is 65 feet. The northern "bays" of the lake are relatively shallow, with the central portion of the lake holding the deeper water.

The primary fishing that takes place here is for walleye, smallmouth and largemouth bass, pike, muskie, perch and bluegill.

Zach Sheldon, a local who works at Skips Sport Shop, just west of Grayling on M-72, fishes this lake quite often and suggests the following for various species on Lake Margrethe:

Walleye: There are lots of walleye in this lake, but not too many above 24 inches. They mostly range in the 17-22-inch category, which, of course, are good eating size. Locate walleye during winter off drop-offs, such as Eagle Pointe and South Bay, as well as West Bay straight out from the public boat landing. Walleye function very well in colder water temperatures no matter the lake. Try fishing open flats and definitely use live bait when the water temperature is low.

Bob Schlachter is an experienced angler on Lake Margrethe and also affirms that walleye fishing along Eagle Point on the northwest end of the lake and South Bay are good areas. He says that, "there is a shallow reef by the National Guard Camp that runs almost to Little Bear Point." It is about three feet deep but drops to about 20 feet. This is a popular fishing area, as well as West Bay where the creek discharges.

In the summer months, Bob uses a simple crawler harness and fishes these same areas for walleye.

Methods: Jigging with a Swedish Pimple or Rapala Minnow, a spoon tipped with a minnow head, or tip-ups with a sucker minnow or gray shiner are the most popular methods. In summer, crawler harnesses are often trolled for walleye.

In the summer walleye are basically fished in the same areas as in winter, drop-offs at Eagle Point and South Bay. Troll as slowly as you can with a harness and bottom-bouncer, or jig off the bottom with jig head tipped with a live leech.

Pike/Muskie: The muskie that were planted here originally were hybrids in the late 1980s, but now the lake is planted with northern muskie, not hybrids. Spearing is the most common method for taking pike or muskie in this lake. Some muskie will range in the 40-plus-inch size in this lake. Even though pike fishing can be slow

Fishing is a great family activity.

during summer, they can still be caught while trolling or drifting with crawler harnesses in the middle grounds where the water is deepest straight out from Eagle Point, as well as in the south end of the lake.

Panfish: You can catch hundreds of perch here, but most will be small, although you can weed out the smaller fish and fish and end up with some nice 8-10-inch eaters. Try the front boat landing area at West Bay, or the South Bay near Camp Grayling. Also check the reef mentioned above in the spring for bluegills. There are plenty of bluegills in certain areas of this lake. The areas on top of the reefs where they spawn is a good location to fish. Bluegills in the 9-10-inch range can be caught here. Also try South Bay by the sand reef. You will also find lots of smaller perch, but many will be keepers.

Bass Fishing: There is some quality bass fishing in the weed beds on the west end of Eagle Point and to the north of the lake up near M-72. Fish the shallows with spinners and harnesses.

Mark Tonello, District Fish Biologist, agrees that there are good smallmouth bass populations in this lake. "The smallmouth bass population is well balanced," he says, "with the majority caught in the last survey over the minimum legal size limit."

DNR Remarks: Tonello also stated that the walleye population in Lake Margrethe appears to be fair currently, primarily due to the VHS disease that prevented stocking in this lake. However, stocking will take place if all goes well in 2012 and beyond. VHS affected many Michigan waters for many years and now we are just starting to see recovery of some of these lakes and other bodies of water.

Muskie, says Mark, are growing well here, same with pike. The recently established Lake Margrethe northern muskellunge fishery is entirely dependent upon stocking.

The Lake Margrethe walleye fishery is also dependent upon stocking. Therefore, 60,000 spring fingerling walleye (Muskegon River strain) should continue to be stocked into Lake Margrethe every third year, starting in 2009. Although some natural reproduction occurs in all or most years, it is not enough to support the fishery. Continued walleye stocking, along with supplemental natural reproduction, should continue to allow Lake Margrethe to be one of the better walleye fishing lakes in the northern lower peninsula of Michigan.

Rock bass are the dominant panfish species in Lake Margrethe.

Perhaps the only downside to the 2007 Lake Margrethe fisheries survey was the lack of yellow perch in the sample. The yellow perch population of Lake Margrethe is currently an uncertainty, but in the past Lake Margrethe has offered good fishing opportunities for yellow perch.

"The other fisheries of Lake Margrethe should continue to manage themselves," says Tonello. Native desirable species like smallmouth bass, largemouth bass, rock bass, and northern pike should continue to thrive in Lake Margrethe.

Note: Tom Lampane, a local guide and Margrethe angler, states that perch fishing is best in the fall. He says that this lake is fished predominately for both large and smallmouth bass. "Walleye tournaments," he says, "have taken a lot of sizeable walleye out of the lake." He noted that he has only seen a few walleye over 24 inches over the past couple of years. However there are lots of non keepers, meaning these fish will be legal in future years. Tom also mentions that there is extremely good pike fishing here and nice size fish. The DNR planted over 45,000 walleye fingerlings in 2011 in this lake, and 6,000 combined northern muskie in 2009-2010. If available, another 60,000 walleye will be stocked as of this writing in 2012.

At a Glance

What: Fishing bass, upcoming walleye, pike, muskie, and panfish

Where: North end of Lake Margrethe

Boat Landing: A public boat landing on the west bay area (off M-72 just past the lake, then south on McIntyre Landing Road, follow signs)

Contacts: Grayling Visitors Bureau, P.O. Box 217, Grayling, MI 49738, Email: visitor@grayling-mi.com, (989) 348-4945, Toll-Free: (800) 937-8837; **Northern Exposure Guide Service** 10045 Portage Heights Ave., Grayling, MI 49738, (989) 348-1875, Tom Lampane, (616) 334-1483

Bait & Tackle: Skips Sport Shop, 5765 M-72 West, (just west of Grayling), (989) 348-7111; **Fuller's, T.E. Guide Service, LLC & Fly Shop and Bait,** 6122 East County Road 612, (Lovells) Grayling, 49738 (989) 348-7951

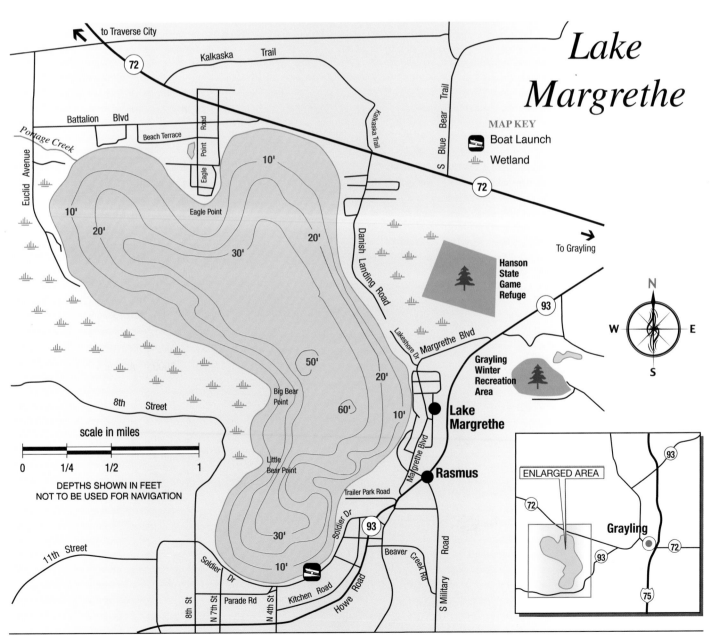

Lake Missaukee

Missaukee County

Lake Missaukee has always been a popular lake with summer residents and anglers. A nice size lake at almost 1900 acres, next to a small, but adequately sized and quaint Lake City. Easy access for people who reside in major cities in southern Michigan, such as Grand Rapids, Kalamazoo, Battle Creek and Jackson.

Fish Biologist Mark Tonello, states that, "overall, Missaukee has got a really good population of bluegills and sunfish in it, and the walleye fishing is improving yearly. The lake also has some pretty decent perch in it if you can find them."

"Panfish populations are booming on Lake Missaukee," according to Matt Bellows from Bait Shop North in Lake City. "Tons of "trash" fish were removed from the lake and the panfish have responded," he says. Missaukee is shallow, but there are plenty of 15- to 20-foot-deep flats near the center of the lake that concentrates winter perch and other panfish.

Panfish: Panfish, such as bluegill, sunfish and crappie, and limited, but nice sized perch are available in Missaukee. For ice fishing, sunfish and 'gills can be found off Green Road in 5 to 15 feet of water. Use a flasher to locate fish. Keep moving and drill plenty of holes. Limits of hand-sized panfish are common. Bluegills are not always easy to locate in the winter here, so most anglers fish for crappie or other larger fish. In spring, you can locate gills in 5-8 feet of water on beds in the coves located in north central area of the lake. Also work the perimeter of the lake in 5-8-foot depths while jigging with waxworms. This is the number one method of catching bluegills, but in

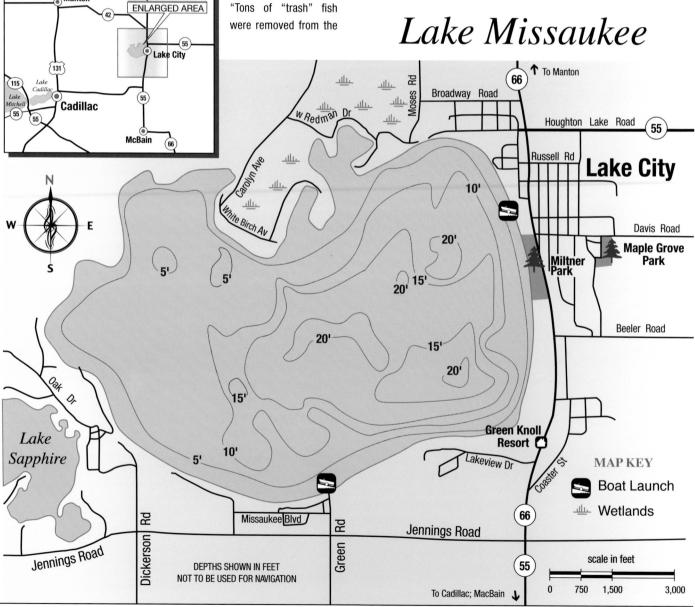

Lake Missaukee

the summer use a #8 gold hook with a bobber. Gills average 6-8 inches and, although not huge, there is a fairly sizeable number of them. One problem with bluegills is finding the weedbeds since the lake is treated for invasive milfoil and the weed beds seem to be moving from time to time.

The crappie fishery is very good here, and you can find them all over the lake. Crappie up to 14 inches can be found in the deeper water where there is some structure. Search them out in the east end of the lake, about 300 yards behind the bait shop in town (104 S. Main), or by the city pier. You will also find rock bass and other panfish in this area.

For perch, use wigglers, minnows and waxworms in hopes of hitting a school of 8- to 10-inchers.

Bass: Smallmouth and largemouth are abundant in Missaukee Lake, however there are many more largemouth available to anglers. As with all bass populations, seek out the shoreline weed bed areas on the northwest side of lake, particularly in the bay area. Look for the 6-8-foot depths. Smallmouth like the depth on east side of the lake, especially the southeast end where there is structure off the highway. According to Matt, there is a 27-foot hole there, the deepest on the lake. Use a crawler harness and bobber, or a topwater lure.

The north central end of the lake is also a good spot for hog bass. They frequent the coves in spring and also search out the weed beds. The average largemouth can reach 7-13 inches here, and many are caught in the 15-17-inch range, upwards of 7 pounds. Matt says you can "catch big bass here all day long."

Rock bass can be found amongst the permanent underwater structures at the southeast end of the lake. The logs in this area are remnants from the logging days and support a nice rock bass fishery.

Pike: Pike in Missaukee have no size limit and a creel limit of 5 per day. Hammerhandles have always seemed to be commonplace on this lake. For pike try fishing the shorelines or northwest corner of the lake. From Green Road in the south end of the lake, all the way to the southwest corner are good spots for pike. Look for the 4-10-foot water depths and the drop-offs. It is not uncommon to pull 30-40-inch pike out of Missaukee.

For ice fishing, tip-ups are common as they are used on most every lake for pike. Simply add a sucker minnow for your offering. Try the coves and mouth of the coves in the north central regions of the lake, and look for the drop-off areas of between 5 to 15 feet off the coves. This approximately 5-15-foot trough runs around the lake. For spearing in the winter months, try the northwest end of the lake. Look for 6-8-foot humps for pike habitat. The Green Road area to the south is also popular.

Walleye: Very nice walleye up to 30 inches are found in Missaukee. They are a stocked fish, and plenty of 18-inch-plus walleye can be caught here. In winter, look for ridges near the coves to the north end of the lake, walleye move into these areas to feed. In summer, troll the outer edges of lake while casting a #6 Rapala Huskie Jerk or similar lure in the evenings along the shallows. The walleye tend to feed in these areas.

Missaukee Lake at one time had a private stocking pond, but eventually it was taken over by the DNR. The pond was not used for many years due to VHS disease, since this particular pond dumped directly into the Muskegon River and it made sense not to take a chance the disease could be release in the river system. Now, however, the pond can be used, but the manpower is currently not available according to fish biologist Mark Tonello.

At a Glance

What: Nice panfish lake, as well as lots of pike, rock bass, and walleye

Where: Lake Missaukee

Regs: No size limit on pike and creel limit of 5 per day

Landings: County park is best launch site with 4 slots and plenty of parking; located at the northeast end of the lake in Lake City. There is also a primitive launch in this same area.

Contacts: Lake City Area Chamber of Commerce, 107 S Main St., Lake City, 49651, (231) 839-4969

Bait & Tackle: Bait Shop North, 104 S. Main, Lake City, 49651, (231) 839-3474, baitshopnorth@gmail.com

Panfishing on Missaukee is somewhat limited, but a meal or two is always available both summer and winter.

As the fish biologist responsible for Missaukee, Mark says that, "there are plenty of largemouth, crappies, rock bass, and some large walleye here." He says, "it is a good lake overall, and one of the better lakes in the area for gills and sunfish." As for perch, Mark says, "they can be hard to find, but if you do locate them they will be nice size."

Lake Mitchell Wexford County

If you read the Lake Cadillac section, you will find that you cannot talk about Lake Mitchell without mentioning its sister lake across the highway. Both are popular fishing lakes, and for good reason.

These two lakes, connected by a channel that flows through Mitchell State Park at the east end of Lake Mitchell and west end of Lake Cadillac, have similar bottom contours and fish species. Both are under 30 feet in depth and warmwater fish species are the norm. Lake Mitchell is 2,580 acres, and 95 percent of it is less than 15 feet deep. Lake Mitchell is dominated by lush patches of aquatic cabbage weed.

You will find walleye, perch, bluegill, pumpkinseed, largemouth bass, and northern pike in this popular body of water.

Panfish in General:
Tonello says Mitchell is a better crappie lake than it is for bluegills. It is not uncommon to catch crappie in the 7-11-inch size. Late afternoons have been producing the most fish, but fishing most anytime will provide results. Anglers on the ice in late afternoons and staying an hour or two after the sun goes down are generally the most successful.

Crappie:
In early spring, shortly after the ice melts, crappie move to shallow-water areas of the coves as well as into the channel that connects the two lakes. This is a good time to fish for them using minnows, maggots and waxworms on teardrops. Light line and very small bobbers are also in order. If you have plastic grubs in your tackle box, you can try those as well.

In contrast, when the first ice forms, fish are generally ready to take on whatever bait offerings available. Crappie anglers will search for schools of fish, which may be anywhere from hovering just below the ice surface to hugging the bottom. Minnows work well.

Bluegills:
The spawning of bluegills (and sunfish) may not begin until late in May, but regardless, the fish will be cruising the shallows. Small black spiders tipped with a waxworm under a bobber often work well. In early summer, bigger hand-sized bluegills are late spawners and typically bed in deeper water. After spawning, these fish head to 10-15 feet of water. Anglers find success fishing bait with bobbers in openings in the weeds. Bluegill anglers generally use grubs on teardrops and search the weedbeds for nice-size fish. Often gills school by size so if you catch little ones, assume the adults are elsewhere.

Note on Bluegills/Crappie:
Steve Knaisel from Pilgram Village says there are the two major coves along the west side of the lake, one being a big cove and the other a smaller sized cove. Along the shoreline bluegills spawn in spring, then as the water warms up, they move out to the mouth of the coves to 6-8 feet of water. Along the edges of the mouth are weed beds where they tend to hang out, with some bass and pike that feed on the smaller fish. There's a shallow hump outside of the smaller cove where the water depth is around 2 feet deep. Just off the hump the water tends to steps down to 4-6-8 feet and is covered with eel grasses and other aquatic vegetation, all good for panfish. Bluegills spawn along the hump, and crappies usually on the outside edges. There is a good sandy bottom here for spawning. Also, at the mouth of the small cove, on the north side, is fox tail (phragmities) and various other reeds. This is also an area worth exploring for panfish.

During winter, fishing for bluegills and crappie follows basically the same pattern of areas, i.e., big cove is first area to find gills while it still supports weed cover and bugs on the weeds that the fish feed on. The mouth area in big

and small coves will find schools of panfish. Then they will move out as the ice thickens. "The area referred to as Blind Island is always a hotspot for panfish on Lake Mitchell," says Knaisel. Minnows usually take the biggest crappies, and spikes and maggots are tops for the bluegills. The zone between Blind Island and the north side of the small cove is almost like a trench and can be dynamite for gills, crappie and pike that feed on smaller fish.

Later in the spawning season, black crappie in the 9-10-inch Master Angler size start to spawn and can be found in 10 feet of water. They spawn around the end of June and into July in this deeper water. Usually they are found along the north side of the lake along the railroad track area where there is a series of drop offs about 70-80 yards from shore. There is not much weed cover here. The same thing happens on the east side of Mitchell between the Country Club and the Sun and Snow Store.

Pike/Walleye:
Mark Tonello, DNR Fish Biologist for this area, states that the walleye population has improved over the past ten years, not so much in producing trophy fish, but lots of walleye in the mid to upper 20-inch size. A 30-inch-plus walleye is rare here.

Tonello says Mitchell is a virtual "pike factory." At times he says they can run on the smaller size, but a fair number of legal 24-30-inchers and a good number over 30 inches are available. Pike fishing is very popular, especially in winter, when both tip-ups and spearing takes place. You can find pike all around the lake, but consider Big Cove and Little Cove off the mouth. Search out the deeper pockets and that is where you will find both pike and walleye

Methods for Pike/Walleye:
Shortly after the pike opener, game fish are often searching for food. A Rapala type lure or spinnerbaits cast in areas of emerging weed beds often find northerns willing to take your offering. The same holds for walleye. At dusk or on dark days walleyes bite. During the first half of May, big shiners suspended with bobbers often work well for both species. Later in the month crawlers and leeches are often used for walleye.

In early summer, use weedless lures for pike and walleye, and typically spinner baits casting through the weeds. In mid-summer, the fish move to deeper waters near weed beds. Deep-running crankbaits and weighted spinner baits can be effective during this time of year.

Drift fishing is also effective using minnows together with weighted jigs. White, yellow, and chartreuse seem to be effective color choices, but something in a crayfish pattern also may work.

As fall starts to drop the water temps, fish crankbaits and spinner baits more slowly. Look for green vegetation. Walleyes begin to feed at night along drop-offs and near the channel between the two lakes. Once again, Rapalas can put fish in your creel. Peak fishing may occur around Halloween or during deer season.

The tip-up still seems to be the weapon of choice for pike and walleye during the ice-fishing season, which is typical of most lakes. But move about the lake until you find the fish. More 30-inch plus size northerns come through the ice than at any other time of the year. Spear anglers are also popular and probably land the majority of big pike here.

Bass:
"Bass fishing", says Mark, "is very very good here, with both large and smallmouth available." However, there are not as many smallmouth as there are largemouth in Mitchell he notes. Try the mouth near the channel at the east end for smallmouth. Tournament anglers love Lake Mitchell, and often take

largemouth in the 14-18-inch size. There are not a ton of 6-7-pound fish here, but overall the bass fishing is very good.

On warmer nights anglers cast Jitterbugs and buzzbaits listening for the unmistakable sound of a lunker largemouth hitting their lure.

Bass, both large and smallmouth are there for the taking. In summer the larger specimens head for deeper water. Mitchell's are found, for the most part, in its southeast corner.

Ice Fishing: Though great catches of jumbo perch are uncommon. Those fishing 10 to 15 feet with minnows or grubs occasionally are rewarded.

Between the two points of the Big Cove is what is some call "The X." It's a 12' hole. The edges are rimmed with living cabbage beds, alive and healthy. Those fishing it mark lots of fish on their electronics. They've been finicky. Light tackle using spikes on tiny jigs will usually entice them. It changes but the color purple should be on your list of jigs.

Tip-up anglers do well here. The bugs live on and eat the weeds. The panfish eat the bugs and the predators, pike and walleye, eat the panfish. Life is great.

Master Angler awards garnered by anglers fishing these lakes stands at sixty-two, including those for bluegills, black crappies, smallmouth bass, pumpkinseeds, and northern pike.

At a Glance

What: Walleye, Pike, Bass, Panfish

Where: Lake Mitchell

Why: An excellent all-around fishing lake

Landings: William Mitchell State Park boat launch on Lake Cadillac that can access Lake Mitchell; **Hemlock Park** (Federal) on the west side of Lake Mitchell in Big Cove, off Pole Road

Contacts: Cadillac Area Visitors Bureau, 222 Lake St. Cadillac, MI 49601, (231) 775-0657 cadillacmichigan.com

Bait & Tackle: Pilgrim's Village, 181 S. Lake Mitchell, Cadillac, 49601, (231) 775-5412

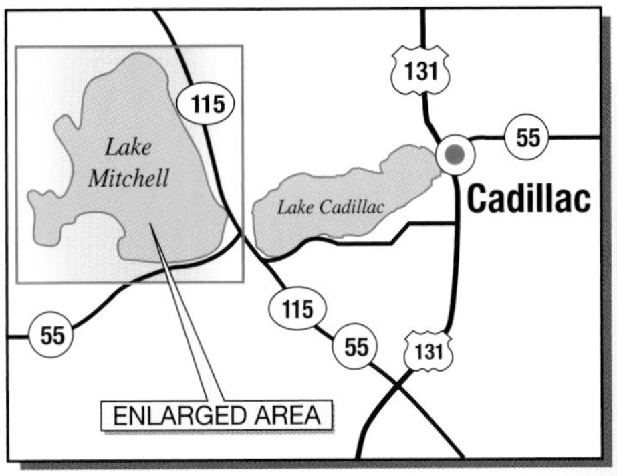

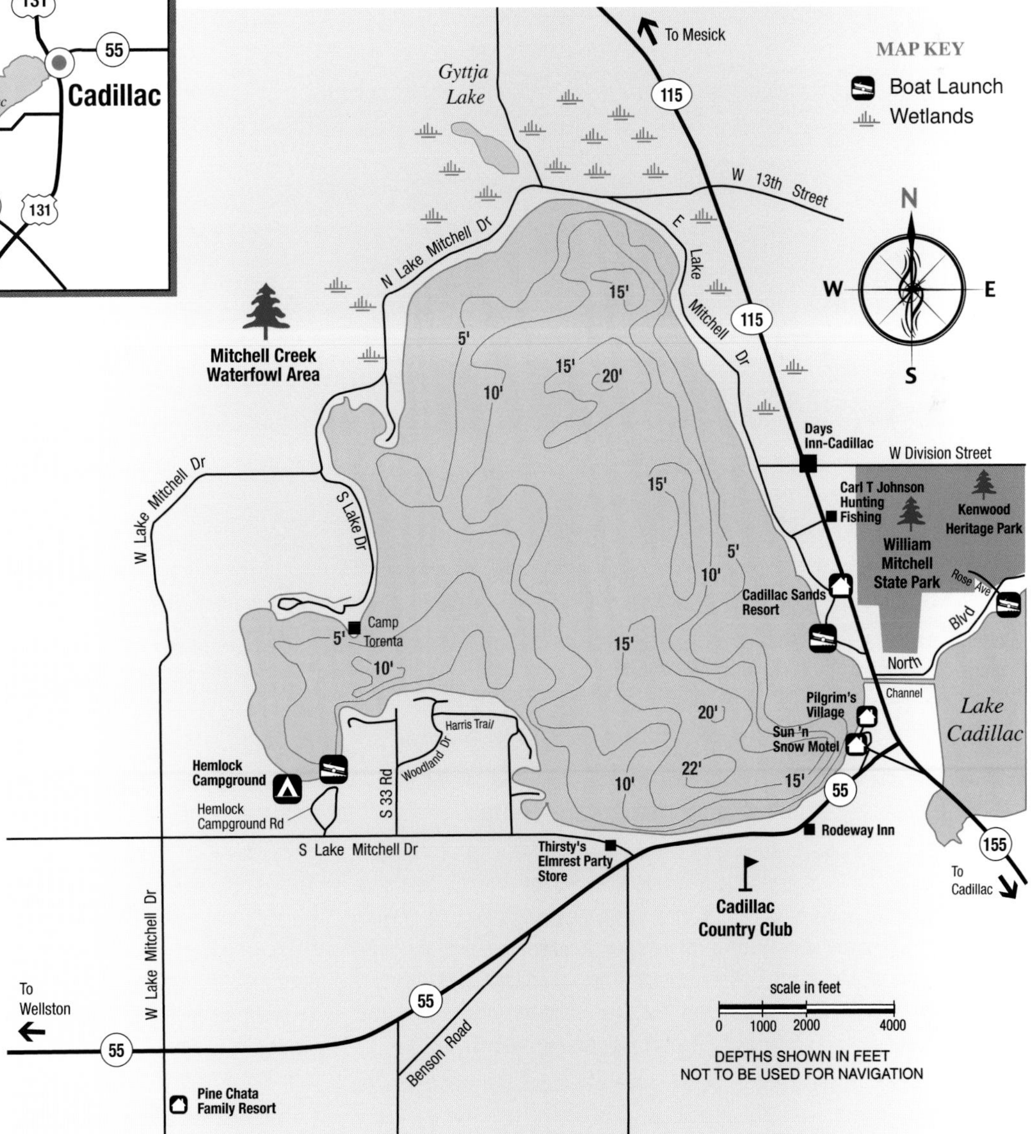

Perch may not be jumbos in this lake, but anglers can often find them in the 10- to 15-foot depths during the winter months.

Lake Mitchell

MAP KEY

Boat Launch

Wetlands

DEPTHS SHOWN IN FEET
NOT TO BE USED FOR NAVIGATION

Lime Lake Leelanau County

Lime Lake, named for the shimmering, emerald color it radiates, is a 670-acre spring-fed all-sports lake located between Leland and Glen Arbor. It has a maximum depth of 67 feet. Once again, this lake is not only beautiful in itself, but located in a fabulous area of the state. A trip to Lime Lake has all the advantages of both fishing and sightseeing for the entire family. Personally, it's the type of lake I love to fish.

Mark Fisher, along with his wife Betsy, own Lakeside Cottages on Lime Lake,

Mark says to not ignore the rock bass in this lake. You can catch upwards of 10-inch rock bass along the structured areas of the lake.

Panfish: According to Fisher, there are plenty of bluegills in Lime Lake but there are only a couple of spots to find them, and unfortunately you just have to look for other anglers on the lake fishing for them. Most fish this lake during the summer months. Once again, locate the weed beds and you will find gills. Perch here can be on the nice 10-12-inch size with great coloring. The south end of the

A good spot for bass on this small beautiful lake is just west of the submerged island in the center of the lake, where the water drops off from five to fifty feet.

and have been there 34 years according to Mark. He fishes this lake as often as possible, and is quite familiar with this beautiful, crystal-clear lake.

Bass: Mark says that there is very good smallmouth fishing on this lake, due primarily to the favorable bottom structure. Some say that the next state smallmouth record could easily come from this lake. Anglers take 16-20-inch bass out of this lake routinely. As bass fishing goes, look for the weedbeds. In the early part of the season, the 10-18-foot water is best, then the fish move out to deeper water as the summer progresses. This is a spring-fed lake with a gravel bottom, so it can remain colder in the deeper, 60-plus-foot area of the lake.

There is a sunken island in the middle of the lake about five feet below the water surface.

lake, in and near the weed beds and where it is shallow, is a good spot to look for these favorite table fare fish. You may catch a lot of smaller perch but keep searching and you can limit out, especially in the early part of summer.

Trout: Brown trout have been planted in this lake for years, but because they are trout they head for deeper, colder water and are therefore harder to catch. There are a lot of alewives in this lake for trout to feed on. Spring is an especially good time of year when the water temp is below 60 degrees, because after the water temperature increases the fish move deeper. Brown trout have been planted in this lake according to DNR records, virtually every year from 2000 until the writing of this book in 2012. The average-size fingerling runs about 7 inches long. Some probably move out of Shetland Creek and head to Little

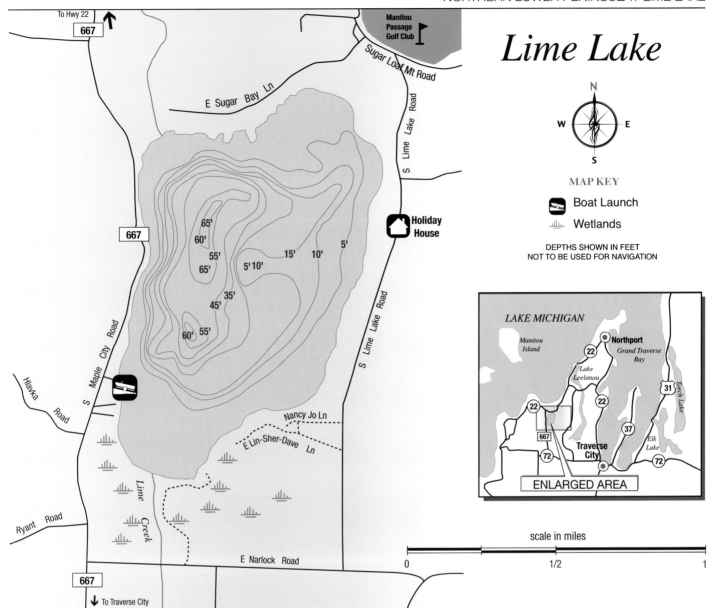

Lime Lake

MAP KEY

🚤 Boat Launch

⬛ Wetlands

DEPTHS SHOWN IN FEET
NOT TO BE USED FOR NAVIGATION

scale in miles

0   1/2   1

Traverse Lake and eventually enter Lake Michigan.

Note: Heather Hettinger, area DNR Fish Biologist, states that the comments made by local anglers relative to trout on this lake are correct in that you can catch a fair number of them if you know what you are doing, but it is often hit and miss. She states that surveys indicate a 3-4-year age group in this lake, and good trout survival, but unless you fish it regularly, it is not easy to find them.

Heather also mentions that she fishes this lake for smallmouth bass, and that it is a "wonderful bass fishery." The last survey showed a 21-inch smallmouth taken. Also, she mentions, there are some very good rock bass, as well as perch and bluegills. Not a lot of bluegills she confirms, but nice sizes.

One of the areas Heather suggests to fish for gills is on the north end where there is a flat, and then a gradual drop off. Work the 12-15-foot water depth. This area is good both winter and summer. In the south end of this lake, there is also a weed bed that can be productive in 12-15 feet of water.

At a Glance

What: Trout, bass and perch

Where: One of the more beautiful lakes settled in a quaint part of the state.

Why: Fishing is good, and other activities are also available while visiting this part of the state

Information/Guides: Leelanau County Chamber of Commerce leelanauchamber.com, (231) 271-9895. **Fisher's Lakeside Cottages,** Mark & Betsy Fisher, (231) 228-6201, (231) 633-5041 (cell), 6200 Maple City Road, Maple City, 49664, email: info@fisherscottages.com

Landings: Located on the southwest side of the lake; S. Maple City Road (Co. Rd. 667), just past Hlavka Road

Bait & Tackle: Narrows Passage Bait & Tackle, 102 St Mary's St, Lake Leelanau, 49653 (231) 256-2547; **The Sportsman Shop,** 5914 S Ray Street, Glen Arbor, 49636, (231) 334-3872; **Cedar Hardware,** 8925 South Kasson Street, Cedar, 49621 (231) 228-5417; **The Fish Hook,** 112 E Philip St, Lake Leelanau, 49653, (231) 256-9496

Manistee Lake Kalkaska County

This Manistee Lake—not to be confused with the Manistee Lake in the county of the same name—is located in north-central Kalkaska County. When many people think of Manistee Lake, we focus our attention to Manistee along Lake Michigan. This relatively small 860-acre lake's deepest spot is only 18 feet, but the outflow of the Manistee River and several creeks entering the lake ensure a steady supply of nutrients. Fish species that live in this lake include walleye, perch, smallmouth bass, bluegills, crappies and northern pike.

The maximum depth is 18 feet, however 95% of the lake is under 15 feet. The North Branch of the Manistee River originates from Manistee Lake, flowing out of the southern end of the lake. There is no lake-level control structure on Manistee Lake. The shoreline of Manistee Lake is about 80% developed with homes and cottages.

"Manistee Lake is a lot like Houghton Lake," said Gary Gile of Jack's Sport Shop in Kalkaska. "The lake is pretty featureless, so there's not much in the way of structure."

The lake generally has a healthy gamefish population. Walleye in particular are fairly numerous, but not as numerous as previous years due to lack of stocking during 2007-2010, this, according to Mark Tonello, due to a fish disease (VHS) that prevented safe stocking. Tonello stated that, "it was better to err on the safe side rather than take a chance of infecting the entire fish population in the lake."

Tonello's 2004 survey produced a 36-inch pike, showing that Manistee Lake is capable of producing some large northern pike.

A fairly recent DNR survey of Manistee Lake indicates that the lake is somewhat unique among Michigan lakes in that, according to DNR records, it has never been stocked with fish. Its tributaries, the Manistee River and Little Manistee River have been heavily stocked with fish, particularly salmon, over the years. Manistee Lake anglers benefit from these stocking efforts, as many adult salmon and steelhead move through Manistee Lake as they ascend the Manistee and Little Manistee rivers for their annual spawning runs.

Native species like smallmouth

bass, largemouth bass, bluegill, pumpkinseed sunfish, crappie, rock bass, northern pike, and walleye should continue to thrive in Manistee Lake.

Most people fish this lake for walleye, and the Manistee Lake walleye stocking program is dependent on the ability of the Department to provide walleye fingerlings that are certified as disease-free. Viral Hemorrhagic Septicemia (VHS) is a fish pathogen that has been responsible for a number of large, high-profile fish kills.

In Michigan, VHS has mostly been limited to Great Lakes waters, but one inland lake (Budd Lake, Clare County) was also found to be infected. When disease-free walleye fingerlings are available, they would be stocked in Manistee Lake. However, if there is any doubt as to whether or not the walleye fingerlings are truly VHS-free, then they would not be stocked.

Tonello stated that, "Native species like smallmouth bass, largemouth bass, bluegill, pumpkinseed sunfish, black crappie, rock bass, and northern pike should continue to thrive in Manistee Lake."

Fishing for walleye at night is most productive, but daytime fishing is also popular.

This photo, re-done as a painting, depicts a couple of pike that are slightly above the norm Manistee Lake.

Dan White, who works at Jack's Sport Shop in Kalkaska and is a frequent angler on Manistee Lake, states that, "bluegills are good along the east side of the lake, along with crappies and pike." It is not uncommon to see 9-10" gills, up to 14-15- inch crappie, and 40-plus-inch pike along the east side where an extensive weed bed exists. Spearing for pike is also common here. Spoons and Rapalas are popular for pike during the summer months, either casting, or even trolling with live bait.

Bass: Bass are plentiful in the lake. Smallmouth can be found most anywhere, according to White, and most anglers use topwater lures, like jitterbugs and hula poppers. Locate fine-gravel areas that drop down into deeper water. Also try using a jig and twistertail. Along the weeds, use spinnerbaits, or Rebel Pop'R's. For the deeper zones a worm rigged Texas style seems to work well.

There used to be some very nice-sized perch, over 15 inches, but they are not as plentiful. Perch are found in the middle of the lake where it is deeper, in both summer and winter.

Methods: Long-lining weed edges with lures like the Shad Rap during evening, or daytime using live bait. Manistee angler Tom Haley, pitches a 1/4-ounce Fireball jig with a half crawler on a fathead and working it along the deeper weed beds with a slip bobber. The first point of land as you view northwest from the public launch is a popular area to fish. Many locals troll or drift a crawler harness' along weed lines and flats for walleye.

Pike/Panfish: If you want pike, try larger spinnerbaits and fish the weeds. This lake has some nice crappies also when you can find them, and nice bluegills as well. A hotspot for nice-size specks is north of the public-access site on the east side where the bottom drops from 10 to 16 feet. A common method is to fish right before dark, using one rod with a minnow on it while jigging the other. Crappies in the 14-inch range are fairly common. The crappies tend to suspend, so a flasher can be a big help.

"There are some big perch in Manistee Lake, too," states Gile. He said that ice-anglers fishing with big blue shiners for walleye routinely catch perch in the 13- to 14-inch range.

Walleye: "Walleyes are an added bonus in this lake," says Gile. "Look for winter 'eyes in the north-central portion of the lake in 10 feet of water."

At a Glance

What: Pike, walleye, smallmouth and panfish

Where: East side of lake for most of the fishing action

Why: Easy lake to fish, shallow and relatively small

How: Crankbaits, spinners, or live bait

Landings: SW side of lake just north of Road 612

Information: Kalkaska Area Chamber of Commerce, (800) 487-6880 www.kalkaskami.com

Bait & Tackle: Jack's Sport Shop Bait & Tackle, 212 Cedar St., Kalkaska 49646, (231) 258-8892

Manistee Lake

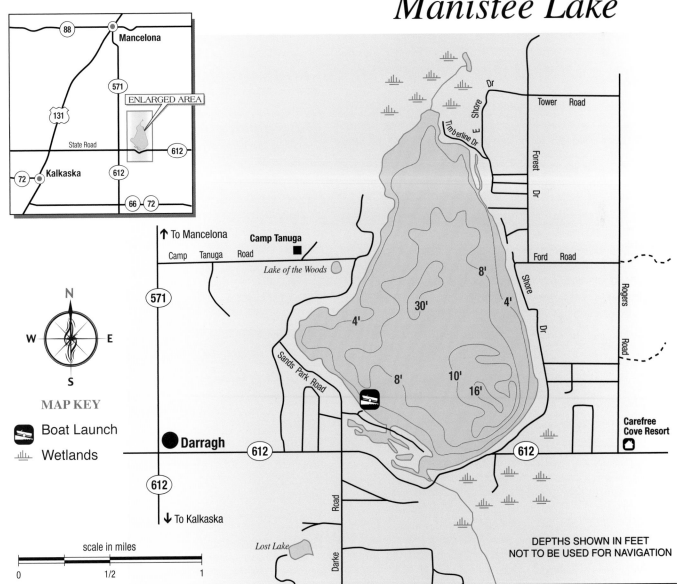

Mullett Lake Cheboygan County

t's hard to write about Mullet Lake without mention of its sister lake across I-75, Burt Lake, both located in the northern tip of the Lower Peninsula. It's like writing about Little Bay de Noc, and not mentioning Big Bay de Noc in the same article.

Burt is more productive, has more natural habitat, and therefore more natural reproduction. According to Tim Cwalinski, DNR District Fish Biologist, "Mullet never did have a supportive fish spawning habitat; i.e., no gravel shoals, no significant weed beds, only sandy shorelines, great for swimmers, but not fish habitat." He went on to say that, "probably two-thirds of Mullet is very deep and not conducive to walleye." Furthermore he says, "a lot of the walleye probably come from Burt or Crooked Lake, lakes that produce walleye."

Mullet Lake fish species include: Largemouth bass, smallmouth bass, crappie, walleye, catfish, sunfish, bluegill, rock bass, perch, walleye, sauger, white bass, striped bass, hybrid bass, brown trout, lake trout, and more. But perch remain the main attraction on Mullet Lake, according to Cwalinski.

Mullet Lake only shares size (over 17,000 acres) in common with Burt; otherwise they are very different fisheries. It's good to have some understanding of this lake in order to choose how and where you may want to fish it, and for what species of fish.

Walleye densities over the years tend to fluctuate, according to Cwalinski. "A lot of the adult walleye move downstream in the Cheboygan River to spawn due to lack of spawning habitat in Mullet," he states (note: fish do not always move upstream to spawn as we are inclined to believe). Then they move to the lower Black River, and the young typically drift to Lake Huron, while others move to Burt Lake, not back to Mullet.

Cwalinski says that, "although walleye populations in Mullet are not high, they are bigger in Mullet versus Burt."

"Because walleye densities are lower in Mullet, perch survive better, but also have slow growth" says Cwalinski. Perch and walleye are density dependant, i.e., fewer fish, they grow bigger, the more you have, the slower the growth. Saginaw Bay is good example of this process; more walleye, slower growth.

Perch increase in size in Mullet due to longevity, because growth rates are slow. Perch are abundant in Mullet and can spawn there because they do not spawn on beds like walleye and some other species, but rather spawn on plants, and most anything upright.

Perch in Mullet average about 2 inches smaller than the average in MI; i.e., if you have a state average perch size, for example, at age 5 of 8.7 inches, Mullet is 6.4 inches. Perch can live, taking out the consideration of predation, up to 10-15 years, but the average is 6-12 years in most lakes.

Another fishable species in Mullet are smallmouth bass which have adapted to the lake and survive on large numbers of crayfish.

South End: Larry Drozdzewsk from Pat & Gary's Party Store (and bait shop) in Indian River states that the walleye fishing has been limited at best, however pike fishing near the mouth of Indian River is very good, with some in the 30- to 40- inch range.

Larry also stated that most bass die of "old age" in Mullet due to the large numbers, especially in the southwest part of the lake, from Indian River up to Topinabee. Bass anglers enjoy both large- and smallmouth fishing in this area. Larry mentions that perch are good also, if you can find them in this very deep lake.

A friend of mine who fishes Mullet fairly often said that at the very southeast end, Pigeon Bay (off the Pigeon River) beginning with Parrott Point, the area is scattered with weed growth and therefore holds nice size pike both winter and summer.

At a Glance

What: Perch, Pike, Walleye, Smallmouth, large Muskie

Where: Mullet Lake north and south end

How: Crankbaits for bass, winter spearing for muskie

Information: Indian River Chamber of Commerce, P.O. Box 57, Indian River, 49749, (231) 238-9325, www.irchamber.com; Cheboygan Chamber of Commerce & Tourist Bureau, 124 N. Main Cheboygan, 49721, (231) 627-7183, www.cheboygan.com

Boat Landings:

North End:

The channel to the Aloha State Park launch is protected by breakwalls on either side and marked by lights at the entrance. At the end of the channel there is a double cement boat ramp.

Just west of Dodge Point is the Mullet Lake Village DNR public boat launch. There is a cement ramp with loading dock, vault toilets and plenty of parking.

South End:

Just north of Topinabee off US 27 there is a small boat landing with a cement ramp.
At the end of Bowersock Road there is public access to the river. It is a hard dirt bottom for small boats.
At the end of Jewell Road, between Round Point to the south and Needle Point to the North.

Bait & Tackle: Pat & Gary's Party Store, 3758 South Straits Hwy, Indian River (Off I-75), (231) 238-6776.

Beautiful sunsets viewed daily from the popular Aloha State Park on the east side of the lake.

Crankbaits worked in close to the weed beds seem to be your best bet. The waters around the mouth of Pigeon and Little Pigeon rivers are great for steelies in early spring. Spawn bags, crawlers, or minnows off the bottom produce good catches of both brown and rainbow trout.

The Southern Sunken Island just south of Topinabee holds walleye year round. Deep crank baits or crawler harnesses in the 15-20-foot depth work well during the summer months. But once again, the walleye population is slim. The area around the flats consists of a rocky bottom, holding smallmouth in the early season along with walleye and pike. Walleye suspend off the steep banks from the sunken island to well north of Topinabee in the summer months.

North End: Just south of Dodge Point, less than a mile in distance, a red buoy marks a small sunken island that comes to within a couple feet of the surface. The area to the north and east of this is known as the flats. There is a transition zone from sand to gravel that runs approximately 25 feet. Work this area in summer and fall for walleye that frequent the flats area.

A flashing green light marks the entrance to Cheboygan River from the north end of Mullet Lake. Stay right in the channel or you will be in very shallow water. The mouth of the river will attract walleye in early spring and fall like most rivers in the area. Evening and nighttime are the best times to anchor and fish the channel with the popular jigs.

Mullet Lake walleye received a recent welcome boost with the stocking of nearly 102,000 summer fingerlings, while Little Bay de Noc received 41,000 fingerlings, according to the Department of Natural Resources.

Each year 1-2-inch walleye fingerlings are stocked in managed waters throughout the state. Unfortunately, only a limited number of walleye eggs were collected once again in some years due to ongoing concerns related to the occurrence of the fish virus, Viral Hemorrhagic Septicemia (VHS), the DNRE said.

DNRE Fisheries Division staff collected walleye eggs in March and April from Little Bay de Noc for pond rearing and eventual stocking into the Bays de Noc this year.

The Inter-Tribal Fisheries Program made available to the Michigan DNRE approximately 143,000 fingerling walleye that they reared in their ponds. These fish were in excess to the tribes' annual stocking targets and were offered to the state for stocking in areas important to both the tribes and the state.

The limited rearing capacity due to VHS concerns has really put a damper on the walleye program, and any additional assistance couldn't have come at a better time.

In addition to the Mullet Lake stocking, ITFAP also provided walleye fingerlings to the DNRE for stocking in Little Bay de Noc, near Rapid River in the Upper Peninsula.

Mullett Lake Fish Stocking

State Stocking Efforts, June, Muskegon Strain

2010: 101,100 spring fingerlings, not marked

2011: 97,951 spring fingerlings, marked

Mullett Lake Area Preservation Society and Private Tribal Stocking Efforts

2010: 10,392 fall fingerlings 6-8 inches in length

2011: 7,500 fall fingerlings 6-8 inches in length

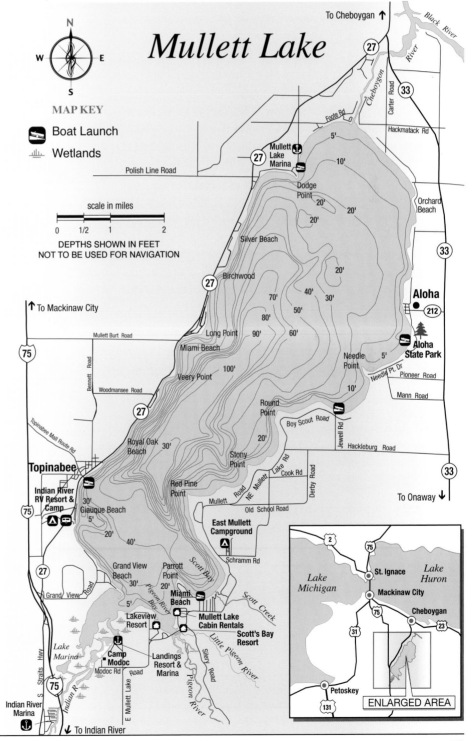

Otsego Lake Otsego County

Although Otsego Lake is only about ten percent the size of Houghton Lake, Michigan's largest inland lake, it has historically received more fish plantings than any lake I know (not official). In 2000 they received almost two million walleye fry, and again in 2006 almost another three million. In addition, northern muskie, pike, and sturgeon have also been added to this fishery over the years. At 1,972 acres, and only a maximum of 23 feet deep, there are a lot of fish packed into this moderately sized lake. Otsego is a long, narrow lake, at 5 miles in length, and averages around 0.7 of a mile wide.

Sturgeon: Joe Verduce once had a fishing store on the west side of Otsego Lake, across from the state park, and has fished this lake extensively. He said he has seen 60-plus-inch sturgeon taken from this lake on a regular basis. He is an avid hook-and-line winter sturgeon angler, a seemingly rare type of winter fishing for one of the oldest species of the bony fish family.

Most of these stocked monsters are in the 25-28-year range, relatively young for sturgeon. Joe's winter fishing methods consist of a 30-inch stainless-steel rod (but a sturdy fiberglass will work), with 50-pound braided line. The sturgeon are virtually all over the lake, but Joe works the 6-8-foot water depth area off the state park since it is easily accessible. The park is plowed during the winter. Other anglers go deeper and that works also. Sturgeon love the smell of the large smelt and are readily attracted to it. Use a #2 or 2.0, 3/4-inch to an 1/8-inch hook for your smelt. There is no sturgeon spearing on this lake.

In summer, after the season opens in mid July, "work the shoreline," says Verduce, "in 6-8 feet of water, using crawlers floating on the bottom. Just anchor your boat, toss your offering overboard, and wait. Once again, use a heavy rod and line."

Walleye: For winter ice fishing, Verduce says that the Point Comfort area is good, and also by the state park, just north of the boat landing, on the beach side. During summer, anglers generally go out towards the center of the lake and troll the shallow trough that runs north to south, just east of the center of the lake. "Only the locals seem to know of this location," says one local angler, "and the weed growth here is very low or nonexistent." This trough runs about three miles long, up to about Point Comfort at the northern end.

Pike: "June and July are generally slow times of the year," says Verduce. In August, the pike season starts to pick up and extends into fall. Spearing, although relatively new on this lake, has also taken off, but be very cautious that you are well aware of the difference between a northern pike, a sturgeon, and a muskie. In fact, Joe said that on the very first day of the pike-spearing season, someone speared a sturgeon, which is illegal on this lake.

Tip-ups are the safest method for taking winter pike. Pike are virtually all over this lake and it is the type of lake, according to Verduce, designed to be a trophy pike fishing lake. Once again, work any potential pike areas, drop-offs, and any weedy areas.

Bass: Both large- and smallmouth bass can be found along the shoreline, structured and weedy areas, generally under the 6-8-foot water depths. When you move beyond that depth, the weeds become very intense and fishing is difficult.

Muskie: There are a few remaining tiger muskie in this lake, but most have disappeared and, like most lakes, the tiger is a thing of the past. But northern muskie can be found in the 24-28-inch range and growing. In future years they should become an excellent target for anglers.

Bluegills: "This is an excellent bluegill fishery," says Verduce. "You can find gills the size of Frisbees," he states. Bluegills in the 10-12-inch range are common, and many are larger. In fact, June through August, this lake has seen over 20 Master Award-winning bluegill taken. Areas to fish are along the shoreline during spring, and around the state and county park.

As with most bluegill lakes, finding weedlines, either emergent or, best of all, submergent, in deeper water is important. The larger bluegills will not suspend far from bottom and a slip bobber is a must.

This park, located on the west side of Otsego Lake, is a popular site for both campers and anglers.

At a Glance

What: An excellent all-around lake for larger predator fish, as well as massive gills

Where: There are several good areas for both larger fish, as well as panfish

Why: One of the overall premier fishing lakes in the state, with good fishing now, and looking to improve in upcoming years

Regs: The hook-and-line harvest season for lake sturgeon shall be July 16 through March 15, inclusive. Fishing for lake sturgeon shall be prohibited from March 16 through July 15, inclusive. Size Limit: 50 inches minimum

Information/Guides: Gaylord Area Convention and Tourism Bureau, 101 W. Main Street, Gaylord, 49735, (989) 732-4000

Landings: Two public boat landings are available. The Otsego County Park site is located on the northwest shore of the lake off West Otsego Lake Dr. There is also a site at the Otsego Lake State Park (state park sticker is required). This access site is best if you plan to fish the southern half of the lake

Bait & Tackle: Corner Store, 4800 West Otsego Lake Drive, Gaylord, 49735, (989) 732-8664; **Northern Sports,** 3819 Old US Highway 27 S, Gaylord, 49735 (989) 448-2014

Cruising and drift fishing along the 15-foot contour lines, which are plentiful in this lake, will bring the angler into these areas of submergent weeds. The deeper area of the lake, west and a bit south of Arbutus Beach Point on the southeast shoreline, can be excellent for gills just after ice-out and after the spawn.

Typical bluegill gear works well, however a glass-bead-head nymph in bright green with a pearl Flashabou tail is a favored fly if you prefer this method.

Perch: Perch are coming back in this lake, not only in the opinion of Verduce, but local fish biologist, Steve Sendek. There are lots of small ones now, generally in the 6-8-inch size, but if you use a larger minnow you will avoid some of the smaller perch that can hassle you. Once again, work the area off the state park, but perch can be found in most of the lake.

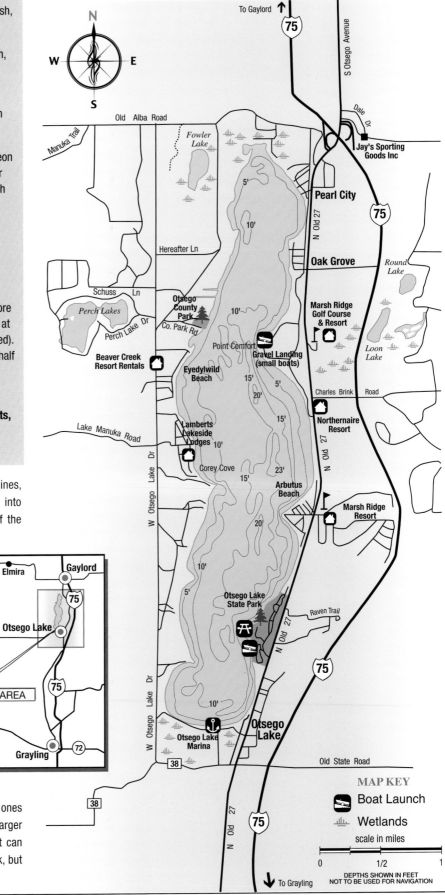

Portage Lake Manistee County

Michigan is blessed with many lakes that are tied in to one of the Great Lakes generally through a channel that may be natural or man-made. These channels provide the influx of whatever fish live in the larger Great Lakes waters, making for at least an excellent seasonal fishery. Portage Lake is one of these lakes. At just over, 2,100 acres, it carries a prime variety of game fish for anglers to pursue. The primary fish species in this lake include yellow and Lake Michigan perch, bluegill, rock bass, walleye, largemouth and smallmouth bass, northern pike, and crappie.

Portage Lake is a consistent producer of some very nice walleyes that remain active throughout summer, partially because it can be tricky to pull fish out of the dense vegetation and structure of this shallow lake. This lake provides enough protection from anglers and other fish, as well as a plentiful food sources, to allow many of them to reach trophy size.

Walleye: The walleye population in Portage Lake appears to be healthy, with some natural reproduction taking place. Adult walleye numbers in Portage Lake are currently sufficient to sustain a consistent fishery.

Jim Simons, a long-time lake resident, says the average walleye in this lake is around 17-19 inches, but he has seen many over 10 pounds. In the winter months, Jim says a good place to ice fish for walleye is off Little Eden Camp located along Andy's Point at the central north end of the lake. Anglers fish for walleye in 20-25 feet of water. Also Jim says that the south shore is good, once again, fishing in about 25 feet of water.

"During the summer months you often have to hunt around for the walleye," states Jim. After the ice moves

Portage Lake

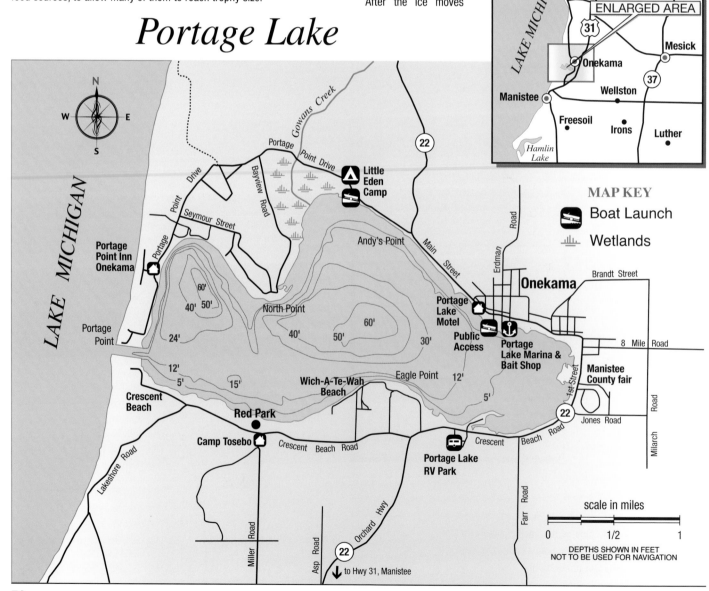

out of the lake, walleye can often be caught around the piers. They may be found in the same areas that support walleye during the ice fishing season. Spring is good in the channel where the lake empties into Lake Michigan. This approximately 300-foot-wide band of water that connects to Lake Michigan is under ten feet deep, but does get dredged about every 2-3 years. Most anglers troll this lake or drift using jigs.

Jigging with a 1/4- 1/8- and 1/16-ounce jig is a good way to hook a walleye in Portage Lake after the weed beds start to develop. It's also helpful to use a sensitive, longer rod to haul in larger fish out of the weeds and brush.

Casting a jig tipped with a worm or leech into weeds and then twitching it until it settles to the bottom is another effective technique. Keep moving it for a few minutes before changing locations in the bed.

Bass:
Jim says that tournament anglers fish the entire lake for bass. In spring, you will find them along the shallows, as well as during the early morning hours all summer long. "There is no one good area on this lake for bass," says Simons. During the summer you can also work the drop-offs that exist around much of the lake. Bass in the 4-6-pound size are often caught on Portage Lake.

Perch:
A fairly recent (2009) DNR survey report indicates that slower-growing resident yellow perch can be found in Portage Lake throughout the year, while larger faster-growing Lake Michigan yellow perch tend to migrate into Portage Lake during the winter months, and back to Lake Michigan in spring.

Perch, averaging around 8 inches, but some over 10, are sought after along the south shore during the winter months. Jim states that there is a hole around 60 feet deep off of Andy's Point at the north end of the lake that holds a lot of fish, including perch. Fish this area right on the bottom in early winter.

During summer, Jim mentions that you might have to work for the perch, but you can locate them in much the same areas as you find them in winter.

Throughout the summer months, only smaller resident perch are caught. However during winter and again after the ice cover thaws, yellow perch appear to move into Portage Lake from Lake Michigan when seeking spawning habitat. Perch fishing for the larger "Lake Michigan" yellow perch can be excellent at times until the water begins to warm in mid-May and the perch begin to move back to Lake Michigan.

Perch upwards of 11 inches, pike up to 34 inches (average 22 inches), smallmouth bass averaging just over 2 pounds each, and all fish were above the state average growth rate. Walleye in particular exceeded the state average length considerably by almost 4 inches.

Bluegill:
Portage Lake has been known to produce excellent catches of bluegill and sunfish at certain times of the year, however the DNR survey in 2009 revealed a considerable drop in numbers of both species. Angler creel estimates confirmed this decline.

Bluegills are located mostly at the east end of the lake, where the shallowest waters are located. You can catch some nice size gills, upwards of 11 inches, but there are also tons of smaller ones. Like most bluegill lakes, you will find them on the beds in early spring.

Management Direction:
The long-term goal for Portage Lake is to maintain the excellent warmwater and coolwater fish communities that currently exist. Species such as rock bass, yellow perch, largemouth bass, and northern pike should continue to thrive in Portage Lake. None of these species are currently stocked by DNR Fisheries Division and they appear to be reproducing well on their own.

Note: The dock located off the town of Onekama is a good place to fish for both bass and panfish, and is handicapped accessible. Crappie upwards of 15 inches can often be found in this same area. Cast for bass and panfish from this dock and, if you are lucky, you might even hook a Master Angler bluegill.

Winter ice fishing is a great time of the year for perch and other game fish on this lake.

At a Glance

What: An overall good fishing lake for large species and panfish

Where: Most anywhere on the lake you can find good fishing

Information/Guides: Manistee CVB, POB 13, Manistee, 49660, (231) 389-9355

Landings: West end of the lake as well as near the town of Onekama.

Bait & Tackle: Portage Lake Marina & Bait Shop, 5159 Main St., Onekama, 49675, (231) 889-3825

Round Lake Mason County

f you are looking for a relatively undeveloped lake to fish for bass and pike, located in the east-central part of lower Michigan, then Round Lake may offer you just what you are looking for. It's often difficult to find a lake that is undisturbed for the most part, and located close to a large part of the population in southern Michigan. This is another Michigan lake that has had a milfoil aquatic weed problem, but has done a good job in reducing it from almost 300 acres (half the lake size), to a small, manageable size of only a couple acres. Milfoil was so thick on this lake that boaters had a difficult time moving through it. The chemical control started in 2008 and has been successful since that time.

Larry Polacek has fished this 580-acre lake and knows it about as well as anyone. He says, due to lack of any significant development, Round lake has fewer noise obstructions than most lakes, and is a good all-around lake. About three quarters of it is owned by a few adjoining farmers.

The maximum depth is 12 feet, a hole on the east-central part of the lake, but averages only 7-8 feet deep. The nearest larger town to this lake is Ludington, about 20 miles to the west.

Bass:
Bass are probably the number one game species in this lake, with some of the larger ones in the 16-18-inch category, according to Polacek. Normally anglers hook some of the larger ones earlier in the season, and eventually they will become less abundant as the season moves through summer. As with many lakes, bass anglers use minnows, rubber worms, or crawlers and troll the lake. Being that there is not much structure in this shallow lake, you can troll just about anywhere since "there are no special areas the bass hang out," says Polacek. Some anglers will also just toss a crawler and bobber overboard and wait in hopes a bass will eventually arrive. On a lazy summer day, this is not a bad way to relax and fish on a small, quiet lake.

Pike:
As with largemouth, being that there is very little structure here the pike seem to roam around the lake in search of prey. During the winter months, some will try spearing pike up on the northwest end of the lake, near the small outlet stream. Others will use the traditional tip-ups with a minnow as an offering. During the summer months, trolling with rubber worms will often net you a nice pike, some up in the upper 28-30-inch size. Not wall hangers of course, but nice size pike nonetheless. Once again, those who seek out pike will often just troll the entire lake.

Panfish:
"Bluegills are on the smaller size," says Polacek, "but crappie can be caught in the 8-10-inch size and larger. In winter, you will do best at the northwest end of the lake for crappie, or in the shallow 12-foot 'hole' at the east-central end of the lake."

Note: There are a few nice size walleye in Round Lake, but they are taken incidentally while fishing other species, such as bass or pike. Some larger ones can be caught in the 26-30-inch range, but no one really targets walleye due to the low numbers.

Fishing is not always a solo event; sometimes you need to take along your best friend.

Round Lake

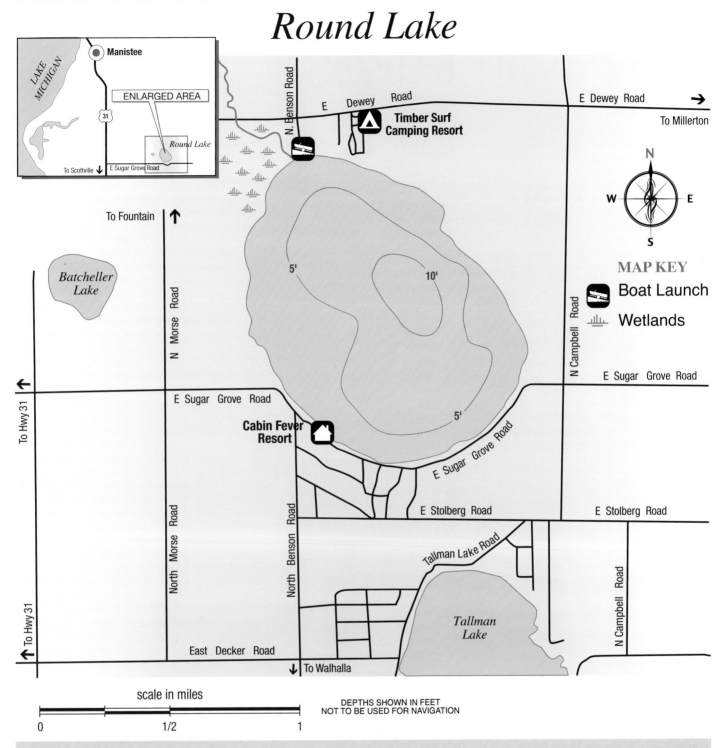

scale in miles

0 1/2 1

DEPTHS SHOWN IN FEET
NOT TO BE USED FOR NAVIGATION

At a Glance

What: Largemouth bass and pike

Where: A small, bowl-shaped shallow lake in the west central part of the lower peninsula

Why: Relatively undisturbed lake, with little development

Information/Guides: Larry Polacek, Timber Surf Camping Resort, 6575 East Dewey Road Fountain 49410, timbersurfresort.com, (231) 462-3468

Techniques: Easy to fish, since there is not much structure, and the lake is small, so you can troll the entire lake

Landings: The only landing on this lake is the township park, located west of the outlet at the northwest end of the lake

Bait & Tackle: Larry Polacek, Timber Surf Camping Resort, 6575 East Dewey Road, Fountain, 49410, timbersurfresort.com, (231) 462-3468.
The closest other bait and tackle shop would be in a larger town like Baldwin or Ludington

Twin Lakes Montmorency County

WEST TWIN LAKE

West Twin is a clear, all-sports lake with good fishing. Troll or still fish for largemouth and smallmouth bass, walleye, northern pike, or catch lots of yellow perch, bluegill and sunfish. West Twin has a sand and gravel bottom around its shoreline, and the lake is wide open and free of obstructions.

West Twin is bigger, at over 1300 acres, deeper and clearer than East Twin. Excellent smallmouth bass up to 4 pounds are present along with good perch and a few pike. Very few weeds exist but there are a lot of drop-off areas with gravel/rock bottom. A deep hole exists near the outlet on the east side of the lake and I have heard of large crappie and even some muskie in this area.

Walleye: Veteran angler Russ Earls says that, "walleye in the winter is not great, unless you go early morning and late evenings." The lake has plenty of 'eyes, he says, "and they are "meaty" as well, most averaging in the 18-23-inch range."

Spring/summer is a good time to fish here, especially when the water temps start to rise. It is best to fish before Memorial Day and after Labor Day due to the heavy boating traffic on this lake. If you fish in the summer months, you need to go early in the day or later in the evening.

In the winter, go by the inlet at the west end of the marina, known as Eagle Point. In the summer you can troll anywhere around this lake, and especially along the shallows in later evening when the walleye move in to prey on minnows and other small fish.

DNR planting records show that in West Twin in 2006, over 67,000 walleye fingerlings were planted, and in 2011 another 98,000 found their way into this lake.

Note: One lure color not to use if you are walleye fishing is orange because you will be besieged by bass.

Smallmouth Bass: Earls says that the smallmouth bass average in the 4-5-pound range and can be caught all around the shoreline where there are docks or structure.

Pike: Pike tend to hang out along the east end of lake in the deeper water, both summer and winter. Russ has seen one pike in the 12-pound size, 42-43-inch length taken from this lake.

Panfish: Russ finds good perch in the shallow bays at the east and west end of the lake. The perch are not big, being mostly in the 6-8 inch size. Bluegills are also smaller, but there are plenty of them and they're a great springtime catch when in the shallows. Rock bass can be fairly decent sized in West Twin, often in the 8-10-inch range. They can also be found along the shoreline in 5-6 feet of water. Spawning takes place in late spring and when water temperatures reach 55 to 60 degrees F.

Legendary retired DNR Director and strong Michigan Conservationist Pete Petoskey resides on West Twin Lake and says that the lake is somewhat sterile and needs some structure to help produce more fish. He says both largemouth and smallmouth bass are popular here. Pete would fish for them near Eagle Point with a fly rod in the evening. He says that you can find perch in the 8-9-inch range now that they are coming back from a walleye overplant that cleaned out many of the perch. "If you find a weed bed," states Pete, "you will most likely find perch."

Both East and West Twin are moderate sized lakes that, although populated with cottages, have a unique uninhabited look.

At a Glance

WEST TWIN LAKE

What: Walleye, bass, and panfish

Information: Lewiston Area Chamber of Commerce, 2946 Kneeland Street, P.O. Box 656, Lewiston, 49756, (989) 786-2293

Landings: A public boat launch with good parking is just west of Lewiston on County Road 612

Bait & Tackle: Lewiston Hardware & Lumber, 4421 Hanson St., Lewiston, 49756, (989 786-2388; **Lewiston Ace Hardware,** 4910 County Road 612, Lewiston, 49756, (989) 786-4910.

At a Glance

EAST TWIN LAKE

What: Walleye, perch

Information: Lewiston Area Chamber of Commerce, 2946 Kneeland Street, P.O. Box 656, Lewiston, 49756, (989) 786-2293

Landings: There is a paved, public boat launch in Lewiston at the public beach

Bait & Tackle: Midlakes Market, 3521 County Road 612, Lewiston, 49756, (989) 786-3227; **Woody's Market,** 4155 County Road 612, Lewiston, 49756, (989) 786-2511

EAST TWIN LAKE

East Twin Lake, at only 830 acres in size, is a pontoon type lake; that is, a lazy, relatively quiet lake, especially during the week, making fishing here relatively easy. Although the lake averages about 7-8 feet in depth, there are some 25-foot depths. These deeper areas are where some of the better fishing can be located. Walleye, lots of smallmouth bass, nice-size perch, bluegills, rock bass, and catfish are the most popular game fish in East Twin.

The Twin Lakes Property Owners Association (TLPOA), founded in the early 1980s, has been promoting the stewardship of both West Twin Lake and East Twin Lake for decades and continues to do so. They are involved in organized programs to protect the water quality of these lakes as well as prevent development-based pollutants from entering the waters here. They are proving that their efforts are successful, since good water quality has remained steady since the 1970s.

East Twin may be West Twin's little sister, but not when it comes to walleyes. The DNR has been stocking walleyes for years and the fishing is hard to beat. There are also plentiful largemouth and smallmouth bass, bluegills and yellow perch. East Twin is an all-sports lake. DNR records show that in 2011 alone, over 80,000 walleye fingerlings were planted. In 2005 and 2006, over 140,000 walleye fingerlings were planted. And for such a small lake, this resulted in some excellent fishing.

Walleye: Don Hunkins is a local angler who fishes East Twin Lake often. He says you can catch walleye over 25 inches, but unfortunately not that often, so don't look for hawgs in this lake, but rather lots of good eating-size fish.

If you plan on ice fishing, most anglers, for whatever reason, are not very successful here. Nonetheless, those that fish here during the winter months, usually work the east and northeast side of the lake for walleye. Anglers also fish at the "hole" about 100 yards off the Lewiston Lodge on Fleming Road at the southwest end of the lake. This location is also good for summer walleye trolling

with Rapalas or your favorite offering. This part of the lake drops to around 26-28 feet deep. You can catch some fish in the 15-20" range by drifting bait behind slip sinkers and trolling minnows at night.

Smallmouth Bass: Smallmouth bass anglers can frequently be seen trolling or casting along the east side of East Twin Lake. This part of the lake has a sandy, rocky bottom, ideal for spawning, so fish often hang out in this area. Smallmouth bass in these waters average around the 20-inch size. Hunkins states that what you lack in numbers in this lake, you make up in the size of the fish. And don't be surprised if you hook into some rock bass in this lake, because they are quite abundant here.

Perch: Once again, you may not run into large schools of perch in East Twin, but they are sizable, not uncommon in the 8-11-inch size, and some upwards of 15 inches. For perch fishing, look for the numerous weed beds, that are easily found. Late-summer perch fishing can be very productive, with limit catches not uncommon.

Note: Tiger muskie were also stocked in previous years, but no more — although it appears that a solid population of this species has been established in the lake through these stocking efforts. The parts of the lake that have deep weed growth, which occurs mostly around the western and southern shorelines, are great for fishing as well.

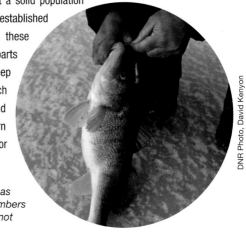

DNR Photo, David Kenyon

Nice-sized perch such as this are not in large numbers in these lakes, but are not uncommon either.

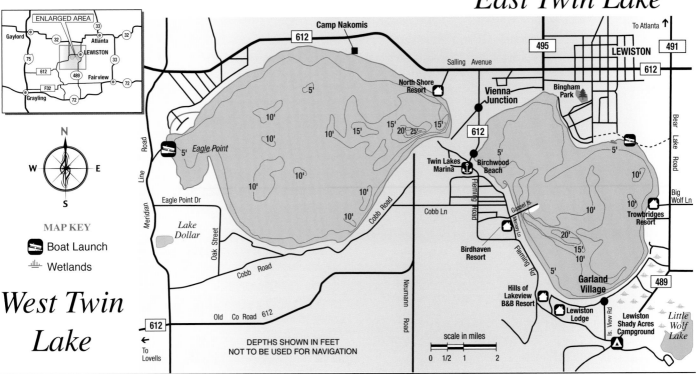

East Twin Lake

West Twin Lake

MAP KEY

🛥 Boat Launch

⚓ Wetlands

DEPTHS SHOWN IN FEET
NOT TO BE USED FOR NAVIGATION

scale in miles
0   1/2   1   2

Van Etten Lake Iosco County

When most anglers think of Van Etten Lake, the first thing that comes to mind is perch, lots of perch all over the lake, states Ross Wellman from a local bait and tackle store. Van Etten is a long, relatively narrow lake just over 1,300 acres adjacent to what was once Wurtsmith Air Force base before it was closed down a considerable number of years back. It was a convenient location for Air Force personnel to fish, or take their families fishing within a short walk from the base. But now the base has been converted to mostly private businesses, housing, and actually part of it is used to repair jumbo jet airliners. Back in the days of the Air Force base, you could be sitting in a boat on Van Etten and have a B-52 approach for landing not much higher than the tree tops and low over the water, the jet engines almost deafening.

Van Etten Lake has a maximum depth of 25 feet and an average depth of 14 feet. It is considered a warmwater fishery, and anglers can expect to find healthy populations of largemouth bass, smallmouth bass, and northern pike. Crappie and rainbow trout can also be found in the lake, and the Michigan DNR stocks Van Etten Lake with walleye.

Steve Sendek, DNR fish biologist who oversees this lake, states that, "Van Etten is a unique lake in a sense that it is low in the Au Sable watershed and has a dam on it, therefore it has a legal lake limit, which creates a problem." He goes on to say that, "because of this, the fish community tends to suffer, and it makes it hard to manage."

Another problem is that all the existing fish eat the smaller planted walleye, making it hard to get over the hump and start to balance out this currently good fishing lake to a potentially great fishing lake. The plan, says Sendek, is to start stocking 80,000 fingerling walleye every other year, and eventually stock muskie to provide more predatory fish in the lake. "Walleye is the one predatory fish that can be effectively managed in this lake," he says. "This is a very productive lake and has lots of nutrients," says Sendek, "and provides

Good eating size perch are a mainstay in Van Etten Lake.

At a Glance

What: Perch bonanza and good crappie fishing

Where: Van Etten Lake in Oscoda

Why: Good fishing lake now, but potential for greatness in near future

Boat Rental: Rainbow Canvas, 4180 N Us-23 - Oscoda, (989) 739-5696; **Jerry's Marina,** 536 Tawas Beach Rd., East Tawas, (989) 362-8641

Landings: Two boat landings are situated at the central west end of the lake, at both the State Forest Campground and Air Force Beach

Bait & Tackle: Wellman Party and Bait Store, 410 S. State St., Oscoda, (989) 739-2869 (note: also cleans fish); **Dam Store,** 1879 W. River Rd., Oscoda, (989) 739-9979

the ideal opportunity for improvement in the fish population as long as we can start to get the balance in order."

Another plan that the state wanted to undertake is to allow the Lake Huron influx of walleye, perch, and pike by opening the dam at the south end of the lake, but the federal government will not allow it, fearing that the lamprey will enter. However, the dam is not a barrier now, and the lamprey control program, as seen by the upper Lake Huron area, has been effective and now considered under control.

Therefore, the bottom line is you can catch a lot of perch from this lake, but keep an eye on it in future years as things hopefully develop with the influx of some predatory fish with the management plan of allowing the zillions of perch to be thinned out and allow the remaining numbers to grow, and provide growth of walleye and possibly muskie.

But the lake continues to be a popular place for downstate cottage owners to fish for a variety of species, however most head out for perch.

Perch: "Perch are my mainstay," says Ross Wellman, owner of Wellman Party & Bait Store. "I sell the bait for people to fish for them, then I get to clean them," he says. Wellman goes on to say that, "my backroom has buckets of perch to be cleaned, and they come in on a daily basis by the hundreds."

Wellman says the perch are not huge by any means, lots of good eating size in the range of 6-7 inches. Ross says there are perch in the 8-10-inch size out there, just not large numbers of them.

For ice fishing, most anglers go to the drop-off area near Air Force Beach and State Forest Campground on the central west end of the lake. The area drops off quickly and is about 10-15 feet deep. This is true for much of the lake however, that is, sharp drop offs near shore. Another place people focus on winter perch is Loud Island at the north end of the lake. But summer fishing is generally good all over the lake with so many perch.

Pike: Pike can be found in the north end of the lake around the island, and in summer you can troll the perimeter of the lake at the drop-offs. Most pike are 30 inches or less in this lake, but they have plenty of food due to the high panfish numbers. Tip-ups are used here, like most inland ice fishing pike lakes, with sucker minnows. Some spearing takes place here, but the water clarity is not good, making spearing somewhat more challenging.

Wellman says that he is seeing more steelhead in the 3-4-pound class showing up in the lake. He believes they are getting through the dam on the south end of the lake. They are being caught on tip-ups set for pike. However he has not seen any taken during the summer.

Walleye: Van Etten is mostly a summer walleye lake, where anglers troll the shoreline drop-offs. In the winter, however, walleye are few and far between for unknown reasons, according to Wellman. Therefore anglers do not target walleye on this lake.

Crappie: Nice size crappie are found regularly in Van Etten. And many are nice size, from 8-10 inches and up to 14 inches. Ice fish around the island at the north end of the lake using minnows, or on the west side of the lake near Air Force Beach. However do not limit yourself to these areas ice fishing for crappie, they can be, and often are, caught most anywhere along the drop-offs.

Van Etten Lake

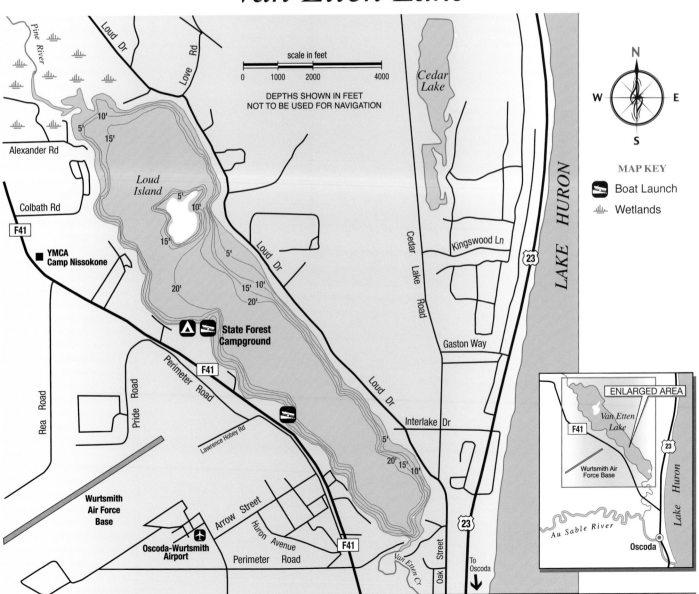

Wixom Lake

Gladwin/Midland Counties

Wixom Lake has always been known as a decent lake for bluegill, sunfish, crappie, perch, bass and some walleye. Wixom Lake plays hosts to several bass tournaments in the summer. Fishing in summer is very popular, as is ice fishing. Wixom is approximately 2,000 acres and has miles and miles of shoreline to explore and fish, with many areas inaccessible to the jet ski crowd.

Great largemouth action, consistent walleye catches, decent-sized crappie, and 30-plus-inch northerns make Wixom Lake an excellent fishery.

Dan Banks, a lifetime resident of this area and now retired, fishes Wixom and other area lakes. He states that most anglers pursue panfish in Wixom Lake. There is good bluegill and crappie fishing in particular, but lots of smaller perch as well. He says the small- and largemouth bass fishing is very good as well, with lots of good habitat for them to both spawn and feed.

Banks says the area north of Al Bright Shores (Estey Road) is an excellent area to fish. The lake (actually a dammed river) narrows here and for about 8 miles north you have lots of sandbars, cattail stands, and holes that hold fish. It is lightly fished, but can be a very rewarding trip, both in fish taken and the wilderness environment.

Panfish: Panfish are the most fished species in Wixom according to Banks. No Master Angler fish necessarily, but decent size and lots of them. "The crappie and bluegill are in the 7-9-inch size," says Banks, "but the perch are on the smaller size."

In winter, panfish can be found off Dundus Road, off the west arm of the lake, actually part of the Tobacco River that eventually runs into Wixom Lake. There is a convenient boat landing there for summer fishing. Another good area for ice fishing is east of M-30, back into Wixom Lake, off the shores of Red Oak Subdivision, which is off Oak Road. First ice is when you will find many

anglers fishing the shallow cuts; there are numerous cuts dotting the edges of both Wixom Lake and the south waters of the adjoining Tobacco River.

Look for the drop-offs along the shoreline both winter and summer. Banks states that it is good to "learn the lake and all its cuts, small bays, and various hidden areas that produce some nice fishing."

Wixom Lake

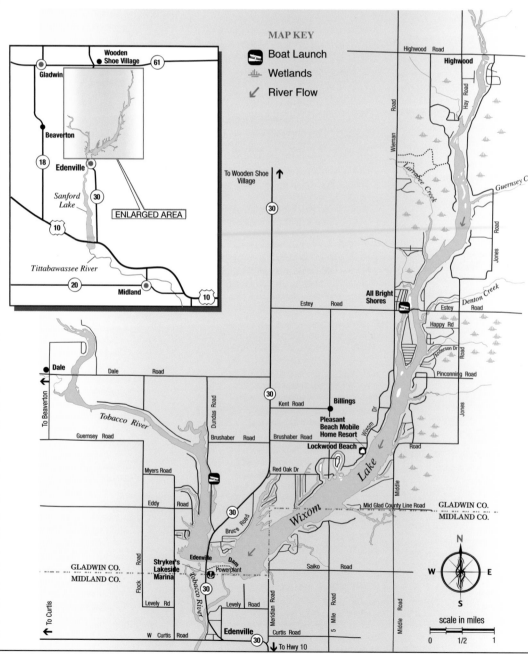

Pike: Winter draws ice anglers to the end of Brushaber Road on the east end of Wixom and along the east shoreline for pike. There are some holes in this area 5-6 feet down to 12-14 feet deep. "Another good location for pike is near the spillway on the west side of the lake, about a quarter mile to the west is a marshy area where pike like to hangout," says Banks.

Banks also mentions the area north of Estey Road as being a good pike area, especially along the shoreline during spring and early summer. Once again, not many people fish this area, especially if they have a large boat which makes it difficult to maneuver this narrow channel. The pike like the stumps and vegetative cover in this area, so be careful with the prop on your engine when moving through this part of the lake.

Bass: Similar to the pike areas, bass also like the narrow channels north of Estey Road, and along the many cuts around Wixom Lake. Banks says that there are both small- and largemouth bass in these areas of the lake, with smallmouth being more prominent. Some of the smallmouth bass can be upwards of 3-4 pounds, with a similar size for the largemouth. As in many lakes, bass also like to hang around structure such as docks or brush extending out from the shoreline. There is also an island near Estey Road that can be a favorite location for both pike and bass. With miles and miles of lake shoreline, you can slowly drift from site to site, casting your favorite hardware alongside such habitat in hopes of landing a scrappy bass.

Kathrin Schrouder, Fish Biologist of Bay City, states that Wixom is mostly managed for muskie and walleye, but anglers don't seem to target walleye in Wixom, however she has heard of some anglers doing well here. Some of the walleye move downstream to contribute to the entire fishery. She agrees that panfish are the main emphasis in Wixom. "Panfish seem to be the most stable fish species in Wixom," she says. She says that muskie are caught in Wixom, but many release them back to the lake. The objective is to allow anglers to occasionally catch a nice size muskie, without creating a vast muskie fishery.

The DNR plantings of northern muskie include 4,000 in 2010, average size almost 10 inches long, and almost 130,000 walleye fingerlings in 2011. Even though many anglers do not target walleye here, there is a decent population, regardless of how many move downstream to the Tittabawassee River and eventually to Saginaw Bay.

Note: Late June the aquatic weed growth in this lake becomes difficult to fish. The channel is about 35 feet deep and the average depth around 10-15 feet deep.

Nice smallies and largemouth can be found in Wixom in many of the cuts.

At a Glance

What: Good panfishing, with a few muskies, bass and walleye mixed in

Where: Along the shorelines, cuts, and north of Estey Road

Why: Lots of water to fish in areas that speed-boaters do not frequent

How: Take your time to get to know this lake, all the productive cuts and shorelines

Information: Midland County Convention Bureau, 128 East Main Street, Midland, 48640, (989) 839-9775

Landings: West side of channel on Estey Road, and east off M-30 just over the bridge

Bait & Tackle: Wixom Lake Bait & Tackle, 5885 M-30, Beaverton, 48612, (989) 689-5005

SOUTHERN

Keweenaw
(Isle Royale)

LAKE
SUPERIOR

LAKE
HURON

LAKE
MICHIGAN

LAKE
ERIE

Oceana
Newaygo
Mecosta
Isabella
Midland
Bay
Huron
Tuscola
Sanilac
Montcalm
Saginaw
Muskegon
Gratiot
Kent
Genesee
Lapeer
Saint Clair
Ottawa
Ionia
Clinton
Shiawassee
Macomb
Allegan
Barry
Eaton
Ingham
Livingston
Oakland
Van Buren
Kalamazoo
Calhoun
Jackson
Washtenaw
Wayne
Berrien
Cass
Saint Joseph
Branch
Hillsdale
Lenawee
Monroe

(LOWER) PENINSULA

Cass Lake Oakland County

Cass lake offers one of the more diverse inland-lake fishing experiences. It has impressive depth and many shallow back channels. Bass fishing, crappie fishing, pike, and walleye can be found here. Cass Lake is also home to good populations of both smallmouth and largemouth bass.

Walleye: Ken Neeley (K D Outdoors), fishes Cass Lake often and states that winter walleye fishing is very productive. "One of the best spots for ice fishing for walleye," he says, "is off Dodge Park." There's a beach in that area and off the beach, to the northeast, there's a drop-off that goes to 40 feet or so off the peninsula. This is one popular area for winter pike. Then if you continue heading east, there is a 100-foot hole. Just northwest of that hole it goes up to 40 feet. Anglers also fish this area for walleye.

Walleye are often caught in the 18-22-inch size range, with some upwards of 25 inches or more.

These same areas are good for summer walleye, plus you can go south out of The Guts area then west to Cinch Bug Island. To the east of the island, it drops steeply along the shoreline. Fish often hang in that area and anglers jig in the spring, but as the water warms, anglers switch to drifting over the entire ledge. Another good spot is east to where the inlet from Orchard Lake enters Cass Lake. The lake here is about 125 feet deep and the shoreline drops off from 2 to 5 feet. Fishing is good along the flats.

Bass: Both largemouth and smallmouth bass can be found in Cass Lake, actually, according to Neeley, they can be found almost anywhere in this lake. The lake receives a large amount of pleasure boating pressure and the bass tend to head for cover, the cover of anything like a dock along the shoreline or a swim platform. The canals are also good hiding places for bass and can result in some good fishing for anglers.

For largemouth, the eastern part of the lake off Ward Point, there are two humps that go from 40 feet to 10 feet. This is a good area for largemouth.

Southwest from this point there is a hole that drops from 10 feet to 60 feet then again moves up to less than five feet. Fish around this five-foot area for largemouth.

As for smallies, when you move out of The Guts into the open lake, go west along the north shoreline. This area can provide you with some smallmouth action where the water drops from 5 to 10 to 15 feet. Also as you approach Cinch Bug Island, look east/northeast. There is an underwater point that goes from 20 to 40 feet. From the start of that point to the 20-foot depth is worth fishing for smallmouth. Another good area is the east end of the lake near the inlet of Dow Lake. The first 20-foot drop is a good area to work, but keep your boat in the shallows. This is also a bass spawning area, according to Neeley.

Use jigging spoons at the ends of points and at bends in the lake's weedlines. Spinnerbaits and buzzbaits work well on pre-spawn flat areas, and some anglers fish with tubes in the shallows when the fish are on their beds.

Panfish: "Crappie," says Neeley, "are popular in this lake and can be caught upwards of 10 inches or so, not Master Angler of course, but decent size." The bluegills and perch however are more on the stunted size, that is, around 6-8 inches for both the gills and perch.

"You can find panfish virtually all over the lake," says Neeley. "You have to remember that this lake is over a thousand acres and fairly deep," he says. "So the panfish move around quite a bit." The shoreline can be fairly weedy, so work those areas for crappie or gills. Perch can be found almost anywhere, so use your electronics and look for schools of fish.

Pike: Winter pike fishing on Cass Lake includes both spearing and tip-ups, typical of many pike lakes. Neeley says that winter pike fishing is good at the north end of Gerundegut (The Guts), as well as in the back bay in this same area. Another good area is to go just east out of The Guts into the open lake area. You most likely will see pike anglers on the ice in both of these areas.

During summer, Neeley mentions that the above two areas are good for pike,

Pike spearing during the winter months is a popular method of adding to one's creel.

as well as Coles Bay at the very northeast end of the lake. "There are two deep holes in this bay," says Neeley, "and some gradual drops." The area is relatively small, so work along the drops. One other good pike area is the far southeast end of the lake in the small bay. This bay is more shallow in its northeast counter bay, but anglers find some good success here in about 25-30 feet of water. As a side note on pike, the adjoining tiny Dow Lake produces some nice catches of pike.

Notes: Many bow fishermen like to shoot carp along the shallows in this lake in spring, and some upwards of 30 pounds can be found here.

Some 10-inch trout were planted in this lake back in mid 2000, but to anyone's knowledge none have been caught nor has there been any record of any natural reproduction.

DNR walleye plantings in Cass Lake are substantial over the course of about ten years prior to the printing of this book. From around 2003 to 2011, over 370,000 fingerlings were planted, 131,000 in 2011 alone. So it's not hard to see why walleye are the main target in this lake with more young walleye soon to be legal size.

At a Glance

What: Walleye, bass, and pike

Where: Cass Lake, a substantial-sized lake in a very populated area of the state

Why: Large numbers of walleye

Information/Guides: Pontiac Chamber of Commerce, 402 N. Telegraph Road, Pontiac 48341, (248) 335-9600, info@ pontiacchamber.com

Landings: Dodge Park at the north end of the lake

Bait & Tackle: Ken Neeley, K D Outdoors, 7688 Highland Rd, Waterford, MI 48327, (248) 666-7799

Cass Lake

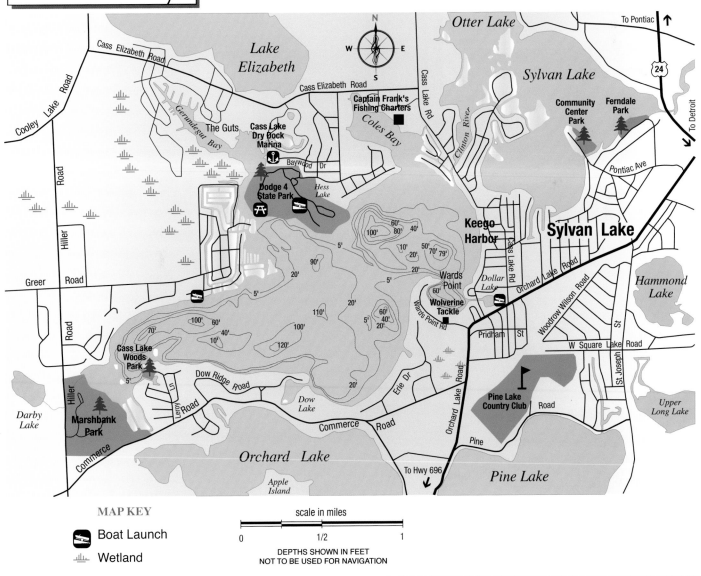

MAP KEY

Boat Launch

Wetland

scale in miles

0   1/2   1

DEPTHS SHOWN IN FEET
NOT TO BE USED FOR NAVIGATION

Chippewa Lake
Mecosta County

Chippewa Lake is a 790-acre lake located in Mecosta County, 9 miles east and 3 miles north of Big Rapids. The lake is in the uppermost headwaters of the Chippewa River. Its outlet, Chippewa Creek, flows through the Martiny Chain and then becomes the West Branch Chippewa River, eventually flowing into the Tittabawassee River in Midland, then to the Saginaw River and to Saginaw Bay, Lake Huron. This lake is Mecosta County's largest lake, with reported depths close to 45 feet.

Tiger muskellunge were stocked in 1980, but few if any exist today.

Bluegill, black crappie, northern pike, walleye and largemouth bass are the prevalent sport fish. Other sport fish, including smallmouth bass, occur in lesser abundance but contribute to the overall recreational fishery.

According to relatively recent DNR records, northern pike were found to be in appreciable numbers and their size structure and age distribution was good.

Walleye stocking has been the only fisheries management action taken on Chippewa Lake in recent years. Evaluations of recently stocked fish have not shown great success and anglers do have nice catches of walleye on this lake. Walleye growth is good here and walleye are known to exhibit some predatory control on panfish but prefer feeding on other forage items, including abundant minnows and small suckers. This allows for the growth and abundance of all panfish.

DNR surveys reveal a somewhat low abundance of crappie, but the size ranged a very respectable 8-12 inches and many that were caught were keepers.

Bluegill, pumpkinseed, northern pike, largemouth bass, and bullheads dominate the fish community in Chippewa Lake and provide good recreational fisheries. No DNR management recommendations are suggested for them.

Ron Dancz from Eastbay Party Store on Chippewa lake, says that "there are lots of pike and walleye in Chippewa Lake. Pike fishing in particular is very good here with many in the 30-40-inch size."

Pike: For pike ice fishing, both spearing and tip-ups with pike minnows are the typical methods used here, says Dancz. Try the shoreline drop-off areas and along the sunken island on the northeast shore.

For summer pike, these same areas are productive by trolling or casting along the drop-offs using spinners or crawler harnesses.

Walleye: Walleye ice fishing is common at the north end of the lake, and in the bay. Also try along the drop-offs that exist around the perimeter of the lake, especially the east end. Summer walleye are caught in these same areas either trolling with Hot 'N Tots or other typical walleye lures.

The current DNR fisheries management prescription for Chippewa Lake requests spring fingerling walleye stocking on a biennial schedule at a rate of upwards of 40,000 walleye with scheduled planting starting in 2011. It should be emphasized that the goal of this stocking effort is to create a more significant walleye fishery and

to provide an additional and highly desirable sport fish for recreational angling opportunities. If surplus walleye are ever available, stocking at a higher rate up to double the previously stated rate would be acceptable. Efforts will be made also to stock the largest size fingerling available.

Walleye stocking in Michigan has always been dependent upon available stock. Chippewa Lake is one of many lakes in the Southern Lake Huron Management Unit stocked with a limited number of available walleye. In recent years, concern over the spread of VHS has greatly reduced statewide production and stocking efforts. As a result, several Michigan lakes which are routinely stocked with walleye have not been stocked. So far, Chippewa Lake has remained on its stocking schedule.

Panfish: Bluegills are very sizable in this lake and can be found, as most panfish, all over the lake according to Dancz. There is no one preferable area to go, except in the spring when they are on their beds along the north and west shore by the park. Both summer and winter they can be found most anywhere on the lake. Crappie fishing is "super" on this lake, especially in winter. Check along

Pike fishing in the fall when temperatures are cooler can be very rewarding.

Chippewa Lake

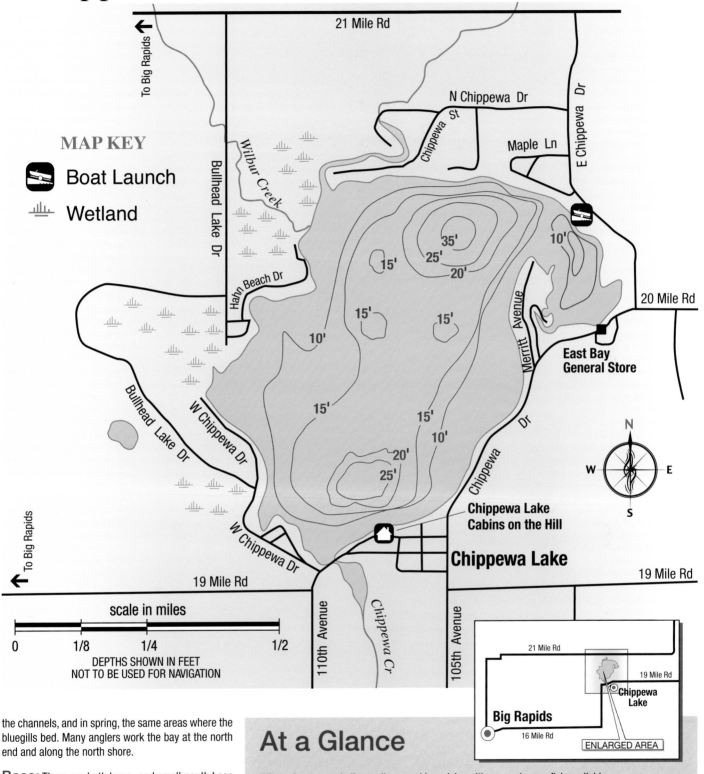

MAP KEY

🛥 Boat Launch

Wetland

21 Mile Rd

To Big Rapids

N Chippewa Dr

Chippewa St

Maple Ln

E Chippewa Dr

Wilbur Creek

Bullhead Lake Dr

Hahn Beach Dr

35'

25'

15'

20'

15'

15'

10'

15'

Merritt Avenue

10'

20 Mile Rd

East Bay General Store

W Chippewa Dr

Bullhead Lake Dr

15'

15'

10'

20'

25'

Chippewa Dr

To Big Rapids

Chippewa Lake Cabins on the Hill

Chippewa Lake

N

W — E

S

19 Mile Rd

19 Mile Rd

110th Avenue

105th Avenue

Chippewa Cr

scale in miles

0   1/8   1/4   1/2

DEPTHS SHOWN IN FEET
NOT TO BE USED FOR NAVIGATION

21 Mile Rd

19 Mile Rd

Chippewa Lake

Big Rapids

16 Mile Rd

ENLARGED AREA

the channels, and in spring, the same areas where the bluegills bed. Many anglers work the bay at the north end and along the north shore.

Bass: There are both large- and smallmouth bass in Chippewa Lake, as evidenced by the many bass tournaments on this lake each year. These fish can be found along the shoreline in most any weed bed. Fish the edges of the beds using whatever popular bass lure you have, including spinner baits and crawler harnesses.

At a Glance

What: A very good pike, walleye, and bass lake with some nice panfish available

Where: Chippewa Lake

Landings: The DNR provides public access on the east side of the lake with plenty of parking, boat launch and restroom facilities. It is well marked just north of 20 Mile Road

Contacts: Mecosta County Area Chamber of Commerce, 246 North State Street, Big Rapids 49307; (231) 796-7649

Bait & Tackle: Eastbay General Store, 19961 E. Chippewa Drive, south of 20 Mile Road

Diamond Lake Cass County

Diamond Lake lies in central Cass County of southwestern Michigan, about 1 mile southeast of the city of Cassopolis, and covers more than 1,000 acres with a maximum depth of 65 feet.

A number of freshwater fish are available in this lake, including bluegill, yellow perch and walleye, along with an occasional crappie and northern pike through the ice. The lake has healthy populations of large- and smallmouth bass, as well as rock bass, but they are difficult to catch.

Scott Crouch, a well-versed angler and guide, states that Diamond Lake is one of the most pristine lakes he knows, but summer daytime non-fishing activity is heavy, especially on the weekends, so nighttime fishing is paramount.

Bass:
"Bass fishing," says Crouch, "is number one on Diamond Lake." "Although there are smallmouth bass in this lake, largemouth is king," he states. Scott mentions that one of the areas to search out bass is the northeast end of the lake, close to the bay area. There is a large weed edge in that part of the lake, just inland from the deeper bowl that exists a short distance offshore. A big flat exists near shore that is about 5 feet deep. Bass will be on the inner side of the weed edge and pike often hang out on the outer edge, especially in spring.

Scott's favorite time and area to fish is "right where the weeds are, especially in the spring," he says. "Fish the weedlines as your "target zone" and as soon as they see a meal, they will attack your bait." Bass can generally be found in the 15-foot-depth zone in spring, and 25 feet in the fall. They are often slightly shallower than pike; pike like the slightly deeper water. "When the crappie and gills hatch, the bass and pike have a bonanza," he says.

Largemouth bass also like the area north of the island. Look for the weed patches in 5-10 feet of water. Good baits to test are minnows, small crankbaits, twister tails, or Yamamotos; fish them in this area along the island in the weedlines.

Bass also hang out on the west end of the lake in the spring. Use spinnerbaits, tossing them just over the top of the weeds. Preseason bass are catch and release, but by the time the season opens it's best to head to the east end of the lake.

"Largemouth bass in Diamond Lake are large," says Crouch, "upwards of 7-8 pounds, with smallies topping out at six pounds." They also have very nice color. Smallmouth are especially good in spring and late fall. In spring go to the southwest corner of the island where you will find good rock structure. You may also find a few walleye in this same area. Twister tails work well. Often you will find that one bass will follow another when pursuing your offering, so be ready to pitch a second bait in that same area after hooking the first one. In fall the fish will be somewhat deeper. Try a Carolina rig, or deeper-running crankbait in the 20-foot zone where the thermocline exists. The fish will generally suspend in about 15 feet of water.

A Carolina rig separates the hook and worm from the lead with a leader. To tie one, slip a lead on your line, follow it with a bead and then tie on a barrel swivel. A leader of varying length is tied to the swivel and a hook tied to the leader. Hook size varies with the size of the bait you plan to use.

One of the best places to fish a Carolina rig is along the gravel points. Fish gather on them in both pre-spawn and post-spawn times, and they can be very scattered. A Carolina rig can locate them by allowing you to make long casts and cover plenty of water quickly.

Brush piles are also good places to fish Carolina rigs. Work the lead to the brush pile and stop it. The worm or lizard will slowly fall and often draw the bass out. If that does not work, pull the lead over the brush and let it fall to the bottom. Then stop it. The following worm will sink slowly and is often more than the bass can stand to resist striking.

Pike:
Pike, some upwards of 20-plus pounds, can be found in this lake. Any sort of twisters or smaller baits work well for pike. Crappie, when found along the weed edges, will be a target for the pike. This is also a good lake to fish even in winter, using tip-ups for the pike. Try the flat at the south end of the island, off Eagle Point Road.

Perch run across the sandbar south of the island, and pike work that same area, knowing the perch are there. Pike will work back and forth in an east and west direction, both winter and summer. You will also find bass, which often will follow the baitfish, working this area. There is also some spearing on this lake, primarily in the same areas, as well as the very north/northwest end of the island along the big flat just before the drop off.

Panfish:
Early spring through early May is the best time for crappie, says Crouch. They are the best eating at that time, whereby in June and July they tend to get soft. Winter is good for both crappie and bluegills. They often sit on the flats along the boat ferry route, as well as to the north of the island on the other flat. Look for the ledges, where the predator fish are. "If you catch a pike," says Scott, "that means there are panfish in the area." Panfish are productive along the northwest and northeast side of the island in both spring and winter. Crappie can be taken in this lake upwards of 14-15 inches.

Walleye:
Walleye are often taken during the winter months, and will average around 4-5 pounds, but can be caught upwards of 10-12 pounds. Work the flat by the ferry route, from east to west where it starts to drop off. Often in the winter you will see them in the 12-20-foot water depths. Look for the weed structure. Start working your lures, or set your tip-ups in the 12-20-foot water depth. Summer months are difficult for walleye due to heavy traffic on the lake. You will need to either go out at night, or early morning. Try the north side of the island using crawler harnesses, deep crank baits, or minnow baits over the weeds. At night also work along the weed edges.

Note:
There are efforts to provide more artificial structure on this lake, such as pine trees and even a sunken sail boat, in 15-20 feet of water on the east end of the island, right at the break. During the summer, it is best to fish mid week, after a couple of days are allowed for the fish to settle down after the heavy weekend water activities.

At a Glance

What: Great bass, panfish, pike, walleye fishing

Where: One of the most productive lakes in southwest Michigan

Information/Guides: Cassopolis, Michigan Chamber of Commerce, 120 South Broadway Street, P.O. Box 154, Cassopolis, 49032, (616) 445-5538; www.infomi.com/city/cassopolis/ (269) 845-0311, CrouchBigFish@gmail.com

Landings: There is a public boat landing at the southwest corner of the lake

Bait & Tackle: Lunker's Inc, 26324 U.S. 12, Edwardsburg, (269) 663-3745; **Trailhead Mercantile,** 209 East Main Street, Niles, (269) 683-3474; **Cranky Hanks Bait Shop,** 24992 Marcellus Hwy, Dowagiac (near Portage) 49047, (269) 462-9272

Survey records indicate that the DNR planted over 52,000 walleye in 2011, so these fish will be legal size within a few years after the planting. This is the first DNR planting since over 58,000 were planted in 2002.

Although bass are considered number one on Diamond Lake, walleye are popular during the winter months and are often in the 3-5-pound size.

Diamond Lake

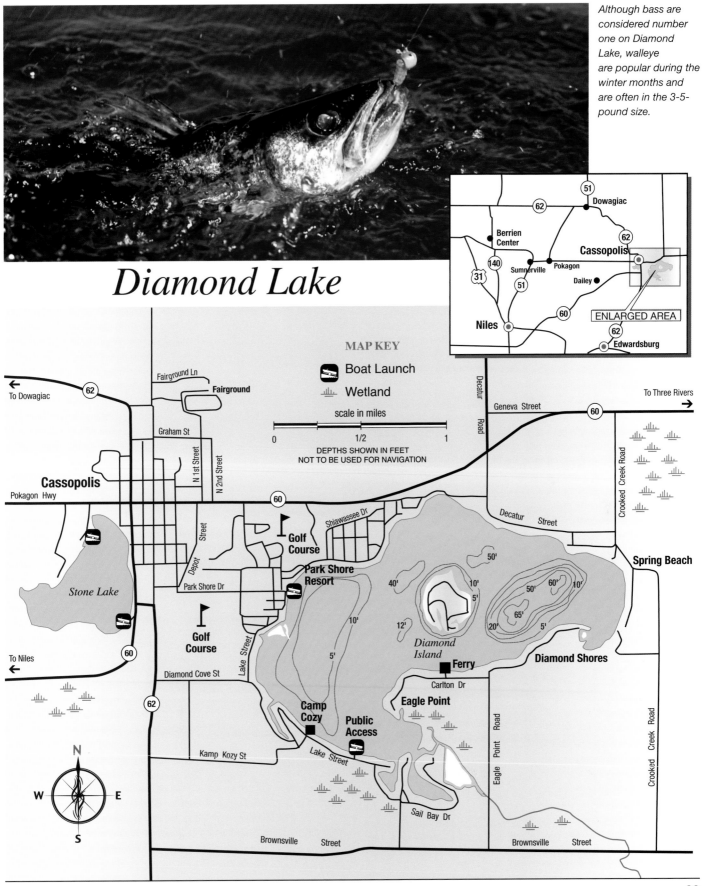

MAP KEY

Boat Launch

Wetland

scale in miles

0   1/2   1

DEPTHS SHOWN IN FEET
NOT TO BE USED FOR NAVIGATION

ENLARGED AREA

Dowagiac
Cassopolis
Berrien Center
Sumnerville
Pokagon
Dailey
Niles
Edwardsburg

To Dowagiac
Fairground Ln
Fairground
Graham St
N 1st Street
N 2nd Street
Cassopolis
Pokagon Hwy
Stone Lake
To Niles
Depot Street
Park Shore Dr
Golf Course
Golf Course
Lake Street
Diamond Cove St
Kamp Kozy St
Camp Cozy
Public Access
Lake Street
Shiawassee Dr
Golf Course
Park Shore Resort
Decatur Road
Geneva Street
To Three Rivers
Crooked Creek Road
Decatur Street
Spring Beach
Diamond Island
Ferry
Carlton Dr
Eagle Point
Diamond Shores
Eagle Point Road
Crooked Creek Road
Sail Bay Dr
Brownsville Street
Brownsville Street

40' 50' 10' 5' 50' 60' 10' 65' 20' 5' 12' 10' 5'

N W E S

Gun Lake Allegan/Barry Counties

Panfishing for gills in the shallows is a great way to spend a day on the water.

Gun Lake in Allegan County is another one of those fishing lakes I would love to have in my "backyard." It has all the makings of a great fishing lake, shallow weed areas, deep holes, numerous small bays and points of land jutting out into the main sections of the lake, and one thing that most lakes rarely have, smaller lakes joined by narrow channels, rather than one big "hole in the ground." I truly enjoy fishing this type of lake. It gives you a feeling of tranquility, and whether you catch fish or not (but you usually will), you simply enjoy a mentally tranquil day on the water.

Gun Lake (south of Grand Rapids and east of Hwy. 131) is 2700 acres, and located between Fountain and Freesoil. Most of the shoreline is built up with private homes and cottages, but there is public access and a park on the south shore. As a side note, this lake map is numbered from 1-6 to help identify certain areas.

This lake, being an average-size inland body of water, yet having some deep holes upwards of 66 feet, is a strong bass fishery with both small and largemouth bass available to anglers.

The one "drawback" to this lake, if you view it as that, is the number of recreational powerboats that can affect the fishing activities. Most anglers get an early start before the skiers hit the water mid to late morning, especially on weekends. But frankly, according to Vern Sinch, a long-time resident and angler on this lake, "the fish seem to be used to the powerboats and it does not seem to affect the fishing activities that much."

Walleye: After a long period of not stocking Gun Lake, the DNR started stocking again around 2009, so legal size walleye should again be available to anglers about the time this book hits the shelves. Whether it be summer or winter walleye fishing, fish the drop-offs on east Gun Lake. Robbins Bay in the northern end of east Gun is also a good location. This area has a water inlet year-round, producing good walleye habitat.

Night fishing is another good way to find feeding walleye. They are generally found in the shallows, making them open to casting and trolling. Troll shallow-running crankbaits or spinners in the shallows well after dark when the fish have had time to make their way there in search of baitfish.

Bass: There are several bass tournaments on Gun Lake, and for good reason: bass, bass and more bass habitat along with good boat landings. The proximity from such cities as Grand Rapids, Kalamazoo, Battle Creek, and other down-state areas, makes it another reason this lake is so popular. There are large- and smallmouth bass in Gun Lake and, according to Sinch, there has been an upward swing of smallies over recent years. The largemouth, in early May, can be found in the channels and shallows.

Bass Methods: Bairds Cove once again is a good bet for bass. When the water warms around mid-summer, east Gun is good for bass, using crankbaits, spinners, jigs and top-water lures. This lake is a good topwater-lure lake when the water is flat, which it often is.

Fishing has changed during 2007 to 2012, due to the introduction of zebra mussels that filter and subsequently clear up the water (not clean up), and the subsequent invasive weed called milfoil. The lake is therefore treated with aquatic herbicides several times each summer for the milfoil.

Algae starts to grow the first part of June, then the water clarity drops down from the usual 8-10 feet to the 1-2-foot level. This makes it harder to find the fish, according to Sinch.

Even the weed growths have been altered by the herbicide, says Sinch. At one time, the area at the north end of west Gun, near the park, had massive numbers of fish, but with the holes created in this area for utilizing fill for building, the adjoining land the area has changed.

Weeds growing on the flat areas are now producing the most fishing activity in these shallow-water spots.

Panfish: The number one fish in Gun are the panfish. Perch, bluegills, and nice-size crappies are plentiful. Perch in the 8-10-inch size and larger, bluegill upwards of 10 inches, and nice-sized crappie can be found during the winter ice fishing months on west Gun, Bairds Cove on the northeast side, and the entire northwest side of the lake. Fish the shallows for these delectable eaters. West Gun is good for panfish anytime of the year.

Area 4 has good underwater contours, a couple of islands, and various points that produce good bluegill fishing in the spring (i.e., first of June into early July). Then the channels produce good numbers of panfish at first ice, especially Robbins Bay channel. This area is also good for late fall crappies as well as spawning in the spring. Robbins Bay, actually according to Sinch, is a good area to fish all year long.

The State Park channel has been good fishing the past few years in both spring and fall, allowing those anglers without a boat to fish from land, including an easy area for kids to fish.

Yankee Springs Island, (area 5), is good for late season bluegills as well as spring spawning on the humps that exist in this area. There are also plenty of bass and pike here. But keep in mind that the perch, says Sinch, are usually not caught in the deeper water, but rather in the shallows. That does not mean they are not in the deeper water, but rather you don't need to fish in deeper water to find panfish. Bluegills are often in open water in schools, but you need to locate them. "Spring is really great fishing on this lake" says Sinch. You can see down around 8-10 feet until the algae starts to invade the lake as the water temps increase.

Winter panfish such as crappies can be caught on minnows, but mousies are the best bait for catching them through the ice.

Pickerell Cove: There is an interesting area at the south end of west Gun, called Pickerell Cove. The southeast corner is about fifty feet wide and about 6-8 feet deep. The main channel is only about 3-4 feet deep. This area is good for perch, bluegills, crappies all year long. Sinch states that there is a nice population of pike that reside here.

On east Gun, during the ice fishing season, bluegills can be found in the corner area at Chicago Point. There are still some rice beds in this area for summer fishing. Crappie usually spawn between Chicago Point and just to the north up to the small bay in the spring.

Bluegills, bass, and pike in this same region (NE corner) of #5-6.

If you are curious about the small connecting Long Lake that runs off Bairds Cove, if you have a small boat or canoe you may be able to get through the tube that connects these two lakes. The water in this small lake is only about 3 feet or so, but many bluegills and perch move into this area in the spring to spawn. So don't hesitate giving it a shot. There is a boat launch here on the west side of the large portion of the lake, but it is only a dirt approach for smaller boats.

At a Glance

What: Fishing a very unique lake

Where: Gun Lake in the western area of the state

Why: Lots of bays, points, and excellent fish habitat

Landings: Access to Gun Lake can be obtained from either the hard-surfaced ramp located on Murphy's Point in the Yankee Springs State Recreation Area, or the ramp found off Marsh Road on the lake's southwest end, Allegan County Park

Bait & Tackle: Gillett's Bait & Hardware, 12258 Marsh Road, Shelbyville (near Kentwood), 49344, (269) 672-5371

Gun Lake

MAP KEY

Fishing Pier

Boat Ramp

Permanent Rice Beds

scale of miles

0   1/4   1/2   1

DEPTHS SHOWN IN FEET
NOT TO BE USED FOR NAVIGATION

Hardy Dam Pond
Newaygo County

Fishing on Hardy Dam Pond, especially for walleye, the number one fish anglers pursue, proves to be a bit challenging on this particular body of water, which, technically, is a dammed-up river, not a pond and therefore somewhat of a misnomer.

It is a manmade impoundment upstream from Hardy Dam on the Muskegon River — a more than 20-mile-long body of still water with meandering river channel cut into its bottom. Fishing that edge sometimes means fishing in 40 to 60 or more feet of water.

You need to be versatile, knowing how to vertical jig, pitch jigs use crankbaits, or crawler harnesses and slip bobbers. Many anglers use a variety of tactics, fishing deep and more shallow, using bottom-bouncers (3-ounce weights that keep the bait on the bottom), and rigged to slide up the line if a fish hits. Others troll a crawler threaded on a Slow-Death hook (Mustad Hook Company), designed to spin slowly while being dragged through the water.

This particular Mustad method is a versatile, year-round power finesse presentation. It can be fished fast or slow, has the attractiveness of live bait and adds good action. The unique hook design creates an enticing corkscrew presentation, allowing for a slow bottom-bouncing presentation that gets bait in cracks, crevices and little corners that faster blade presentations skip over.

To Rig: Attach a bottom-bouncer weight to your main line. Add a 4-6-foot, 10-pound monofilament leader and attach hook. Thread half a night crawler up the hook shank over the hook eye. There should be 1/4" to 1/2" of night crawler hanging off the hook.

To Fish: Use your trolling motor and keep speeds from 1 mph to almost nothing. The key is to keep just enough speed so the crawler spins. Can also be used effectively when drifting.

Hardy Dam Pond, according to DNR fish biologists, contains a self-sustaining population of walleye of moderate to low density. The pond is not stocked, but was during the 1940s and '50s. Hardy Dam does not need to be planted by the DNR because it has good habitat for a self-sustaining population of walleye.

Ken Clark, noted charter captain that has fished Hardy Dam Pond many times, concurs that the number one fish anglers seek here are walleye, followed by smallmouth bass, then perch and bluegills, and finally pike, which tend to run on the smaller size.

Walleye: Captain Clark mentions that walleye here are best fished during spring and fall, unless you go early in the day because there are often a lot of go-fast boats speeding up and down the river, disrupting fishing opportunities.

Clark likes to drag a plain hook and a crawler in 10-12 feet of water around Hardy Pond, often connecting with fish. Many, however tend to be small. He focuses on the fall months, and uses a ½-ounce Hopkins

Jigging Spoon in deep water, that is, around 65 feet or so. Remember that by the dam the water is about 100 feet deep.

Spoon color, weight and even style and design can make a difference in your presentation, depending on the type of water you are fishing. Try to match the forage that walleyes are feeding on to the color of the lure.

Walleye, for instance, weighing around five pounds and under prefer to eat 1-2-inch forage. So if that is the size fish you are targeting, staying with a spoon with that size profile is very important. However, if you are fishing the Great Lakes or other bodies of water with larger forage, then bumping the spoon size up will put more fish in the boat (Hopkins Jigging Spoon).

The average walleye taken here are not wall hangers by any means, being around 16 inches or so, but some can be in the 20-inch-plus range. Walleye are migratory and spawn once in the river, then they head downstream through the turbines to bigger water to grow. The problem is that walleye instinctively migrate down river when they get sexually mature, between 15 and 16 inches. It has been estimated that about 26,000 go through the dam each year and are

Hardy Dam Pond

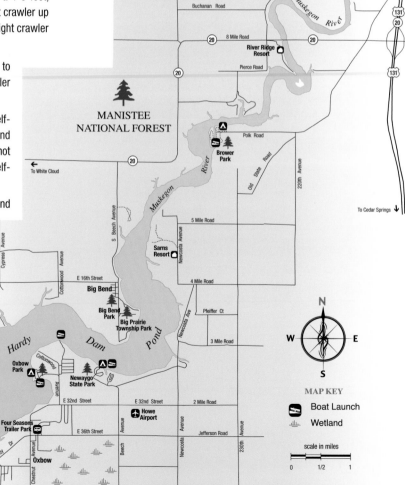

Walleye are just one of many species anglers fish for at the popular Hardy Dam site.

unable to return to spawn. A significant percentage do not make it and are killed. That's why you don't get larger fish here on a consistent basis.

If you have not fished this area before, try the waters in front of Brower Park to start. Brower's can also be good for smallmouth bass, some largemouth, bluegills, and even pike. Bass up to 4 pounds can be had in this location. Work the weed area along the shoreline. There have been a fair number of bass tournaments on this body of water, so figure there are some nice size bass here.

Panfish: Panfish, bluegills and perch tend to move around here, and you may need to work for them. The bigger gills like deeper water, meaning 20-plus feet, but if you find them you could be in for a treat, like 10-inch gills. Perch, once again, in the fall can be rewarding, but fish in the 30-plus depth of water for them.

During a day's fishing on Hardy you may land a nice 28-inch northern pike, or a sizable 20-inch smallmouth bass, so be prepared for other types of fishing action here. You almost have to talk about fishing here in general, rather than

specifics. For example, you may use crankbaits over the top of the weeds for walleyes and the many smaller northerns, or you can bounce-bottom with blades and minnows in the deeper water for walleyes. Bright colors have been the best for cranks and blades.

Walleyes have also been known to hit up by the bridge, and pike will often take a Mepps spinner and spinner baits and walleye will often hit on a harness in a bright color. Almost anything goes in these waters.

At the top end of Hardy towards Parkers landing you may find some nice walleye or a smallmouth or two.

Note: Remember that Hardy Dam Pond, being that it is a dammed river, can become a problem during the ice fishing season in that it may cause the ice to fluctuate and even weaken, so caution must be maintained when venturing out on it.

Fish that are often planted by the DNR in this body of water include channel cats, northern pike, smallmouth bass, bluegills, and crappie.

At a Glance

What: Walleye, bass, pike, bluegill, crappie

Where: A unique fishery, once a river, now considered a large deep pond

Why: Offers good variety and challenge

Information/Guides: Mecosta County Area Convention & Visitors Bureau, 246 North State Street, Big Rapids 49307, (231) 796-7640; **Newaygo County Tourist Information Center,** 4684 S. Evergreen – M37, Newaygo 49337, (231) 652-9298, Extension 10. **Brower Park** is located on the Muskegon River and provides access to 18 miles of navigable river in the backwaters of the Hardy Dam. The park's 280 acres boasts 230 campsites, 10 camp-n-cabins and almost 8000 feet of river frontage. No pets allowed. Administrative Office, (231) 832-3246

Landings: Numerous locations along the impoundment (see map)

Bait & Tackle: Parsley's Sport Shop, 70 State Rd, Newaygo 49337 (231) 652-6986; **Hardy Grocery & General Store,** 7607 E 36th St., Newaygo 49337, (231) 652-3386 (about a half mile from the dam); **Frank's Sporting Goods,** 165 S. Cass St., Morley 49336, (231) 856-7778, www.orders@ frankssportinggoods.com; **Hilltop Shopping Center** (west side of the dam), 6398 East 36th Street, White Cloud, (231) 689-6470

Kent Lake Oakland County

Kent Lake, known as Kensington Park, is a shallow body of water along I-96 and anyone who resides anywhere near this lake is well aware of the many outdoor activities available here. It provides countless hours of fun and entertainment for locals and visitors alike. I fondly remember it as my high school senior skip day outing location where my classmates and I enjoyed a day of picnics and other activities. But fishing is also popular in this sizable lake.

Bass:
Gerry Gostenik, who is very familiar with Kent Lake, says that previously there was probably close to a 50/50 population of large- and smallmouth bass in this lake. The smallmouth are in the 4-5-pound range, and largemouth around 5-5.5-pound maximum. Prime places to key in for Kent Lake's smallmouth are along the twisting river channel, near points with access to deep water and along the riprap along Interstate 96. Largemouths are more prevalent in the back bays and around the many islands in this 1,000-acre lake.

"I would say that the bass population in Kent Lake is now about 60/40 smallmouth," states Gostenik. There are still some good largemouths in the lake, but the smallmouths seemed to have benefited most from the clearer water as a result of the zebra mussels. There seems to be more gravel now along the old river channel and it is solid beds when the bass are spawning.

As the summer progresses, around June, the lake starts to see lots of aquatic vegetation and you will need weedless lures. Bass tournaments and other fishing pressure will also increase dramatically. Therefore the easiest time to fish this lake is spring and fall. When summer arrives, the smallmouth head to deeper water. This is not a novice lake to fish during the summer months for the reasons mentioned above. You will need to work your lures in the occasional "holes" in the vast weed growths, then if you get a hit, tugging out the bass will be a challenge.

The weeds are a source of oxygen, attracting baitfish and crawfish, which, in turn, are food for the bass. Weeds also offer a place for the bass to lie in ambush for a potential meal, and also offers shade from the hot summer sun.

I have good success by tossing spinnerbaits along the edges of the weed beds. This allows you to target active bass that are sitting near the edges of the weed bed, waiting for schools of minnows to pass by. If they are active, you will almost always provoke strikes this way. To target active bass in the center of the weed masses, try a jerkbait or spinnerbait over the weeds if possible. In the early morning, a topwater lure such as a Buzzbait over the weeds might work. In weeds that extend all the way to the surface, you may want to target the active bass with a weedless spoon like a Moss Boss, or even a weedless in-line spinner. Check out some of the Terminator Lures. They carry a line of titanium weedless in-liners that can work wonders in weedy situations. For less active bass, try slowing down your presentation.

Other best bass fishing locations in Kent Lake are the submerged stumps, and there are hundreds of them in this lake. Look for them along the shallow bays. You will also probably find a "few" submerged picnic tables along the shoreline that were tossed in by partygoers.

Walleye:
Walleye catches had been increasing and a population estimate conducted back in 1994 and 1995 resulted in an estimate of 3-4 adult walleyes per acre in the lake. Due to this high population density of walleye and the poor condition of the panfish fishery, walleye stocking was suspended after 1996 to allow the panfish populations a chance to recover. A small number of fall fingerling walleye (3,000) were stocked in 2001 to maintain the walleye fishery that had developed in the lake. The most recent walleye stocking as of this writing was in 2011 when over 32,000 fingerlings were planted by the DNR.

Panfish:
There is a good population of bluegills, and decent crappie fishing as well. The gills are not large according to Gostenik, but you can catch a lot of them along the shoreline when they are spawning. For crappie, head to the boat basins and work these areas. Remember there is only a 10 mph speed limit on this lake so leave your "go-fast" bass boat at home. You may not have much luck fishing for bluegills in the deep water at Kent Lake, but when you're near the shoreline, look for trees or bushes where bluegill might be hanging out. The

At a Glance

What: Bass fishing

Where: Kent Lake, also known as Kensington Park

Why: Excellent bass fishing in a park setting

How: Good spring and fall traditional fishing, but summer offers a challenge due to heavy weed growth

Regs: 10 mph speed limit

Information/Guides: Novi Chamber of Commerce, 41875 W 11 Mile Rd., #201, Novi, 48375, (248) 349-3743, www.novichamber.com

Landings: Two sites, one located at the mid east part of the lake off Huron River Parkway, and the other at the very southwest end of the lake of Labadie Road

Contacts: Gerry Gostenik on the Web at www.greatlakesbassfishing.com

Bait & Tackle: Holden's Party Store & Deli, 2055 South Milford Road, Milford 48381, (248) 685-1260, www.holdensdeli.com

Kent Lake

ENLARGED AREA

Fenton

75

23   24

75

59   Waterford

Pontiac

Milford   1

Brighton   96   Farmington Hills

696

Southfield   24

N
W   E
S

MAP KEY

Boat Launch

Picnic Area

Wetland

scale in miles

0   1/2   1

DEPTHS SHOWN IN FEET
NOT TO BE USED FOR
NAVIGATION

Huron River

Dawson   Road

Milford Guesthouse B&B

Martindale Road

Garner Road

Pearson   Road   3'

4'

Hickory Ridge Trail

5'

Buno   Road

Bruno   Road   6'

Milford Road

Kensington Metropolitan Park

Beach Dr   Fishing Docks

Highridge   Maple   Dr   Maple   Road

Labadie   Road   Drive   Maple   Maple Beach

7'   Martindale Beach

5'   8'   8'

Wildwing Lake   7'   9'   7'

Kensington Road   Highridge   Dr   Fishing Pier   8'

Kensington Metropark Golf Course   Huron   River Parkway

96   96   Pontiac Trail
To Brighton   To Detroit

Huron River   Grand   River   Road

Dam   New Hudson

Kensington Road   Kent Lake Beach   Road

Kent Lake Road

bridge where I-96 crosses is generally a very good location for pulling in some bluegill.

Historically there has been an excellent bluegill and black crappie fishery in the lake, but from about the mid 1990s this declined significantly according to angler reports. Survey data also showed a sharp drop in bluegill numbers. Michigan DNR Fisheries Division stocked over 214,000 fingerling bluegills in 1997 to address this decline, but the only result was the larger number of smaller gills. If you like to fish the old natural way with a bobber and worm, bluegill at Kent Lake will likely cooperate with your offering.

Note: There is only a 10 mph speed limit on Kent Lake, and it is strictly enforced, so although you will not get from point A to point B fast, the lack of speed makes for overall good fishing. Ice fishing here is very limited due to the lack of fish species available during the winter.

When fishing for bass in the shallows, rock beds are often your best bet.

Lake Chemung Livingston County

Lake Chemung is located between Howell and Brighton in central Livingston County. Although a natural lake, the Alger Creek outlet has been dammed, enlarging the lake to an estimated 313 acres. Alger Creek flows out of Lake Chemung to Thompson Lake and then discharges to Bogue Creek of the South Branch Shiawassee River. The South Branch Shiawassee River flows to the mainstream Shiawassee River and to Saginaw Bay of Lake Huron.

Presently, Lake Chemung is in good condition in terms of its overall fish community. The lake offers decent angling opportunities for several species including bluegill, pumpkinseed, sunfish, largemouth bass, black crappie, and northern pike.

Dave Hoerauf, a local from Midwest Sports Shop in Brighton, fishes this lake often, and says that "there is some good fishing here for largemouth bass, pike, and crappie." Other species of fish such as bluegills, perch, and walleye are not

a significant fishery currently. "The gills and perch are small, but lots of them," he says, but "also there are some larger ones, unfortunately not many."

Although the following is a more technical report on this fishery, it will provide you with an overview of the fish population in this lake.

Bluegill: The DNR 2008 survey of Lake Chemung shows that of a total of 1,645 bluegill surveyed, the average size was just over 6 inches and comprised 52% of the total fish catch, making bluegill a major fish population in this lake. Bluegill ranged from 1 to 9 inches with 70% of the fish meeting or exceeding the acceptable harvest size of 6 inches.

Sunfish: That same survey indicated a total of 217 sunfish averaging 9.2 inches comprised 7% of the total catch. Sunfish ranged from 5 to 11 inches with 99% of the fish meeting or exceeding the acceptable harvest size of 6 inches. This makes sunfish a small part of the overall fish population in this lake.

Perch: A total of 109 yellow perch averaging 5.5 inches comprised 3% of the

Lake Chemung

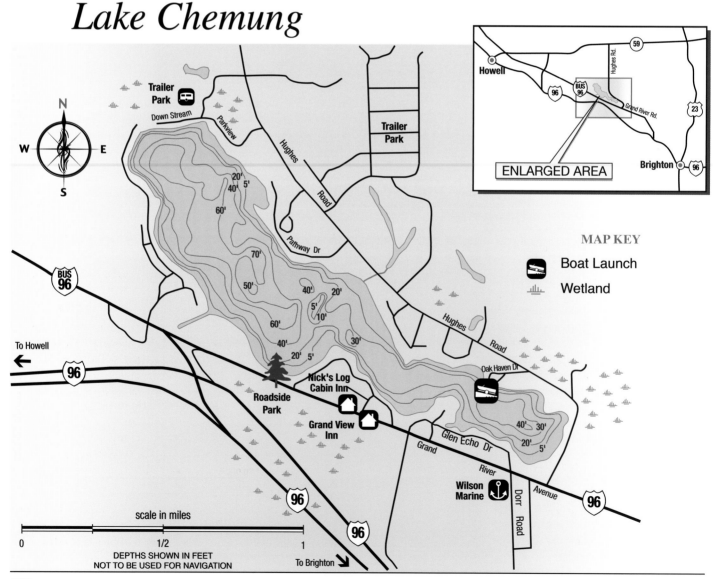

total catch. Yellow perch ranged from 3 to 7 inches with only 2% of the fish meeting or exceeding the acceptable harvest size of 7 inches, once again making perch an insignificant part of the lake population.

Crappie: A total of 51 black crappie averaging 9.0 inches comprised 2% of the total catch. Black crappie ranged from 7 to 10 inches and all fish met or exceeded the acceptable harvest size of 7 inches. Hoerauf says that you can catch crappie in the respectable 9-11-inch range across from the boat landing in the corner of the lake (the very southwest cove near Wilson Marine). This area is good both winter and summer for crappie. Also during the winter, crappie can be found suspended in about 20 feet of water in this same southwest area of the lake.

Overall, most of the panfish are abundant, but not sizeable. So if you like smaller tasty size fish, this lake has plenty of them.

Largemouth Bass: A total of 48 largemouth bass averaging just over 12 inches comprised 2% of the total catch. Largemouth bass ranged from 5 to 19 inches, with 31% of the fish meeting or exceeding the legal harvest size of 14 inches.

The largemouth bass population of Lake Chemung appeared in excellent shape. Relative abundance, size range, growth, and age distribution were similar to 2001 indicating a healthy and stable fish community. The presence of multiple year classes and the tendency for bass anglers to practice catch-and-release preserves large fish for multiple recapture and assures a highly desirable fishery.

Most largemouth bass can be found using conventional methods all around the lake, looking for weedbeds, docks, and other structure.

Pike: A total of 22 northern pike averaging almost 22 inches comprised less than 1% of the total catch. Northern pike ranged from 17 to 26 inches, with 14% of the fish meeting or exceeding the minimum harvest size of 24 inches. For pike, Dave recommends going west of the boat launch, off S. Hughes Road. Anglers can find some 20-30-inch pike in this area during the winter using tip-ups with pike minnows. Dave has seen pike upwards of 10-12 pounds however. This area drops off from around 5 feet, to 20 feet, then to 30 feet in depth. It also freezes up first on the lake, making it the first area for ice anglers to fish.

Walleye: Over 21,000 walleye planted in 2011, and approximately 35,000 combined in 2004 and 2006. For walleye fishing, most are caught in this lake in the winter months. Dave says that summer walleye are difficult to find and

Crappie are fun to catch and great in the fry pan.

catch, "they just don't seem to go by the conventional methods," he says. That is why many people do not fish this lake in the summer. It's a busy lake and if you do fish, early morning is best during summer.

Notes: Although black crappie and northern pike populations are not as abundant as other sport fish, they appear in sufficient numbers to provide reasonable recreational fisheries. Relative abundance, size structure, and growth compared similarly to past assessments suggesting stable populations.

Some panfish anglers find success here in 5-25 feet of water at the small end of the lake using the Glo Demon lure. The popular Demon size 10 is the most effective size for panfish. The Demon size 12 is a premier ultra-light lure for ultra-finicky fish. Tipped with a single spike (maggot), the Demon 12 is a tremendous shallow-water bluegill producer. The Demon size 8 is great for perch and crappie or any other fish keying in on a larger-profile lure. Be aware that shallow fish are often finicky, so you must tempt them with a tiny lead-head jig or teardrop with just a single maggot or waxworm. Usually, this is fishing that's a matter of scoring one here and one there, then moving to a new location. Fishing close to dark can also add to your creel.

Caution: Be aware of the rock pile about 500-600 yards out from the Grand River Roadside Park not far from where the lake narrows. A Wilson Marine employee says that there are boulders in this area 4-5 feet in diameter and every year many lower units and props are victims of these boulders.

At a Glance

What: Smaller fish, but lots of them

Where: Southeast end of Lake Chemung

Information/Guides: Greater Brighter Chamber of Commerce, 218 East Grand River, Brighton, 48116, 810-227-5086, www.brightoncoc.org

Landings: Off South Hughes Road on far northeast side of the lake (Oak Haven Drive)

Bait & Tackle: Midwest Sport Shop, 10049 Grand River Rd, Brighton, 48116, (810) 227-3141

Lake St. Clair Macomb County

"Fish hard, and think like a muskie" were Homer LeBlanc's fishing words of wisdom. I met Homer, who resided on a channel connecting to Lake St. Clair, one Saturday when I was to meet Charter Captain Don Miller on the nearby popular lake. We met at Homer's house, where his basement was virtually loaded with countless antique lures, photos, and other fishing artifacts. It was easy to create a lasting impression of this giant amongst muskie anglers. His basement was, in fact, a fishing museum.

Author of a book entitled, *Muskie Fishing: Fact and Fancy, Lore and Lure,* Homer was constantly inventing and making lures for muskie fishing. He operated the State of Michigan's most successful charter boat and guided for over 30 years. He also had his complete, distinct line of tackle that he made and sold.

As Captain Miller said, "Homer may never have set the world's record for the largest catch, but no one disputes the fact that he caught the most." When I would ask him how many he caught, he would candidly reply, "thousands." It was no wonder he was referred to as Mr. Muskie.

French explorers discovered Lake St. Clair in 1679, calling it Lac Sainte Claire in honor of Sainte Claire of Assisi whose feast day fell at that time. It was Sainte Claire who established an order of Franciscan nuns called the Order of the Poor Claires. Government officials and map makers later changed the spelling to the present form of Saint Clair, or St. Clair.

In general, Lake St. Clair's geographic proximity within the Great Lakes basin gives it its unique character as a world-class fishing destination. The swift-flowing St. Clair River brings clean, cold and nutrient-rich water into the lake, where it is channeled in a wide delta consisting of the North, South and Middle Channels, plus the main shipping channel. These nutrients spawn baitfish which, in turn, spawn bigger fish. From Muskie to smallies, yellow perch to walleye, and from giant channel catfish to pike, you will find them all in Lake St. Clair (and you might get surprised with other fish that tug on your line from time to time).

Muskie: Captain Miller says that muskie have really come back in Lake St. Clair, from the days when you might hook 2-3 in a day, while today you can easily see 8-10 or more on a typical charter trip. Muskie in Lake St. Clair run from 10-22 pounds, some in the 30-plus range, and even a few over 40 pounds. Don states that there are more gizzard shad available for them to feed on, and that has allowed them to not only grow in numbers, but size as well. "There is more

girth to these fish today," says Miller. Don will see upwards of 500 muskie this year alone during his charter trips. Testimony to the comeback of muskie here.

As for where to fish, Don says the entire lake supports muskie, whether casting mid-summer in the shallows of Anchor Bay, or trolling off the area by Selfridge Air Force Base, St. Clair has lots of muskie. Grassy Island (Grass Brunner Island) off the north channel is also a good place to search for muskie. Fish west of the island anywhere from 5 to 12 feet of water. "The area off 14 Mile Road near St. Clair Shores is also good," says Miller. One more location to search out these giants is off Grosse Point around the dumping grounds. Fish in the 15-foot water depths.

As for lures, there are many to attract muskie according to Miller. A couple of popular ones include the Believer (Drifter Tackle Company) which is very popular in the 8-inch size, as well as Double Bladed Bucktails. These are generally trolled between 5-40 feet behind the boat. Muskie are not intimidated by your prop or prop wash. I have seen them grab a lure as someone reaches for it in the water next to the boat.

Keep in mind that, like sturgeon, many of these fish are old-timers that are best released back to the waters they come from for a future battle.

Smallmouth: Although the muskie is king in Lake St. Clair, smallmouth are not far behind. You can go most anywhere for bass in this body of water, but the area between 9-14 Mile Road, where there are lots of weeds, is a good start. Smallmouth upwards of 4-7 pounds are not uncommon, with the bigger fish seeming to be out toward the shipping channel in 16-17 feet of water. Shad raps, Rapalas (watermelon color), Bombers, and Storm's Hot N Tots are favorite lures. Anchor Bay is another good area to search for smallies, up by New Baltimore. Try grub baits in this area.

Pike: Mitchell's Bay and Anchor Bay are loaded with pike, along with the area near St. John's Marsh. Also try the Metro Beach area and the waters off Grosse Point in the shallow water. Pike range in size generally between 3-15 pounds, with some over 20 pounds. The average size for pike in this lake is around 7-8 pounds according to Miller. Weighted spinner baits, spoons, and the trusty Daredevil are good choices for lures, but you can always try a smaller Believer. In the winter, tip-ups in Anchor Bay, and spearing around the marinas, are common methods like on most lakes.

Panfish/Perch: Jumbo perch between 10-14 inches are not uncommon in Lake St. Clair. The best time to fish for these tasty fish is in late summer and

At a Glance

What: Giant muskie, pike, perch, smallmouth bass

Regs: Canadian fishing license needed when fishing Canadian waters. www.mnr.gov.on.ca/en/Business/OC/2ColumnSubPage/STDPROD_091032.html

Information/Guides: Detroit Metro Convention & Visitors Bureau, 211 W. Fort St., Ste. 1000, Detroit, 48226, (313) 202-1800. Don Miller, professional guide, (734) 395-8820, millerssportfishing.com

Landings: There are almost countless boat landings along this body of water, here are some in Macomb County: **Brandenburg Memorial Park,** 50050 Jefferson Ave., Chesterfield, 48047, (586) 949-0400; **Clinton River Cut-Off,** 36110 Jefferson Avenue, Harrison Township, (586) 465-2160; **Harley Ensign Memorial,** 32995 South River Road, Harrison Township, (586) 463-4165, **Metro Breach,** 31300 Metropolitan Pky, Harrison Township, 48045, (800) 477-3172; **Selfridge AFB,** 44200 N Jefferson Ave.

Bait & Tackle: Lakeside Fishing Shop, 25110 Jefferson Ave. (corner of 10 Mile), St. Clair Shores, (586) 777-7003. Been there for several decades

early fall. The mouth of the St. Clair River, off Grosse Point, and St. Luke's Bay on the Canadian side of the lake are good bets. In the river channel, the large freighters stir up the river bottom, drawing in not only the panfish, but predators as well. Crappie are a good bet in Anchor Bay in the shallow waters. You can fish for them in this area both summer and winter.

Note:
Canadian fishing licenses are available on the Internet: www.mnr.gov. on.ca/en/Business/OC/2ColumnSubPage/STDPROD_091032.html

Sturgeon:
Just a note on sturgeon in this lake. There definitely are some large sturgeon here, and there is a location along the shipping channel, about 2-3 miles south of the mouth of the St. Clair River and just before the St. Clair light that hold sturgeon. Decker's Landing off the North Channel is also a productive location. But sturgeon are not often sought out due to the more productive muskie in this lake.

Walleye:
Walleye in the 2-5-pound range, with some upwards of 5-7 pounds are not uncommon in these waters. Try the area off the spillway off 14 Mile Road. Bottom-bouncers, crawler harnesses, and small spoons are generally used by anglers. Then when the fly hatch ends in June, it is best to drag hard plastics such as Bombers or Hot N Tots off the mouth of the Detroit River, by Peche Island, or out by the channel in 16-17-foot water. The waters off Selfridge AFB are also good.

Notes:
Muscamoot Bay is between the south and middle channel, near Harsen's Island, just down from Goose Bay. Grass Island (or Grassy Island as it is also known), is in the center of Anchor Bay and is submerged. When heading out of Selfridge head east at 80 degrees, it's 6 miles to the island. Fish the west side. Raise your bait during the day. Often you will find that panfish will be feeding on zooplankton in mid day and the predators will move up to feed on the panfish.

Muscamoot Bay:
GPS coordinates for Muscamoot Bay are N 42.55783 and W -82.66071.

Some Facts:
Length: 26 miles, Width: 24 miles, Average depth: 10 feet, Maximum depth: 21 feet, Water surface area: 162 sq. miles, Canada: 268 sq. miles, Shoreline length, (including islands): U.S. Mainland: 59 miles, Islands: 84 miles, Canada: Mainland: 71 miles, Islands: 43 miles. The smallest lake in the Great Lakes system, Lake St. Clair is not considered to be one of the "Great Lakes," however, it is part of the Lake Erie basin.

Homer LeBlanc (Mr. Muskie, on the right) along with his Believer lures, is a legend on Lake St. Clair. Seen here with Tom McGarrity of Saginaw, and Charter Captain Don Miller, Homer would always say "I may not have caught the largest muskie, but I no doubt caught the most."

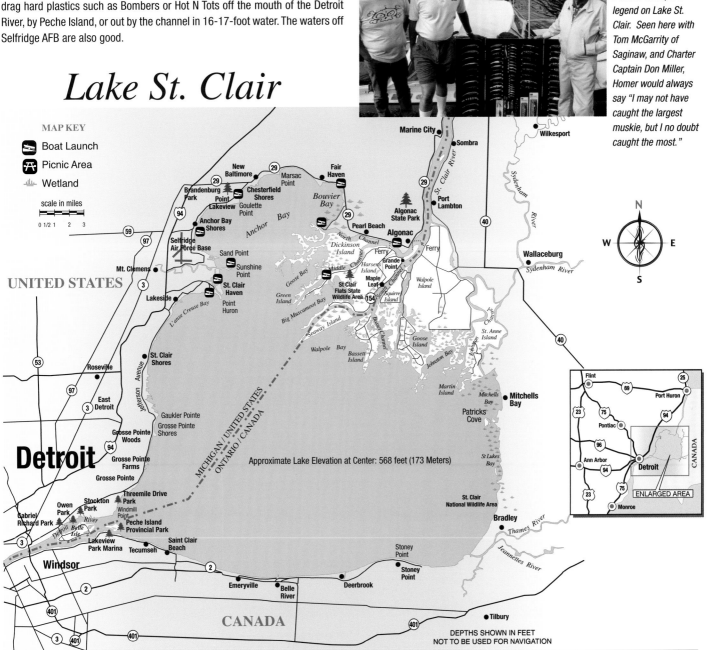

Lake St. Clair

MAP KEY
- Boat Launch
- Picnic Area
- Wetland

scale in miles
0 1/2 1   2   3

DEPTHS SHOWN IN FEET
NOT TO BE USED FOR NAVIGATION

Maceday Lake Oakland County

Maceday Lake is one of a major series of lakes in Oakland County, all connected by the St. Clair River. But one difference is that Maceday is probably the best trout lake in the county, primarily as a result of its depth at just under 120 feet versus the shallower adjacent lakes. The nearest lake to Maceday is the adjoining Lotus at only 65 feet in depth, with the former being 235 acres and the latter at a slightly smaller 219 acres. The depth variation is what keeps any significant trout migration out of Maceday to the other lakes in this lengthy chain.

Maceday Lake is located east of Maceday Lake Road and west of Airport Road in Waterford Township. The clean, clear nature of the lake allows the deeper and colder waters to remain well oxygenated all summer, providing habitat for various species of trout.

Splake: Fishing guide Ken Neeley, of KD Outdoors, who fishes many lakes in this part of the state, says that Maceday has a significant population of splake, a rather rare fish species in most any of Michigan's vast array of lakes. The splake in Maceday can be caught upwards of 12 inches according to Ken. Looking at DNR planting records, you will find that from 10,000-15,000 seven-inch splake have been planted in this lake virtually every year from 2001 until the time of this writing in 2012. Neeley says the best spot on the lake to fish for these tasty hybrids, a cross between a lake trout and a brook trout, is to go near the boat landing at the south end of the lake and work the area that drops the off to the deepest part of the lake.

Overall, this hybrid trout is an excellent game fish, although here too, it reveals its split personality. Some fight much more like speckled trout while others fight deep and doggedly like lake trout.

Splake and brook trout have very similar coloration patterns, making it very difficult for the untrained eye to distinguish between the two species. Splake tend to have a slight fork in the tail, a trait passed down from its lake trout parent, while brook trout tend to have no fork or "square" tails.

Splake have been culturally produced since the 1870's and the hybrid is genetically stable and capable of reproducing. However, splake reproduction, to my knowledge, has never been documented outside of the hatchery environment.

Maceday Lake

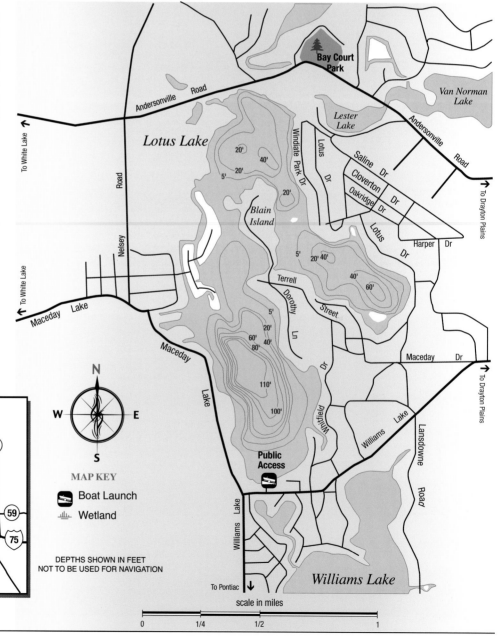

ENLARGED AREA

MAP KEY

Boat Launch

Wetland

DEPTHS SHOWN IN FEET
NOT TO BE USED FOR NAVIGATION

scale in miles

0   1/4   1/2   1

At a Glance

What: A top inland trout lake in southern Michigan

Where: Waterford Township, Oakland County

Why: A somewhat rare chance to catch splake, a hybrid (cross between a laker and brook trout)

Information/Guides: Waterford Area Chamber of Commerce, 2309 Airport Rd., Waterford, 48327, (248) 666-8600; **Ken Neeley, K D Outdoors,** 7688 Highland Road, Waterford, 48327, (248) 666-7799

Landings: Boat landing at south end off Williams Lake Road

Bait & Tackle: Ken Neeley, K D Outdoors, 7688 Highland Road, Waterford, 48327, (248) 666-7799, map: www.michigan.gov/dnr/0,1607,7-153-30301_31431_31560-67601--,00.html

Fish splake like you would speckles. Through the ice you can start near shore in an area where there's a gradual drop-off, then run your line from about 10 feet, out to 30 feet. This tends to work best if you have other anglers fishing with you. Jig with flashy spoons, in silver and gold colors, or try a Williams Wobler. For still lines, go with a simple hook and minnow. Shiners seem to work best for splake. Work the spoon just off the bottom with short lifts and drops. Keep a tight line on the drop, as many hits come on the way down. The Williams Ice Jig is a favorite and used in the summer months as well. Work the spoon to the top and all the way down. Be more aggressive or subtle, change jigs and/or colors until you find the right combination for that day.

A small Mustad hook tipped with the tail half of a minnow and a split shot eight inches above works well for splake as well.

Another method is to use a piece of minnow, a piece of canned shrimp, and run about four inches off the bottom; look for the 35-degree water temp if possible. Splake have a strong tendency to school which often gives rise to short periods of intensive angling success.

When fishing splake through a shanty, keep a clear glass juice bottle full of minnows on the lake bottom; the splake tend to chase schooling minnows and the little guys flashing around in the bottle helps attract the big ones your way. Always check to make sure this technique is totally legal.

Lake Trout: In late October to early November, the DNR planted 500-600 retired breeding lake trout in the 25-30-inch range, some upwards of 10 pounds. Three hundred lake trout about 7 pounds, and 25 inches long, were stocked in 2010. Initially the trout stay in the more shallow water, then move to deeper water. Once again, the main area to fish is from the boat landing to the deep hole.

For these lakers, jig the deep hole with live bait, with suckers or chubs.

Largemouth Bass: Neeley says that there is a "good solid largemouth bass population in this lake, upwards of 5 pounds or more in size." The best fishing is to move from along the drop-offs along the shoreline on the east and west side of the lake, as well as in the canals. During mid-summer you can look for bass under the docks where they tend to search out shade.

Panfish: Ken says that crappie (8-10-inch average) and bluegills (8" common), are both a winter and summer fishery. The best area to search for these two species is between the two lakes, north of Blain Island where there are a couple of 20-25-foot holes. In the summer crappie can also be found in the canals, and of course the gills are always on their spring beds.

Pike: Neeley mentions that pike are not in high numbers in this lake, but the ones that are here are sizeable, upwards of 30-plus inches. In winter, tip-ups are the favorite method just north of the deep gravel pit up to the no-wake zone between the two lakes. In summer, pike fishing is fair he says, but anglers might try the 10-20-foot depths along the weedlines.

Note: Regardless of whether Maceday Lake is stocked within the past year or so (2012-13), Jim Francis, a DNR fisheries biologist located in Southfield, said there is plenty of lake trout, splake and rainbow trout action to test the angler. "We got enough trout to last a few years," he said. "Ultimately, they'll live there a long time because it's a good lake for trout. Most guys are jigging but on open water some will troll cowbells and little Rapalas. "Frankly," he says, "any technique that works on Higgins Lake or other inland trout lakes will work here."

Maceday Lake is a Type C trout lake. Besides various cold-water trout, anglers also go for largemouth bass and even bluegill in the warmer top waters, said Francis, who noted an "All Species" fishing license must be purchased to fish for trout on Maceday Lake.

Maceday Lake is one of a few lakes that has not only bass, pike and panfish, but lake trout and even splake.

Mott Lake Genesee County

Mott Lake is a 684-acre impoundment of the Flint River located in northeast Genesee County. The impoundment is approximately 3.5 miles in length with the upper boundary generally accepted at the ending of Vassar Road. The lake was created in 1972 with the construction of C.S. Mott Dam and was intended to provide recreational opportunities for the area.

Development of the Mott Lake shoreline is considered light. In 2008, eight dwellings were counted in 11.6 miles of shoreline. Genesee County Parks and Recreation Commission is the majority landowner and administers their property for lightly developed recreational purposes.

This lake has an extensive history of fisheries management by the DNR. Historic management objectives sought to provide and maintain a diverse warmwater fish community with particular emphasis on bluegill, black crappie, channel catfish, largemouth and smallmouth bass, northern pike, tiger muskellunge, and walleye.

Back in the mid-1970s, an assessment found an over-abundance of common carp and Mott Lake was included in a major chemical reclamation of fish in the upper Flint River drainage. An estimated 113 tons of carp were removed from Mott Lake. Post-reclamation fish stocking included the introduction of rainbow trout for an interim fishery, as well as bluegill, channel catfish, largemouth bass, pumpkinseed sunfish, tiger muskellunge, and walleye. Benefits from the 1976 fish reclamation were short lived as carp re-established themselves in high abundance within a few years.

Management through fish stocking continued for channel catfish and largemouth bass until 1978; for tiger muskellunge until 1991; and for walleye until 1992. Tiger muskellunge stocking was discontinued due to poor survival. Bluegill, pumpkinseed sunfish, largemouth bass, channel catfish, and walleye stocking were discontinued when self-sustaining populations developed. No fish have been stocked in Mott Lake since 1992.

The average water depth is approximately 8 feet and an estimated 95% of the total surface acreage is considered less than 15 feet deep.

Back in 2009, a DNR fish survey of Mott Lake revealed that of a total of 2,293 fish caught by them, the total catch represented 20 various species, with the majority being catfish, round goby, bluegill, and walleye, comprising 87% of the total catch by number.

Renee Whitt, who owns the Bain Master Bait Shop at the south end of the lake, is very familiar with Mott Lake and states that just this past year (2011) she had seen five master angler walleye caught here, all being in the upper-20 to lower-30-inch size.

Walleye:
A total of 104 walleye averaging 13.6 inches comprised 5% of the total catch by number, and the average size of the walleye collected were just over 12 inches compared to almost 18 inches from trap-net gear. Thirty-five percent of all walleye collected met or exceeded the minimum harvest size of 15 inches.

Most of the walleye are caught near Genesee Road bridge (by Lions Club Park). Whitt states that Mott is more of a summer fishing lake, and not much ice fishing here for whatever reason. She says that "another good walleye fishing location is where the river channel runs into the lake at south end." Anglers troll here using the soft plastic Mimic Minnow (by Northland Tackle), or the Road Runner jig (by Blakemore). She indicates that the average walleye here is in the 17-21-inch size. (NOTE: Map of Mott is good for walleye also).

Bass:
Although collected in low numbers, smallmouth and largemouth bass showed up as an important component of the sport fishery. During the DNR survey, smallmouth bass ranged from 5-16 inches with 19% of the catch meeting or exceeding the legal harvest size of 14 inches.

Smallmouth and largemouth bass have been a small but consistent component of the Mott Lake fish community.

Whitt says that there are a significant number of largemouth bass taken from Mott, and most anglers work the north end of the lake, north of the Genesee Bridge. Work the shoreline, and the areas where there are fallen trees and brush. There are many good bass holes at the north end. Also try the shallows around the many small islands. Renee says the Gary Yamamoto Kreature Lure is a proven lure on Mott. The 4-inch Kreature can be cast weightless for a slow, horizontal descent. Raise your rod tip, and you can burn it back across the water's surface like a buzzbait. The lure's performance is improved when Texas rigged for flipping or Carolina rigged for those bottom-hugging fish.

Bluegill/Crappie:
A total of 333 bluegill averaging 6.4 inches comprised 15% of the total catch by number. Bluegill ranged from 1-9 inches with 71% of the fish meeting or exceeding the acceptable harvest size of 6 inches. Bluegill longevity appeared to peak at age 6 and older fish are either harvested or die of natural causes.

Once again, the panfish fishery on Mott is not active during winter according to Whitt. In fact, Renee closes her bait shop during the winter months. But the spring and summer months are popular. Many anglers use Gulp bait, in black shad color. The Berkley bait resembles real corn. It is recommended that you keep the bait off the bottom and in the strike zone.

"The one-inch Berkeley bait in the black shad style is the most popular color," says Whitt. Artificial minnows in a liquid are popular as well on Mott Lake. Fish

Many anglers dismiss catfish as a table fare, but they are excellent eating and provide a battle on the end of a line.

where Branch Road is closed, across from Bluebell Beach. This is the most popular area for gills and crappie in the 8-10-inch size.

Catfish: Another primary change in the Mott Lake fish community has been a significant increase in channel catfish. Channel catfish were first observed in high abundance in 1995 and they have remained in high numbers since. Numbers of channel catfish collected with trap nets in 1995, 2001, and 2008 were 435, 600, and 859, respectively, indicating a significant increase in this species in a relatively short time-frame.

"Catfish in Mott Lake are abundant," says Whitt, and "cats usually will hit most anything you throw at them," but she says the most popular offering is the Premo Sticky Catfish dip bait by Magic Bait. Many anglers fish with long lines along the shore, or standing on shore, making it easy on a nice spring or summer day to fish without having a boat. Renee has seen a 38-inch cat from Mott Lake, but most are in the 20-30-inch size.

Note: The decline in gizzard shad is believed to be associated with the high abundance of channel catfish in this lake and to a lesser degree walleye and other predatory species.

At a Glance

What: Walleye, bluegills, catfish

Where: Mott Lake impoundment

Why: There are some sizable walleye and catfish in this lake.

Regs: No-wake boating rules are in effect for Mott Lake.

Landings: Boat launch between Coldwater and Genesee roads. Bluegill Boat Launch is a paved and barrier-free facility capable of launching moderated sized boats with parking for approximately 75 vehicles and trailers.

Contacts: Genesee County Convention & Visitors Bureau, 502 Church Street, Flint, 48502, (810) 232-8900.

Bait & Tackle: Bain Master Bait Shop, 3180 E. Carpenter Road at south end of lake, (810) 736-1444.

Notes: Branch Road ends where Coldwater Road starts at the curve. It is closed just past the parking lot. You need to go north off Carpenter Road to access this area.

Mott Dam area is fished for walleye, but there are restrictions for fishing near the dam, and not very good markings currently to indicate such restrictions.

Mott Lake

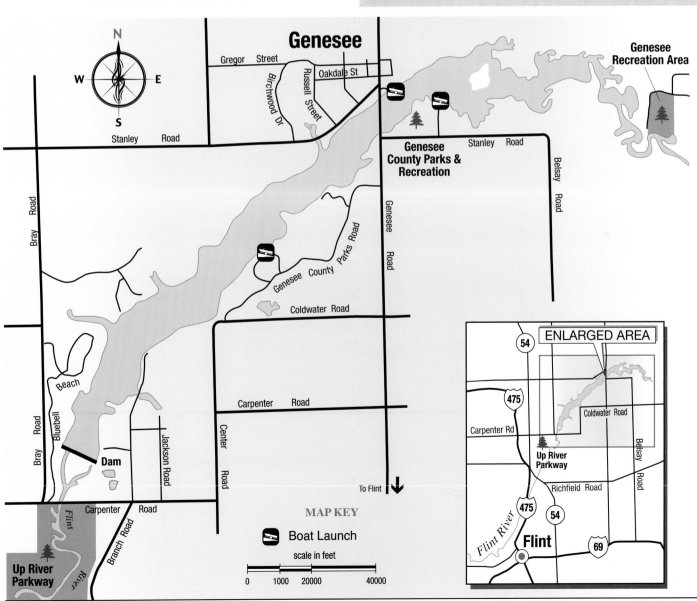

Muskegon Lake
Muskegon County

Muskegon Lake is a moderately sized 4,100-acre lake with a maximum depth of 79 feet. Located in a popular fishing area, it's within a rifle shot of Lake Michigan. Large- and smallmouth bass, pike, perch, bluegill, crappie and even catfish are found here.

The average depth of this popular lake is around 30 feet, with the deepest area in front of Bear Lake Channel at around 45 feet, and the south side by old car ferry docks at 70 feet. The west end, along the sand docks is about 45-50 feet.

Ron Spring, who lives in this area, and a long-time angler of Muskegon Lake, says that pike "average around 6-8 pounds, and some up to 12-14 pounds, which is a more sizeable pike than any other lake in this area of the state."

Where to Fish: In summer, Ron suggests fishing the weedbeds on the north side of the lake, or south side. Summertime however is not the most popular time for pike fishing in this lake.

Ice Fishing for Pike: Muskegon Lake is a great place to catch some table-fare-sized pike, but you may also catch a wall hanger. Pike in the 26- to 30-plus-inch range are very common and 15- to 20-pounders are caught every winter. Use minnows for pike, or jig through the ice. Ron states that "tip-ups

Casting for sizeable bass is a popular activity on Muskegon Lake.

baited with smelt are most effective during the ice fishing season." Regular-sized suckers and golden shiners will take the average sized pike, but for the lunkers try jumbo herring. Slammer tip-ups are the tools of choice. Fish the area along the north side, keeping in mind that access is poor here; the state park is best for access, or the east side at the Muskegon Conservation Club, however membership might be a prerequisite for utilizing this access point. Prime fishing locations are also off the South Branch of the Muskegon River, off Fisherman's Landing, and Second Street. Fish the drop-offs in the 10-20-foot range.

Walleye: Basically fish the same areas as pike; i.e., north or south side. Most anglers use crawler harnesses during the summer months, working the edges of weeds and drop-offs, especially in front of Bear Lake Channel. There is a ledge that runs about 10' deep out to the black buoy. This is the most popular area for summer walleye.

During winter the ice is treacherous along the east side of this lake due to the warm-water discharge from Consumers Power Plant. Anglers often use a boat here even during the winter since part of this area is always open.

Jigging spoons with a minnow head through the ice is a popular choice for walleye. Husky jerk or swim bait such as Northlands and Storm lures often work well in the spring.

Bass: Ron says that "bass is a popular fishery in Muskegon Lake. Work the edges of the weedbeds on the north and south ends of the lake, casting rubber worms for both large- and smallmouth bass, or troll a crawler harness." Bass are good size in this lake. Tip: Smallmouth bass fishing is generally slow when the water temperature drops to below 40 degrees. When this happens, fish deep and slow. Try some deep primary points and drop-offs using jigs, plastics and deep jerk baits will be your best bet to boat a smallmouth. Bass fishing can also be good at the 15- to 22-foot depth. Dragging shiners is also a good choice.

Panfish: Lake Michigan perch move into Lake Muskegon in the fall and stay all winter. Fish the south side during the winter months. Perch move into the west end of the lake also, near the sand docks, and then move out around the end of March. They can even be found in water under five feet during the winter. Perch are often not huge here, but 8-10-inchers are not uncommon, and some can reach over 12 inches. Bluegills are also abundant here. Fish the weedbeds on the north and south sides and along the bays. Crappies can be caught summer or winter in the deeper water. They are often suspended about 4-5 feet off the bottom.

Crappie fishing is sometimes at its best when the water temperature drops. Crappie will be in large schools and follow the large shad schools around in the deeper water. So locate the deepest parts of this lake and look for schools of fish. Then drop your plastics or live bait down to the bottom of the shad school. Many crappie anglers can catch good numbers and good-sized crappie during the winter months.

Catfish: Muskegon Lake is a good lake to fish for channel cats and other varieties as well. Use leeches for these fighters and work the bottom of the lake.

At a Glance

What: One of the better pike lakes in the area and good catfish lake

Where: Muskegon Lake

Information/Guides: Muskegon CVB, 610 W. Western Ave, Muskegon, (231) 724-3100, www.visitmuskegon@co.muskegon.mi.us

Landings: The state park on the NW side of the lake is the best access area

Bait & Tackle: Adam's Angler, 2008 Lake Ave., (231) 744-5992; **Shoreline Service Bait & Tackle,** 2080 Lakeshore Dr, (231) 759-7254

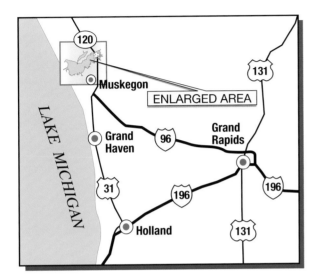

Catfish Tip: The catfish family comprises of blue catfish, flathead catfish and channel catfish. Since catfish are warmwater fish, they are not very active in colder water temperatures. They are still feeding, but catfish will only be found very deep and feeding very slowly. Therefore catfish are generally fished more during the warmer months.

Muskegon Lake

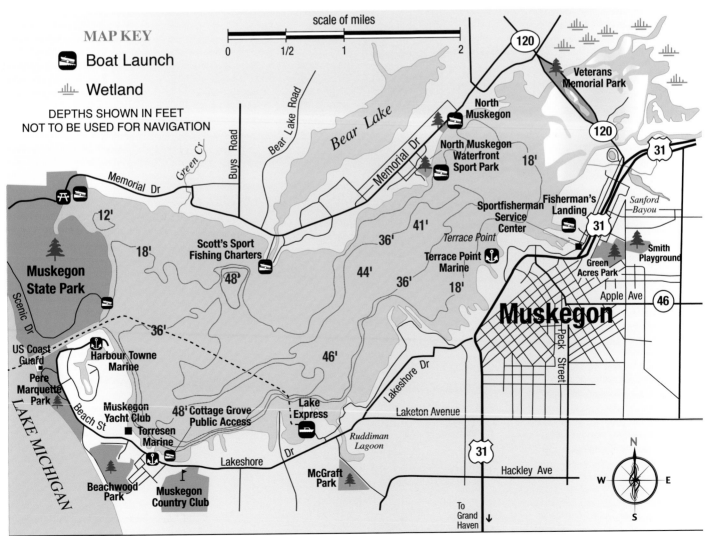

Nepessing Lake Lapeer County

Lake Nepessing, a small 414-acre lake located in the southwest corner of Lapeer County, has a maximum depth of 25 feet, in the southwest corner of the lake. This is also the area of the lake where it drops off quickly, going from 5 feet to 25 feet in a very short distance.

In addition to the prized largemouth bass in this lake, you can find pike, muskie, walleye, bluegill, crappie, sunfish (a recent state record here) and perch.

Les Noblett, owner of Hilltop Party Store for over 18 years (also sells bait and tackle), says that Nepessing is rated as one of the top lakes in the state for largemouth bass.

Nate Scharrer, who fishes strictly bass on this lake, agrees. Largemouth bass can range from the lower teens to the upper 20-inch size; and there are lots of them. "It's not uncommon," says Nate, "to catch largemouth here averaging in the 17-19-inch range."

Walleye: Walleye are planted every other (even-numbered) year by the DNR, the last planting as of this writing was over 22,000 in 2010. Nepessing is a spring-fed lake, which turns over about 4 times a year. Walleye can be fished both winter and summer on the north and east end of the lake. Look for drop-offs and in the evenings fish the shallows. Many anglers fish the 15-foot depth at the north end of the lake near the public-access site.

The weed areas of the lake used to be at the south and east end, but with aquatic weed treatment (milfoil), these areas change from time to time. There are some weed areas in the center of the lake as well as the north side. Although walleye exist in this lake, they are not always easy to find.

Panfish: Les states that ice fishing for panfish usually takes place at the north end of the lake, but many anglers also go to the south end, along the drop-offs. Also try the sunken island near the southwest/south-central shore.

These same areas are good during the summer months, except when the gills are on their beds in early spring.

Perch generally range in the 8-10 inch size, not large by any means, but large enough to keep. Crappie on the other hand, are sizable, ranging from 12-15 inch. A state record sunfish was taken here back in 2009 that was almost 13 inches and weighed 2.15 pounds. Anglers tend to be successful fishing for crappie at night using lanterns jigs as the most popular lure.

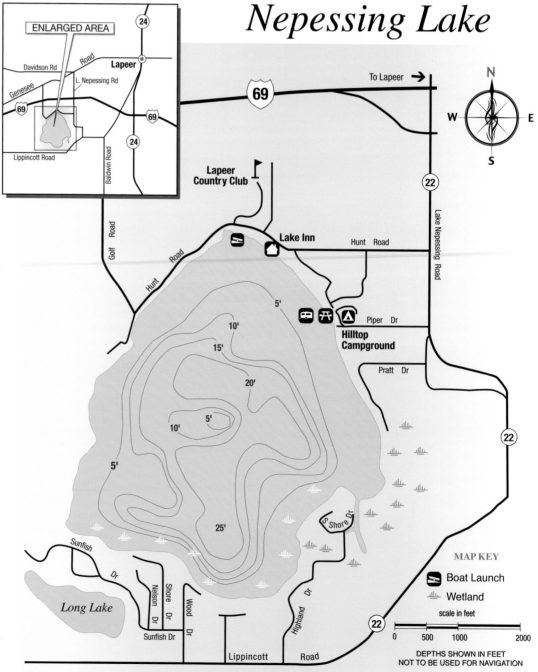

Muskie: For the hybrid tiger muskie, some anglers troll the waters from south shore to the sunken island area towards the southeast, and back again, going from deeper to shallow water. The biggest known muskie taken from here was 53 inches back around 2007.

Pike: Pike fishing takes a back seat to bass here, but nonetheless some decent pike can be caught. Try fishing along shore using one of the favorite offerings consisting of a purple worm with white stripe. Naturally the weed areas can also be productive, and along the drop-offs. Pike can range up to 30 inches or more, but not much bigger, in this lake.

Bass: Bass tournaments are commonplace on Nepessing for a good reason; it is highly rated as a quality largemouth bass lake.

Nate Scharrer, a noted bass angler on this lake who heads up a college fishing team at Western Michigan University, states that the best way to fish this lake if you are unfamiliar with it, is to "work around the many docks that extend from the shoreline." He says an effective method is to simply troll along the shoreline and cast your favorite bass lure, whether it be spinner baits, rattletraps, soft plastic worms, or top-water lures. Nate likes the Texas rig (www.bassfishingusa.com/Rigging/rigging1.html) , using a 5-inch plastic worm. Work the early part of the morning, especially when the temperatures are going to be up above 70 degrees since that is a difficult time to get the bass to move out of their shaded, protected area.

The terrain varies around the shoreline on Nepessing. The middle of the lake has some good weedy areas, but you have to horse lures through them. Try jigging with a trailer, or spinner baits in these weedy areas, or rattletraps, but you will either have to horse your lure through the weeds, or use a protective hook. Soft plastics also work well in the weedy areas according to Nate. Purple or black seem to be the favorites.

There are 101 different ways to fish bass, regardless of the lake, but one thing is for certain, Nepessing has plenty of them to try all your lures.

Note: No spearing allowed here since they do not want undersized muskie accidentally taken.

DNR Photo, David Kenyon

At a Glance

What: Largemouth bass

Where: Lake Nepessing in Lapeer County

Why: One of the better bass lakes in the southern half of the state

Landings: There is a boat landing at the very north end of the lake off Hunt Road, just across from the entry to the country club

Contacts: Hilltop Party Store, (810) 664-2782

Bait & Tackle: Hilltop Party Store, Hilltop Campground, 1260 Piper Drive, Lapeer, (810) 664-2782, www.hilltopcampground.net

This angler pulls a typically sized Nepessing perch from under the ice.

Sand Lake Lenawee County

Panfish, including some very nice bluegills, are available in Sand Lake.

for bluegill and crappie. A fairly healthy sunfish population also exists here.

Anglers on Sand Lake generally use the tried-and-true 1/16-ounce white jig for shallow spring crappie, but live minnows are also effective. A live red worm or piece of crawler is usually all you need to catch bluegill, though they also seem to find crickets irresistible, especially in summer.

Nick Glancy, who resides near Sand Lake and fishes it on a regular basis, said it is a good lake for bluegills, crappie, and perch. You can catch 7-9-inch perch on a regular basis and some up to 10-12 inches.

S and Lake, a 442-acre lake near the town of Springville, has a maximum depth of 55 feet and is noted especially for its bluegill, crappie, and largemouth bass populations. But there are walleye, northern pike, smallmouth and rock bass as well.

Sand Lake is part of a cluster of similar lakes, such as nearby Wamplers Lake, Evans Lake, Iron Lake, Kelly Lake and others that also provide good fishing opportunities.

In a state with more than 11,000 inland lakes, small lakes like this one can become lost in the significant variety of fishable waters. But don't overlook this fish-producing lake, to do so would be a mistake. Sand Lake harbors a multitude of fish as noted above, and is an ideal place to cast a line from a small vessel, such as a kayak, canoe or float tube. The bottom of the lake varies between peat, gravel and sand and it supports a variety of aquatic vegetation.

Panfish: Spring and summer are top times to fish in Sand Lake. Crappie fishing peaks relatively early. A 2010 report by the DNR indicates that crappie were biting in shallow water in early to mid April. Bluegill and largemouth bass fishing starts up a short time thereafter as these fish move shallow through May and spawn in June. Ice fishing in January and February can also be productive

Most anglers target panfish in the area about 100-150 yards off the east-side boat access site. The water here drops off from 5-6 feet to about 18 feet and is good for ice fishing or spring fishing. While you are fishing for panfish with your favorite tear drop and minnow, you can set up a tip-up in hopes of catching a walleye.

Nick says this is not a very good summer fishery due to boating, jet skiing, and other lake activities that disrupt fishing. If you go during the summer, try early morning or later in the evening.

Largemouth Bass: Largemouth bass will strike plastic worms and other soft plastic baits as they often do on most any other lake, but spinners, crankbaits and jigs are also worth trying. Topwater lures can entice strikes from bass, especially early morning and later in the evening. Fish around shallow brush, the edges of vegetation and the docks that line parts of the shoreline. The point on the southeast corner of the lake can also be productive.

DNR fish biologist, Jim Francis says that the last survey back in 2003 noted smallmouth existing in Sand Lake, which is a good thing since many lakes do not have a good smallmouth population. For what it's worth, most of the smallmouth back in 2003 were in the 4-18-inch size.

Sand Lake

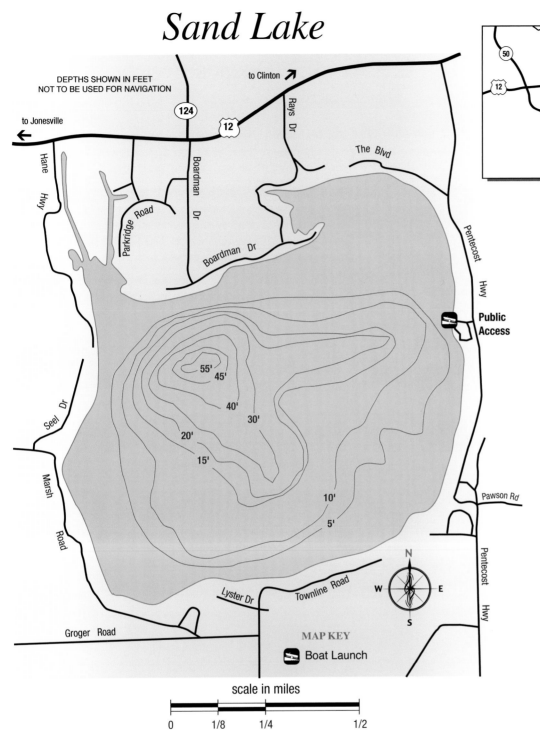

DEPTHS SHOWN IN FEET
NOT TO BE USED FOR NAVIGATION

Public Access

ENLARGED AREA

scale in miles

0   1/8   1/4   1/2

MAP KEY

Boat Launch

Many tournament anglers fish here as well. Glancy states that you can catch some nice 2-4-pounders on a fairly consistent basis. Try fishing the north end of the lake around the bend. Many of the homes there install their docks early and you can pitch various bass lures near the docks and floating rafts.

Walleye: 2,200 walleye, with an average length of just over 8 inches, were planted in the fall of 2008 and 4,000 back in 2003 by a private lake group.

Nick states that Sand Lake is one of the two most common walleye lakes in that area, or in Lenawee County for that matter. Ice-fishing anglers target walleye across from the access on the west side of the lake (off Lake Drive) where the channel exists. In spring, troll this same area where it drops off from 15 to 55 feet. There is also a sand bar in this area that is productive during the winter months. Often you can see a red marker where the drop-off exists.

Note: Timing is important for productive fishing, as well as safety. On many lakes, safe ice does not form until January, and ice fishing often lasts into March, depending on the weather. The best ice fishing is often in areas where "green" vegetation exists during the winter, especially spots with a mix of rocks and weeds, and where both deep and shallow water are nearby. Live grubs, worms and larvae are productive baits, and many ice fishermen use small jigs with soft plastics as well. Larger fish, such as pike and walleye, will strike live minnows.

At a Glance

What: Panfish, largemouth & smallmouth bass, walleye

Where: Sand Lake in SE Michigan

Landings: East side of the lake off Pentecost Road; relatively new landing constructed by DNR.

Contacts: Lenawee County CVB, 209 N. Main St., Adrian, 49221, (517) 263-7747, (800) 536-2933, www.visitlenawee.com, email: lccvb@tc3net.com

Bait & Tackle: Knutson's, Brooklyn, M-124 and M-50, (800) 292-0857; **Irish Marina,** (517) 592-6006, on M-124 about 1-1/2 miles off US-12; **Yoder's Tackle,** (517) 467-2468, 11700 M-50, south of US 12

Silver Lake Oceana County

Silver Lake is another lake located along the scenic Lake Michigan shoreline dotted with scores of quaint towns and many tourist attractions. This lake abuts beautiful sand dunes, and you can fish for walleye, largemouth and smallmouth bass, pike, bluegill, and crappie.

This 700-acre lake can be a jewel of a walleye fishery. Silver Lake is relatively shallow at 20 feet average, but ranges from a few feet on the east end to around 28 feet on the west, or the dune, side. A shallow shelf of sand extends out from the state dock, anglers in larger boats might need to walk them out to deeper water.

The one time I fished this lake some years back, I remember that it was not long before I hooked a couple of walleye, albeit throwbacks, but then the next several were all above keeper size. The largest I remember was around four pounds. But along with the walleye, I caught pike (under 30 inches), and a few rock bass.

Dan Monnor, who is very familiar with Silver Lake angling, states that most people target walleye on this lake, but it has many other species of game fish, including pike, largemouth bass, rock bass, and crappie.

Panfish: Ken Clark, a well-known charter captain from White Lake, north of Muskegon (www.fishmascharters.com), states that Silver Lake has a good population of fish, but primarily largemouth bass, some smallmouth, and good numbers of perch. "Bluegills can be caught in the 8-10-inch size" he says, "most generally in and along the edges of the weed lines."

Sizable crappie in the 12-inch average size are common in late winter (last ice) and early spring by the channel at the northeast end of the lake.

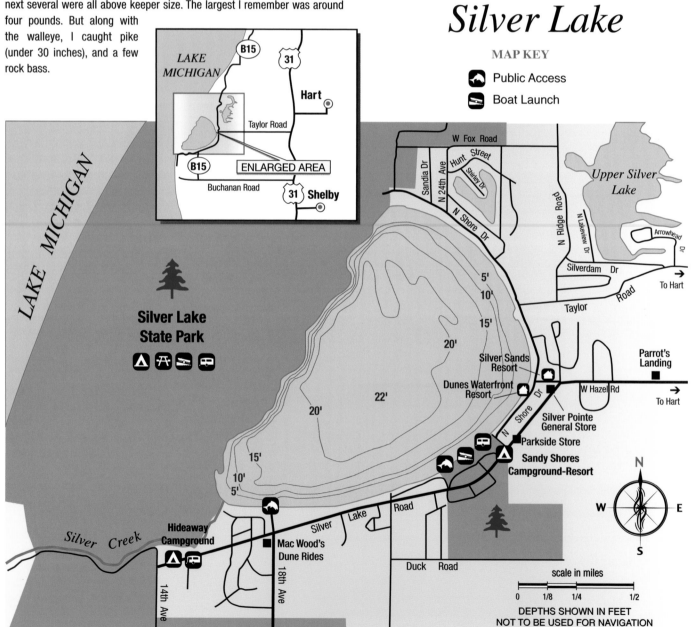

Silver Lake

MAP KEY

Public Access

Boat Launch

There are no weeds along the west end of the lake adjacent the sand dunes, so the best bet is to start along the north shore in the spring or in the southeast corner of the lake. You may also find a school of crappie in these same areas.

Captain Clark likes to fish just before dark when you can see suspended crappie going from deep to shallow water in the spring/summer months.

Perch in the 10-12-inch size range can also be found in Silver Lake. Since this lake is like a bowl, and small in size, you can easily work your bait for panfish and cover the entire lake in a couple of hours. When you locate a school of perch, for instance, ease down your anchor and work that spot until they move on or quit biting; then move on again. This works for both summer and winter fishing.

Ice fishing for panfish in the 15-19-foot depth near the State Park can be very productive on Silver Lake. The fish here will travel between different depths and along the weed edges. Clark's favorite winter lure in this lake is the Jigging Rapala with no minnow. He feels the addition of a minnow changes the normal jigging action of the lure, and not necessarily for the better.

Walleye:
Winter walleye anglers can be found working the west side of the lake, near the dunes. This area is deeper and walleye tend to hang out here during the winter. Swedish Pimples and Rapalas are the popular lure choices. In summer, walleye move to the 15-18-foot weedline on east side of the lake. Trolling with Rapalas is the most common method used here. Tip-ups can also be used along the south end of lake.

Monnor says that Silver Lake "overall is a popular fishery and has a nice walleye population. There aren't very many inland lakes in the area where you can set your sights on walleye, but Silver is one place you can," he says.

The lake is stocked by DNR. It receives 28,000 to 40,000 fingerling walleye every other year. Thirty years ago, the lake was stocked with walleye fry, but state fisheries managers switched in the 1990s to planting fingerlings up to 2 inches long. As of this writing, the last stocking on record was 2010 when almost 40,000 fingerlings were planted in June.

As a side note, Silver Lake walleye are best fished from dusk to dawn. Walleye are low-light feeders, and have adapted by developing large light-sensitive eyes, positioned to see up rather than down. Therefore they are more apt to be caught in low light or nighttime lighting conditions.

Captain Clark says that the walleye here can be in 21 feet of water or they might be suspended. "Trust your electronics" he says. You can "get a lot of walleye when a hatch is going on," he says, noting that walleye will often suck bugs off the top of the water like a trout. So when trolling, run some of your lures 3-5 feet below the surface because walleye are not always on the bottom. Silver Lake is clean enough that the fish can see quite high. Clark will run planer boards with crawler harnesses for the best action here.

If you troll too slowly near shoreline you will catch a lot of bullheads when using a crawler harness, so if you wish to avoid this, pick up your trolling speed.

Pike:
Monnor says that winter time is great for spearing pike up to 30-40 inches, although most are in the 20-30 inch range. There is no size limit, so beginners do not have to worry about accidentally spearing an undersized pike. The most popular area for taking winter pike is near the south end of the lake around the outlet (Silver Creek). Anglers also use tip-ups here with pike minnows in this same area. There doesn't seem to be much of a pike summer fishery on Silver Lake, probably due to the other popular species such as walleye and bass.

Bass:
Silver Lake is also known for its healthy population of 12-14-inch rock bass. Once again, as with crappie, the northeast end of the lake near the channel is a popular site for taking these scrappers. There are weeds in this part of the lake during summer, but they are not very abundant.

Captain Clark has caught many largemouth in the 4-5-pound range along the weed edges, actually often when fishing for walleye. Clark is a "walleye junkie," so to speak, and favors this species over any other, but is quite knowledgeable about many other game fish in a number of inland lakes, as well as the Great Lakes.

Notes:
Monnor says you can fish this lake in May without much summer lake activity, and it can become full of weeds in some areas mid and late summer. Many early summer boating anglers use planer boards, and each rod has 10-pound line, with 1-ounce inline weights to get the bait to the bottom. A crawler harness with a spinner blade completes the recipe. This allows you to cover a significant amount of the lake in a short amount of time.

At a Glance

What: Walleye, rock bass, and pike fishing

Where: Silver Lake near Lake Michigan

Why: One of the better walleye lakes in the area

Regs: No size limit on pike

Contacts: Hart Silver Lake Mears Chamber, 2388 N Comfort Dr. Hart, 49420, (231) 873-2247

Landings: North Shore Drive and Silver Lake Rd. all along the east and southeast end of the lake has access sites, four of them to be exact. The best access sites are the state park, the landing at the end of Hazel Road on the east central area of the lake, and the one at the south end at the end of Scenic Road. The access site just south of the state park is not a very good site and would best be avoided. **Note:** Although there are four public access sites, only one landing has a dock, at the state park by the hotel

Bait & Tackle: Country Boy Bait & Tackle Bait Shop, 704 S. State Street, Hart, 49420, (231) 873-1820

Ultralight tackle is great for finicky perch, and when you land a couple of jumbos, like the author's son, Jeff, did, it makes it all the more exciting.

Tamarack Lake Montcalm County

Tamarack Lake, located near the town of Lakeview, is a predominately shallow lake approximately 310 acres in size situated in the Muskegon River Watershed, Montcalm County. There are several small islands within the lake that produce some good fishing for panfish. The lake also has some good structure for focusing on bass and pike.

A 2008 lake survey funded by the Tamarack Lake Board, states that the fishing experience on this lake is perceived as above average by anglers, especially for pike and largemouth bass. Largemouth bass of 3 to 4 pounds are not uncommon and draw the attention of several bass clubs that host local tournaments on this lake. Large crappies, northern pike and bluegill sunfish are often targeted by anglers fishing through the ice. Tamarack has the potential to support two additional gamefish species including channel catfish and sunfish.

Tamarack Lake is a shallow, warmwater inland lake whose lake level is maintained via water-control structure. The majority of the lake is less than 10 feet deep.

Bluegills: John London, a local who is familiar with this lake, says that bluegills are often found along the southeast side of the lake, off Tamarack Road in 7-10 feet of water. Darrell Johnson, who owns Tamarack Sports about a quarter mile down the road, states that you can catch bluegills all day long, but most are in the 8-9-inch size or smaller. During summer the areas around the islands are good for gills, as well as the southeast shore, and to a limited extent the west shore. There are many good bedding sites off the west shore and around the islands.

Crappie: Darrell Johnson says that crappie are more often found on the west side of the lake, off the cemetery grounds and north of the city park on the southwest side of the lake. You can also find them along the north side of the large island over the sand flat, both winter and summer. There are some pockets of crappie along the southeast side of the lake near the 17-18-foot hole. Crappie in the 10-11-inch range are not uncommon in this lake.

Perch: There are perch in this lake, even some larger ones upwards of 14-16 inches according to Johnson, but this has not always been the case. The lake has seen improvements in perch numbers and size over the past couple of years from the time of this writing. Try the north side of the islands in spring, but generally you can find them all over the lake at other times of the year.

Largemouth Bass: There are bass tournaments on Tamarack Lake which indicates at least some decent bass fishing here. Darrell indicates that largemouth bass can be found in the 3-5-pound range in most all areas of the lake due to the varied bottom structure. You might first try the southwest shore and northwest corner of the lake near the cemetery. One other good area is the southeast corner near the deeper hole. Typical bass lures are used on this lake.

DNR Photo, David Kenyon

This young angler proudly shows off a nice pike taken on a trip with dad.

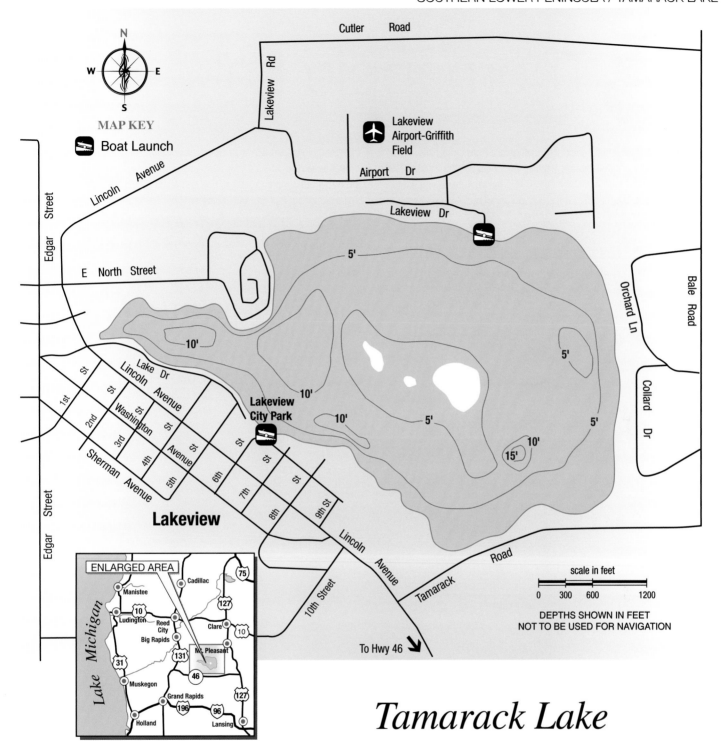

Tamarack Lake

Pike: There are some pike in this lake, and although mostly in the hammer-handle size, Darrell says that they are starting to rebound and anglers are finding some 20-30-inch pike, and even some in the 30-inch-plus size. Anglers don't have much luck yet ice fishing for them, but during spring and summer you can try around the islands and also the southeast side of the lake.

Walleye: Johnson states that the only plantings of game fish in this lake were walleye by the DNR back around 2010 when 750 fingerlings were planted. Few, if any, walleye currently exist in this lake.

At a Glance

What: Largemouth bass and panfish

Where: Around the islands and the east and west shorelines

Why: Some nice-size largemouth bass are taken from this lake.

Landings: North end of the lake off Golf Drive Road

Bait & Tackle: Tamarack Sports, 9599 N. Greenview Rd., Lakeview, (989) 352-7527 (SW side of the lake about a quarter mile)

Thornapple Lake Barry County

According to various local fish biologists, Thornapple Lake in Barry County has ideal muskie habitat, and some of the muskie taken out of this lake are testimony to this belief. Aquatic vegetation is abundant to a depth of 4 feet and primarily consists of coontail and various pondweeds.

Thornapple Lake is 409 acres in size and up to 50 feet deep, averaging about 30 feet deep. The lake isn't big, and you won't find any clear water there due to it being an eutrophic lake (i.e., rich in nutrients like phosphates, nitrates, and organic nutrients that promote a proliferation of plant life, especially algae).

Steve Walker is a veteran angler on Thornapple and states that anyone fishing this lake must treat it like a river, not a lake, because it does have a pronounced current due to the influx of river water at one end and an outlet at the other.

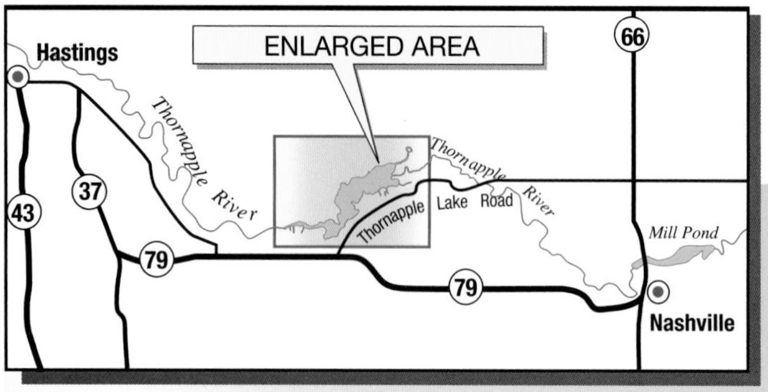

Hastings

ENLARGED AREA

66

Thornapple River

43

37

79

Thornapple Lake Road

79

Thornapple River

Mill Pond

Nashville

Thornapple Lake

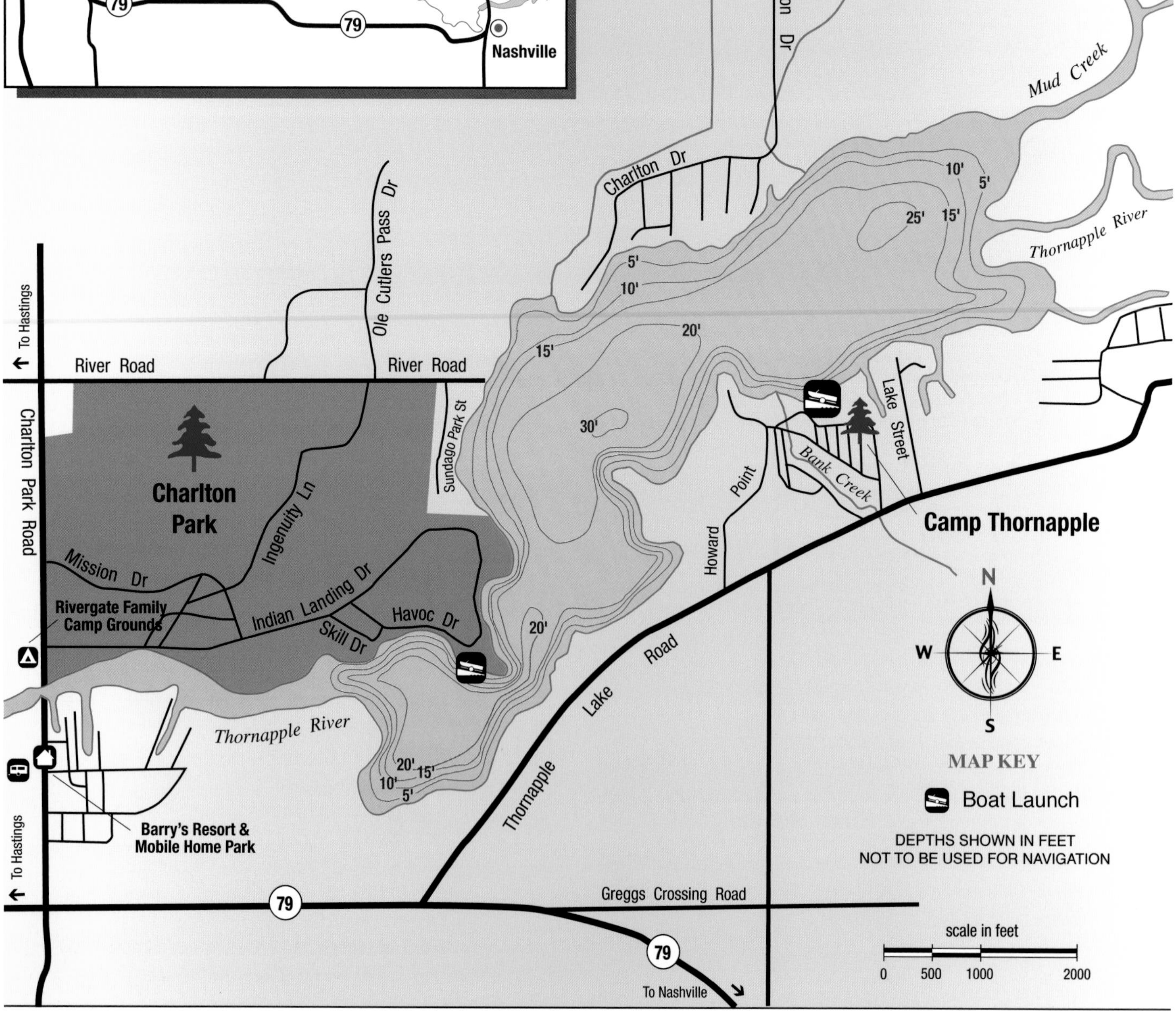

Charlton Dr

Mud Creek

Charlton Dr

10'

5'

25' 15'

Thornapple River

Ole Cutlers Pass Dr

5'

10'

20'

River Road

River Road

To Hastings

15'

Sundago Park St

30'

Charlton Park Road

Charlton Park

Ingenuity Ln

Lake Street

Point

Howard

Bank Creek

Camp Thornapple

Mission Dr

Indian Landing Dr

Skill Dr

Havoc Dr

20'

N

Rivergate Family Camp Grounds

20'

Thornapple Lake Road

W E

Thornapple River

20' 15'

10'

5'

S

To Hastings

Barry's Resort & Mobile Home Park

MAP KEY

Boat Launch

DEPTHS SHOWN IN FEET
NOT TO BE USED FOR NAVIGATION

79

Greggs Crossing Road

scale in feet

79

0 500 1000 2000

To Nashville

"You need to have a river mentality on this lake, that is, a need to understand current lines, depth contours, and basically how a river works," says Walker. "Know the weed lines and how they relate to each other with the bottom contours. With a stronger current, the larger fish will hang back in an eddy and wait for food to pass by, so you need to fish the edges of the deep side of a weed line, not necessarily the deep water."

Another issue, according to Walker, is that this "lake fluctuates after a rainfall, meaning it will rise a week or so after a heavy upstream rain, and then it takes about three weeks to get back to normal. The lake can either shut down after a storm or turn on," he says.

Steve mentions that, "for those of you who know how to fish the Grand River, you can fish Thornapple."

Muskie:
Thornapple Lake is home of the current state-record muskie, weighing in at 49 pound, 12 ounces. That giant fish was taken in 2002. It's not unrealistic, however, to think that a new state record is swimming in Thornapple's murky depths today. The water in Thornapple is somewhat turbid but loaded with nutrients, providing this natural habitat for trophy-size muskie.

Muskies will attack and consume nearly any living animal, including small rodents, waterfowl and muskrats, according to state fish biologists. They have been known to take ducks, but they don't tend to go after pets or humans.

Big fish mean big baits and anglers routinely employ oversized spinners, body baits and plugs when targeting Thornapple muskies.

Hotspots are at the inflow of the Thornapple River near Charleston Park and off of High Bank Creek. The west end of the lake tends to have more breaklines and distinct weedlines, while the shallows throughout the lake contain submerged vegetation. Thornapple receives over 1,000 fingerling muskies on a regular basis, which helps explain why the fishing is so good.

Thornapple is one of the two muskie broodstock lakes, along with Hudson Lake in Lenawee County. They provide the eggs and sperm that create the 20,000 to 30,000 12-inch fish that will be planted in muskie lakes all over the state.

Some anglers tend to think that too many muskie in a lake can destroy other fishing opportunities, but biologists try to stock these predators at a lower rate than once was the case.

Stocking now takes place at somewhere between one to five fish per acre, and waters where other prey are available like suckers or gizzard shad are chosen to minimize eating other favorite game fish.

DNR has planted almost 6,000 muskie in Thornapple Lake since 2008, ranging in size from 7-11 inches, and a few larger.

Walleye:
DNR planted almost 90,000 walleye in the early 2000s. Anglers often work 1/4-ounce. Hot 'N Tots in chartreuse with white bottom color, but other similar colors may work well at times. As for walleye, Walker says "Thornapple is an excellent fishery." In the winter, anglers work the north shore line along Sundago Park Street, and east of Charlton Park. There is a pronounced drop off from 14 to 25 feet and a gravel bed. The two points by the public access, off Thornapple Lake Road, are also good areas for winter walleye. The average sized 'eye in this lake is in the 18-24-inch range according to Walker. In summer the south basin where it narrows by Charlton Park is good for trolling. There is a contour by the beach area. Also try the north end which has a sand bar and weed bed where the two rivers enter Thornapple Lake.

Crappie:
Thornapple Lake produces some nice crappie, averaging 9-11 inches. Popular lures include a size-9 jig or a Jig-N-Minnow. When you find a school of crappie, float over them, or use the 10-20-foot depth contours with weed growth and look for fish in these areas.

Bluegills:
Bluegills are known to hang out in this lake and are popular, especially during the winter.

For panfish, Steve says to move diagonally northeast from Charlton Park across the lake to where there is a bowl-shaped area along the east shoreline. This area is good for crappie and bluegills. The crappie are nice size in this lake averaging 7-11 inches. There are tons of bluegills and lots of perch in this lake, but most are on the smaller size since the pike and muskie do not let them age to a respectable size.

Bass:
Walker says that smallmouth bass can be found all around the edges of the lake where there are trees and brush. The smallies are nice size in this lake, he says.

Thornapple Lake produces some monster muskie.

DNR Photo, David Kenyon

At a Glance

What: Muskie, walleye, and bass

Regs: No pike fishing since this is a State DNR breeding lake for pike

Landings: There is a DNR ramp located off Thornapple Lake Road with a good ramp and parking for about 15 vehicles. There is a DNR boat launch on the southeast side of the lake

Information: Hastings Area Chamber of Commerce, (269) 945-2454; www.mibarry.com; **Barry County Chamber of Commerce and Barry County Economic Development Alliance,** 221 W. State St., Hastings, 49058, (269) 945-2454

Bait & Tackle: Bob's Gun & Tackle, 2208 W. M-43 Hwy, Hastings, 49058, (269) 945-4106; **Al & Pete's Sport Shop,** 111 S. Jefferson St., Hastings, 49058, (269) 945-4417

Union Lake Oakland County

Union Lake is only one of a myriad of lakes in a highly populated section of Oakland County, near the city of White Lake.

Union Lake is a good winter fishery for perch and crappies, and is famous for producing big catches of bluegills, walleye and bass. Its big crappies, upwards of 15 inches, are often overlooked.

Oakland County's 465-acre Union Lake is deep, with one hole topping 100 feet, but it also has several humps that rise inside 10 feet of the surface.

Panfish: Perch, bluegills, and crappie are sizeable and abundant in Union Lake; in fact Ken Neeley, a tournament angler and owner of KD Outdoors (Bait & Tackle) on Highland Road in Waterford, says that Union Lake is one of the better perch lakes in the area.

As for ice fishing, Ken would focus on the bay off the public landing at the west end of the lake. The drop-off edge of the bay is about 40 feet deep, and the fish are commonly found between the 10-20-foot depths. Barnsberry Road at the south end of lake has a peninsula that juts out from shore, almost at the central area of the south end. This is a good area also to seek out panfish. The other bay at the southwest end of the lake, all around the shoreline in the 5-20-foot depths, is good for panfish. Perch in the 12-inch range (plus), and crappie in the 12-15-inch size, along with 8-10-inch bluegills are not uncommon in this lake.

For this little angler and his dad, the fish may just have well been a 10-pound walleye based on his bright smile.

DNR Photo, David Kenyon

At a Glance

What: Nice-sized panfish, pike, walleye and both large- and smallmouth bass

Where: Covering much of the west and east end of the lake

Why: Panfish are sizable in this lake, and perch fishing tops many Oakland County lakes

Information/Guides: Ken Neeley, KD Outdoors, (248) 366-4093

Landings: Northwest side of the lake off Union Road

Bait & Tackle: KD Outdoors, 7688 Highland Rd, Waterford, 48327, (248) 666-7799, www.k-d-outdoors.net; **Six Lakes Party Store,** 9266 Cooley Lake Rd, White Lake, 48386 (248) 366-4093

In the spring/summer, these same areas can be productive for panfish.

Minnows are always a good bet when it comes to jumbo crappies or perch, but you can interest a school of most any panfish by using teardrops and ice flies baited with waxworms.

Walleye: Winter walleye can be found along the north end of the lake, around both the sunken island at the west side and the one more toward the east/central end of the lake. The one on the east end comes up to about five feet and then drops off to about 50 feet in depth. The other good walleye area during the ice fishing season is the flat zone at the east end or east bay area.

The average size walleye in Union Lake is around 18-20 inches, with many in the lower to mid 20-inch size.

During the warmer months, the sunken island and flats area at the east end, as well as all along the north shore, are productive for walleye. Anglers troll or drift over the drop-off area using jigs and minnows early in the year, and as the season moves to mid and late summer anglers switch to body baits using side planers. Try using a crawler harness at night along the flats in the east end of the lake. Look for late-fall green weed lines along the shoreline and work those areas.

DNR walleye plants in this lake were over 250,000 fingerlings in the early 2000s, but in 2011 they planted almost 100,000 walleye fingerlings, making them ready for the fry pan within a couple of years or less.

Pike: Pike are caught in Union Lake using both spear and tip-ups during the ice-fishing season. The same areas you find panfish, however, inside the 5-foot depths, are worthwhile exploring. "The key," according to Neeley, is to find the greenest weed beds in the lake, in both west bays." You can easily take home pike in the 20-30-inch length, however Neeley says there are a lot of legal size fish here, not the hammer-handle size. You can also expect to see some in the 30-plus-inch size.

Bass: Both smallmouth and largemouth bass are present in this lake, although largemouth are more prolific. In fact, Neeley states that Union Lake is one of the better bass lakes in Oakland County, and as a tournament angler he should know. He regularly catches largemouth upwards of five pounds, and smallies in the 3-3.5-pound size.

Fish the northeast shoreline where the long underwater points meet, as well as in the 10-foot flats at the east end, and in the bay near the west-end boat landing. At the landing, there are some 25-30-foot areas that can be productive for smallmouth.

The bass also spawn on the east-end flats and the northwest side of the lake.

Largemouth can be found in the same areas as the smallmouth, plus try the southwest bay, where there is a 65-foot hole. Fish in and around this deep hole.

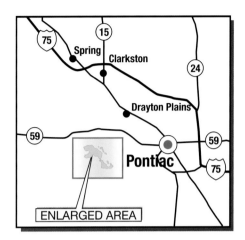

Union Lake

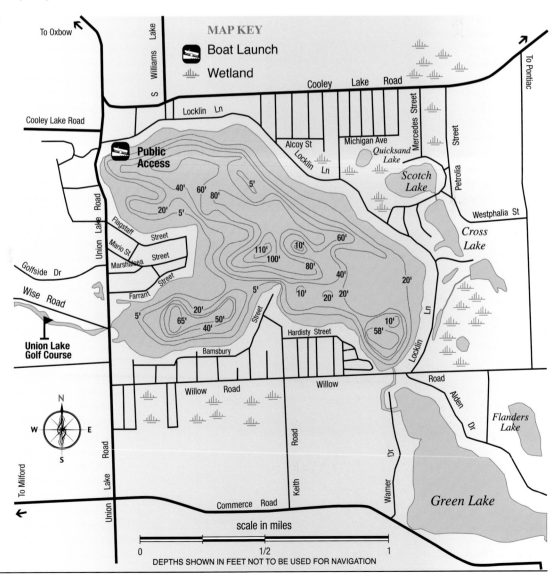

MICHIGAN

Keweenaw
(Isle Royale)

LAKE
SUPERIOR

Keweenaw

Houghton

Ontonagon

Baraga

Gogebic

Marquette

Iron

Alger

Luce

Chippewa

Schoolcraft

Dickinson

Delta

Mackinac

Menominee

LAKE
HURON

LAKE

MICHIGAN

Emmet

Cheboygan

Presque
Isle

Charlevoix

Montmorency

Alpena

Leelanau

Antrim

Otsego

Grand
Benzie Traverse

Kalkaska

Oscoda

Alcona

Crawford

Missaukee

Ogemaw

Iosco

Manistee Wexford

Roscommon

Mason Lake

Osceola Clare

Gladwin

Arenac

Huron

Newaygo

Isabella

Oceana

Mecosta

Midland

Bay

Tuscola

Sanilac

Montcalm

Saginaw

Muskegon

Gratiot

Lapeer

Saint
Clair

Kent

Genesee

Ottawa

Ionia

Clinton

Shiawassee

Macomb

Allegan

Barry

Eaton

Ingham

Livingston

Oakland

Van
Buren

Kalamazoo

Calhoun

Jackson

Washtenaw

Wayne

LAKE

Berrien Cass

Saint
Joseph

Branch

Hillsdale

Lenawee

Monroe

ERIE

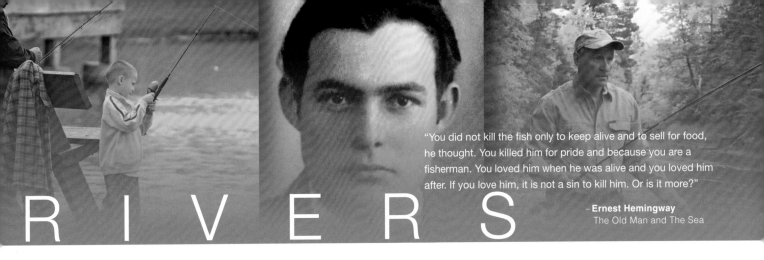

"You did not kill the fish only to keep alive and to sell for food, he thought. You killed him for pride and because you are a fisherman. You loved him when he was alive and you loved him after. If you love him, it is not a sin to kill him. Or is it more?"

– **Ernest Hemingway**
The Old Man and The Sea

RIVERS

Au Sable River (A Blue-Ribbon Trout Water)
Iosco County

Back in 1959 a group of 16 men gathered in a cottage along the Au Sable River and eventually formed what is today known as the highly regarded Trout Unlimited. The site was chosen along an area of the river worthy of this distinction. The Au Sable River, with its stable water-flow and excellent water temperatures, make it some of the premier trout water in the country, and that says a lot being situated in a state that has so many excellent trout waters.

The Au Sable has a stretch of water that is aptly named, "Holy Waters," consisting of almost 9 miles of year-round catch-and-release fly-fishing only, running from Burton's Landing to Wakeley Bridge. However the term "Holy Waters" can also be used for the entire stretch of the Au Sable as far as

Classified as a Type 7 trout stream, where the regulations are no-kill, catch and release only, and artificial flies only, anglers from all over the world come to fly-fish its fabulous populations of trout.

There are numerous fly hatches on the Au Sable, adding to the allure for anglers. Hatches occur as soon as the spring days begin to warm, usually in late March and early April.

Early on in the season, the black stoneflies emerge, followed by the popular Hendricksons and the larger mayflies, often signaling the start of the fly-fishing season. Then, in rapid succession, little black caddis and mahogany and sulphur mayflies add to the feeding frenzy.

June and July bring hatches of large and plentiful bugs—brown drakes, *Isonychia* (white-gloved howdies), the giant Michigan mayfly (*Hexagenia limbata*) as well as tiny but prolific *Tricos*.

August through October brings on the terrestrial insects, including grasshoppers, inchworms and beetles along with a variety of species of small mayflies known collectively as "blue-winged olives."

There is no doubt that the Au Sable River has one of the most prolific and diverse insect communities of most any Michigan river.

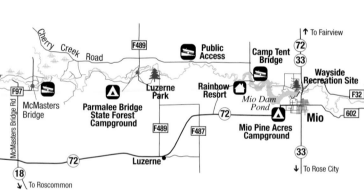

1. Burton's Landing
2. Louie's Landing
3. Keystone Landing
4. Thendara Road
5. Gates Au Sable Lodge

I am concerned; or maybe Sacred Waters would be more appropriate for the remaining stretch.

The name Holy Waters was coined in the early 1970s by the late Cal Gates, owner of Gates' Au Sable Lodge, a fly-fishing mecca located on the south bank of the famed stream.

What is covered is only a quick sampling of fishing on this magnificent river. Books have been written describing the nature of this river and all it has to offer.

The Au Sable winds through gently rolling wooded landscape, spotted with few homes along the way, from its headwaters north of Fredrick eventually emptying into Lake Huron to the east.

On the Au Sable, one can expect a healthy dose of small to medium-sized rainbows, browns, and brook trout, with the chance of landing a nice sized brown. As an added bonus, there is an influx of steelhead from Lake Huron that draws large numbers of anglers.

The section of the Au Sable River known as "The Holy Water" supports an excellent self-sustaining population of brown trout. Its cold clear waters, combined with its stable flows and stream depths, provides the kind of habitat that allows trout to thrive. In fact, this river system is unique among all rivers in the United States in that it has the most stable flow of any stream in the country.

Steve Sendek, very knowledgeable DNR Fishery Biologist who works out of the Grayling District Office, states that, "the trout population within the Au Sable Holy Waters is certainly one of the best, if not the best, in the state." He further states, "this river boasts an incredible population of brown trout, brookies, and a small resident population of rainbows.

"Few trout streams anywhere have been studied as extensively as the Au Sable," he says. The DNR maintains detailed data sets on the Holy Water, which indicates how truly unique a habitat it is.

A few key locations that Sendek says are favorable for fishing are listed below. Additions were also made from Trout Source (troutsource.com):

Keystone: The wide water here makes it easier to keep flies from snagging brush as well as helping to not spook fish. Wading is relatively easy downstream on the solid-bottom half-mile or more, then walk back on the public land along the south shore. Take M-72 to Keystone, north to the river.

Guide's Rest: This stretch is owned by Trout Unlimited and is publicly accessible a mile or so on both sides of the river. You can begin at the north parking area and work your way down to the south parking area. Walk back on the road that connects the two.

Mc Master's Bridge to Mio Pond: The confluences of the North Branch just below McMaster's and Big Creek below Parmalee Bridge add jolts of fresh, cold water to the Au Sable, helping form a 200-foot-wide trout river to be reckoned with. Here the river again picks up its gradient and gravel bottom while retaining the prolific *Hex* hatches. The river is big, with lunker browns ranging from 20-26" to match. Access is somewhat limited, but the river can be waded in summertime. However, many prefer to float this 16-mile section of the river using craft ranging from float tubes to the flat-bottomed Au Sable River boats.

Headwaters (Fredrick to Grayling): The headwaters of the Au Sable, just north of Fredrick, marks the beginning of a nearly 80-mile stretch of blue-ribbon trout water. These waters are classic American freestone in nature, clear and gravel-bottomed, dominated by brookies with the occasional brown. Pressure along this 13-mile stretch from Fredrick down to Grayling is minimal thanks to other local freestone attractions and limited access. At Grayling, the river bends eastward towards its Lake Huron descent. Just below, the East Branch injects a welcome shot of cold water. Unfortunately, both sun-wilted humans and trout alike revel in fresh, cold river water making the fabled fishing town of Grayling a haven for canoeists and water fanatics. Luckily, the trout have grown accustomed to the ruckus and success can be easily achieved in this area.

Holy Waters (Grayling to Wakeley Bridge): Burton's Landing, several miles downstream from Grayling, marks the beginning of what Michiganders consider the Au Sable's Holy Waters. This 9-mile stretch from Burton's Landing down to Wakeley Bridge is regulated by year-round fly-fishing-only and catch-and-release. Both North Down River Road and South Down River Road straddle the river along this stretch. From the north, the best access point is the Whirlpool Road turnoff. From the south, access points are Burton's Landing, Louie's

Landing, Keystone Landing, and Thendara Road. This stretch is crossed at mid-point by Stephan's Bridge Road which provides excellent access, coupled by a full-service Orvis fly-shop at Gates Au Sable Lodge. Access below the bridge is limited, so a float trip might be the best way to comb the waters properly. Habitat in the Holy Waters is feestone in nature and the fishing is excellent. Gradient is medium with a rocky bottom creating an ideal habitat for the Hendricksons, Olives, Caddis, and Tricos which hatch consistently between early May through October. Fishing pressure is relatively high so you will be faced by a breed of trout not easily fooled.

Knight Tract: There are some very nice trout that exist in this stretch, and you can work your way down to Wakeley Bridge, approximately a day's worth of fishing. Then walk back on the road. M-72 to Wakeley Bridge Road, north over the river.

Both North Down River Road and South Down River Road straddle the river along this stretch. From the north, the best access point is the Whirlpool Road turnoff. From the south, access points are Burton's Landing, Louie's Landing, Keystone Landing, and Thendara Road. This stretch is crossed at mid-point by Stephan's Bridge Road which provides good access.

At a Glance

What: Fishing the Holy Waters on the famed Au Sable River

Where: Starting several miles downstream from Grayling, a nine-mile stretch from Burton's Landing to Wakeley Bridge.

Why: One of the prized trout fishing rivers in the country.

How: Night fishing is the best time to catch big trout, but be careful in the dark whether floating or wading. It is highly advised to scout the territory in daylight to become familiar with your surroundings.

Regs: No kill zone, catch and release only.

Techniques: Anglers don't need an especially long fly rod, a 7 ½- to 8-foot will do, with 35-weight fly line. Sometimes, a 10-foot leader and thin tippet is needed to fool these selective trout. Matching the hatch is about the only way to fool Au Sable wild trout.

Access: Varies considerably; sites listed in body of article.

Bait & Tackle/Information: Old Au Sable Fly Shop, 200 Ingham St., Grayling, 49738, (989) 348-3330, www.oldausable.com; **Skips Sport Shop,** 5765 M-72 West Grayling, 49738, (989) 348-7111, www.skipssportshop.com; **Gates Au Sable Lodge,** Grayling, 49738, (989) 348-8462, www.gateslodge.com

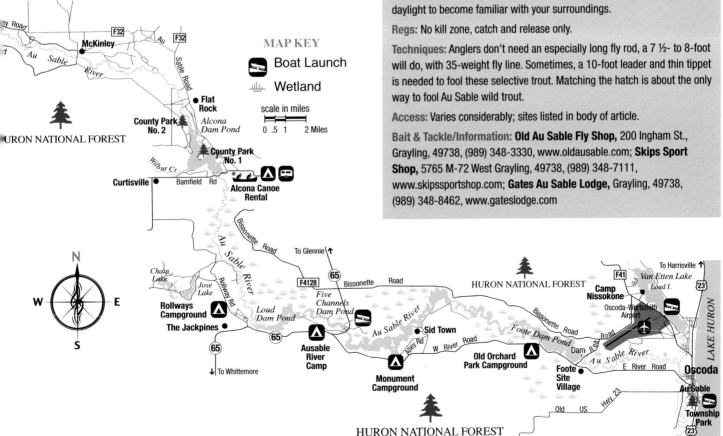

Betsie River Benzie County

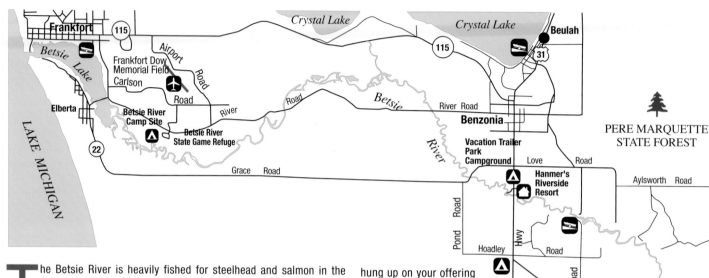

The Betsie River is heavily fished for steelhead and salmon in the spring and fall. It is a tributary to Lake Michigan, and also has a very good population of resident trout. Hatches can be prolific providing exciting dry-fly fishing. The river averages 40-50 feet wide in most areas and is one of the most scenic in the state.

The Betsie is best known for its migratory fisheries, specifically for chinook salmon and steelhead. Some migratory brown trout and coho salmon are also caught. Chinook and coho are not stocked in the Betsie system, rather the runs are comprised primarily of wild fish, or strays from other rivers.

The resident trout populations of the Betsie River will never rival those of other nearby rivers such as the Platte or Little Manistee, but nonetheless offers some great fishing opportunities. Salmon survival and growth in the Betsie will continue to be limited by high summer temperatures, particularly in low-flow years.

River guide Brent Borcherdt has fished the Betsie and other area rivers long enough to almost know the resident fish by name. He fishes downstream toward County Line, to M-115, then to the dam for browns and steelhead. His expertise is outlined season by season below.

Seasonally, let's start with spring and move through the winter months and show the changes in fishing opportunities.

Spring:
When steelhead fishing, M-115 to Fred's Landing (about three miles east of Beulah and marked) is a good start, allowing for about 5-6 miles of easily fishable waters without a boat. You can enter the river at the M-115 bridge as well. The river here has good gravel, deep pools, and easy to wade. It's ideal for steelies because between each pool is a gravel bed. Brent says that this stretch is "very user friendly." Trout Unlimited and the DNR worked hard on the Betsie to improve it for browns, and it is slowly making a comeback.

As for bait, Borchert says the basic steelhead stuff works well, along with caddis flies, pheasant tails, nymphs, and egg flies in a variety of colors. When steelhead are in the river, they do not act like the resident brown trout in that they are not as particular in the offering. The native brown trout will "look at a size 6 hook and want a size 5," so to speak. But steelies are from Lake Michigan and are not as interested in lure choice, but rather proper drift and line size; for example using a six-pound Maxima, or if the water is gin clear, a fluorocarbon line. This is much more important, so don't get hung up on your offering for steelhead.

Another popular site for spring steelheaders is the old Homestead Dam location near Benzonia. The river averages 100 feet wide or more here and features excellent gravel bars, deep pools and runs from the dam to US-31. Anglers can gain access to the river at the dam, US-31, River Road and Grace Road. The Betsie River is popular with drift boaters who use deep-diving crankbaits in hot colors to provoke spawning rainbows into striking. For those who prefer to wade, you may wish to rely on yarn, flies, spawn and flashy spinners. Rainbows approaching 20 pounds are not unheard of on the Betsie.

Summer:
Trout fishing takes place a bit further upstream from the spring outing. Move up around the County Line Road area and fish upstream.

Fall:
In September the salmon show up. The lower Betsie gets its first push of fish in mid August and fishing action takes place from Grace Road to Upper and Lower River roads, west of Beulah. Kings and cohos pool-up before spawning and stage in these areas. They will readily jump on streamers and crankbaits, along with regular flies floated through their holes. This action runs through the fall. In October, the fishing action moves up to Fred's Landing and Homestead Dam, where they move on the gravel. Steelhead arrive in October and November into these same stretches of water.

Winter:
Steelhead will look for natural, smaller eggs so try the bigger nymph patterns. The steelies will have seen lots of eggs by now, and become picky on egg patterns, so the nymphs offer something a bit different, such as the stonefly patterns.

The Betsie is a diverse river, with plenty of good access. You don't need a boat to get to good water to fish for salmon and steelhead.

Note: The upper section of the Betsie, above where the Little Betsie empties in, is a small river plagued with fallen trees, shallow runs, quiet pools, and some very nice trout. This upper area, from Green Lake to where Grass Lake Creek flows in, is not known for being a very productive stretch of trout water. It only averages around 30 feet across with a sand and gravel bottom. Although trout populations are still good, they are better below Grass Lake Creek where the Betsie picks up some volume, cooler waters, and has deeper pools.

Platte River: For those of you who are reading the information on the Betsie, here is a quick rundown on neighboring Platte River. The Platte, from an historical standpoint, was Michigan's first river to receive salmon plantings in the later 1960's. It has enormous runs of coho in the fall. The river is relatively shallow and you have very good sight-fishing. Areas to consider would be Goose Road, and any road leading out of Honor where there are bridges over the river. The water is all productive, super shallow, and gin clear. Use the same bait as the Betsie for fall fishing.

Betsie River

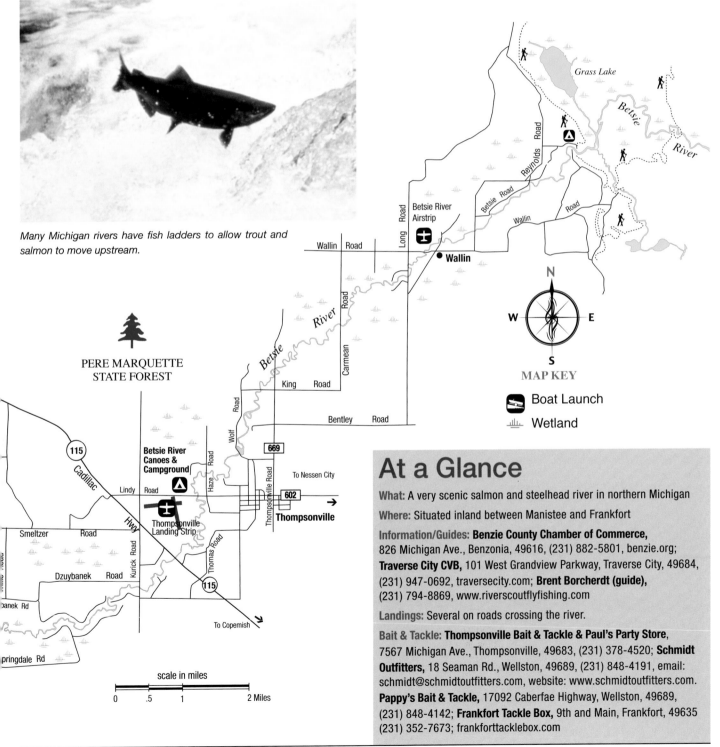

Many Michigan rivers have fish ladders to allow trout and salmon to move upstream.

MAP KEY

Boat Launch

Wetland

At a Glance

What: A very scenic salmon and steelhead river in northern Michigan

Where: Situated inland between Manistee and Frankfort

Information/Guides: Benzie County Chamber of Commerce, 826 Michigan Ave., Benzonia, 49616, (231) 882-5801, benzie.org; **Traverse City CVB,** 101 West Grandview Parkway, Traverse City, 49684, (231) 947-0692, traversecity.com; **Brent Borcherdt (guide),** (231) 794-8869, www.riverscoutflyfishing.com

Landings: Several on roads crossing the river.

Bait & Tackle: Thompsonville Bait & Tackle & Paul's Party Store, 7567 Michigan Ave., Thompsonville, 49683, (231) 378-4520; **Schmidt Outfitters,** 18 Seaman Rd., Wellston, 49689, (231) 848-4191, email: schmidt@schmidtoutfitters.com, website: www.schmidtoutfitters.com. **Pappy's Bait & Tackle,** 17092 Caberfae Highway, Wellston, 49689, (231) 848-4142; **Frankfort Tackle Box,** 9th and Main, Frankfort, 49635 (231) 352-7673; frankforttacklebox.com

Big Manistee River (Part 1)
Manistee County

Whether you fish for trout or salmon on this fabulous river, the action will often be productive.

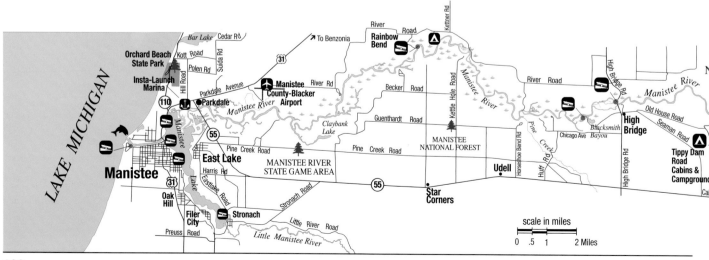

The Big Manistee River runs approximately 232 miles through Michigan's northern lower peninsula, through the villages of Sharon, Smithville, Mesick, Wellston and enters Lake Michigan at Manistee. It is considered to be one of the best trout fisheries east of the Rockies. The river rises in the sand hills in southeastern Antrim County. These deep glacial sands provide it with a remarkably stable flow of clean cold water all year, making it a popular river for fishing.

Known as the "Big Manistee," because of its neighbor the Little Manistee, the Manistee is one of the most diverse fisheries in the country. With plants of 55,000 Michigan steelhead and another 34,000 summer-run steelhead each year — and improved natural reproduction — it may have a bigger stock of steelhead than any river in the country.

Every year anglers come to fish for the thousands of steelhead and salmon that enter its lower reaches. The water is big and, in some areas, tough to wade. A drift boat will certainly help to cover the water. The river below Tippy Dam flows aggressively towards Lake Michigan over a sand and rocky bottom. Plenty of fallen logs, deep pools, and swift runs, all help to create classic holding water for steelhead and salmon. Bear Creek is a feeder to the Manistee that is found on the north side of the river. This creek is also an excellent fishery for steelhead and can be found along River Road near where it enters the Manistee or off of Coates Highway to the north.

Mike Marsh is a river guide in this area of the state, and quite familiar with this popular trout stream. He fishes and guides both the upper and lower part of the river, and outlines seasonal fishing opportunities below.

Big Manistee River

Map continued on page 130

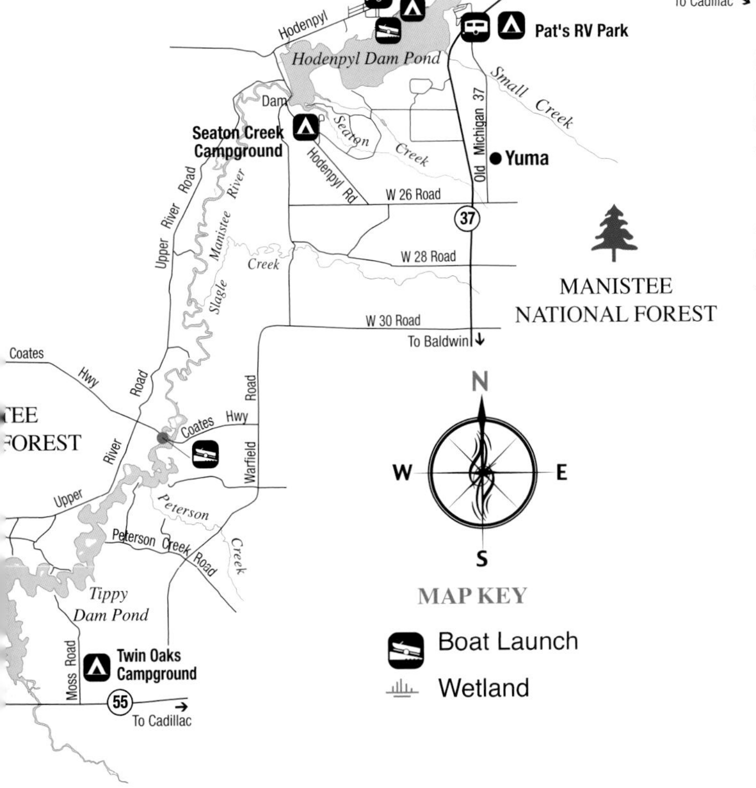

From Tippy Dam downstream to Lake Michigan the Manistee River is nationally known as a migratory-fish angling hot spot. Both the spring and fall runs of steelhead surpass most rivers in the nation. Fly-fishing anglers from around the world visit the gravel bars near the dam and the national forest woodlands on either side of the river further downstream.

During those springs when the snow suddenly melts and the river goes sky-high, steelhead blast upstream until they run into Tippy Dam. Other years, they might just trickle up, thus providing steady action for anglers farther downstream.

In fall, the entire river below Tippy Dam will explode with salmon, lake-run browns, coho, kings, resident browns, and steelhead. Marsh states that all access points along the river are good bets to land any of these fish. The river is not complicated, being fairly large like the Muskegon, making it popular with amateur and more experienced anglers alike.

Thundersticks and spinners are common offerings by anglers in the fall, with flies being used the rest of the season. Streamers and nymphs will produce at almost any time. Steelhead and salmon can be caught on the usual Great Lake fly patterns, such as egg flies, Woolly Buggers, wet flies, and nymphs.

In the winter months, steelhead are king. The entire river system contains these fighters. Some anglers pull Hot N Tots from drift boats, others use streamers, bottom-bouncers, or Thundersticks. The early spring season is very similar to the winter fishing.

Continued on page 130

Big Manistee River (Part 2)
Manistee County

Continued from page 129

In the summer months, there are plenty of rainbows, small browns, and salmon smolts, which are a young salmon about two years old in the stage of development that assumes the silvery color of the adult and is ready to migrate. Walleye are also available in Tippy Lake.

Doug Samsal is another guide who has fished the Manistee below Tippy Dam for close to 30 years and has seen changes in the river that many current guides have not. Doug states that the Manistee's principal change is the clarity. It use to be "greenish" looking many years ago and it used to rage up and down, where now, it is clear and stable and often you can see the bottom in deeper holes. As for the fishing itself, without a doubt, in the past there were more fish, and they were bigger. You used to see 30-plus-pound kings in September, but is it still great fishing? Doug says definitely yes! Certain areas of the river you could see the water "boiling" with fish in the spring. "There are definitely more people

on the river today, and that can be good and not so good," he says. The good is that people are fishing. The not so good is the river is very busy during certain times of the year. "We still have some very good years, and we seem to be on the upswing in some areas," says Doug.

Now we are also finding more people casting crank baits for kings, but the kings don't seem to chase these lures as much. So we resort back to our "old" methods such as traditional spawn on a bobber, or wiggling a plug in a hole. This stuff does not work on the gravel, normally the kings would chase plugs, but now we had to move back to the tried-and-true methods. "You have to be flexible," he says. It will be interesting to see this upcoming year and beyond if the kings chase the crank baits.

Overall however, if you're looking for an excellent Lake Michigan tributary for exciting steelhead, salmon or for a great trout fishery, consider the Manistee River.

Bass: As a side note, in addition to the superb fly-fishing for trout and salmon, the Manistee is also ranked Michigan's third-best smallmouth bass river. In July and August when the water temps put the trout off, fishing for wild smallmouth bass heats up. The Manistee produces many 2- to 4-pound. bass as you float the river and cast streamers and "pop the top" with all kinds of top-water flies and poppers. A six-weight fly rod is the ticket.

Fly-fishing on the Manistee for trout, salmon and other fish species is a popular activity.

Map continued from page 129

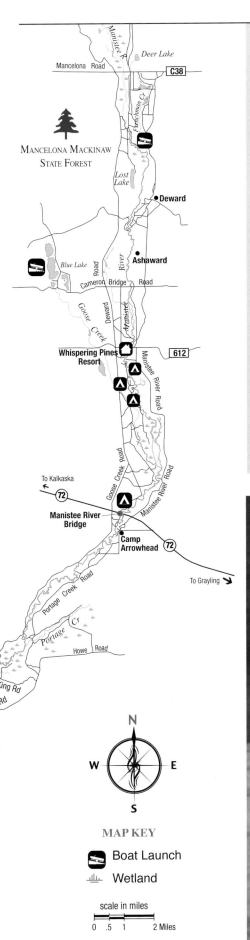

At a Glance

What: Great salmon and steelhead fishing

Where: Along much of the Manistee River

Special Regulations: There is an area for artificial flies only, located from M-72 downstream to CCC Bridge. This is a productive stretch of river that has a lot of good holding water and some trophy fish as well. The special regulations put upon this stretch have helped to preserve this great resource

Information/Guides: **Mike Marsh, Marsh Ridge River Guide Service,** (231) 920-7527, www.marshguide.com. Also check out **Evolution Sportfishing Charters,** 16896 Timberdunes, Grand Haven, (231) 920-7527; **Doug Samsal,** www.manisteerivercharter.com, (231) 668-2894; Manistee Visitors Bureau, 310 1st Street, Manistee, 49660, (231) 398-9355; www.visitmanisteecounty.com

Landings: Good access to the Big Manistee can be found at Insta-Launch Campground in Manistee, Bridge Street, Rainbow Bend, Bear Creek, High Bridge and Tippy Dam. Bank-fishing is pretty much restricted to the area around Tippy Dam. The river is best fished from a boat

As a note for those of you moving to the upper part of the river, above Tippy Dam, access to this section can be found near M-38 (Mancelona Road) and is best fished with a light fly rod (2-4 weight). Below Mancelona Road you will find access in the town of Deward off of Fayette Road, County Road 612 Bridge, the CCC Bridge, and Sharon Bridge. There are also plenty of other areas to access the upper river

Bait & Tackle: **Schmidt Outfitters,** 18 Seaman Rd., Wellston, 49689, (231) 848-4191, email: schmidt@ schmidtoutfitters.com, www.schmidtoutfitters.com; **Pappy's Bait & Tackle,** 17092 Caberfae Highway, Wellston, 49689, (231) 848-4142; **Frankfort Tackle Box,** 9th and Main, Frankfort, 49635, (231) 352-7673; frankforttacklebox.com

MAP KEY

Boat Launch

Wetland

scale in miles

0   .5   1   2 Miles

When the hatch is on, the Manistee is the place to be for great trout fishing.

Carp River Marquette County

The Carp River makes a noisy, tumultuous journey through Marquette County on its way to Lake Superior. The final 5 miles of the river from Carp Lake to Lake Superior drops over 600 feet and there are long stretches of rapids, white water, and many small falls. At Carp River Falls the river drops over 30 feet while taking a sharp curve.

Carp River is a 22-mile-long river formed from the outflow of Deer Lake in Ishpeming Township north of Ishpeming.

The Carp is one of the best-kept secrets in the Upper Peninsula. Clear, cold waters rampaging over granite rock and boulders with a gravel bottom offering the angler a variety of fish all the way up to Carp River Falls about 5 miles upstream. From the river mouth in the Marquette Lower Harbor local anglers give moderate pressure to this river but nothing like a downstate quality stream. Fly-fishing and/or spin casting, generally with spawn, is the ticket here. Easy parking and lodging almost next door make the Carp an excellent destination river.

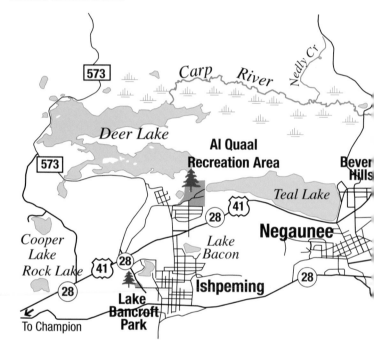

Eric Miltz Miller not only fishes the Carp, but as of this writing, performs research on it as a student at Northern Michigan University and therefore is very familiar with this river, as well as many of the rivers around Marquette where he lives.

Spring: Miltz Miller says that in the spring there is a phenomenal run of steelhead in this easily accessible river. You can park on either side of Highway 41, a short drive east of Marquette near the mouth of Lake Superior, and work the river upstream for about 2-2/12 miles. If you have a buddy with another car you can work up to the next road south toward the ski hill and then drive back to your other parked car. Or you can park at the ski hill and work up toward Morgan Falls. This later section has less pressure, is easier to pick up fish, and the water is faster. Eric says that the fish seem to be more active in this upper section, and it is not uncommon to pick up steelies in the mid 20-inch range, and some larger. There are some deeper pools in the river, but most of the river is wadeable.

Summer: Brookies are in the water all year, and can even be fished in the summer months due to the colder water temperatures. Most ethical anglers will not fish brookies during the summer when it becomes warmer because the fish are more susceptible to dying. If you have fished the Au Sable near Grayling, the Carp is smaller in size as a comparison. Brookies are more abundant as you move up stream according to Miltz Miller, and many are in the respectable 12-15-inch size.

Fishing in a river setting for trout is a great way to relax and take home a tasty meal.

The area of the river that runs up toward Negaunee is slower, and mucky, so you will need a canoe or small boat. But this area also supports a lot of nice-sized brook trout.

Fall: In the fall you will see a few salmon in the river, mostly coho, but also some decent-sized kings, and if you are fortunate you may hook onto a pink salmon that are occasionally found in the river.

Browns are also a bonus fish in this river. Many are in the mid 20-inch range, Eric has seen some upwards of 30 inches. For the browns, use streamers or an egg imitation. You can fish them all season through the winter. The river generally does not freeze totally, especially near the ski hill where the current is swift.

Carp River

MAP KEY

⊥ıllı Wetland

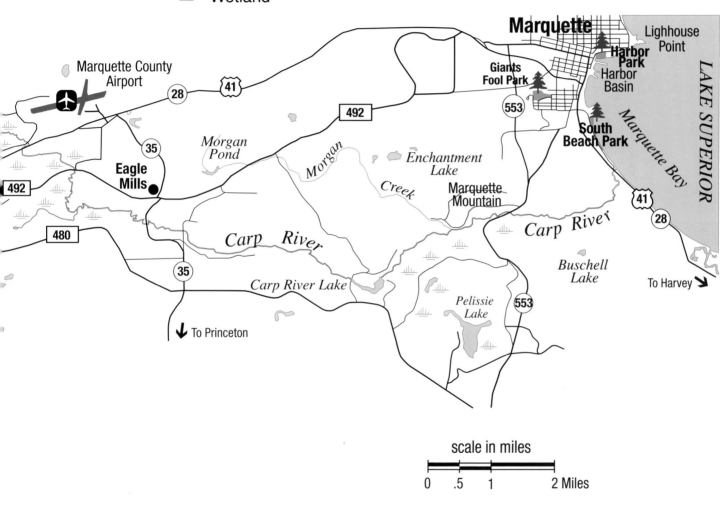

At a Glance

What: Great steelhead and sizable brookies and browns

Where: A small, swift, but wadeable river near Marquette

Why: This is a finesse river that offers plenty of action to both fly and traditional anglers

Information/Guides: Marquette County Convention & Visitors Bureau, 337 West Washington St., Marquette, 49855, (800) 544-4321, or (906) 228-7749, frontdesk@marquettecountry.org

Landings: Easy access off Highway 41

Bait & Tackle: Gwinn Bait & Tackle, 56 N. Billings St, Gwinn, 49841, (906) 346-3330; **Phil's 550 Store**, 52 County Road 550, Marquette, (906) 226-9146; **Gander Mountain,** 3465 U.S. 41, Marquette, 49855, (906) 226-8300

Clinton River Oakland/Macomb Counties

The Clinton River drains approximately 763 square miles of Southeast Michigan into Lake St. Clair. The mainstem is 79 miles long with 260 miles of major tributaries. Most of the watershed is included in Oakland and Macomb counties, a portion in Wayne County, with a very small section that reaches into St. Clair and Lapeer counties.

The Clinton River Spillway is a 2-mile-long canal that connects Clinton River to Lake St. Clair. Located in Macomb County's Harrison and Clinton townships, the spillway is not as frequently fished as the main river, but still contains ample populations of game- and panfish. The Spillway is easily accessible and provides year-round angling opportunities.

Fish Species: The Clinton Spillway is on the Michigan DNR's list of Better Fishing Waters for black crappie, yellow perch and northern pike. It also contains largemouth bass, bluegill, sunfish, channel catfish and the occasional walleye or muskie. The spillway also sees a limited steelhead run in spring and fall, but most of these fish run in the Clinton River proper, which empties into Lake St. Clair located about 4 miles up the shoreline.

Spring and early summer are the best times to fish the spillway for most of the species that reside here. Black crappie fishing peaks a little earlier, spawning in late April or early May. Ice fishing is also popular among local anglers here, and January and February generally offer the safest ice for this activity.

Methods: Jigs, plastic worms and crankbaits take their fair share of bass. Catfish like smelly baits fished near bottom. A live worm on a hook is usually all you need for bluegill and perch, but small jigs will also tempt these panfish. Crappies usually bite small jigs or live minnows fished under a float. Being a man-made canal, the Clinton River Spillway has a largely uniform bottom without a lot of variation. Look for areas with changes in depth, changes in bottom type and vegetation, as all of these things tend to attract fish.

Access Sites/Notes:

Clinton River at Yates Park, Rochester Hills:

Yates Park (located at the intersection of Dequindre Road and Avon Road/22 Mile Road) is probably the most popular fishing spot for steelhead in the Clinton River watershed, and draws a substantial crowd at the dam. Fewer anglers go downstream below the cider mill, where there are literally miles of parkland all the way to Ryan Road. Anglers must enter and fish off the north bank; the south bank is private land owned by the Detroit Sportsmen's Congress. If you are in the river and fishing from the north bank, you are on public land and won't be trespassing.

Clinton River at River Bends Park, Shelby Township:

River Bends Park (entrance at Ryan Road south of 22 Mile Road) is a continuation of Shelby Township's great parkland along the river. The park covers both banks

Whether fishing in a boat, or from the bank, taking kids out fishing is important now more than ever.

DNR Photo, David Kenyon

all the way nearly to Utica, with the interior park roads providing a lot of fishing access. (Check with Shelby Township Parks & Recreation for hours and fees.)

Clinton River at Dodge Park, Sterling Heights:

There is a nice run of spawning pike through Sterling Heights in the spring, so there's a good chance of steelhead in this area as well. Sterling Heights Nature Center on Utica Road east of Van Dyke is a good access point with parking.

The river at Wolcott Mill looks like ideal steelhead water, and there is plenty of access from the Metropark from the Mill Entrance off of Kunstman Road in Ray Township.

Lower River at Shadyside Park, Mt. Clemens:

The lower river is wide and deep, so you'll need a small boat. Shadyside Park has a boat launch ramp.

Main Branch:

The main branch of the Clinton River below Yates Dam in Rochester Hills to Lake St. Clair receives an impressive annual spring run of steelhead (rainbow trout). Yates Park owned by the City of Rochester Hills is a popular destination for local fishermen and provides public parking. Other gamefish of interest that can be caught in this section include walleye, white suckers, bass, pike, and assorted panfish.

The main branch of the Clinton River above Yates Dam provides opportunities for the angler to catch a variety of fish species including brown trout, suckers, and a variety of panfish.

Note: Fish plantings by the DNR have been substantial during the past decade or so. In 2011 and again in 2012 a combined 3,000 (10-inch) browns were planted in March by the MDNR. During the period 2008-2012, 150,000 (7-inch) rainbows were planted. And a combined 300,000 rainbows were planted between 2002 and 2007.

At a Glance

What: A variety of warm water fish, plus a run of steelhead in the spring and fall, with many access sites

When: Spring and fall are the best times to fish this river; summer is a busy boating time

Information: Detroit Metro Convention & Visitors Bureau, 211 W. Fort St., Ste. 1000, Detroit 48226, (313) 202-1800, Visitor Information (800) DETROIT (338-7648), vic@visitdetroit.com

Access/Landings: Shadyside Park in Mt. Clemens is located at the start of the spillway where it connects to the Clinton River. You can launch a boat from the park and there is shore access to both the river and the spillway. Another access point is Tuckers Park in Harrison Township, which features a paved path that runs parallel to the spillway

Bait & Tackle: Selfridge Sport & Tackle, 45200 Jefferson Ave., Chesterfield, 48047, (586) 949-2998; **Lakeside Fishing Shop,** 25110 Jefferson Ave., St Clair Shores, 48081 (586) 777-7003; **Anglers Point Marina Bait Tackle,** 28955 Wm P Rosso (End of Hall Road/M-59), Chesterfield, 48047, (586) 949-9223

Clinton River

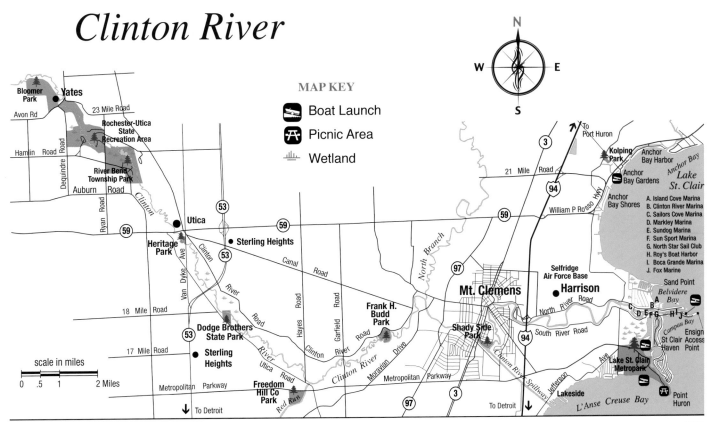

Detroit River Wayne County

Detroit has long been known for Red Wing Hockey, being often referred to as Hockey Town, and rightly so, but more recently it has developed a well-deserved reputation for some of the best walleye fishing in all of Michigan, right on the Detroit River. This 32-mile stretch of river wedged between Detroit and Windsor, Ontario is a premiere fishery for walleye in particular, but perch, bass, and an occasional muskie also call this river home.

Charter Captain Todd Robbins is about as well versed on Detroit River fishing as anyone. He knows when the fish arrive, where they move, the somewhat varied current, and most importantly how to fish for them.

Spring Walleye: Todd says that "in the spring, when the water temperature hits the magical 42-degree temp, usually occurring around the second week in April, the walleye move in to spawn." The fish may not be huge in numbers at this time, but they are definitely increasing daily, making for some very good action. "This is the start of six weeks of great walleye fishing," says Robbins. Then most of the females move back out of the river and the males remain.

Robbins states that the Detroit River is very diverse. The fish first move out of Lake Erie near the warmer waters at the Trenton Edison hot-water discharge situated at the mouth of Lake Erie. Usually this water is around 4-7 degrees warmer, and is like a magnet to walleye. Anglers work the ledges in waters no more than 20 feet deep. "But just because you hear that they are taking walleye here does not mean they are not elsewhere," says Robbins, "because you will start to find walleye throughout the river."

Captain Todd fishes from the tip of Grosse Ile up to Zug Island during this early part of the season. He advises starting shallow in the early morning, then moving out to deeper water as the sun rises and the day warms. Fish generally are everywhere when the water moves up to the 45-degree mark, so don't be tempted to look for a pack of boats. Actually, the fish can be spooked and will move elsewhere, even in 30 feet of water when you have boats packed in a small area.

Vertical jigging is the preferred method and Todd uses a standard one-ounce jig that works well in the 4-6 mph current. If winds blow from the north, the current can easily pick up to 6-8 mph. That's the reason for the heavier jig, to keep it vertical and on the bottom so you can feel the strike.

As for lure color, Todd likes black and white (pearl), but the more natural the color the better. Contrary to popular belief, walleye can see black lure colors even in dirty water. The Wyandotte worm in purple is a "killer" bait and probably the number one color. Smelt are now nonexistent in these waters, so a bait simulating a small lamprey is more appealing to walleye. Green and camo colors also work well for Todd. Also consider jigs with a minnow-shaped head.

Walleye fishing on the Detroit River is as popular as the Detroit Red Wings.

MDNR Photo, David Kenyon

At a Glance

What: Incredible walleye fishing.

Where: All along the 32 miles of the Detroit River

Regs: Keep in mind that there are U.S. (Michigan) regulations and Canadian (Ontario) regulations. Canadian Fishing License website: www.mnr.gov.on.ca/en/Business/OC/2ColumnSubPage/STDPROD_091032.html

Information/Guides: Detroit Convention & Visitors Bureau, 211 West Fort Street, Detroit, 48226, (313) 202-1800; Todd Robbins, (734) 231-7329 cell; www.ready2tackle.com; email: todd@ready2tackle.com

Landings: Trenton has the most popular boat landings, at Metro Park and Elizabeth Park. They are probably less than a mile apart and both are very nice landings. The mid sections of the Detroit River are limited. The Wyandotte boat landing off Jefferson is a good site. Ecorse, off Jefferson, is also a good site to drop your boat in, but it is much smaller than the aforementioned landings. Further north, just south of Zug Island, is a landing at Belanger Park

Landing Detail: Erie Metro Park Boat Ramp, 32481 Jefferson Avenue, Rockwood, 48173, (734) 379-5020; **Elizabeth Park Ramp,** 202 Grosse Ile Parkway, Trenton, 48183, (734) 675-8051; **Wyandotte Ramp,** 711 Jefferson Ave (Biddle), Wyandotte, 48192, (734) 284-6774; **Ecorse Ramp,** 4633 W. Jefferson Avenue, Ecorse, 48229, (313) 216-7770; **Belanger Park Ramp,** Belanger Park Rd, (east of Jefferson), River Rouge; **Delray Ramp,** Jefferson & Ft Wayne, Detroit (just an OK landing); **St. Jean (Reids) Ramp,** St. Jean Street, Detroit (good ramp at the north end of the river)

Bait & Tackle: Bottomline Bait & Tackle, 32660 Jefferson Avenue, Rockwood, 48173, (734) 379-9762; **Riviera Market & Party Store,** 4500 W Jefferson Ave., Trenton, 48183, (734) 676-8405; **The Dip Net Bait Shop,** 4464 Jefferson Avenue, Ecorse, (313) 388-5811

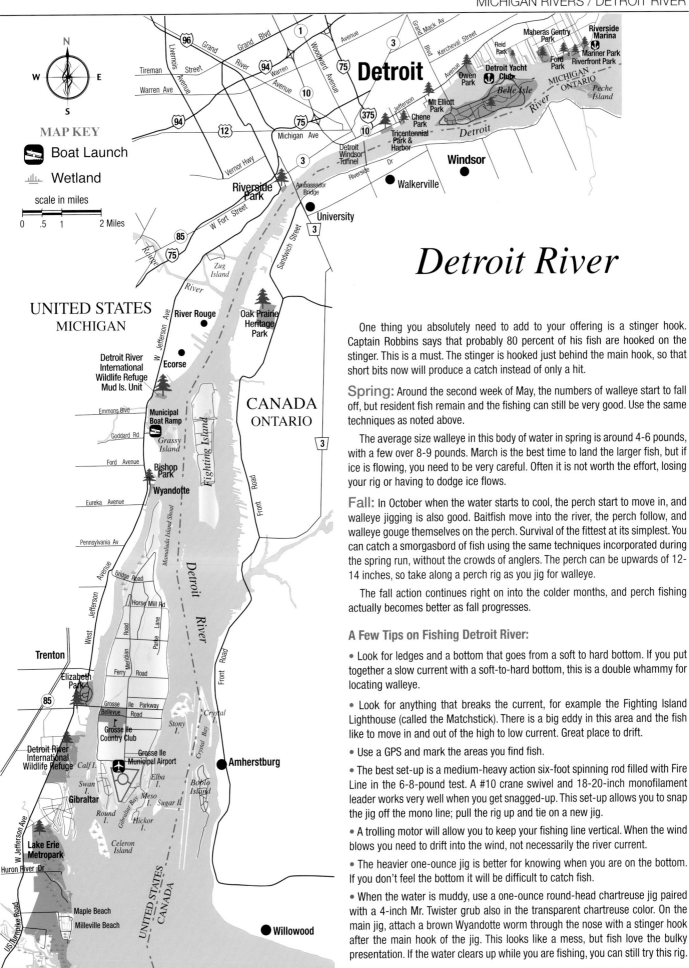

Detroit River

One thing you absolutely need to add to your offering is a stinger hook. Captain Robbins says that probably 80 percent of his fish are hooked on the stinger. This is a must. The stinger is hooked just behind the main hook, so that short bits now will produce a catch instead of only a hit.

Spring: Around the second week of May, the numbers of walleye start to fall off, but resident fish remain and the fishing can still be very good. Use the same techniques as noted above.

The average size walleye in this body of water in spring is around 4-6 pounds, with a few over 8-9 pounds. March is the best time to land the larger fish, but if ice is flowing, you need to be very careful. Often it is not worth the effort, losing your rig or having to dodge ice flows.

Fall: In October when the water starts to cool, the perch start to move in, and walleye jigging is also good. Baitfish move into the river, the perch follow, and walleye gouge themselves on the perch. Survival of the fittest at its simplest. You can catch a smorgasbord of fish using the same techniques incorporated during the spring run, without the crowds of anglers. The perch can be upwards of 12-14 inches, so take along a perch rig as you jig for walleye.

The fall action continues right on into the colder months, and perch fishing actually becomes better as fall progresses.

A Few Tips on Fishing Detroit River:

• Look for ledges and a bottom that goes from a soft to hard bottom. If you put together a slow current with a soft-to-hard bottom, this is a double whammy for locating walleye.

• Look for anything that breaks the current, for example the Fighting Island Lighthouse (called the Matchstick). There is a big eddy in this area and the fish like to move in and out of the high to low current. Great place to drift.

• Use a GPS and mark the areas you find fish.

• The best set-up is a medium-heavy action six-foot spinning rod filled with Fire Line in the 6-8-pound test. A #10 crane swivel and 18-20-inch monofilament leader works very well when you get snagged-up. This set-up allows you to snap the jig off the mono line; pull the rig up and tie on a new jig.

• A trolling motor will allow you to keep your fishing line vertical. When the wind blows you need to drift into the wind, not necessarily the river current.

• The heavier one-ounce jig is better for knowing when you are on the bottom. If you don't feel the bottom it will be difficult to catch fish.

• When the water is muddy, use a one-ounce round-head chartreuse jig paired with a 4-inch Mr. Twister grub also in the transparent chartreuse color. On the main jig, attach a brown Wyandotte worm through the nose with a stinger hook after the main hook of the jig. This looks like a mess, but fish love the bulky presentation. If the water clears up while you are fishing, you can still try this rig.

Fox River Alger/Schoolcraft Counties

The Fox River rises from a semi-open marsh draining the Deadman Lake in eastern Alger County about 10 miles southwest of Grand Marais. It flows in a southeasterly direction for 35 miles mostly in Schoolcraft County until it empties into the Manistique River near the village of Germfask. It is noted as an excellent brook trout stream, and is widely accepted that this is the river Ernest Hemingway fished when he wrote the Nick Adams stories and not the Big Two-Hearted. No one knows for sure, but they are both excellent brookie streams.

The Fox and its East Branch have been included in Michigan's Natural Rivers Program. In addition, 18 miles of the Main Stream above Seney and 15 miles of the East Branch from M-77 to the Luce County line have been designated Michigan Blue Ribbon Trout streams.

MAP KEY

ﻬﻬ Wetland

scale in miles

0   .5   1   2 Miles

At a Glance

What: Great brook trout river on an historic river

Where: A very scenic area of Michigan's Upper Peninsula near Grand Marais

Why: Enjoy the serenity of this river while stalking some sizable trout

Information: Grand Marais Chamber of Commerce, PO Box 139, Grand Marais, 49839, (906) 494-2447; www.grandmaraismichigan.com

Landings: Various access points

Bait & Tackle: Grand Marais Outfitters, N 14277 Lake Avenue, (906) 494-3333; website: www.grandmaraisoutfitters.net

It is still possible to catch the 2- or 3-pound brookies here although most are in the 10-11-inch range. The river is a beautiful pristine trout stream largely unchanged since the days when Hemingway fished this area. It is not an easy stream to fly-fish or canoe due in part to all the tag alders hanging over the river, but those anglers with some skills at both pursuits will be thoroughly rewarded.

In general the Fox has been known for its excellent brook trout fishing. The upper portions of the Fox, which includes the Main Stream above Seney and the East Branch above M-28, are prime trout waters. The stream bottom is primarily sand and silt, but contains enough scattered gravel to provide adequate brook trout spawning habitat. The brook trout fishery in the East Branch is probably the best in the system, but brown trout are starting to replace the brookies, which are the preferred fish of most local anglers. Brown trout now comprise about 50 percent of the trout population in the upper East Branch.

Wading is not difficult except for some of the deeper pools on the Main Stream. Both live bait and artificial flies are used with success.

Main Stream:
The more easily accessible Main Stream is approximately 35 miles long and within 4-5 miles from its headwaters, it flows through Casey Lake and eventually into Schoolcraft County. The bottom structure is mostly sand with some sections gravel based. The current is considered moderate. This part of the river flows through stands of spruce, pine, balsam and many other conifers. A belly boat can be an asset due to some of the deeper holes. The vast majority of this part of the river flows through public lands, and consequently has more fishing pressure.

Wagner Dam is a good access site along with the Fox River State Campground; a few two-tracks off CR-450, also known as Fox River Road, also provide good access to the river.

A unique feature with the Fox is that there are no steelhead or salmon to compete with trout. "The river also maintains an ample supply of cold groundwater," says District Fish Biologist Darren Kramer, "providing for stable, year-round flow and rarely allowing the water to exceed the upper 60-degree temps."

The overall difficulty of access helps curb fishing pressure, but the word "difficult" is subjective; what's difficult for one person is not for another, so don't let it stop you from experiencing this river. The DNR at one time annually planted 6,000 yearling brook trout to the Main Stream to augment native reproduction, but Kramer states that, "since 2005 no plantings were needed due to good natural reproduction, which is a good thing for any body of water."

East Branch:
This portion of the river rises from springs located in northeast Schoolcraft County and flows south along M-77 for several miles along which many smaller tributaries discharge into the Fox. Eventually it ends up north of Seney, then swings back to the southwest and eventually to the Main Stream.

Fishing pressure on the East Branch below M-77 is heavy, probably the heaviest in this river system. Excellent catches of brook trout up to two pounds, along with an occasional brown trout, are taken. The best fishing is obtained by parking on the west side of the M-18 bridge, motoring a small boat upstream to the Spreads and then fishing the holes and undercuts back down to the Soo Line Railroad Bridge. The East Branch used to have a more sizable population of trout compared to the Main Stream, but this has since equaled out over the years. In this segment of the river, there's a strong population of brook trout and brown trout.

Trout can be caught along this Branch above M-28. Along M-77, the river varies between around 10 to 30 feet wide and contains pools deeper than six feet, so caution is advised.

The East Branch from M-77 to M-28 is difficult to fly-fish, unless you have advanced skills to handle tight spots. If you fish this section, you may be rewarded with some nice-sized brookies. Spinners work well in this stretch, along with nymphs and streamers for the fly-angler. Muddler Minnows are also worth trying.

There is an abrupt change in the Main Stream and East Branch below M-28, and a corresponding change in the fishery. Both streams are now wider and have a leisurely flow to the confluence with the Manistique River. Stream cover consists of an abundance of windfalls, log jams, undercut banks, overhanging brush, and deep pools. Because of the bottom type, however, very little brook trout spawning habitat is available. Fishing pressure is light, producing a few pike, walleye, and perch.

Note: Thanks to Hunt-Up Guide, www.hunts-upguide.com, for assistance with this particular river.

The Fox River in Michigan's Upper Peninsula, a river the to that Hemingway fished, is not only beautiful, but a great brook trout stream also.

Grand River Kent County

The Grand River spans more than 260 miles, offering a diverse array of fishing opportunities. Draining parts of 18 counties and almost 6,000 square miles of the lower peninsula, it is the state's longest river. From its source near Jackson, the river generally flows northwest until it empties into Lake Michigan at Grand Haven. Although there were some apparent issues with the overall cleanliness of The Grand, it's significantly cleaner and safer than it was a few decades ago, according to the Great Lakes Commission.

The Grand is home to game fish such as catfish, pike, large and smallmouth bass, walleye, coho, steelhead, and some sizeable gar. You will find the river stocked with game fish, thanks to a local culture that emphasizes catch-and-release fishing and the planting of coho salmon near Lansing. It's not uncommon for anglers to pull large fish from the river, running in the range of 1 to 4 pounds for smallmouth bass.

Fishing guide Mike Marsh grew up in this part of the state and knows the Grand very well. He likes to fish the river March through April in particular for steelhead around the mouth of the many tributaries that empty into the main river channel. There are fish ladders that allow the spawners up river past Grand Rapids.

In May, Marsh says smallmouth bass upwards of 3 to 4 pounds are common in the Grand Rapids area. In June catfish and gar pike are sought after. As September moves in, the waters start to cool providing conditions that coho enjoy. Anglers start to fish for them at the Grand Rapids 6th Street Dam around

mid September. Kings will also start moving up river, along with steelhead. Spawn bags and Cleos are popular choices for anglers seeking out salmon and steelhead.

Marsh says that most fish species remain active into October until the water temperature falls below 50 degrees. He also notes that walleye are available year-round and salmon run the river when the water hits 60 degrees.

A Note: Upriver from Grand Rapids the water runs between 4-8 feet deep, so a boat is in order.

Many people in Grand Rapids fish the river for recreation, stationed on the Riverwalk along the river's east bank or from within the river just below the fish ladder at the 6th Street Bridge. If you're willing to deal with people traffic, try fishing the center of the river from atop the Fulton Street bridge.

Sixth Street Dam Profile:
During low flows all of the rapids are accessible to wading anglers in this area, but as the river rises you need to limit wading to certain locations. There is a staff gauge on the ladder structure above the ladder and there is a United States Geological Survey gauge in the lower rapids.

The favorite fly-angling areas near the dam are Center Run and the Flats. The Flats are found on the eastern side of the river and are a shallow, fast sweep of water over bedrock just below the dam. On the western side, the water is much deeper and the area near the dam is called the Boils. You can fish this area if you can find a spot to fish during the busy fishing season. Marsh says that Center Run is named for its location and it's where the main flow of the river occurs. There are three slightly deeper areas or dips in the Center Run he says, where the fish tend to lie.

Just above the expressway there is a traverse trough that extends almost the whole width of the river. You can't wade through it but you can fish above and below it.

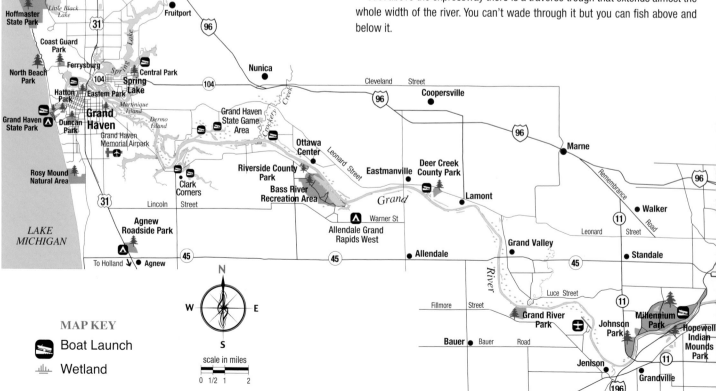

MAP KEY

Boat Launch

Wetland

scale in miles

0 1/2 1   2

At Bridge Street, between the first and second coffers and its abutments, good cover is available for the fish. Wading can be difficult here because of strong currents and an uneven bottom. Use your wading staff but don't try it if the water level is at 5.7 or above.

Lyons Dam: Access to Lyons Dam is available on each side of the river below the dam, which is located on Bridge St. in the town of Lyons. Fish tend to hold and feed near the dam. To fish the apron area below the dam it's best to enter the river from the eastern or ladder side. The bridge just below the dam also deserves lots of attention, especially the first two areas between pillars on the western side. Below the bridge, the main flow and deeper water is on the western side of the river. You can roll cast from shore, or wade out from the eastern side when the water is not too high. Streamers work well here.

Webber Dam: Below the dam, off Divine Hwy., just south of the town of Lyons, can be excellent steelhead, walleye and smallmouth bass fishing. Above the dam is also good. Smallmouth fishing, and excellent walleye fishing, is also good here if you can find them you will also find excellent walleye fishing. There is a public-access site on the eastern side of the river that can be reached from Maple Road and then Park Boulevard. When the water is relatively low, with only one turbine running on the dam, you can wade all the way across the river here and swing streamers or drift nymphs downstream, but you will need to return to shore to wade further downstream. Fish continue to hold all along both sides of the island as well.

Portland Dam: The ladder at Portland Dam (located downstream from Bogue River Recreation Area, off Lyons Rd. in Portland) is on the south side of the river and there is a public-access site there. The power channel can hold fish but the better fly-fishing is found in the main river. At modest water levels you can walk downstream to where the channel tails out and cross it to the rocky main flow. From here, you can wade almost up to the dam. With a wading staff and great care you can cover most of the water below the dam.

Rogue River Tributary: The Rogue River, a tributary of the Grand River that flows out of Newaygo County through the city of Rockford and into the Grand River just north of Grand Rapids, is the Grand's only large cold-water tributary. Even though it is a relatively secondary water for trout, both browns and rainbows survive year-round in the lower river. The real draw here for fly-anglers is the trout fishing from Algoma Avenue down to the confluence with the Grand. In this reach the river rapidly changes from a relatively narrow soft-bottomed stream to one that is broad with a firm gravel.

DNR Photo, David Kenyon

The 6th Street Dam is a popular place for anglers when the salmon are heading up stream.

At a Glance

What: A variety of fishing opportunities in a large city setting

Where: All along the Grand, both up and downstream from Grand Rapids

Information/Guides: Grand Rapids CVB, 171 Monroe Ave NW, Suite 700, Grand Rapids, 49503, (616) 459-8287, (800) 678-9859, mailbox@ ExperienceGR.com; **Mike Marsh, Marsh Ridge River Guide Service,** 10069 River Bend, Baldwin, 49304, (231) 920-7527

Landings: Various access sites as outlined in the text portion of this river

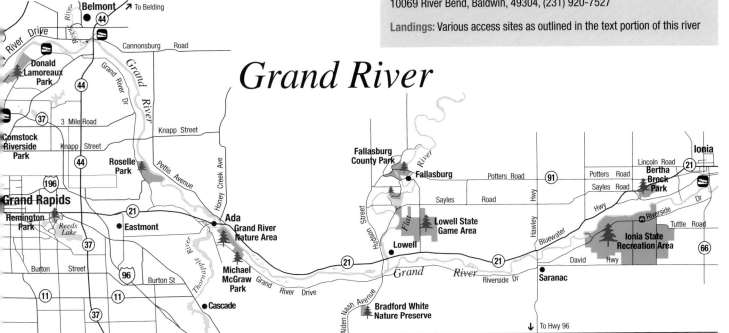

Grand River

Huron River Wayne County

The Huron River is located in southeast Michigan and flows into Lake Erie. The river flows 125 miles from the Huron Swamp northwest of Pontiac to Pt. Mouilee on Lake Erie, dropping from 1,018 to 572 feet above sea level along the way. Bass, bluegills, sunfish, crappie, carp, catfish all abound in various Ann Arbor locations on the river. There are multiple public-access points in Ann Arbor to the river. Anglers fly-fish, as well as fishing from the banks or boat.

DNR Fish Biologist, Jeff Braunscheidel with the Lake Erie Management Unit, states, "there are many different parts of the river and each have significant fishing opportunities." The lower part of the river from Belleville Dam down is stocked with approximately 60,000 steelhead each spring.

"As for steelhead fishing," says Braunscheidel, "it's best in the southeast part of the state, and a big draw for anglers." All four bordering states to Lake Erie, as well as Ontario, have steelhead stocking programs so the lake is well managed. Most anglers access the river by boat. There are a few areas accessible by wading, but you need to be knowledgeable about those locations and careful if you fish them. Other anglers fish from shore throughout the year for the varied species of fish available to them—steelhead, salmon, suckers, smallmouth bass, and an occasional muskie.

A friend of mine who resides in this area of the state fishes the Huron often and stated recently that the river produces well for him most of the time. There was a time when you were lucky to even see another angler with a steelie, but now you can often land a couple given the right time of year. He often works his way up from Lake Erie and fishes the deeper holes along the way by anchoring upstream from the hole and drop-back fishing with crankbaits, like Hot n Tots or spawn. During the winter months, he uses large chrome-colored lures. When drift fishing, be sure to keep your offerings close to the bottom, and also keep in mind that snags are evident and lost tackle is a way of life on this river.

The preferred rod is an 8-12-foot noodle rod with soft action allowing you to not only fight the steelies with light line, but to more easily cast a single egg or fly. Keep in mind that you need to wear out the fish before it becomes hung-up in one of the many possible snag locations.

In the past, most steelhead action took place below Flat Rock Dam, but since the fish ladder was installed steelhead move up even further, as far as Belleville Dam 17 miles upstream.

Steelies can range in size here and get as big as anywhere in the state, averaging in the 10-12-pound range. There are also a few stray kings here, mostly from the eastern end of Lake Erie. The walleye, according to Jeff, can be up to 10 pounds or more.

The time to fish for steelhead is late fall, mid-November, right through winter if the river does not become hard. March and April are good for the spring run. There are a few walleye in the river when the March season opens.

Summer fishing is mostly for smallmouth bass, and some small pike, all in the lower river.

The upper part of the river above Belleville Dam is a totally different stretch, with impoundments at various locations up through Ann Arbor. There is plenty of public land that you can wade for smallies, and a three-mile stretch that runs from Dexter downstream is a catch-and-release-only area for smallies.

Braunscheidel says, "this is probably the only catch-and-release smallmouth area in the state." It provides a great bass fishery that allows many anglers to enjoy using fly rods.

Where to Fish: For wading anglers, the stretch from the mouth of the river to 17 miles upstream contains many good opportunities. The west bank from Belleville Dam down to New Boston can be waded close to shore, but once again be cautious of the deeper water. The Hur-Roc Park area is popular for steelheaders, as well as the area west of US-24, Telegraph Road, Flat Rock Dam, which is also popular several hundred yards below the main dam. There is a two-foot-high control dam that anglers work both sides of the river from just below the dam to several miles downstream. There are no boats allowed on the pool between the smaller control dam and Flat Rock Dam, so anglers line the shore and fishing can be difficult at times.

West of I-75, off the Jefferson Road bridge, is a section of water that attracts many anglers. This section consists of a lot of meandering water, with several long deep runs accessible by boat or fished from shore. Parking is available along Huron River Drive, but respect any private property in this area.

DNR Photo, David Kenyon

Along with many other game species, catfish are popular in the Huron River.

Huron River

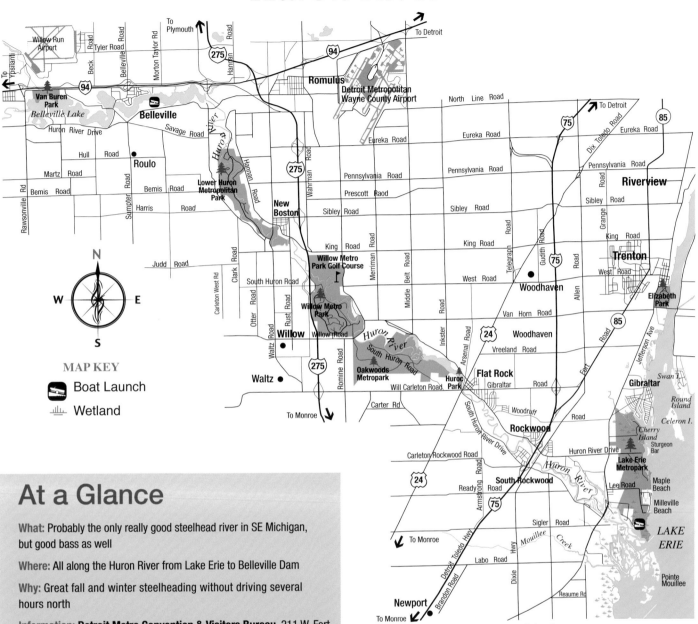

At a Glance

What: Probably the only really good steelhead river in SE Michigan, but good bass as well

Where: All along the Huron River from Lake Erie to Belleville Dam

Why: Great fall and winter steelheading without driving several hours north

Information: Detroit Metro Convention & Visitors Bureau, 211 W. Fort St., Ste. 1000, Detroit, 48226, (313) 202-1800, Visitor Information (800) DETROIT (338-7648), vic@visitdetroit.com; visitdetroit.com

Landings: There are many boat landings below Flat Rock Dam, including a very nice State DNR landing several hundred yards south of Telegraph Road with entry from North Huron River Road in Flat Rock. Another landing is off Jefferson in Rockwood, north of the bridge. Another is south of North Huron River Drive in Flat Rock. The Pointe Mouilee SGA also has a landing where the Huron River opens to Lake Erie

Bait & Tackle: Bottom Line Tackle, 32660 W. Jefferson, Rockwood, 48173, (734) 379-9762; **South Street Tackle,** 205 South St., Belleville, 48111, (734) 697-0990; **Little Dipper Bait and Tackle,** 26464 W. Huron River Drive, Flat Rock, 48134 (734) 782-4277, Email: littledipperbt@aol.com; **Jeff's Bait & Tackle,** 1756 N. Dixie Hwy., Monroe, 48162, (734) 289-4901; **Matthew's Bait & Tackle,** 14011 LaPlaisance Road, Monroe, 48161, (734) 241-4757

There are many sections where shore anglers can cast to small riffles and some of the deeper pools below Flat Rock and Belleville dams. Access here is relatively easy. Also, between Flat Rock and Belleville cities, much of the west bank is open to the public as part of the Metropark authority.

Common Bait and Lures: For steelhead, anglers who frequent this river use a variety of tackle, including a black and green Woolly Bugger suspended below a bobber, or a one-inch pink-colored twistertail and plastic worms. During fall and spring, a single waxworm hung below a sensitive bobber seems to work well. Use splitshot to get the offering just off the bottom of the river. Spawn of course is always a preferred bait, and a single egg firmly placed on a strong hook and 4-6-pound-test line is often effective. But do not rule out all options, including spinners, spoons, and flies.

Some of the impoundment sites are also stocked for walleye.

Little Garlic River
Marquette County

Located about 10 miles north of Marquette on County Road 550 the Little Garlic is a notable steelhead river, especially during the early part of the season with the spring run-off. Filled with large granite rocks and boulders the river is fishable either at the river mouth or upstream from the DNR parking lot just west of County Road 550. You can trek upstream about three miles to the falls. Just below the falls there are many small pools that hold many spawning steelies.

Eric Miltz Miller not only fishes the Little Garlic, he does research on it as a student at Northern Michigan University. The Little Garlic is one of the many home waters in this area fished by Robert Traver, aka John Voelker, who wrote *Trout Magic, Trout Madness,* and *Anatomy of a Fisherman.*

Both the Little Garlic River, a pristine brook trout stream that is a spur of the famed North County Trail, and the surrounding forest are a pleasure to visit. Four tranquil miles from the trailhead, the path arrives at Little Garlic Falls, a scenic stretch of cascades, rapids, and swift water running through a rocky cleft. The North County Trail, by the way, is a hiking trail that extends from South Dakota to New York and passes through Michigan.

Spring Steelhead: In the spring Eric states, there is a "really good run of steelhead." They will mostly end their spawning duties before the season opens. The river is very wadeable, very popular with anglers, and also good for surf casting for not only steelhead, but whitefish also at the mouth where it empties into Lake Superior. The fish in the lake are feeding on eggs that drift downstream and out into Lake Superior waters. Anglers often use chartreuse-colored eggs or variations thereof. The "chuck-n-duck" rig works best, especially in streams that are small and rocky.

The whole idea behind the unique chuck-n-duck fishing is to turn fly-angling on its head. Whereas in traditional fly-fishing, the line is cast and the fly goes along for the ride, in chuck-n-duck fishing a weight is cast and the fly line and fly are pulled along, similar to spin-fishing (except the line does not come off a reel). While it is quite possible to perform this feat with typical fly lines and some big split shot, evolution of chuck-n-duck seems to be the better alternative. Fishermen noticed a fly fished with classic methods would drift above the fish holding in these areas—and the fish would not rise to meet the fly. If they could get their flies to drop quickly into the pockets and pools, and drift at the same

Fly-fishing is a popular method of fishing smaller rivers and streams such as the Little Garlic.

Little Garlic River

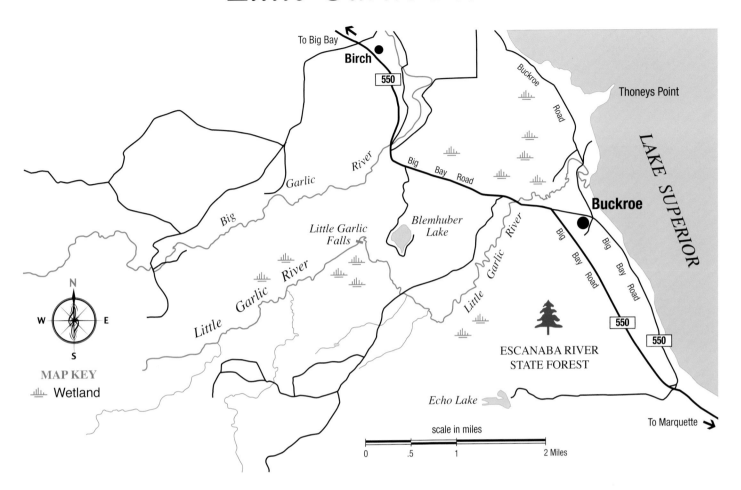

level as the holding fish, they might be at equal odds with their spin-angler counterparts. The result was chuck-n-duck fishing. Chuck-n-duck fishing is not for everyone, but it's an effective angling technique, one worth learning if you occasionally find yourself in a situation where drifting a nymph along the bottom of a distant lie is the difference between catching and casting practice.

One problem along this river that should be mentioned is access. Much of this area is owned privately, so be careful where you set foot on land. However the part of the river that people fish is generally accessible along Highway 550 by the bridge. This stretch is also the most crowded to fish during the prime season, but if you take the two-track off of 550 that crosses the river one more time, it becomes less congested during prime fishing season.

Brookies: *"Brookies on the Little Garlic are tough to get to,"* says Eric. "Most are in the waters along the private lands, but if you care to explore, and gain access to the third bridge at the headwaters, the water there is cold enough to fish all summer and has a great brookie population," he says. Few anglers work their way that far upstream. During Eric's river research, he has seen a few brookies upwards of 20 inches, a wall hanger for sure. In addition, there are many brookies in the 8-10-inch size at the headwaters. So if you enjoy hiking, take a GPS along and head to this area of the Garlic for some great brookie action.

Note: As a side note, there is a brown and coho run in the fall, but no resident browns. You can find them in the 20-inch range, making the effort worthwhile.

At a Glance

What: Great steelhead, brook trout fishing

Where: A 3½-mile stretch of the Little Garlic River

Why: Some of the best fishing for both steelhead and especially brook trout

Information/Guides: Marquette County Convention & Visitors Bureau, 337 West Washington St., Marquette, 49855, (800) 544-4321, or (906) 228-7749, e-mail: frontdesk@marquettecountry.org

Landings: None; access off Highway 550

Bait & Tackle: Gwinn Bait & Tackle, 56 N Billings St, Gwinn, 49841, (906) 346-3330; **Phil's 550 Store,** 52 County Road 550, Marquette, 49855, (906) 226-9146; **Gander Mountain,** 3465 U.S. 41 Marquette, 49855, (906) 226-8300

Little Manistee River
Manistee County

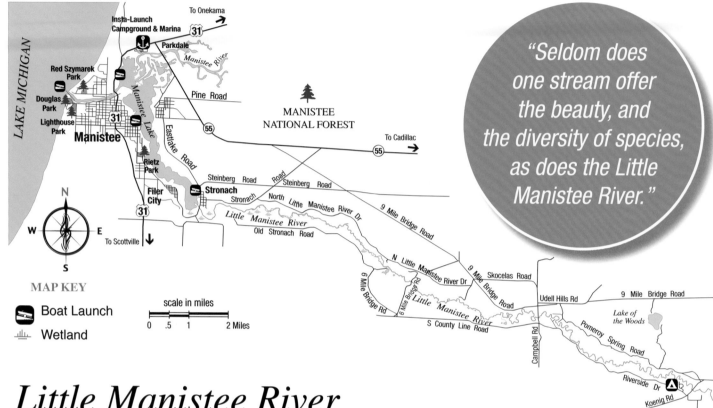

"Seldom does one stream offer the beauty, and the diversity of species, as does the Little Manistee River."

MAP KEY

🛥 Boat Launch

⟰ Wetland

scale in miles

0   .5   1   2 Miles

Little Manistee River

District Fish Biologist, Mark Tonello, says that, "the Little Manistee River is such a productive steelhead river that there's no need to plant." The majority of the 10,000 fish that return to the Little Manistee between the spring and fall runs are naturally reproduced.

The Little Manistee River is located in the southern portion of Manistee County, and northern area of Lake and Mason counties. It originates near the small town of Luther in northwest Michigan and includes 67 miles of mainstream and approximately 41 miles of 16 tributaries. The Little Manistee joins the Big Manistee River at Manistee Lake which empties into Lake Michigan at Manistee.

This river presents anglers with quite a challenge. Rapid stream flow, log-filled and loaded with snags, can result in trying to land a feisty steelhead to the net a somewhat difficult accomplishment. But anglers still visit their favorite holes in anticipation of the April 1 opener on this magnificent river.

Brent Borchert has fished the Upper Manistee River for many years and is very knowledgeable on this river. He states that the fishing is very good north of M-72, north of the Deward area. It is smaller water with rainbows, brookies, and browns, and is only open during the regular trout season. But it is good fishing all season. There is a lot of wadeable water, and the fish may be smaller, but it is a "fun area to fish," he says. Generally they use dry flies, Adams, caddis, and stonefly imitations.

As you move downstream, the area from M-72 to the CCC Bridge is flies-only, and has trophy regulations, that is, only one fish can be kept per day over 18 inches.

Brookies are a favorite fish species anglers pursue along the beautiful Upper Manistee River.

Photo courtesy of Mike Marsh

This is about a 12-mile stretch and has very good access on both sides of the stream. The fish are also "picky" in this stretch, being older and wiser, so you have to match the hatch, such as Brown Drakes, or *Hex* hatches.

From the CCC bridge to Highway 131 the water is bigger and some sort of boat is in order. There is good streamer-fishing for big browns, upwards of 28 inches or more. Once again, you will need to match the hatch. Multiple areas are used to gain access in this stretch. Sharon Bridge near Military Road, Sharon to Smithville (M-66), then Coaster Rd. to M-131. "This entire area is a bit tricky to wade," says Brent, "so you need to be smart if you wish to walk it."

There are huge browns here; it is especially good in spring and fall, and summer is a match-the-hatch season. The river meanders a lot and there are many sizable holes to fish. The brookies seem to be in the Sharon Bridge area, where you can even land some walleye as you get closer to M-131.

The brookies are in the 10-12-inch size in the upper stretches of the river. Brent says that this river has some of the best brown trout fishing anywhere in the state.

From M-71 upstream, there are also many feeder streams with very nice fishable water, much of it ankle deep with many 2- to 3-foot holes.. "Trout are not as wary here, compared to the larger browns further downstream," says Brent.

Brent also states that beyond the emerging aquatic insects anglers should pay close attention to the terrestrials, including flying ants, grasshoppers, beetles and many more. Size generally does matter with these bugs, so just try to match what you see on the streamside vegetation or on the water. Much of the year you can expect to see plenty of Blue Winged Olives (BWOs) in sizes ranging from 16 to 22; these are a staple for just about any trout fisherman, and trout love 'em.

Obviously there are more types of bugs that come off on this river, but the above mentioned are the ones fly-anglers and fly tiers should be most concerned with.

Anglers also use crawlers and spinners to fish the upper Manistee.

Notes: The CCC Bridge is located about 40 miles east of Traverse City, 20 miles south east of Kalkaska and 12 miles west of Grayling, Michigan.

Floating bobbers with spawn is a good way to avoid some of the snags. Others flip spinners or work plugs into the deeper holes on heavier line, which gives a better chance at landing fish. Rolling spawn is another alternative. Some of the best fishing on the Little Manistee occurs in May, long after most anglers have given up for the season.

The stretch of the Little Manistee between Johnson's Bridge and Nine Mile Bridge is one of the most heavily fished. Much of the streamside property is privately owned, but anglers can gain access at several crossings, including Fox, Dewitt, Pole and Eighteen bridges. Farther downstream, Nine Mile and Six Mile bridges provide access.

At a Glance

What: A prolific producer of browns and brookies on this beautiful stretch of the Manistee River

Where: All along the upper stretches

Regs: The CCC Bridge and the CCC Bridge campground are focal points of the fly-fisherman who fishes the Manistee. The bridge is the lower boundary of the "Flies-Only" section of water, with M-72 being the upper boundary. This water is open year round and has special regulations, so be sure to check the latest fishing guides before fishing this area

Information/Guides: Traverse City Convention & Visitors, 101 West Grandview Parkway, Traverse City, 49684, (231) 947-0692, traversecity. com. **Brent Borchert** (guide), (231) 794-8869; **Doug Samsal,** www. manisteerivercharter.com, (231) 668-2894

Landings: Numerous access sites for entering the river

Bait & Tackle: Schmidt Outfitters, 18 Seaman Rd., Wellston, 49689, (231) 848-4191, email: schmidt@schmidtoutfitters.com, www.schmidtoutfitters.com. **Pappy's Bait & Tackle,** 17092 Caberfae Highway, Wellston, 49689, (231) 848-4142; **Frankfort Tackle Box,** 9th and Main, Frankfort, 49635, (231) 352-7673; frankforttacklebox.com

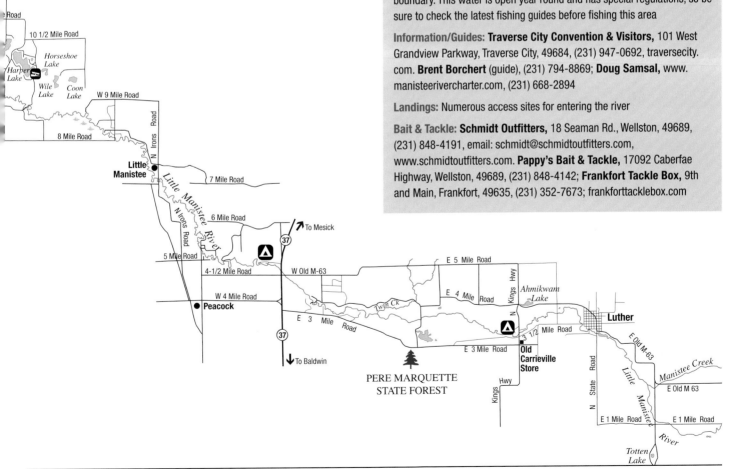

Menominee River
Gogebic County

The 100-mile stretch of the Menominee River from above Iron Mountain to Menominee provides a beautiful setting. There are over 100 tributaries that enter the Menominee River in this 100-mile stretch. The shoreline and river corridor is very wild and scenic with multiple ownerships including private, corporate, and state and county governments. Large blocks of the shoreline and adjacent uplands are owned by We Energies and timber companies such as International Paper, plus the Michigan and the Wisconsin Departments of Natural Resources, and county governments in Wisconsin. Numerous campgrounds and boat-access points along the river cater to wildlife watchers with canoes. There are nine hydroelectric power dams and reservoirs on the river; each has a portage for small boats.

One of the most scenic and popular natural attractions in the river corridor is Piers Gorge. It contains some of the fastest-moving water in Michigan and Wisconsin. It is not navigable for general canoeing (class IV to V white water), but still offers beautiful scenery and good wildlife viewing from shore.

The river also offers some of the best fishing for smallmouth bass in the Upper Peninsula. The dams on this river and the reaches below them are loaded with smallmouths, along with some walleyes and northern pike says Mike Mladenik, a guide on this river from across the MI/WI border in Crivitz, Wisconsin. The Hattie Street Dam is the first one up from Green Bay and that reach is the best for walleyes; there are lots of smallmouth bass that are larger than average.

Along its course the Menominee River has been converted into a series of large reservoirs. The waters contained in these reservoirs are some of the area's deepest and cleanest "lakes". Many of the lands around those waters are managed for recreational use, which ensures conservation and restricts shoreline development. The lakes are pristine, wild shores of forest lands instead of rows of cottages and docks. The region through which the river flows was formerly a center of iron-ore mining.

The name of the river comes from an Algonquian term meaning "wild rice", or "in the place of wild rice," named for the Menominee tribe who lived in the area and subsisted on the plant.

Summer: In general, summer fishing can produce smallmouth bass, channel catfish, and an occasional pike when trolling. Walleye are caught but many are small during the summer months. Try crawler harnesses or Rapalas. Shore anglers often fish in the late evening and target walleye and smallmouth bass. Smallmouth bass and rock bass are generally caught by casting crank or tube baits. You can start catching giant smallmouth in early May with many 6-pound-plus fish caught at this time.

Some anglers still-fish near the mouth of the river catching bluegills and yellow perch, but most of them are small. A few shore anglers mainly target smallmouth bass or walleye. Night crawlers and leeches worked the best.

Bass: Mike says the bass can reach upwards of 20 inches, and many are only slightly smaller, in the 17-19-inch range. "Smallies," he says, "are found most anywhere in the river." He goes on to say that, "you need to follow the basic rule of thumb, that is, in the summer, fish the moving water, and in the spring and late summer or fall the deeper reservoirs are the best fishing." These reservoir areas are 20 to 30 feet in depth, with other parts of the river being in the 5- to 10 foot depths.

Mike fishes all summer by drifting the rocky and grassy areas. There are good top-water bites in spring and summer, using most any bass lures, including poppers.

Walleye: By far the most popular walleye hangouts are in the two-mile stretch near the mouth, where it empties into Lake Michigan. Also, in the spring, all the areas below the many dams are very good walleye fishing locations. Most of these areas are fished with a boat.

Sturgeon: The sturgeon are mainly about half way up the river, from Waseca downriver. Mike says that they can be from legal size up to 60 inches or so. Anglers bottom fish using live bait, such as crawlers.

Notes: The 100-mile river corridor has many access points, and maps showing these areas are produced by We Energies, a major landowner on the

At a Glance

What: Smallmouth bass, walleye, and sturgeon

Where: From the mouth of the river, upstream below the many dams, and other locations

Why: A great smallmouth bass fishing river. While fishing, it is common to see bald eagles, osprey, deer, bear, otter and other wildlife. There is no better place to relax and get away from it all than on the Menominee River

Regs: Being a boundary river, Michigan & Wisconsin fishing licenses are both legal on the river regardless of where you fish

Information/Guides: Mike Mladenik, Guide, N6550 S. 6th St., Crivitz, WI 54114, (715) 854-2055, smguide@centurylink.net. **Chamber of Commerce,** 601 Marinette Ave., Marinette, WI 54143, (715) 735-6681, mandmchamber.com; **Chamber of Commerce,** 2511 10th, St, Menominee, MI 49858 (906) 863-2679

Landings: Many small landings along the river from the mouth upriver. Also a DNR landing in Menominee at the city marina.

Bait & Tackle: Hook Line 'N Sinker, 516 N. US Hwy 141, Crivitz, WI 54114, (715) 854-2073; good source for sporting goods, including live bait, and latest fishing information

Menominee River

river (canoe trail maps are available from area outfitters for a nominal fee; "Wilderness Shores" pamphlets are free from We Energies), or the Michigan and Wisconsin DNR. From Norway, drive south on US-8 about 2 miles and follow the signs to Piers Gorge. The road ends at a parking lot at the gorge.

High winds can ravage fishing on many lakes, but not on the Menominee River. There is always possibilities on the river. This is a world-class smallmouth fishery.

Finally, you may approach this river from Michigan and be a native of Michigan, but keep in mind that not far away is Green Bay, WI, home of the Packers, so be cautious about wearing a Lions shirt in this area. (smile)

Caution: The river current at Piers Gorge is very strong. Do not wade or swim, and keep small children and pets away from the water's edge.

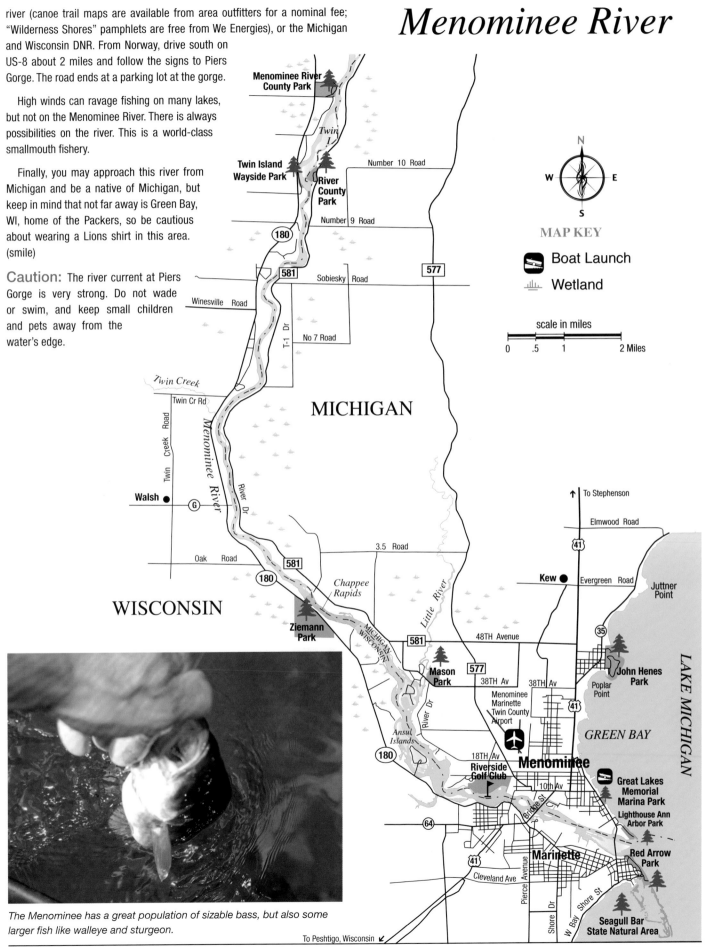

MAP KEY

Boat Launch

Wetland

scale in miles

0 .5 1 2 Miles

Menominee River County Park

Twin Island Wayside Park

River County Park

Number 10 Road

Number 9 Road

Sobiesky Road

Winesville Road

No 7 Road

Twin Creek

Twin Cr Rd

MICHIGAN

Menominee River

Walsh

River Dr

Oak Road

Twin Creek Road

WISCONSIN

Chappee Rapids

Ziemann Park

To Stephenson

Elmwood Road

Kew

Evergreen Road

Juttner Point

3.5 Road

Little River

48TH Avenue

Mason Park

John Henes Park

Poplar Point

GREEN BAY

38TH Av

38TH Av

Menominee Marinette Twin County Airport

18TH Av

Riverside Golf Club

Menominee

Ansul Islands

Great Lakes Memorial Marina Park

Lighthouse Ann Arbor Park

LAKE MICHIGAN

10th Av

Bridge St

Red Arrow Park

Marinette

Cleveland Ave

Pierce Avenue

Shore Dr

W Bay Shore St.

Seagull Bar State Natural Area

To Peshtigo, Wisconsin

The Menominee has a great population of sizable bass, but also some larger fish like walleye and sturgeon.

Muskegon River Muskegon County

One of the reasons the Muskegon River between Croton Dam and Newaygo is so productive is the fact that it has some of the finest spawning gravel of any stream in Michigan. This river averages 150 to 200 feet wide and therefore is more suited to utilizing a watercraft of some sort. Wading and bank fishing is more restricted to access sites at Croton Dam, Pine Street, High Rollaways and Henning Park. There are launch ramps at each of these sites also.

Spring steelhead on the Muskegon generally start to run the river in late March, and will peak in April. But May is also a productive month, so don't always look for peak runs as the only time to fish this beautiful river. If the river is high, drift boaters can enjoy great sport from Croton Dam to Newaygo.

Rainbows that have wintered in the lower river begin their spawning activity as early as the beginning of March some years, and the run is bolstered by waves of spring-run fish in April. During most years, fresh-run fish are available through May, long after most of the crowds have disappeared. The Muskegon gets an annual plant of about 65,000 Michigan winter steelhead that is supplemented by improving numbers of naturally spawned fish.

Fish will be staging behind gravel beds and plugs like Wiggle Warts or Hot-N-Tots can trigger ferocious strikes from shifty steelhead. Metallic colors are also a good bet. Many of the fish are intentionally snagged or "lined" as fast as they go on the beds. A better option is to work the dark water behind the beds or the deeper runs for drop-back or fresh-run fish. Spring is also excellent for steelhead, using spawn, flies. It's also excellent for browns with the same bait. Just pick your hole and enjoy the action, according to Mike Marsh, who guides this river.

Author's daughter, Michelle, along with canine angler Grace (Mike Marsh's "partner"), show off a nice smallie taken on the Muskegon River.

Muskegon River

1. North Muskegon Waterfront Sport Park
2. Bear Lake Beach Park
3. North Muskegon
4. Veterans Memorial Park
5. Terrace Point Marine
6. Fisherman's Landing

In the summer months, there are great mayfly and caddis hatches. Blue wings and stoneflies are favorites of the rainbows and planted browns. Summer steelhead and smallmouth bass are caught on crayfish into September, then the salmon return throughout the entire river system. Many anglers release the smallies to help guarantee a future for these sizable fighters.

In fall, down from Croton Fall Dam, and all the downstream, coho and steelhead arrive and stay through the winter. The fish are big, the river is big, and the action is fantastic.

And don't forget the excellent walleye fishery in this river; some very nice sized walleye can be caught here.

Once the water drops and clears, most anglers sight-fish for spawning steelhead. Typically, anglers run from bedding area to bedding area, lining fish just about as fast as they can get on the gravel, but the fish become super-skittish. A better tactic is to fish the deeper runs and pools for fish that are dropping back and

for fresh-run fish on their way up. Another alternative to beat the crowd is to head downstream from Newaygo, where the fishing pressure is much less intense and there's plenty of good water. Try below the public access just south of Newaygo, Felch Avenue, Old Woman's Bend and Bridgeton.

Note: During summer, it is best to fish weekdays to eliminate the weekend crowds, not only other anglers but canoeists as well.

Fishing pressure drops off dramatically between Newaygo and Bridgeton, even though there is some beautiful water in this section of the river. Drift boaters will find more free area to work and bottom-bouncers will find fish that have not been continually harassed.

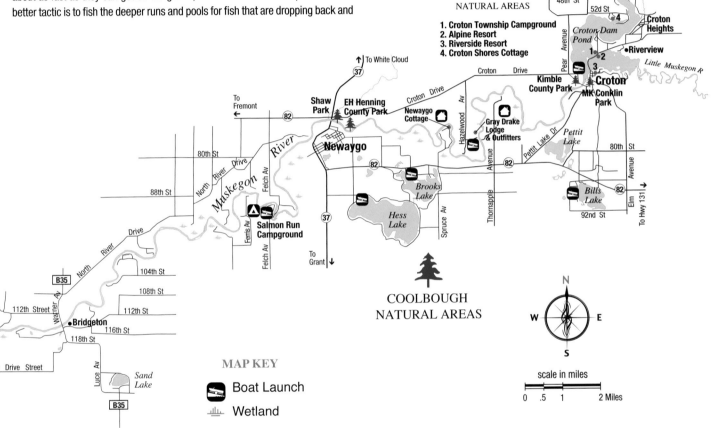

At a Glance

What: Top steelhead and bass river

Where: Between Croton Dam and Newaygo

Why: Some of the best spawning habitat in the state

Information/Guides: Muskegon County Convention & Visitors Bureau, (231) 722-3751, www.muskegon.org; **Mike Marsh, Marsh Ridge River Guide Service**, 10069 River Bend, Baldwin, 49304, (231) 920-7527

Landings: Croton Dam, Pine Street, High Rollaways and Henning Park. Good access to the river is available just below Newaygo at a DNR access, at Felch Avenue, Old Women's Bend and at Bridgeton

Bait & Tackle: Parsley's Sport Shop, 70 State Rd, Newaygo, 49337, (231) 652-6986; **Ed's Sport Shop,** 712 Michigan Ave., Baldwin, 49304, edssportshop@yahoo.com, edssportshop@att.com, (231) 745-4974; **Pappy's Bait & Tackle,** 17092 Caberfae Highway, Wellston, 49689, (231) 848-4142

Pere Marquette River
Mason County

The Pere Marquette River (PM) is without doubt one of the finest overall trout, steelhead, and salmon fisheries in the Great Lakes area. In general, this marvelous river meanders its way through vast stretches of land and eventually empties into Pere Marquette Lake and then to Lake Michigan. The regular trout season on this river is superb for resident browns. High-energy steelhead enter the creek from Lake Michigan in early fall and provide excellent fly-fishing throughout the winter till early spring. Salmon enter the creek in late summer and provide good angling through mid-fall. Quality hatches of mayflies, caddis, and stoneflies exist which provide tremendous dry-fly angling for the river's resident trout.

Mike Marsh, of Marsh Ridge River Guide Service, has fished this river and several others in this part of the state for most of his life. He fishes steelhead all winter and into May; browns are a good bite from the later weeks of March through mid-May using streamers as an offering; downriver the *Hex*, gray drakes and Hendricksons are hot selections in late May and into early June. Then it's night fishing at Walhalla utilizing drakes at dusk; night fishing produces nice 18-25-inch fish, but during the daylight hours, only the smaller 16-inch average fish are generally netted. Late August arrives and so do the kings, which are popular right through into September while they migrate upriver. Flies, Thundersticks, spinners and streamers are successful offerings. This fishery will last until later October. Then the steelhead and coho arrive in late October as the waters cool, and will stay well into the winter months.

Marsh says the average size range for rainbows will be 10 to 16 pounds, the browns are in the 6- to 15-inch range, but many are 20-plus inches. But don't bet on the larger browns without some skills that are beyond this writing. Years of patience, and angling proficiency are something you gain by doing, not just reading.

The jewel of the PM is the Flies-Only section that extends from M-37 south of Baldwin to Gleason's Landing. This seven-mile section features extensive gravel stretches that attract scores of spawning fish. Anglers often spot the redds and spawning activity, then drift egg flies, streamers and nymphs in front of the rainbows, hoping to coax them to bite. The area is popular with fly-anglers and drift-boats floating down the river. No-kill regulations have done little to lessen fishing pressure. The water in this section has characteristic pools, riffles, and runs that hold large trout and steelhead quite well. The upper regulations area is easy to wade while the lower section near Gleason's Landing is deeper and quite a bit faster.

Weekends are busy on this river, especially during prime fishing, so plan a weekday trip if you can. Expect plenty of fish from 5 to 12 pounds, and trophies topping 17 pounds are taken with regularity.

There are some nice holes below Bowman's Landing, with plenty of wood and timber cover that trout seek out, but the river is slow moving and a good time to fish this stretch is on a cool or cold rainy day.

The Middle Branch of the PM is small averaging approximately 25 feet in width. Sand, gravel, and silt make up much of the bottom of the river. A few boulders, fallen trees, and a lot of sharp bends help to create seams and holding water for the trout. There are impressive resident browns that can reach twenty inches in this area. The main river is larger, averaging approximately 50-60 feet below James Road and larger yet below the junction of Baldwin River.

Sulak to the Branch Bridge and Upper Branch Road to Walhalla is a good winter float trip for steelhead. Everyone fishes the flies-only stretch so much during the season that the fish are wary and difficult to land, unless the water turns dark due to storm runoff. If you are an experienced angler, the "miracle mile" can be very productive.

In spring, the browns and steelies are good throughout the entire river system. Early spring is best, using nymphs, #12 stoneflies, or micro eggs that resemble an egg that has been in the river for some time, bouncing along the bottom. Streamers are also a favored bait.

Marsh states that, "excellent fishing exists all the way from Baldwin to Walhalla." The best access points include Bowman's Bridge, MacDougal's, Rainbow Rapids, Sulak, Upper Branch Bridge, Lower Branch Bridge and Walhalla. Anglers use rolling spawn bags, chucking in-line spinners or pulling plugs from a drift-boat.

In winter, Hot-N-Tots are productive if you wish to row the river. The best area is from the MacDougal's all the way downriver.

During summer the water is too warm downstream toward Lake Michigan, so is mid river above Indian Bridge. There is a lot of marsh land in this area and mayfly hatches. It's a more peaceful stretch of river with overhanging trees and brush, providing much needed summer shade. The river is also wider and deeper, so bigger fish hang out here looking for an occasional grasshopper or cricket to float by, providing an easy meal.

According to Marsh, late May through early July is usually the peak of the dry-fly fishing with mayflies on the river including Hendricksons, Blue Winged Olives, Gray Drakes, Brown Drakes, and Michigan Caddis, one of the largest mayflies. Stoneflies include a variety of species, with Little Black Stones being most popular, especially as nymphs for steelhead. Large brown trout can be found gorging themselves on any of these insects. The *Hex* hatch is one of the most popular for big fish, especially on the lower river below. Terrestrials are also an important part of the summertime fishing. Steelhead flies are tied in multitude of colors, including black and brown to shades of pink and chartreuse.

The last week of August and first three weeks of September the browns get off the bite. The salmon move in first, followed by the coho and steelhead in October. The steelhead have nice coloring at this point, and the river is gangbusters throughout its entire length.

Drift boating down the Pere Marquette River during the winter can put you in a spectacular winter wonderland.

Pere Marquette River

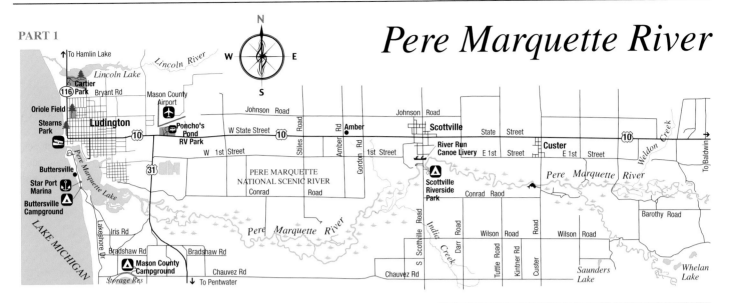

PART 1

Gleason's Landing to the mouth is a long and very productive section of river with deep pools, strong runs and riffles that tend to hold some very nice sized steelhead and large resident trout. Drifting a black stonefly nymph or egg pattern behind a fallen tree or in a deep run here could produce a ten-plus-pound steelhead or a twenty-plus-inch brown.

"Below Gleason's Landing the river gains speed and wading becomes more difficult," says Marsh. Most anglers float-fish this section of river. If you decide to wade this section, be cautious and be sure to move slowly. It can be a dangerous and very deceptive river, yet at the same time you can put yourself on some of the most productive trout and steelhead water in the state. There is approximately twenty miles of fabulous fishing from Gleason's to where it empties into the lake.

Note: Keep in mind that there is a flies-only stretch on this river from Baldwin (M-37), downriver to Gleason's Landing.

At a Glance

What: Steelhead and salmon

Where: One of the finest trout streams anywhere

Information/Guides: Mike Marsh, Marsh Ridge River Guide Service, (231) 920-7527, www.marshguide.com. Also check out **Evolution Sportfishing Charters,** 16896 Timberdunes, Grand Haven, (231) 920-7527

Landings: Access to the river is fairly easy to find and is located in many areas. The upper river, and especially the upper regulations area, has several access points. Route 10, MI37, and other side roads will lead you to the river and its access points. A few access points include Switzer Bridge (Middle Branch), Ledge Hole, and Gleason's Landing

Bait & Tackle: Baldwin Bait & Tackle, 9331 S. M-37, Baldwin, 49304, (877) 422-5394, www.fishbaldwin.com; **Ed's Sport Shop,** 712 Michigan Ave., Baldwin, 49304, edssportshop@yahoo.com, edssportshop.com, (231) 745-4974

PART 2

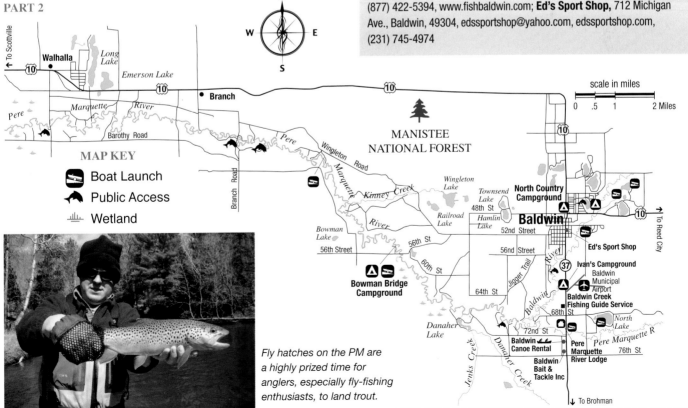

MAP KEY

- Boat Launch
- Public Access
- Wetland

Fly hatches on the PM are a highly prized time for anglers, especially fly-fishing enthusiasts, to land trout.

Rifle River Arenac County

When I think of the Rifle River, two things come to mind: sucker fishing and canoeing. As early spring arrives, the river bank is packed with anglers with nets and fishing poles trying to catch, what some refer to , as the "poor man's walleye." As nightfall occurs, campfires bring light to the banks and the party starts.

Fishing for suckers is simple and cheap. To fish for them, an angler doesn't need fancy equipment or a boat. They don't taste as good as prized walleye, but if smoked or canned, suckers can be a pleasurable treat (see recipe website at end of story).

Suckers run the rivers to spawn in the spring. A general rule of thumb for the sucker run is to wait until the first good rain after ice out to start targeting them. The suckers will start running slow, but by early April, the heavy action should begin. Depending on the year, the hot action will last for a week or two.

The Rifle River is probably the most popular of all the sucker rivers in lower Michigan. Sucker fishing is an event in Omer, where the town holds an annual sucker fest. Even if you don't fish, there are plenty of activities to keep your interest.

All you need for sucker fishing is a simple rod-and-reel set-up. Any rod and reel has the potential to catch suckers but I prefer a medium-light pole over 6 feet long and a spinning reel. Fishing for suckers on ultra-light tackle is a fantastic way to enjoy the battle of these bottom feeders. Suckers feel more like salmon when using an ultra-light rod. For line choice, 6- or 8-pound monofilament will do the trick.

The majority of suckers find their way into an angler's bucket with a good old-fashioned hook and worm. No fancy lures, no color choices, no electronics. You don't even have to worry about where the suckers are holding in the water column. Suckers favor a ball of worms a couple inches from the bottom of the river and that's about it. Simple.

There are a couple of typical methods many anglers use to present the hook and worm to a sucker. One experienced sucker angler I know takes an egg sinker with a hole in its center and then threads it onto his line. Make sure to use enough weight to get the offering to the bottom of the river. After this is done, he ties a medium-sized hook to the end of the line. This method will allow the egg sinker to move along your line allowing the hook and worm to always be in the sucker's line of sight no matter the depth.

If you want to get a beginner out (child or adult) this is about as easy, inexpensive, and effective as any method of fishing, utilizing the barest of necessities for fishing tackle. Even hooking up most any rod with an Eagle Claw snelled hook and a sinker consisting of a large old rusty nut from your home workshop goes a long way to enticing a sucker or two into taking your bait offering.

If you prefer to get sophisticated, try a barrel swivel tied to the main 10-12-pound-test line, followed by 12-18 inches of monofilament line about two pounds lighter than the main line. The tag end of the knot attaching the leader to the swivel is left on, providing a location for attaching enough split shot to keep it all on the bottom of the river, and helping reduce snags. A night crawler tipped at the end should do the trick. When tying the leader, make sure it is longer than three inches. In Michigan, it is illegal to fish with anything shorter. If experiencing snags, apply the method from the above technique.

If you are experiencing a lot of snags, instead of tying the hook directly, tie a barrel swivel to the end of the line. After the barrel swivel, tie a 3- to 4-inch leader out of lighter pound-test followed by the hook. When snagged, the hook and leader will be the only thing that breaks off.

Given the right day, you can easily take home a bucket full of suckers. In Michigan, there are no creel limits, so take all you can eat, as long as you do it without waste.

Suckers are actually great eating with a mild flavor. Many anglers prefer the smoked flavor of sucker, but some standard fish recipes work well also.

Sometimes it's simply nice to prop your lawn chair along the bank of a sucker-filled river, grab a good book, set out your line and enjoy the spring day. And if you take a kid or even an adult beginner along, the resulting experience may lead to a lifetime of continued fishing adventures.

The Rifle may be known for its spring sucker fishing, but it produces other species as well. Steelies are not as common as some other Michigan rivers, but they are worth giving a try when the waters turn colder (Oct/Nov), right into spring. Dale Farrell, a local angler quite familiar with the Rifle, states that "it is not uncommon to catch a nicely colored steelhead in the 28" range." If you search the 5-6-foot holes near embankments you can often hook a steelhead. If you fish a hole for 10-15 minutes without any luck, move on to another hole.

They will move in from Lake Huron right up to Rose City. You can try spawn bags in the spring, but simple spoons often work well. On the Au Sable to the north, Hot-N-Tots often entice fall/winter steelhead, so you can try them on the Rifle as well.

Occasionally you might hook on to a brook trout, or even a salmon, but these are not as common as steelhead.

Note: Sucker recipes: www.southendwalleyeslayer.com/sucker2007.pdf

The sucker run on the Rifle is an annual springtime "festival" for many anglers.

At a Glance

What: Sucker fishing on Rifle River

Where: Omer (M-23)

Why: One of the best sucker fishing spots in the state

How: Simple equipment with lots of action off river banks

Regs: No limit

Bait & Tackle: Wright's Sports Store, 100 N Huron Rd (M-23) Au Gres, 48703, (989) 876-8720 (crawlers, wax worms, spawn); **Dean's Live Bait & Tackle,** 2260 M 33, Alger, 48610, (989) 836-2460; **Frank's Great Outdoors,** email: info@franksgreatoutdoors.com, (989) 697-5341, 1212 N. Huron Rd. (M-13), Linwood, 48634 (full-service bait and tackle)

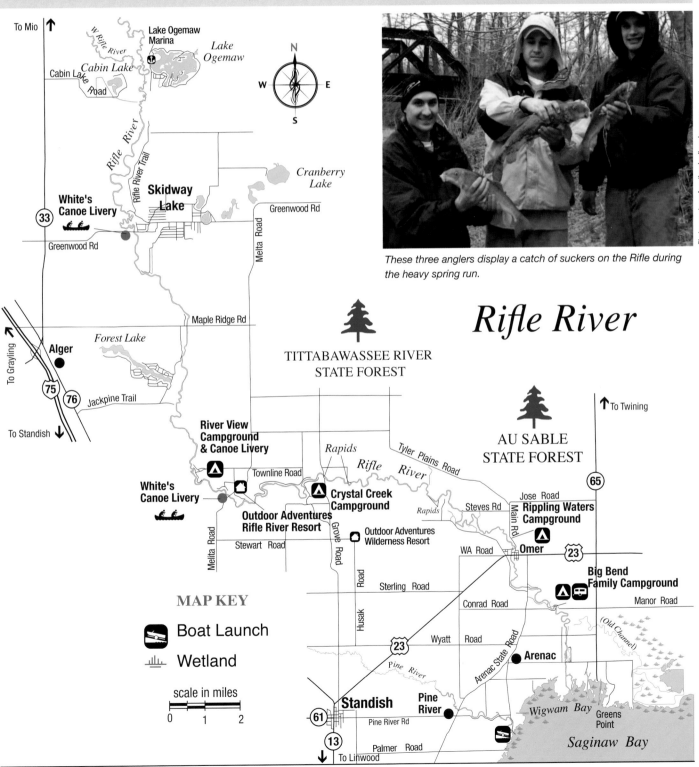

Photos courtesy of southendwalleyeslayer.com

These three anglers display a catch of suckers on the Rifle during the heavy spring run.

Rifle River

TITTABAWASSEE RIVER STATE FOREST

AU SABLE STATE FOREST

MAP KEY

🛥 Boat Launch

〰 Wetland

scale in miles
0   1   2

Saginaw/Tittabawassee Rivers
Saginaw/Bay Counties

The majestic Saginaw River travels a 22-mile-long journey carrying water from the Tittabawassee and Shiawassee rivers northward to the Saginaw Bay (yes, rivers do travel north). From here, the water continues on to Lake Huron. By passing through Bay City and Saginaw, the Saginaw River provides passage for shipping routes carrying goods from one place to another. In addition, this river system is also a favorite among walleye anglers, being a site for the popular Shiver on the River Contest held each year. It is common for the top anglers in this contest to weigh in 11-plus-pound walleye.

Approximately half the record-setting walleye in Michigan are taken from this area of the state.

In the early days, spring and fall were hotspot times to hunt for walleye. Now the summer season is joining the mix. Not to be left out is the wintertime ice-fishing season. Ice shanties and snowmobile anglers can be seen far and wide staking claim to a portion of the ice they hope will score big in the walleye department. As for locations to ice fish, just drive along the river and look for the scores of anglers or ice shanties. There are no real secret spots here, only "secret" days when the fish may be biting better than some other day. But that's fishing.

MAP KEY

🚤 Boat Launch

〰️ Wetland

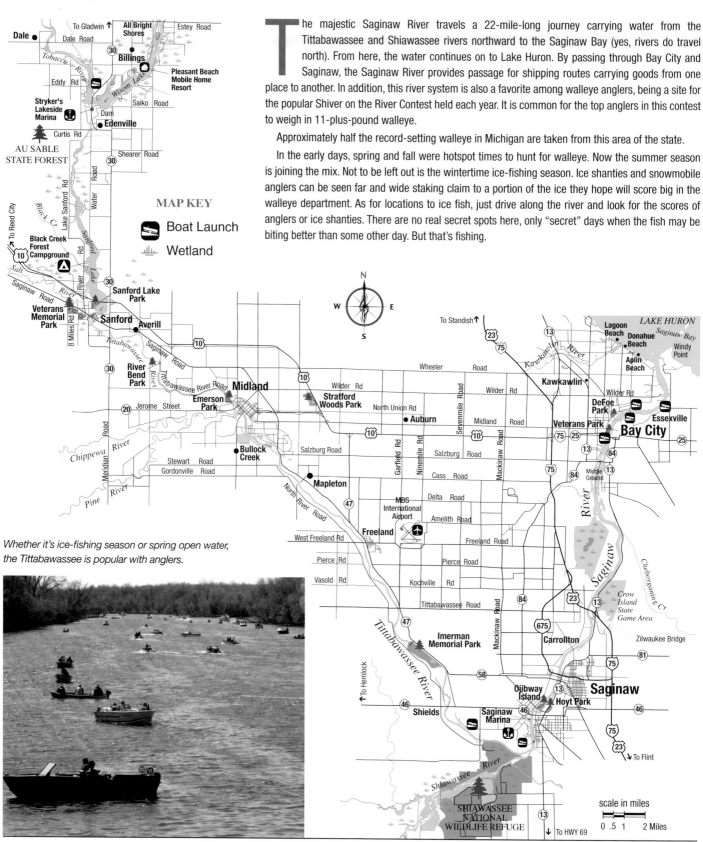

Whether it's ice-fishing season or spring open water, the Tittabawassee is popular with anglers.

scale in miles

0 .5 1   2 Miles

One of the best physical features of walleye is their ability to reflect light. This strength gives the fish an amazing ability to see clearly in dark or muddy waters. For this reason dimly lit times of day are their favorite feeding times.

Effective Walleye Fishing Rigs

At any time during the hunt for walleye there are several options an angler can select. The simplest yet most effective way has four elements that work tremendously when placed together on a single line. The four elements are a lead weight, spinner blade, beads and a hook. Sure there are fancier elements to place on a line in a variety of combinations. The end results will not be nearly as effective as with this combination.

The key here is the lead-weight-head jig. Walleye love lead-weight-head jigs. This could be due to any number of things. Among them being that walleye view the lead-head jig as a strange yet familiar object in the water. They strike almost without warning so as not to let this object slip away. Anglers welcome this favoritism for jigs. It is among the most affordable options for anglers. A variety of colors and sizes are available on the market, allowing anglers to mix it up every now and then.

Two variations of lead-head jigs are available. One is a flip-tail jig and the other is a skirt-tail jig. Pair either one with a minnow or other live bait selection on the hook for great results. Walleye prefer to eat crawfish, small crustaceans and night crawlers. Keep a healthy stock of each in your tackle box to keep walleye on the end of the line.

The second type of effective walleye rig is the Blakemore Roadrunner. This rigging has been around almost as long as walleye have been manning the waters. Even so, it is still a very popular and effective rigging technique for reeling in elusive walleye. One of the greatest aspects of this rig is the fact that it cannot be used incorrectly.

At night walleye prefer night crawlers, small plugs, bullheads, leeches and minnows. Feeding time is from dusk to dawn. These are the hours when the waters are at their darkest and walleye can do their best hunting. These are also the hours anglers need to strike with the best rig combinations known in the fishing community.

Saginaw River

Like any system with a bounty of catchable fish in it, the techniques used vary and are many, depending on your intended prey and often the time of year you're fishing for them. Few lures can beat the Jigging Rapala for sheer numbers of fish caught through the ice on the Saginaw. Jigged near bottom, with a morsel of minnow meat hooked to the belly hook of the lure, and your chances for success are greatly increased. And during the open-water seasons few things beat a jig-and-minnow offering. Jigging the right-sized, weighted tidbit straight up and down letting it hit bottom, while slowly drifting in complete unison with the current, catches the majority of all the species available, especially walleyes. Trolling crankbaits like the Dave's Ka'Boom Winning Streak, the Storm ¼-ounce Hot-N-Tot or Rapala #7 Shad Rap all take their share of walleyes during the day and some real monsters during nighttime.

In my experience, November and December are the best times to intercept a truly big walleye. The spring fishery is also good, but the legal walleye season re-starts almost too late to intercept the spawned-out females before they drop back out of the river and back into the Saginaw Bay system. So many of the fish caught are the smaller 2- to 3-pound male hold-overs.

Tittabawassee River

A primary tributary of the Saginaw River, the Tittabawassee River, unlike neighboring Shiawassee, is "relatively clear." Walleye staging in preparation for the spawn seek out deep pools with current breaks created by logs or boulders. While casting crankbaits can at times be an effective presentation on the Tittabawassee, a more productive technique involves casting jig-and-plastic

combos from an anchored boat or from shore.

The Tittabawassee nurtures thousands of spawning walleyes late winter into spring, as well as their offspring after they hatch. Her twisting wooded shorelines, sand with occasional gravel-strewn bottom is perfect habitat for river-run walleyes, pike, some largemouth, and many huge smallmouth bass. Virtually every freshwater species known to the Great Lakes can be found in varying numbers during certain seasons in the Tittabawassee River system.

The only downside to this gem is her unfriendly attitude towards any boats larger than 17 feet and sporting motors with long shafts. The Tittabawassee is very shallow and dangerous during high water. Long stretches of water 1-foot deep are not uncommon. Also, many hazards abound, including abandoned old bridges and their cement supports, pier heads, and pylons left behind in the river. You can fish from its convergence with the Saginaw River, up-stream to the Dow Spillway Dam in Midland.

As far as techniques go, nothing beats a jig-and-minnow cast while anchored or hopped while slipping the current, for every species of fish swimming in the river. You can catch everything from fall salmon and steelhead to spring white bass and catfish on this offering and technique. The key is finding and recognizing the preferred holding areas of each species during each season or in each fluctuation of the water table. Holes, slots, deep runs or wing dams all hold fish at some point. It's when the water fluctuates that some of these spots get better or worse, during wet or winter thaw periods or when the Sanford Dam is releasing or holding water back from Sanford Lake, well upriver of the Dow Spillway. Once one has a handle on the tricky nature of this river, it can provide you with some real fishing memories.

At a Glance

What: Some of the best walleye fishing in both winter and summer

Where: From Freeland area on the Tittabawassee River, to the mouth of Saginaw Bay via Saginaw River

Information/Guides: Great Lakes Bay Regional Convention & Visitors Bureau (Main Office), 515 N. Washington Avenue, Third Floor, Saginaw, 48607, (800) 444-9979; **Walleye Express Charters**, Captain Dan Manyen, 1686 S.E. Boutell Road, Essexville, 48732, (989) 893-4802, www.fishingsaginawbay.com

Landings: The DNR has a good ramp and large parking lot very near the mouth of the Saginaw River; 3 docks and 6 boat slips. Exit #164 off I-75 (Wilder Rd.). Take Wilder east past all the shops, turn left at the light at Patterson Rd. just as the road curves to the right. Take Patterson north almost to the end, turn right at Don's Quick Stop. Follow that to the end. It's $6 per day or $24 per year, and that can be used at most DNR ramps in the state. Other sites include: Zilwaukee just south of the Z-Bridge, Rust Avenue Boat Launch Saginaw, Imerman Park (Tittabawassee River access off of Midland Road just south of Tittabawassee Road, Saginaw Twp.), Center Road (Tittabawassee River access off Center and Michigan in Saginaw), Wickes Park Saginaw, (Saginaw River access), Veterans Memorial Park on west side of the river in downtown Bay City (Saginaw River access).

Bait & Tackle: Michigan Sportsmen Bait Tackle & Hunting Supplies, 612 W Center Rd, Essexville, 48732, (989) 893-6550; **Frank's Great Outdoors** is the next closest location listed, on M-13, Linwood, just south of Anderson Road; **Gander Mountain.,** Tittabawassee & 675 (NW corner), Saginaw; **Cabela's,** Bay & Tittabawassee Rds., Saginaw. There are hardware stores in Freeland (Tittabawassee River access) that also provide some fishing supplies.

St. Clair River St. Clair County

The St. Clair River in southeastern Michigan is one of the most productive walleye fisheries in the state. According to the Michigan Department of Natural Resources, the river system attracts fishermen from all over the country each spring and summer. Walleye are an aggressive species, making them fun to catch, as well as popular table fare. Certain methods of catching walleye are known to produce results depending on the season, time of day, location and lure choice.

Doug Samsal, who also guides on the Manistee on the west side of the state, has found a summer home along the St. Clair River, having guided here for over 10 years. His experiences on both the river and Lake St. Clair prompted him to develop a video titled, "Spinning & Bait Casting Made Easy." He notes a tremendous number of anglers who frankly do not know how to cast, and often blamed the poor technique on poor equipment, when in fact, many of them had expensive rods and reels. Sounds like a golf story. "It does not matter," says Doug, "whether you have an expensive outfit, or a Snoopy one, the problem is in the technique." The video can be found on his website: www.manisteerivercharter.com.

Doug says that walleye average around 19 inches, muskie in the 41-45-inch average range, and smallies three pounds. Walleye can easily be caught upwards of mid to upper 20-inch range.

Walleye: Doug starts his guide service the first part of April, but says he could start early in May on the St. Clair River. He says that walleyes and muskie are in the river in early spring, but not the smallmouth bass, aside from a limited number of resident fish. The smallies will move in to the river system during the heat of summer.

This later arrival is a result of the long journey the fish must take each year to return to Lake Huron from their spawning waters in Lake Erie to the south. Therefore, fish the river beginning in late spring when the fish return and again when they head back to Lake Erie. The river's position between lakes causes it to act like a thoroughfare for walleye, which results in substantial numbers of fish found in the waters each season.

In the early part of the spring season, Doug fishes the area from Marine City down to Algonac. "This is a hot spot for walleye," he says, but as the season progresses, every branch off the St. Clair will have good numbers of walleye. Work the 18-35-foot depths, and deeper at times, even as deep as 60-plus feet. Crawler harnesses, crankbaits, as well as jigging will work at this time. As the summer moves on, drifting with crawler harnesses and working tube jigs are the main methods of landing walleye. The waters between Stag Island and Blue Water Bridge are highly fished areas.

Jigging in St. Clair River proves most productive, with many anglers using ¼- to ½-ounce jigs, usually either chartreuse or orange. Maintain a vertical presentation while jigging, and add live bait to the jig to help improve your success. Trolling is another popular method to be used later in the season. Anglers often use Rapalas, Wiggle Warts and spoons for trolling. As fall approaches and the fish become less active, you may find jigging in deep water with spoons leads to more bites.

Keep in mind that walleye are a light-sensitive species and commonly stick to darker areas of the water. At midday you are likely to find them in the deeper waters near the bottom, where light is less intense. However in the early morning and later in the evening, you should cast into the weed beds and other shallow areas near the bank. This is where walleye come to feed before the heat and light of the day have penetrated the shallow waters.

Muskie: Muskie are often seen "jumping all over the place," says Samsal, and it is not uncommon to land a few nice-size fish. Doug states that muskie don't care so much about the type of lure you toss at them, but rather the presentation. In the river Doug likes to cast or even jig for them using crankbaits, jerkbaits,

The St. Clair River is known for great runs of walleye, but is also a very popular bass fishing river.

St. Clair River

spinner baits and soft plastics that go deep. "Cover every depth," he says. One of the most consistent colors however is anything that resembles perch. Many local anglers know how important color is, so they often paint new lures that quickly become favorites. Muskie can change their feeding style for various baits, so you need to be flexible. Work different lures, and fish different areas of the river.

Smallmouth Bass: During a bass tournament one summer as this book was being developed, the anglers with Bassmaster's would often mention how spoiled we were to have such a great fishery in this area of Michigan. Tremendous walleye and muskie fishing, and fantastic smallmouth bass as well. When the smallies move in to the river system in good numbers, anglers use mostly soft plastic tube jigs, drop shots, and fish them deep, that is, in the 25-40-foot depths. "Most people don't think deep," says Sandal. But it pays to know where all the sunken objects are in the river and you can easily become snagged.

The bass are constantly on the move in the river, and just when you think you have a location tagged, they move on you. "They are like ghost fish," says Samsal. "They move a lot in the river, and you have to move with them."

At a Glance

What: Walleye, muskie, smallmouth bass

Where: Along the entire St. Clair River system

Information/Guides: Blue Water Area Convention & Visitors Bureau, 520 Thomas Edison Pkwy., Port Huron, 48060, bluewater@bluewater.org, (800) 852-4242, (810) 987-8687; Doug Samsal, www.manisteerivercharter.com, (231) 668-2894

Landings: I-94 Bridge Municipal Ramp, on the Black River, provides access to St. Clair River and Lake Huron. There are 49 parking spaces with toilets and courtesy piers. Operated by the City of Port Huron; **Marysville Boat Launch:** This site (along with one just north of it) provides access to St. Clair River. About 40 parking spaces, 4 ramps with courtesy piers, toilets. Operated by Marysville; Algonac Municipal Ramp: Provides access to the N. Channel of the St. Clair River. There are 40 parking spaces and a courtesy pier. No toilets. Operated by City of Algonac; **Fair Haven Boat Launch:** Provides access to Lake St. Clair, 47 parking spaces, toilets, and a courtesy pier. Operated by Michigan DNR; **Snooks Boat Launch:** Provides access to the N. Channel of St. Clair River. There are 35 parking spaces and toilets are available. This site has limited water depth. Operated by Michigan DNR

Bait & Tackle: Anderson's Pro Bait, 2731 Pine Grove Avenue, Port Huron, (810) 984-3232, www.andersonsprobait.com; **Gander Mountain,** 4055 24th Avenue, Fort Gratiot, 48059, (810) 385-6700, www.gandermountain.com

St. Joseph River Berrien County

In 1969 the Michigan Department of Natural Resources (MDNR) began stocking and managing the lower 23 miles of the St. Joseph River for trout and salmon. To expand this fishery, Michigan constructed a fish ladder at Berrien Springs Dam in 1975 which extended trout and salmon fishing opportunities an additional 10 miles upstream to Buchanan Dam.

The St. Joseph River project is truly unique. The success of this joint project would not have been possible without the cooperation and support of the two DNR agencies, USFWS, Indiana-Michigan Power Company (American Electric Power), private industry, local communities, Michigan Salmon and Steelheaders Association, Michigan Steelheaders and others. Unique features of the project include underground viewing chambers at four of the five ladders. Here biologists monitor fish passage with time-lapse video or computers. This allows for 24-hour evaluation of fish passage. The Berrien Springs and South Bend ladders also have facilities to enable easy capture of spawning fish (primarily steelhead) to supply eggs for the hatchery system.

"We don't get a lot of Chinooks moving into the St. Joe until late in the year because the river is so warm," offered charter captain and river guide Russ Clark. "The fishing can be tough because the salmon just blast right up to the dam, but anchoring with plugs, like Flatfish or Hot-N-Tots, can produce some pretty good catches at times. If you use spawn you might pick up a bonus Skamania steelhead too." Clark said the best river fishing in September is usually in the first few deep holes below Berrien Springs Dam.

Clark said the best fall chinook fishing in the big lake is right off the pier heads at St. Joe/Benton Harbor. "The hottest fishing usually starts right around late August and lasts until mid-September," offered Clark. Stitching the color line off the river mouth trolling very slowly with J-plugs and Spin Doctors is dynamite, he says. The usual chrome, chrome/redhead, lime/black back are good colors for plugs. Try a white/glow Spin Doctor and seaweed fly on a diver.

The north parking lot and wheelchair-accessible paved walkways at Silver Beach provide quick and easy access to South Pier at the mouth of the St. Joseph River. This popular fishing location offers anglers access to shore and pier fishing opportunities. Fish typically caught here include lake perch, rainbow trout (steelhead), brown trout, coho salmon, chinook salmon, whitefish and catfish.

Captain Russ fishes the St. Joe from the end of September to the following March or mid April. The river is shallow, only around 5-10 feet deep, with rocks and other submerged debris, so caution needs to be observed.

Salmon, both kings and coho, enter the river in September and anglers anchor and fish spawn on the bottom, or troll using plugs such as Hot-N-Tots or Wiggle Warts. Salmon in the 15-20-pound range can be caught this time of the season.

As October arrives, salmon fishing tapers off and steelhead start to make their way upstream for their winter stay. You can fish steelies the same way you do salmon, either anchored or trolling. The river can freeze, and when it does anglers move upstream to the dam where it is 12-15 feet deep. Casting with spinners, Wobble Glows, or spawn bags are popular methods here.

A Wobble Glow is a small piece of cork that is rounded on one end and has a flat angle on the other end causing it to wobble in the current. There is a hole through it so you can slide it on your line. Slide a bead or two on the line, then tie a hook on. They come in many colors and sizes. They have proven to catch a lot of fish.

This action will continue to the end of March or even into April.

Walleye are also caught here during the winter, upwards of 10-12 pounds, however it is not a strong fishery, says Clark. Jigging with minnows, or summer drifting with crawlers on the bottom, can often land you a nice 'eye. Most of the larger walleye are caught in the winter however.

Up river is the town of Berrien Springs, home to Berrien Springs Fish Ladder on St. Joe River, allowing salmon and steelhead to move past the dam. There are several public-access sites for catching steelhead, coho salmon, walleye, smallmouth bass, panfish and pike in this area also. The best fishing near the fish ladder is from April to November.

Salmon and steelies are a great fall fishery on the St. Joe.

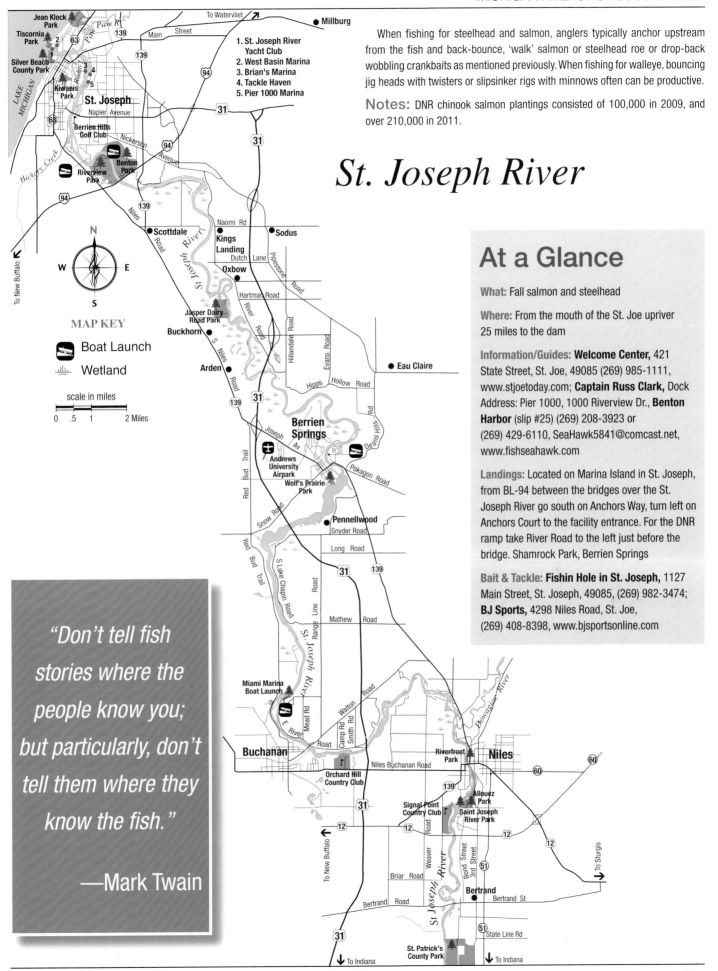

When fishing for steelhead and salmon, anglers typically anchor upstream from the fish and back-bounce, 'walk' salmon or steelhead roe or drop-back wobbling crankbaits as mentioned previously. When fishing for walleye, bouncing jig heads with twisters or slipsinker rigs with minnows often can be productive.

Notes: DNR chinook salmon plantings consisted of 100,000 in 2009, and over 210,000 in 2011.

St. Joseph River

At a Glance

What: Fall salmon and steelhead

Where: From the mouth of the St. Joe upriver 25 miles to the dam

Information/Guides: Welcome Center, 421 State Street, St. Joe, 49085 (269) 985-1111, www.stjoetoday.com; **Captain Russ Clark,** Dock Address: Pier 1000, 1000 Riverview Dr., **Benton Harbor** (slip #25) (269) 208-3923 or (269) 429-6110, SeaHawk5841@comcast.net, www.fishseahawk.com

Landings: Located on Marina Island in St. Joseph, from BL-94 between the bridges over the St. Joseph River go south on Anchors Way, turn left on Anchors Court to the facility entrance. For the DNR ramp take River Road to the left just before the bridge. Shamrock Park, Berrien Springs

Bait & Tackle: Fishin Hole in St. Joseph, 1127 Main Street, St. Joseph, 49085, (269) 982-3474; **BJ Sports,** 4298 Niles Road, St. Joe, (269) 408-8398, www.bjsportsonline.com

1. St. Joseph River Yacht Club
2. West Basin Marina
3. Brian's Marina
4. Tackle Haven
5. Pier 1000 Marina

MAP KEY

Boat Launch

Wetland

scale in miles

0 .5 1 2 Miles

"Don't tell fish stories where the people know you; but particularly, don't tell them where they know the fish."

—Mark Twain

St. Mary's River Chippewa County

The St. Mary's River, connecting Lake Superior to northern Lake Huron, is a unique river in its diversity. It's a busy shipping channel, a waterfowl hunting hotspot, and holds a tremendous variety of sport fish, including walleye, northern pike, whitefish, rainbow trout, four species of salmon, smallmouth bass, herring, and a host of other species (up to 80 or so). If you enjoy exploring and enjoy a serene environment while fishing, the St. Mary's may be just your ticket.

Walleye: Walleye abound here due to the vast structure found from the shallow bowls like Munuscong, or the abrupt rocky points and reefs near Sugar and Neebish islands, or the crystal-clear water of the main river where huge boulders expose themselves in depths exceeding 20 feet. And, just off the main channels, as well as the vast sand flats with their undulating and ever-changing furrows, is where walleyes like to hold.

This river favors no one single tactic, hotspot, hot depth, or color. It will challenge you and that is exactly what makes fishing here so enjoyable.

If you prefer jigging, try the expansive shallow flats of Munuscong Bay or deeper jiggers have the waters off of Sugar and Neebish islands to fish. Trollers, either with crawler harnesses or crankbaits, have the entire river to work with as pieces of structure are scattered throughout the system. Keep in mind that large freighter's frequent this river and obviously have the right of way; no playing "chicken" with these thousand-footers.

Whitefish: For whitefish, it's best to break the river down into two sections in the Soo area. The upper river, the water up from the locks to Brush Point, and the lower river, below the locks, including the Edison Hydro Plant. Be sure to have light-tipped rods for whitefish. No horsing these light-mouthed fish.

Usually (not ice fishing), whitefish are caught in early spring or in the fall when they migrate to areas with current, such as rivers or narrow flows in the lake system. Whitefish have very small and tender mouths, which is why most people who catch whitefish were walleye fishing while using really small hooks and minnows or small jigs.

At a Glance

What: Numerous fish species in the St. Mary's River, especially whitefish

Where: East end of Michigan's Upper Peninsula

Why: River fishing doesn't get any better for such a diverse number of species

Information/Guides: De Tour Village, www.detour@detourvillage.com, (906) 297-5987, P.O. Box 161, De Tour Village, 49725; Sault Ste. **Marie Convention & Visitors Bureau,** 536 Ashmun Street, Sault Ste. Marie, 49783, 800-MI-SAULT, or (906) 632-3366, info@saultstemarie.com

Landings: There are a couple of boat landings just east of town as well Raber Bay Landing north of Lime Island, 26816 S. Raber Bay Dr., Goetzville, 49736, (906) 297-5812. Detour Harbor Marina DNR, 600 N Ontario St., De Tour Village, 49725, (906) 297-5947

Bait & Tackle: Woody's One Stop Shop carries an assortment of live bait. 1198 East Portage Avenue, Sault Ste. Marie, 49783-2470, (906) 632-7361

In very early spring, whitefish generally migrate into a river system or stream to feed on walleye, pike and sucker eggs that are being dropped during the spawn. The best way to fish for spring whitefish is in the river with 4-pound-test line and really tiny hooks with a single salmon egg, grub, a little ball of Berkley Power Dough or the best bait, Wax Worms. Have a small float and let the bait float down stream and over the deeper pools that are behind the gravel spawning beds.

In the fall, whitefish migrate into rivers and spawn in the same spawning beds as walleyes. During the spawn, whitefish feed during the day which is the exact opposite of most fish. You will find that as soon as it gets dark, the fish lose all interest in food and concentrate on their spawn.

Generally, whitefish will stay shallow all winter. In spring, they feed on walleye eggs again and do not go deep until after they gorge themselves on the spring mayfly hatch.

A small jig suspended beneath a float or casting bubble near the surface still takes lots of whitefish and won't attract as many pike. This rig can also be drifted or slowly retrieved across rocky reefs and points without hanging up. Just before dark, whitefish sipping emerging insects from the surface film often hit dry flies presented on a fly rod or casting bubble, or small compact spoons like Little Cleos.

A good choice of rod would be a 9-foot fly rod in the 6-weight style. Nothing fancy, any inexpensive model will do just fine. Long steelhead rods, as in 9- or 10-footers will fit the bill also.

Most anglers go with a 6-pound line, attaching a three-foot leader of 2- or 4-pound test with a small barrel swivel, and adequate weight to get the bait down. If you decide to fish the upper river for whitefish, plan on fishing water from 20 to 30 feet deep with a considerable current.

When whitefish bite, a sense of weight at the end of the line is often all there is. Rather than feeling a bite, most times there's just a slight impression that something is at the end of the line. And when you set the hook, you will sometimes literally rip their lips off, even with a fly rod. So a quick, firm and short hook-set is all that is needed.

Downriver, below the locks, the tried-and-true hotspot is the power plant, but don't anchor here. Instead, you actually toss a hook, or anchor in a pinch, over the cement wall and catch the grass behind it. The force of the water coming out of the turbines is severe so you'll need a 20- to 40-foot length of rope tied from the anchor or hook and attached to the front eye or cleat of the boat. Strip about 12 feet of line off the reel, and toss the rig up into one of the turbine holes.

Salmon and Steelhead: Beginning in May and extending into June is when spring steelhead become available. From early-mid June through early August, Atlantic salmon become most prominent. Mid August through early October is when you'll find chinook and pink salmon. October brings a run of cohos, and steelhead enter once again, too.

When wading the rapids be aware that the bottom is rocky so bring studded felt-bottomed wading boots and a wading staff. Be very careful how far you wade out into the rapids, as they can be hazardous. Trolling activity starts in mid-June with Atlantics. Spoons are the bait of choice and the place to be is from the Sugar Island Ferry Dock up to the Edison Soo power house.

Late July you'll find chinook hanging out around the mouth of Garden River, which enters St. Mary's from Canada along the north channel across from Sugar Island. By mid-August chinook will be everywhere, from the Neebish Island area up to the locks and the Edison Soo plant. Spoons, J-plugs and Bomber-style baits all take fish. Trolling pretty much ends for the salmon species by late September.

Bass: Smallmouth bass are probably the most underutilized fish in the Soo area. That means pressure for these fighters is light to nonexistent and you'll have the water pretty much to yourself. Munuscong, Neebish, Sugar and

Potagannissing Bay are the hot spots. Early in the season you'll find them in the shallows looking to spawn. This June fishery is downright on fire in Munuscong and Potagannissing, with Lake Nicolet and Waiska Bay not far behind. Simple jig and crawler rigs take a lot of fish but you may want to toss some cranks in chartreuse or yellow and white.

The water will be stained with tannins so the hotter colors seem to work best. After the spawn, look for the fish in 8 to 16 feet of water. There must be structure in the form of old pilings, rock humps or the like to draw the fish in. Isolated weed beds are another prime choice. Now is the time to work Jig-n-Pigs, tubes and other soft baits. Don't be afraid to go big on bait size either, these smallies like a real man-size meal. Late summer and fall is prime time for these fish. Cranks are probably your best bet, as are stickbaits. For some reason the clown-finish lures produce amazingly well, but the natural finishes also do quite well. Weed beds will hold good numbers of fish right into fall.

Pike/Muskie: With good populations of prey species and clean waters spotted with an abundance of weed beds these two supreme predators are in fish heaven. Everything they need is right here. Early season fishing, say from the opener until mid June, is a shallow-water fishery most years. Big jerk baits, surface plugs and in-line spinners really shine at this time of year. Perennial hot spots include Izaak Walton Bay, Waishka Bay, and Munuscong. As summer wears on and the water warms you'll need to slow-troll the deeper weed beds, say the 12- to 18-foot depths, in order to find success.

Big stickbaits seem best now. It's late summer and into fall when this fishery really gets exciting. The fish become more active as the water cools, and it's now when casting again takes the forefront. Work the edges of those midsummer weed beds carefully, making sure your bait gets into every nook and cranny. These tooth-filled fish are waiting for prey and they won't be afraid to rip the rod out of your hands if they take a liking to your offering. Don't ask why, but orange is a very hot color now, particularly on Lake George and in the Upper River. Down on Munuscong, natural colors seem best but fire tiger finishes are also a good bet. This is the time for the entire arsenal—spinner baits, erratic cranks and big buzz baits all working magic. The night bite is particularly heart-stopping with the buzz-style baits. (Thanks to the Soo Convention & Visitors Bureau for their input into this section).

St. Mary's River

MAP KEY
- Boat Launch
- Wetland
- River Flow
- Ferry

The St. Mary's River has numerous species of game fish that travel from the Great Lakes up river, as well as some permanent species that reside in this river.

Two Hearted River
Luce County

The Big Two Hearted River is rated among the top ten trout streams in the U.S. Although Pulitzer Prize winner and noted author and journalist Ernest Hemingway used the Two Hearted name, it is thought that the story indicates that Hemingway was really describing a different trout stream, the Fox River near Seney. The story, set after World War I, was first published in 1925 as part of the collection. *In Our Time* and republished in 1972 as part of *The Nick Adams Stories*. He decided to name the story after the Two Hearted River, because he believed that that river's name had a more poetic feel. The Fox River is also the river that Hemingway fished while he was in Michigan. The time Ernest spent in Seney in 1919-1920 is what inspired the writing of *"Big Two Hearted River."*

A short excerpt from his book is as follows:

"While Nick walked through the little stretch of meadow alongside the stream, trout had jumped high out of water. Now as he looked down the river, the insects must be settling on the surface, for the trout were feeding steadily all down the stream. As far down the long stretch as he could see, the trout were rising, making circles all down the surface of the water, as though it were starting to rain."

Big Two-Hearted River *by Ernest Hemingway*

The Two Hearted and its four branches run west to east across northern Luce County for over 100 miles. The system drains a watershed of over 180 square miles of mostly remote lowland forests, marsh and bog. The high quality of the tea-colored water reflects relatively undisturbed natural conditions. The Two Hearted is the only Michigan stream to be designated a wilderness river under the states' Natural Rivers program. Most of it can be fly-fished and fishing pressure on the upper reaches is low to moderate.

Local angler and resident Mike Kimbler has fished this river for 25 years, and he is only 31 years old at this writing. So to say he knows it, is like saying Ernest Hemingway was a comic book writer. A few words of advice from Mike are fitting as he is well suited to comment on this magnificent river.

Mike starts to fish the Two Hearted for trout as soon as it warms up, usually around the end of March or beginning of April. Later in April the fish are on the beds, and Mike usually stops fishing to pursue walleye elsewhere. Anglers continue to fish here another few weeks.

Steelhead in the 25- to-30-inch size are common (8-9 pounds). He likes to fish from the Reed and Green Bridge off County Road 374, about six miles from the mouth of the river.

You can fish this river all year, and Mike says it is one of the best brookie rivers around, maybe in the country. He has caught them close to 20 inches (three pounds), but most average around 8 to 10 inches. Many of the feeder streams have nice brookies, including the south branch which has some very nice deeper holes.

During the summer, Mike has great luck fishing for brookies using Panther Martin spinners and crawlers. In the fall, for coho, Mepps spinners and spawn will provide you with some good action.

The steelies stay here all winter, but brookie season ends at the end of September.

Hemingway Passport Photo 1923.

MAP KEY

Boat Launch

Wetland

N
W E
S

LAKE SUPERIOR

Two Hearted River Campground

Rainbow Lodge

Jeep Trail

Mouth of 2 Heart Road

423

Coast Guard Line Road

Two Hearted River

412

North Pike Lake Road

412

Two Hearted Canoe Trip

Coast Guard Line Road

Reed & Green Campground

374

LAKE SUPERIOR STATE FOREST

410

410

Connor Lakes

LAKE SUPERIOR STATE FOREST

Wabash Creek

14

At a Glance

What: Great brook trout fishing, some of the best around. Nice steelhead as well

Where: Upper stretches of the famed Two Hearted River

Regs: Trout season regulations in effect

Information: www.exploringthenorth.com; **Newberry Area Tourism Association,** P.O. Box 308, Newberry, 49868, (906) 293-5562; **Paradise Chamber of Commerce,** (906) 492-3219, paradisecoc@jamadots.com

Landings: Access all along the river

Contacts: Two Hearted River Fishing Report, Jeff Ross, **Winter Haven Motel & Pine Stump Junction Rentals,** Newberry, 49868, (906) 658-3314 or 3357, jrwinterhaven@gmail.com

Bait & Tackle: Grand Marais Outfitters, N. 14277 Lake Avenue, Grand Marais, 49839, (906) 494-3333, www.grandmaraisoutfitters.net

scale in miles

0   .5   1   2 Miles

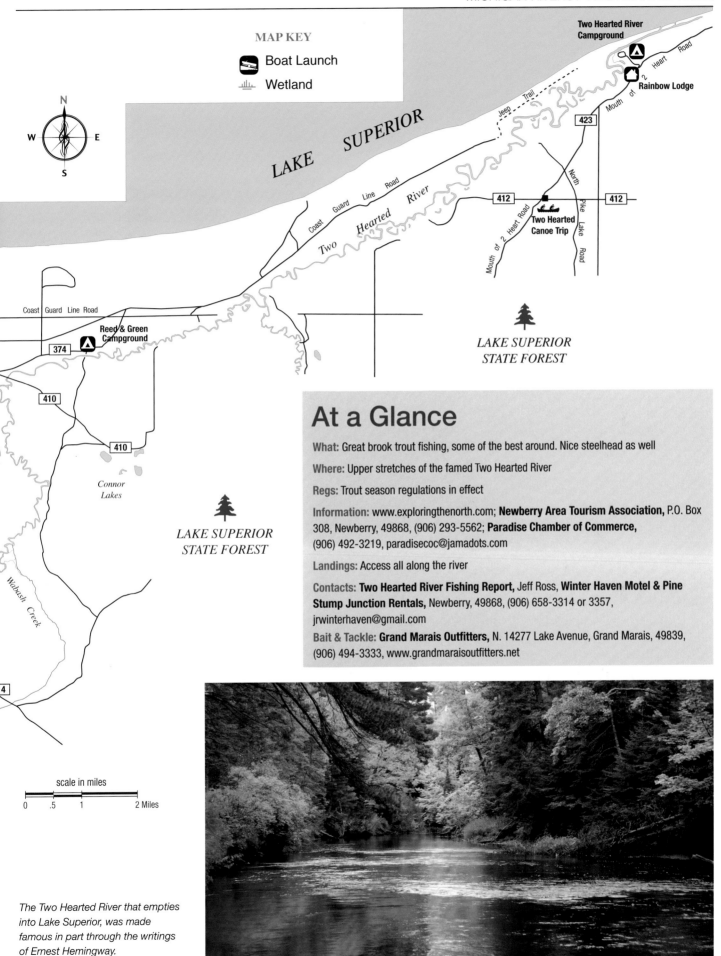

The Two Hearted River that empties into Lake Superior, was made famous in part through the writings of Ernest Hemingway.

M I C H I G A N

Keweenaw
(Isle Royale)

Keweenaw

Houghton

Ontonagon

Gogebic

Baraga

Marquette

Iron

Dickinson

LAKE

SUPERIOR

Alger

Delta

Schoolcraft

Luce

Mackinac

Chippewa

LAKE

HURON

Menominee

LAKE

MICHIGAN

Emmet

Charlevoix

Leelanau

Benzie

Grand
Traverse

Manistee

Mason

Oceana

Muskegon

Ottawa

Cheboygan

Antrim

Kalkaska

Wexford

Lake

Newaygo

Mecosta

Montcalm

Kent

Ionia

Allegan

Van
Buren

Berrien

Cass

Otsego

Crawford

Missaukee

Roscommon

Osceola

Isabella

Gratiot

Clare

Midland

Clinton

Barry

Kalamazoo

Saint
Joseph

Eaton

Calhoun

Branch

Presque
Isle

Montmorency

Alpena

Oscoda

Alcona

Ogemaw

Iosco

Gladwin

Arenac

Huron

Bay

Saginaw

Tuscola

Sanilac

Shiawassee

Genesee

Lapeer

Saint
Clair

Livingston

Ingham

Oakland

Macomb

Jackson

Washtenaw

Wayne

Hillsdale

Lenawee

Monroe

LAKE

ERIE

Charlevoix

Alpena

Oscoda

GREAT LAKES

Northern Lake Huron
From Alpena to Mackinaw City

The very northern Lake Huron area from Alpena up to Mackinaw City is a serene area of the state, unlike the more developed, touristy west side of the state. The traffic is manageable, homes on the water are more affordable, and fishing opportunities, both inland and along the Lake Huron shoreline, are endless. I often drive the M-23 route along the Lake Huron shoreline rather than down I-75 through the central part of the state. It takes me about an hour or so longer, going through all the small towns along the way, but I never tire of it.

As for fishing these Great Lakes waters, Jim Johnson, DNR Fish Biologist who covers the northern Lake Huron area, states that, "the numbers of quality lake trout caught are now in the 8-14-pound size category, which is quite high." They are being caught from Hammond Bay down to Alpena. Part of the reason for these numbers of lakers is due to a fishing reduction agreement with the tribe in that area of the state, along with good lamprey control methods in the late 90s along the St. Mary's River on east end of Upper Peninsula. This has cleaned up some major problems in Lake Huron, and now many of the lakers are of wild origin, so the trout are recovering nicely.

Coho Salmon: In the Rogers City area, salmon fishing has held up according to Johnson. Salmon are averaging in the 12-14-pound weight category for three-year-old fish. There are not many over 20 pounds, but the current weight range is about what the normal was in the 1990s.

Steelhead: Johnson also mentions that the steelhead are good in all ports along northern Lake Huron. "We have seen one of the highest catch rates in 2011, averaging 5 pounds and good numbers of steelhead, " says Jim.

Brown Trout: One unfortunate note is that the brown trout fishery has all but collapsed. With reductions in forage fish (e.g., alewives) for the predators, they apparently went after the brown trout, causing a significant reduction in these once highly sought after fish. To make matters worse, the brown's life expectancy is only about 3 years, very few make it to 4-5 years old. Steelhead, as a comparison, are still going strong at 4-5 years old. Lakers average 12-13 years old, and some live up to 30 years or more.

Atlantic Salmon: Northern Lake Huron is one of the best Atlantic salmon fisheries, from Alpena to Rogers City. Fishing activity is very good from May into June, when at this point they head up the St. Mary's River in the eastern upper peninsula to spawn. Many people who catch an Atlantic salmon think they caught a brown trout. You can catch them by casting from shore, or in the harbors, making this a fun fishing activity for people without boats.

Presque Isle harbor has some excellent walleye fishing, according to Johnson. He says that the next best area is Thunder Bay. Many walleye are caught along the shoreline, and this runs from Thunder Bay south to the Thumb of the extensive Lake Huron area. The best times to fish for walleye are on cloudy days or at dawn or dusk.

Another assist to the fish populations in Lake Huron has been cormorant control. Johnson says that there has been a resurgence of smallmouth bass, perch and walleye. This fish-eating bird population is now back to the 1980s level and at a level where they are not a threat to these gamefish populations.

Perch: Hoping for a recovery of cisco in northern Lake Huron, the always popular perch may start to increase in size and numbers. Currently the fish are still on the small side, 6-8 inches in the Thunder Bay down to the Tawas Bay

area. Should the cisco continue to increase, the walleye will switch to these rather than perch, thus allowing the perch to thrive again. Walleye used to eat alewives, gizzard shad, and perch, in that order. Without the other forage fish to eat, walleye will focus on perch. An example is all the gizzard shad in the Saginaw Bay, allowing walleye to focus more on them and less on perch. Thus, perch are being caught in good numbers in the 6-14-inch size.

Don Rang (fishalpena.com) is a veteran charter boat captain who works out of Alpena. Don catches a mixed bag of fish when he goes out on Lake Huron, and works hard to bring in 15-20 fish each trip. Don likes to start in spring through early summer, when fish are in close and the water is still at an ideal temperature; however, you can still fish this area in mid-summer by heading out a ways from shore. And Don will do it. His charter, like most, runs spring through early fall.

Don's methods include starting in the Alpena area and moving wherever he has to go to catch fish. The majority of fish caught are lakers, granted, due to the large numbers in Lake Huron. He will run four downriggers with spoons, flashers, green and white fly, using numerous color combinations. Sometimes he will run 2-3 colors, other times 6-8 or more different colors. The important thing, Don states, is to look for the proper temperature. For salmon it is 54 degrees, and for lakers, 52 degrees. But you also need to run lines out of this temperature zone to search for other suspended fish, like walleye. Sometimes he will hook walleye at 100 feet or so.

Fishing at all zones will catch more fish, he says. It is not uncommon to bring in 3-4 steelhead, upwards of 6-10 pounds, during a trip. You never know what is going to hit your offering on any given trip.

Don runs Dipsey Divers, lead core, planer boards, and is always trying a different combination of lures and colors. He says, on darker days, use darker lures, and vice versa; however, his saying is that "if it doesn't glow, it doesn't go." For steelies and even salmon, reds, oranges, greens, and blues seem to work well.

Speed is another factor. Most trolling speeds are between 2-8 mph. The trick is to go slow for lakers, but with the newer flashers, like Dream Weaver's brand (Spin Doctor), you can control them more at most any speed. With dodgers you need to go slow or they will spin out of control.

Don feels the smelt are gradually coming back, which means forage fish for predators. He has caught many lake trout and, upon stomach inspection, has seen upwards of 30 smelt in the stomach. Predator fish need these kind of smaller fish to feed on in order to survive, and to prevent eating other game fish.

In the harbor at Alpena, you can troll in the early part of the season for walleye. Occasionally you may pick up another species of fish, such as a brown trout; an added bonus.

Northern Lake Huron

At a Glance

What: Salmon, lake trout, steelhead, walleye

Where: Northern Lake Huron

Charter and Guide Services: Captain Dick Rang, Lake & Stream Fishing Charters, 13395 Park Rd., Lachine, 49753, Business: (989) 379-2617, Cell: (989) 464-6436, email: rangd@charter.net, fishalpena.com; **Wipe Out Charters,** Rick Konecke, 916 Ford Ave., Alpena, 49707, (989) 356-3220 email: rick@wipeoutcharters.com; Captain Ed Retherford, 220 Richardson, Alpena 49707, (989) 657-2681, (989) 356-9361; **Bounty Hunter Charters,** Larry Sanderson, 4029 Elcajon Beach, Alpena 49707, (989) 354-3855, email: bountyhunterch@hotmail.com; **Brunings Charter Service,** Capt. Tim Bruning, 259 N. First Street, Rogers City, MI 49779, (989) 734-3463; Capt. Rick Colonna, 12558 Orcutt Hwy., Millersburg, MI 49759, (989) 733-5443, www.tlcbirdpreserve.com

Landings: Ports are available in most of the cities located along the M-23 route. In particular, Rogers City, Cheboygan, Alpena, and Presque Isle

Contacts: Alpena Convention & Visitors Bureau, 235 W. Chisholm Street, Alpena, 49707, (989) 354-4181

Bait & Tackle: Adrian's Sport Shop, 335 North Bradley Highway, Rogers City, 49779, (989) 734-2303; The Dry Dock, 450 N. Bradley Hwy, Rogers City, 49779, (989) 734-2924

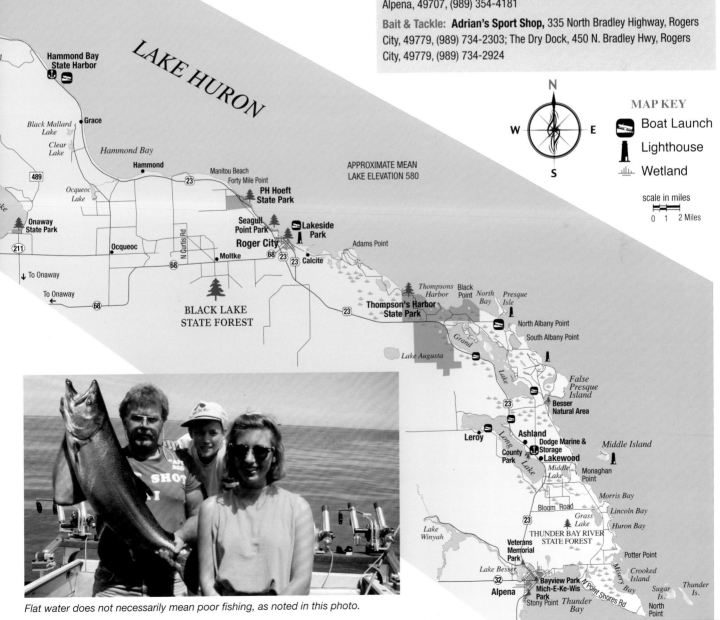

MAP KEY
Boat Launch
Lighthouse
Wetland

scale in miles
0   1   2 Miles

Flat water does not necessarily mean poor fishing, as noted in this photo.

Port Austin Grindstone City Area

As the Port Austin website states, this area is nestled on the shores of beautiful Lake Huron, and encompasses northern Huron County with its 90 miles of shoreline. It continues to state Port Austin and the surrounding areas are quiet and picturesque, enhanced by the beauty of the lake, wooded areas and rolling farmlands. Opportunities abound to enjoy many outdoor activities that the lake and local beaches have to offer. To the west of the Village of Port Austin, beyond Oak Beach, is an area of numerous parks, beaches and recreational facilities. To the east are many historic areas—from Grindstone City and harbor, to the restored lumber town of Huron City, now a museum, to Lighthouse Park featuring historic Pointe Aux Barques lighthouse.

Captain John Atwell, of Port Austin Area Fishing Charter Service, says that there are only a few wild salmon still existing in this area of Lake Huron, but the walleye and lake trout fishing are very good. Perch fishing has unfortunately been slow in the area, but decent perch show up to the south in Caseville in early spring and again in fall.

John summarizes the fishing opportunities as follows:

Walleye: Walleye at the tip of Michigan's Thumb will average in the 18-21-inch size, with some in the upper 20s to low 30-inch size on occasion. Starting in early July, it is relatively easy to pick up a limit of walleye here. But don't head out here for spring walleye, because according to John, they are slow to non-existent.

In mid-summer, however, head to 20-60 feet of water, using bottom-bouncers such as Reef Runners, Long A's or Hot 'N Tots. Fish will start showing up about six miles west of Port Austin. Then, as the summer warms and water temps rise, the fish will move east meeting up between Port Austin and Grindstone City on the other side of the Thumb. Another school of walleye will move up along the east coast of the Thumb from the St. Clair River, resulting in plenty of hot action at the tip of the Thumb. In September, like a ghost, they disappear; you basically have a 90-day window for walleye in this area, i.e., June, July, August.

If a storm from the north kicks up in August, you can kiss the walleye action goodbye. And they will not return. If the water temp moves below 70 degrees, you will also be hard pressed to find walleye. Right now, as of this writing, there is an estimate of a million and a half walleye in the Saginaw Bay, and this should continue to explode in upcoming years.

Lake Trout: During the spring "you will most generally find lakers out by the lighthouse," says Atwell. Anywhere by the "green can" or Flat Rock Reef, you can hook on to lakers using spoons, body baits, in black and purple, gray and black, or silver and blue. Also use some glow-in-the-dark stuff as well. In the summer they will move 10-13 miles northeast of the lighthouse in 120-130 feet of water. Sometimes they will move west to 140-150-foot depths in August, but could move back to the 120-foot depth if there is a break in water temperatures. In September you will once again find them in 95-110 feet of water, then even shallower by the end of September, often in the 75-80-foot depth.

Lakers are in the 6-18-pound range. Use spinners off the bottom with glow colors, and Luhr Jensen dodgers on the front end of the offering.

Steelhead: Steelies start showing up in July and can run 6-12 pounds. John suggests 12-18-pound lead-core off planer boards using bright-colored spoons and body baits. The overall size of the fish will increase as summer progresses.

Caseville: Perch fishing has always been a mainstay for this area of the Saginaw Bay. I have fond memories of fishing off the pier when I was a kid, and you can still do it today. Early spring and again in September through November is a good time to seek out not only perch, but walleye as well. Perch are not the size I remember, as the larger ones seem to have been replaced by those in the 6-9-inch size; great for young kids and for the dinner plate as well. Other than July and August, walleye can be plentiful off the pier. It is not uncommon to pick up some 17-21-inch walleye much of the summer season.

Harbor Beach: Just a note on Harbor Beach to the south. This area of Lake Huron is generally good in May, but the fishing action starts to taper in June and becomes very slow until around mid September. You can pick up some browns and kings, along with a few other species, during these times close to shore.

Walleye in the Great Lakes are not only abundant, but nice size for eating as well.

Port Austin

Note: As of this writing, the Bella Vista Inn, Sunset Bay Resort & Hersel's on the Bay at 6024 Port Austin Road in Caseville are considering a perch charter operation once again. They have a boat and were negotiating an agreement for this service. You may wish to try contacting them at (989) 856-2500 or (989) 856-2650; email: bella@avci.net.

At a Glance

What: Walleye, lake trout, perch

Where: Michigan's Tip of the Thumb and adjoining towns

Information/Guides: Port Austin Area Charter Service, Lake Huron Fishing Charters, Capt. John Atwell, P.O. Box 489, Port Austin, 48467, (517) 230-4326, www.fishportaustin.com. **Caseville Chamber of Commerce,** 6632 Main, Caseville, 48725, (989) 856-3818, email: ccofc@avci.net; **Thumb Area Tourism Council,** Inc., 1111 W. Caro Road, Suite B, Caro, 48723, (989) 672-0323, info@thumbtourism.org; **Pt. Austin Chamber of Commerce,** 2 West Spring St., P.O. Box 274, Port Austin, 48467, (989) 738-7600, website: www.portaustinarea.com

Landings: Boat landings are available at all the sites mentioned above. Just follow the signs when you enter these small towns

Bait & Tackle: Walsh Gun & Tackle, 5020 N Caseville Road., Caseville, 48725, (989) 856-4465

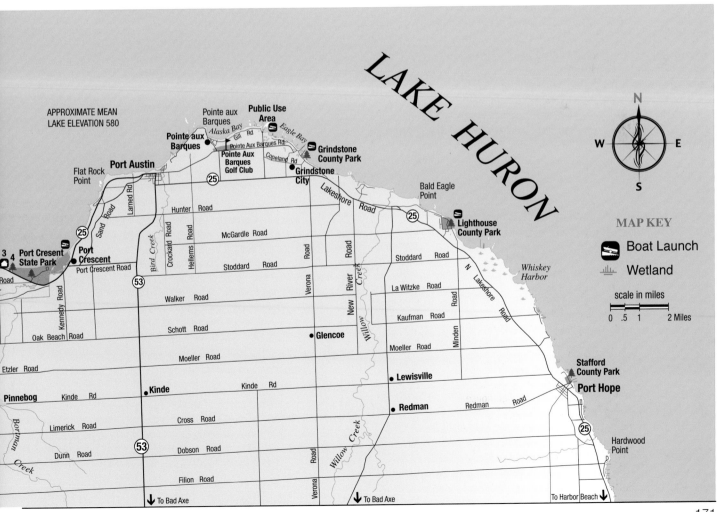

Saginaw Bay

(Part 1)

Bay/Tuscola/
Huron/Arenac Counties

Saginaw Bay has a special place in my hunting and fishing experiences, having grown up not far from its shoreline and fished or hunted just about every square foot of its surface area. My fascination with this unique body of water resulted in my purchasing property and building a home along the west bank not far from the popular fishing town of Linwood. A book can be written on fishing Saginaw Bay, but for the purpose of this particular book, a synopsis of where to go and mostly how to fish for walleye will be laid out below. There are lots of variations and styles for both winter and summer fishing tactics, but these will give you a heads up and hopefully land a few more fish on the ice or in your net. Keep in mind that perch, bass, catfish, and other game fish abound in this unique body of water.

Fishing success has always fluctuated on "the Bay," but lately it has been fantastic. When you read fishing reports on the Internet, or other media, you might see something like this: "The Bay is still poppin' and most guys haven't seen action like this in a decade; both sides of the Bay are hot hot hot! Crawlers, Crawlers, Crawlers, that's all you need to know. Low and slow!! From Kawkawlin to AuGres and across the Bay is all I can say!" (July 2012, saginawbaywalleye.com).

But large bodies of water like Saginaw Bay are in a constant state of change. Examples include the food web that constantly changes and forces predators like walleye to adapt feeding habits. The past couple of years, the Bay experienced an abnormally high concentration of gizzard shad according to local DNR fish biologists. These forage species have historically seen frequent spikes followed by a decline. Often significant die-offs of these fish occur in winter when water temperatures drop below the levels gizzard shad can tolerate.

Saginaw Bay is within the top five destinations in the country for walleye, year after year. Given the right conditions and angling experience, a limit of walleye can be expected on almost a daily basis. However, walleye movements change day to day, making fishing Saginaw Bay a challenge. The walleye can be close to shore, or many miles away from access points. Popular access spots for Saginaw Bay on the west side are Linwood and Erickson roads, but there are many others as listed elsewhere in this section.

The easiest way to describe fishing activities on the Bay is to break it up between winter ice fishing and warm-weather fishing.

Ice Fishing: For those who enjoy pursuing walleye across Saginaw Bay's winter icy surface, the action can be up and down, but always an adventure. During this past winter, for instance, fishing success on the ice has been only limited to the shoreline for perch and some evening walleye due to poor or non-existing ice. But that is not typical. Most years you can venture out to some of the favorite holes and search out these tasty predators. For walleye, when the ice becomes safe enough to venture miles out off shore, the area northeast of Linwood is always a favorite location. Anglers head out northeast from Coggins Road a few miles north of Linwood, or slightly southeast off of East Neuman Road, located one mile south of Pinconning Road. You will easily see the "city" of walleye enthusiasts once you head out on the ice. Another popular spot is off the Bay City State Park toward the mouth of Saginaw River. The best fishing is generally 4-5 miles or so off the State Park in 15 to 24 feet.

Early and late in the day are typically the hottest periods to fish on the bay, but anglers who keep moving and punching holes can stay on the fish all day. Some days you can find a good bite at midday. Be sure to watch for pressure cracks, and always have a compass available. If the winds blow the snow around, you can easily become disoriented.

Ice-Fishing Methods: Jigging is the method that produces the highest percentage of walleye from Saginaw Bay, more than other methods such as tip-ups or other set lines. Because three lines per person are allowed in Michigan, the most successful anglers favor jigging two rods and setting out one tip-up as their third line. Jigging tactics involve the use of leadhead jigs, jigging spoons and jigging/swimming style baits.

Medium-action ice rod and reel, spooled with 6- to 14-pound-test line, is your best bet for walleye. Fluorocarbon leader of 6- to 10-pound test is suggested. Lures in various sizes and colors, including body jigs such as Rapala Jigging Raps or jigging spoons like Northland Macho Minnows and Bay de Noc Lure Company's Do-Jiggers, as well as Northland Puppet Minnows are angler favorites. Other tackle include small ball-bearing swivels and snaps for jigging, and size-10 to -6 single hooks, and assorted split-shot complete your angling tackle box.

In the jigging category, a "stand up" type jig is the best choice since it ensures that the hook point will be in position to deliver the best hook-set. For walleye fishing, a light-wire hook that can be easily penetrated into the tough jaw of a walleye is favored as opposed to jigs with tempered hooks designed for bass. Examples of a stand-up jig for winter fishing include the Bait Rigs Odd Ball and Northland Lipstick Jig. Both these jigs perform best when tipped with a lively emerald shiner minnow hooked through the lips.

Anglers are starting to realize that the best tip-up design is one that covers the hole, preventing light from entering and the hole from refreezing. A number of manufacturers produce excellent products in this category.

A tip-up rigged for walleye should feature 10-12-pound-test monofilament as the main line and a 24-inch fluorocarbon leader of 8-10-pound test tied directly to a No. 6 treble hook. A couple of split shot on the line above the leader is ample for keeping the bait positioned a couple feet off bottom.

For bait, nothing beats a very lively emerald shiner minnow hooked lightly through the skin of the back so the minnow is positioned horizontally in the water.

Jigging spoons like the classic producer Swedish Pimple, made in Michigan by the Bay de Noc Lure Company, have been a favorite for many years on the winter walleye scene. Regardless of the many other lures on the market that have come about since the advent of the Swedish Pimple, it still continues to produce when tipped with a minnow head or a small shiner minnow.

Do Jiggers, also from Bay de Noc Lure Company, Silver Streaks, Little Cleos by Acme Tackle, Cobra Spoon by Wolverine Tackle, and the Luhr Jensen Krocodile Spoon are also popular lures. It seems like a number of ice anglers are using lipless crankbaits for jigging, in a manner similar to the Chubby Darter by Salmo. These baits tend to have lots of rattles and work best when walleye are very active and feeding aggressively. Like other jigging/swimming baits the Chubby Darter has good action, but a slightly slower drop rate that at times can result in a strike. Finally a note that as walleye become more active the jigging spoons and jigging/swimming lures start to bring walleye on the ice.

Staying mobile on "The Bay" is important. Too many anglers head directly to an area they have heard is producing fish, pop up their shelters and sit tight all day long.

It's a good idea to stay for an hour or so in the morning and then again in the evening when walleye are most active. During the day it pays to move around, hitting various locations and searching for schools of fish. Doing this however, means keeping your gear to a minimum and well organized to allow for making those midday moves without the hassle of time-consuming tear-downs.

Continued on page 174

Fishing the bay during the hard-water months for nice-sized perch offers the advantage of being close to shore and in water under two feet deep, as shown in this photo of the author fishing in front of his home near Pinconning.

At a Glance

What: Specifically walleye, although great perch fishing here as well

Why: Walleye have been a mainstay since introduced in the bay and are here to stay

Information/Guides: Great Lakes Bay Regional Convention & Visitors Bureau, 100 Center Avenue, Bay City, 48708, (989) 893-1222, www.visitgreatlakesbay.org

Landings: There are more landings around the bay than I care to list, but here are a few of them: There's an abundance of parking at the Au Gres boat launch located just in from the mouth of the Au Gres River and plenty of docks for boat entry and removal. At the mouth of the Saginaw River is another DNR boat ramp with ample parking and slots for boat entry. Another good location is at the end of Linwood Road, at the Linwood Marina

Bait & Tackle: Michigan Sportsmen Bait-Tackle & Hunting Supplies Bait Shop, 612 Center Avenue, Bay City, 48708, (989) 893-6550; **Frank's Great Outdoors** in Linwood at (989) 697-5341 or online at www.franksgreatoutdoors.com

Saginaw Bay (Part 2)

Bay/Tuscola/Huron/Arenac Counties

Photo courtesy of Free Style Charters, Ludington

Walleye often hang out around the islands off of Bay Port and are easily accessible.

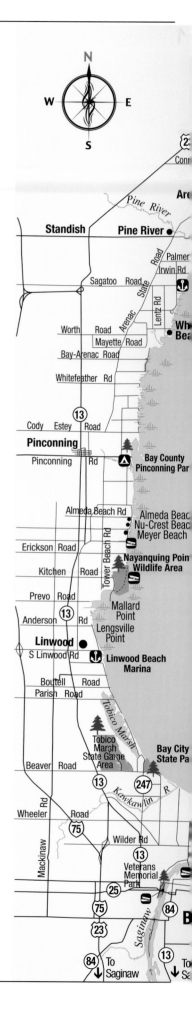

Summer: Try straight out about 5 miles between Point Au Gres and Lookout Point in 40 feet of water for nice summer walleyes. Hot N Tots 60 to 100 feet back or a crawler harness with 2-ounce clip weight at 40 feet, 100 feet back. Vary the depths to find where they are suspended.

Captain Dan Manyen states that in his experience with the jigging/swimming category the classic "Jigging Rapalas in a size 5 or 7 are hands-down the most popular option." "Another similar lure," he says, "is the Moonshine Shiver Minnow that comes in a wider assortment of colors compared to the Jigging Rapala."

And of course the old standby Storm Lures Hot N Tots is always a productive lure. From its inception, these lures, along with its variations (Rattle Tot), have been king for catching walleye on the Bay. I know of no other lure that produces as well as these lures.

Speed is always important for trolling for walleye on the bay. When trolling, you'll want to keep adjusting your speed until you have a couple of strikes; then take note of the speed and try to maintain it. Spinners work best when fished slowly, from .07 to 1.5 mph. Crankbaits work best in the 1.2 to 2 mph range. There are times, however, especially in warm-water conditions, when high-speed trolling cranks work well, at speeds upwards of 3 mph.

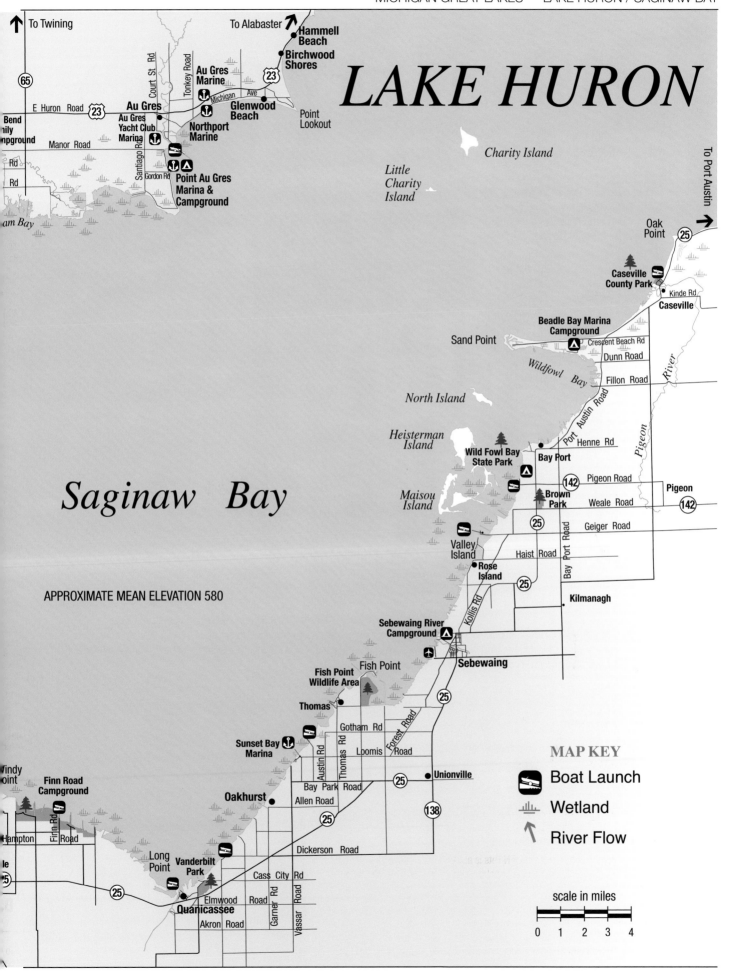

LAKE HURON

To Twining

To Alabaster

Hammell Beach

Birchwood Shores

Au Gres Marine

Michigan Ave

Glenwood Beach

Point Lookout

Au Gres

E Huron Road

Bend
mily
mpground

Au Gres Yacht Club Marina

Manor Road

Northport Marine

Gordon Rd

Point Au Gres Marina & Campground

Rd

Rd

am Bay

Charity Island

Little Charity Island

Oak Point

To Port Austin

Caseville County Park

Kinde Rd

Caseville

Beadle Bay Marina Campground

Sand Point

Crescent Beach Rd

Dunn Road

Wildfowl Bay

Fillon Road

River

North Island

Port Austin Road

Pigeon River

Heisterman Island

Wild Fowl Bay State Park

Henne Rd

Bay Port

Pigeon Road

142

Pigeon

Saginaw Bay

Maisou Island

Brown Park

Weale Road

142

25

Geiger Road

Bay Port Road

Valley Island

Haist Road

Rose Island

25

Kilmanagh

APPROXIMATE MEAN ELEVATION 580

Kollis Rd

Sebewaing River Campground

Sebewaing

Fish Point

Fish Point Wildlife Area

Thomas

Forest Road

25

MAP KEY

Gotham Rd

Boat Launch

Sunset Bay Marina

Loomis

Austin Rd

Thomas Rd

25

Unionville

Wetland

Windy
oint

Finn Road Campground

River Flow

Bay Park Road

25

138

Oakhurst

Allen Road

Finn Rd

Hampton

Road

25

Dickerson Road

scale in miles

Long Point

Vanderbilt Park

Cass City Rd

Quanicassee

Elmwood Road

Garner Rd

Vassar Road

Akron Road

0 1 2 3 4

5

Grand Haven Ottawa County

Photo courtesy of Free Style Charters, Ludington

A Lake Michigan hot spot for steelhead, browns and salmon.

As Grand Haven's website states, from its roots as a highly commercial port-of-call for ferries and passenger liners, Grand Haven has evolved to become a place of serene family enjoyment, hosting lively outdoor recreation, a thriving downtown, history, culture and festivals on the shores of Lake Michigan and the Grand River.

In March of 2012, Grand Haven was named as one of *Travel+Leisure Magazine's* "Best Secret Beaches on Earth" alongside exotic destinations like Turkey, Australia, France, and Thailand.

You can fish here and then take a stroll through town, shopping and visiting places to eat. Grand Haven has it all, especially for people residing in lower Michigan who do not have the time to take a longer trip north.

One of Grand Haven's lifelong residents, and now a charter captain, is Mike Nelson, of Nelson Charters. Mike has fished this area all his life, and became a charter captain over 20 years ago.

"The easiest way to explain fishing off of Grand Haven is to look at it month by month," says Nelson. "The fish vary considerably as to where they are located, their size, and methods of catching them," he states. So let's look at this great fishery on a month-to-month basis.

April: Brown trout fishing is "pretty good in April," says Nelson. You can catch them along the shore using orange Rapala's on a long line in 8-15 feet of water. This is the time of the year when it becomes economical, especially for the smaller boats, to fish close to shore. Brown trout during this early time of the year will most generally be in the 5-8-pound size. A side benefit of this fishing is that you might pick up a bonus walleye while trolling. There are not many in Lake Michigan, but some 5-7-pounders can be caught on occasion.

Salmon such as chinook and coho, in 60-80 feet of water, are also available in the 5-7-pound size. In early spring they tend to start off on the smaller size, and get bigger by mid-summer and beyond. Most can be found offshore in 200

feet of water, plus you can also find steelies that are just starting to come out of the rivers.

May: May is similar to April, however the fish are bigger, in the 12-15-pound range. But now you need to head out to 150 feet of water, while fishing the suspended fish at around 50 feet down, using downriggers, lead core, Dipseys, and spoons.

At a Glance

What: Fishing the big predators off a fabulous area of Lake Michigan.

Why: Fabulous fishing and other great activities.

Information/Guides: Nelson Charters, 15801 Stanton, West Olive, 49460, (616) 846-4344; email: mike@nelsoncharters.net, Cell (616) 990-4421. **GHACVB Visitors Center,** 225 Franklin Avenue, Grand Haven, 49417, (616) 842-4499, email: web@visitgrandhaven.com

Landings: There are a dozen or so boat landings in this area of Lake Michigan, and you can view them on their website: www.visitgrandhaven.com/boat-launches. **Municipal Marina,** 101 N. Harbor Drive, Grand Haven, 49417, (616) 847-3478. Grand Haven, Michigan is a favorite destination of sailors and power boaters. You can boat from Lake Michigan, Grand River, and Spring Lake. With 57 slips, Municipal Marina is located near Chinook Pier. Dockside facilities include electricity, pumpout, water, ice, restrooms, showers and public telephone. The boat launch is located on Harbor Island, just west of US-31, south of the drawbridge. A pass is required to launch your boat. Daily and seasonal passes are offered. Daily passes are available at the launch ramp. Seasonal passes may be purchased at the Treasurer's Office in City Hall, 519 Washington Avenue, Grand Haven, Michigan 49417 or by calling (616) 842-3210

Bait & Tackle: Fish On Bait & Tackle, 1366 Cleveland Ave., (M-104), Nunica, 49448, (616) 935-6985, www.fishonshop.com; **Lakeview Marine & Tackle,** 24 S. Beechtree St., Grand Haven, 49417, (616) 842-2770, www.lakeviewmarineandtackle.com

June: Once again, June is similar to the previous month, however the fish are even bigger and now you switch from spoons to flies. Salmon trolling flies are used with a dodger or flasher with this popular technique used in Lake Michigan for both trout and salmon. The dodger or flasher gives more action to the fly and causes the fly to flutter, making it look like a fish chasing baitfish. Be sure to tie the fly on a lure head and not the hook as to allow the fly to slip up the leader when a fish bites and starts to fight. This method will provide longevity to the fly.

July: "July can be gangbusters," says Nelson. "Coho and kings are moving up in size, and the steelies move in close to shore, depending on the water temperatures," he states. "Look for fish in the 80-120-foot depth, and fish from high up in the water column down to about 100 feet." Spoons and flies are popular during July, with the blue and green colors being the favorite.

Steelhead tend to move in due to water temperatures while the baitfish are in closer to shore. But there are still a lot of steelies off shore as well. A particular good time to fish for them is after a thunderstorm, as the storm will bring in insect life which are deposited on the water surface. The fish will feed on these insects. The fish are now in the 20-pound-plus class.

Lots of alewives are available for them to feed on. The alewives, as of this writing, are in their second year of a seven-year growth rate, making them about medium size. The fish caught now will be filled with this forage fish.

This fishing activity will continue right on in to late summer and early fall.

October: If July is gangbusters, then October "is phenomenal," says Nelson, for both steelhead and salmon. The fish are big, the air temps are comfortable, and boating pressure is lighter, making for an excellent opportunity to head out on the water. The fish are also moving in closer to shore and fishing is easier.

Perch: Perch are not fantastic, like in Saginaw Bay, but nonetheless you can catch some nice 9-12-inchers in the "perch hole," according to Mike. The perch hole is southwest out of Grand Haven, about a mile out. You will know when you are there when the depth moves downward from 50 to 60 feet. April and July seem to be good months for catching perch in this area. Use the typical perch rigs, shiners, pieces of shrimp, and wigglers. Take them all with you because you never know what might be their favorite menu item on any given day.

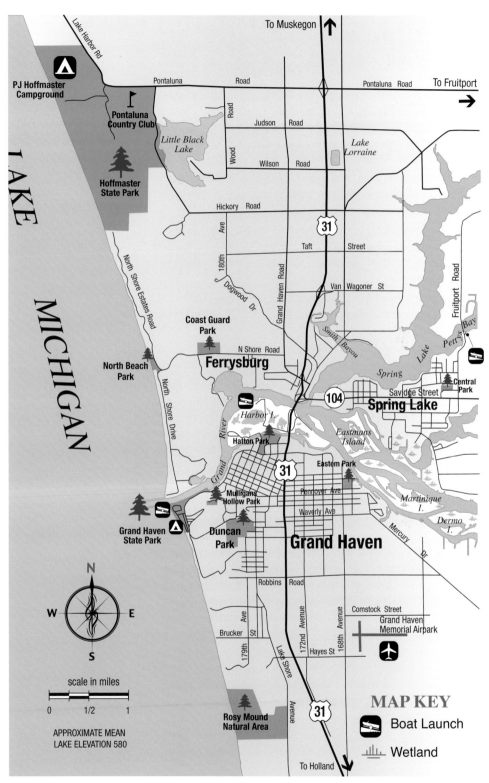

Grand Haven

MAP KEY

Boat Launch

Wetland

The advantages of chartering a boat to fish the big waters of the Great Lakes include: the charter captain knows almost daily where the fish are located; provides all supplies (i.e., rods, lures, bait, etc); is cheaper if you don't own a boat; you can split the charter fee with friends. It frankly pays to charter, especially if you are only an occasional angler. If nothing else, you will learn the techniques of a real pro and can apply them as best you can later on.

Nelson makes a point about people who have lived in Michigan all their life and never been on Lake Michigan. "Michigan has finally caught up to states like Florida where you can go on a charter trip and have your catch prepared at a local restaurant," he says. People should take advantage of this benefit, spending a relaxing day on the water and then eating your catch afterward at a local restaurant makes for a great day.

Grand Traverse Bay
Grand Traverse County

With the clear, blue waters of Lake Michigan and scores of crystalline inland lakes just a short cast from its quaint shops, gourmet restaurants and sugar-sand beaches, Traverse City is rapidly gaining fame among serious bass anglers and their families as the ideal venue for the fishing trip of a lifetime.

And unlike many other Great Lakes areas, fishing here on windy days is more doable, since the narrow bays and high adjoining land features often provide good protection from potential heavy wave action.

Local angler Chris Noffsinger, who has guided on Grand Traverse Bay for over 23 years and is now a pro bass angler, says that Grand Traverse has "some of the best smallmouth fishing in the world." That's saying a lot, and probably well deserved.

But Chris should know. In 2011 he caught five smallies over 7 pounds. He says it is not uncommon to catch six-pound bass, and 3-5-pounders are very catchable all day long in both the East and West bays.

When asked for some of the best areas to fish for bass, he states, "you can catch them almost anywhere in the bays, from top to bottom."

Pre-spawn smallmouth action can be fast and furious right after the catch-and-release opener, Noffsinger said. "The water temperature is generally in the 40s at that time of the year, with the big females staging on offshore drop-offs and breaklines, waiting for the water to warm a few degrees before moving onto adjacent shallow flats," he said. "They'll bust Gulp minnows on drop-shot rigs, suspending jerkbaits and twister tail grubs."

"The smallmouth spawn occurs in stages," he said, "and the amazing clarity of the water means unbelievable sight-fishing."

"You'll see big smallmouth bedding in the bays from May through July," he said. "Wear Polarized sunglasses while slowly cruising the edges of sand flats under trolling motor power, and you'll often spot scores of monster smallmouth on their nests. Bedding fish will gobble up a tube bait or small jig without hesitation. If the wind kicks up a chop on the surface, preventing you from seeing bedding fish clearly, cast a spinnerbait across spawning flats and slow-roll it back to the boat – chances are a big bronzeback will crush it."

Fall brings some of the fastest bass action of the year to the Traverse City region, Noffsinger has found. "Those big smallmouth will be packing in the groceries in anticipation of the cold winter ahead. Dragging a tube bait along a steep drop-off will usually get your line stretched by a hard-pulling smallie."

And since Traverse City boasts over 80 motels and resorts, it's easy to find comfortable and affordable lodging with ample parking room for your trailered boat. There are plenty of boat launches close to town, so you can get in and out of the water quickly.

Cam Garst is another experienced charter captain who works this area. Cam starts to troll for salmon the first of August and continues the action into the mid fall. Lakers precede the salmon starting in early May and run through the first part of August. Lakers average 5-6-pounds and salmon run in the 15-18-pound average, but this will vary somewhat every year.

There are jack salmon available to anglers in GTB in the spring. These are somewhat smaller planted fish but provide good table fare. If anglers return the smaller jacks, they will eventually grow in four years to sizable 15-pounders.

Most of the fishing is done in West GTB, south of Power Island. Garst says you need to know where the active schools are located when fishing for lakers. Salmon, on the other hand, are often located in front of the Boardman River, making fishing for them before their run upstream relatively easy.

"The lake trout," states Garst, "are basically all over the bay, but the exact location can and often changes daily." They will naturally follow the baitfish and are temperature oriented, enjoying colder mid-40-degree water temps. In early spring they will be in water as shallow as 10 feet, but as summer progresses, they will move to 140 feet in this 650-foot-deep bay.

There are more salmon in the West Bay because salmon are planted in Boardman River and they do not need to move far out for their ideal water temperatures or forage fish.

Fishing methods Captain Garst uses for lakers include cowbells as an attractant with a glow spinner behind it or peanut. A Luhr Jensen dodger is also a useful add-on. For salmon, plugs, spoons, dodgers, and flies are the choices. The "fish catcher" (check with local bait shops) simulates dying alewives, as it goes in a circular motion when trolled. A very effective lure. For colors, chartreuse for lakers always seems to work, and anything bright and silvery. When fishing deep in the summer, anything that catches light will work.

Note: One nice feature West GTB has that you don't find elsewhere on big water in Michigan is the fact that even on windy days you can find a place to fish. The narrow bay running more east to west, and the high peninsulas on the north end south ends help protect these waters. Many anglers tuck up behind Power Island when there is a north or northwest blow.

(Thanks to Mike Norton, Traverse CVB for assistance with some of the information in this article.)

At a Glance

What: Great bass fishing, along with trout and salmon

Information/Guides: Traverse City Convention & Visitors Bureau, 101 W. Grandview Parkway, Traverse City, 49684, (800) 940-1120 or (231) 947-1120, www.traversecity.com. **Northern Adventures Fishing,** Chris Noffsinger, 19739 Bronson Lake Road, Interlochen, 49643, (231) 620-7000, email: bronzebacks4fun@aol.com; www.northernadventuresfishing.com. Cam Garst, showtimecharters.com, (231) 218-1495, (800) 817-5807, email: cgarst@showtimecharters.com

Landings: Starting from the northeast (East Bay) and working around to the northwest (West Bay): Antrim County, **Elk Rapids Marina,** Grand Traverse County:, **Acme** (East Arm) Marina, East Arm boat ramp (Old Mission Peninsula is located at Haserot Beach on Old Mission Harbor. The Township boat launch is also at this location), Bowers Harbor (Old Mission Peninsula) Clinch Memorial Ramp (Traverse City), Leelanau County: **Elmwood Township Marina** (just north of TC), West Arm Ramp (Bingham Twp.), **Suttons Bay Marina,** Northport Marina.

Bait & Tackle: Northern Angler Inc., 803 W Front St, Traverse City, 49684, (231) 933-4730; Orvis Streamside, 223 E Front St, Traverse City, 49684, (231) 933-9300; **Narrows Passage Bait & Tackle,** 102 S Saint Mary's St, Lake Leelanau, 49653, (231) 256-2547; **Interlochen Bait & Tackle,** 10033 US Highway 31, Interlochen, 49643. (231) 276-7115

Grand Traverse Bay

LAKE MICHIGAN

GRAND TRAVERSE BAY

APPROXIMATE MEAN
LAKE ELEVATION 177

MAP KEY

Boat Launch

Public Access

Wetland

Little & Big Bay de Noc
Delta County

On a trip to the Bay de Noc area some years ago, I visited Escanaba, a town that I had not visited since I was much younger. I was impressed by the quaintness of the town, the many beautiful homes along the bay, and the reasonable cost of living in that area. I always thought of Escanaba and that area of the Upper Peninsula as the "banana belt" since it does not receive all the snow that often hits their neighbors not far north along the Lake Superior shoreline.

Between the Little and Big Bay de Nocs, there is a combined shoreline of 211 miles, exhibiting a variety of sand beaches, marshes, limestone cliffs and even a ghost town. They boast the most coast with freshwater bays in the country.

If you are traveling from the lower peninsula, expect about a two-hour drive from the bridge west to this beautiful area of the U.P.

Fishing on the Bay de Nocs is a book in itself. What you are getting here is the "Reader's Digest" version, but enough information to get you going.

When not chasing walleyes on Saginaw Bay, Denny Keysor of Flushing can often be found on the wide expanses of Little Bay de Noc.

Although ice fishing in some areas of the state during some years of above average temps, ice on the Bay de Nocs is more predictable; safe ice usually forms by late December, making it one of the best locations to ice fish early in the Great Lakes region. Shanties appear overnight on the ice as winter anglers try for walleye, perch, pike, splake or smelt.

During the ice fishing season there are some areas that, like many large bodies of water, need a word of warning. The real obvious areas to watch for thin ice are the river mouths – the Whitefish River, Days River and Escanaba River. The narrow passages through Gladstone and the shipping channel from the Escanaba ore docks are two other thin-ice spots.

An additional spot to avoid is the north end of Butler's Island near Kipling where weak ice is always present. Though the water is shallow enough there to avoid the danger of drowning, having any sort of motorized vehicle drop through the ice can lead to a very expensive day on the ice.

The best advice is to stay on established tracks to ensure safe ice. However, like any body of ice, it is advisable to use caution when venturing out on new ice or ice not previously used, to test the ice every 20 feet or so, and use the buddy system. Always check with local county/city officials or bait and tackle shops for the latest ice information.

Keith Wils, well known and experienced charter captain out of Gladstone, states that walleye and perch are the two main species of fish that anglers pursue on Bay de Noc. "The majority of anglers fish Little Bay versus Big Bay, due to the more extensive and varied structure and smaller area", he says.

A discussion with Regional DNR Fish Biologist Darren Kramer reveals the fact that during the 2000 decade, the fish population has changed somewhat in this area, probably due to habitat changes for the most part. Clear water causing more light penetration, resulting in walleye, for instance, to moving to deeper water during certain times. The walleye once caught toward the inner bay near Gladstone are now being caught toward the south end of the bay near Escanaba. The good news is that the walleye are still there, and it is not uncommon to hook an 8-plus-pound walleye or larger, although the larger sizes are slightly down from years back.

Walleye stocking programs continue with walleye fry being released in Big Bay and Little Bay on alternating years, i.e., one year in Big Bay, the next in Little Bay. However there are some private stocking efforts that take place according to Captain Wils. In 2010 for instance, 12,000 walleye were stocked in Little Bay, and 7,000 in 2011 through a joint venture with Chamber of Commerce and donated money.

As for ice fishing, once again moving a bit south in the bay to where the walleye have moved is probably your best bet for hooking some of these tasty fish.

Kramer mentioned that the splake stocking program was terminated back in mid 2000 due to poor returns, however the same number of brown trout are being stocked. Even with this increase in stocking of browns, the fishing has been challenging for unknown reasons, other than possibly habitat changes. Stocking under the ice has been tried to prevent bird predation, and other methods were used to try to increase the trout numbers, but so far the results are marginal. Studies continue to try to resolve this problem.

Captain Wils says that, "for walleye, your best bet is to take into consideration the winds and how it may have stirred up the water, because if the shallow water becomes "dirty" the walleye will stay in the northern end of Little Bay." However, if the water is clear, they will move more south toward Escanaba.

You can start your fishing by trying to locate the drop-offs and reefs off the river mouths at the north end of the bay. Start fishing in the shallow areas at first light, then move out to deeper water as the morning progresses (most of the time). Later in the afternoon, this process is reversed.

Other prime areas to search out for walleye, according to Wils, are near river mouths and along shoreline points. Look for submerged bars and rocky areas near shore. A couple of the better winter walleyes sites are off Kipling and east side of Butlers Island.

Ice-Fishing Methods:
Jigging probably accounts for 75% of the walleye on the bay. The most productive depths for winter walleyes on Little Bay de Noc range from 15 to 30 feet. Look for humps that rise up around the 10- or 12-foot depth, and then slowly work down the slopes. Swedish Pimples, Jigging Rapalas, Moonshine, tip ups with sucker minnows are old and proven standbys on the bay, but also consider a jigging shad lure in purple, especially when the fish are aggressive.

Perch:
If the walleyes aren't cooperating on the bay, there are always perch. Schools of perch roam the 20- to 30-foot depths during the winter and can be counted on for consistent action. Small minnows are a top choice, but wigglers and wax worms are a close second. Most perch run 9 to 12 inches, but bigger ones are common. Try the same areas where the walleyes are except in slightly deeper water. Big Bay de Noc is also very good for perch, however there is much more area to cover. Mid April is a favorite time of year for perch.

Walleyes and northern pike can be taken with a Swedish Pimple and minnow on tip ups or pike can be speared. Perch are typically taken using minnows, or if you prefer crappies you can head over to the Escanaba yacht harbor and try a combination of wrigglers and minnows by Kipling dock. Most winter walleye fishing is centered on the reefs in 15 to 25 feet of water. These fish generally start in the shallows early in the day then move deeper as the day progresses.

Swedish Pimple and Do Jiggers are the lures of choice for winter 'eyes on Little Bay. Tip the lures with a minnow head. Most use a ripping motion to attract attention and then allow the lure to flutter downward. Walleyes inhale the lure on the fall. Expect to catch plenty of walleyes in the 4- to 6-pound range, although special regulations on Little Bay De Noc allow only one walleye over 23 inches per day.

Fall Fishing:
Although Little Bay De Noc has great walleye and smallmouth fishing starting in the spring when the fishing season opens, October can turn into trophy-walleye season. From the first part of October until the Bay is covered with ice sizable walleyes are here for the taking. These walleye can be caught using jigging live bait or spoons, drifting crawler rigs, trolling crawler rigs or trolling crankbaits (popular night bite). Probably the most effective for these trophy walleyes is trolling crankbaits over deep water.

A not-so-uncommon ice fishing report (example): Ice conditions improved however there are still areas throughout the bay that are dangerous. A couple vehicles fell through the ice on the northern end of Butler Island. This area is always dangerous and should be avoided at all times. Anglers are ice fishing in the northern bay and off Gladstone, however any ice south of Gladstone should be considered dangerous. Pressure cracks have been a real problem this year as they seem to be moving around on a daily basis. *Use extreme caution when crossing them!* Walleye reports were good and the Gladstone area produced the best for those jigging Rapalas 6 to 8 feet off the bottom in 25 to 30 feet of water. Some caught fish from the Center Reef when jigging Rapalas or using tip-ups with sucker minnows in 18 to 28 feet of water. Several large walleye and good numbers of pike were reported in this area. The best walleye catches are early morning or between dusk and an hour after dark. For those looking for whitefish, the ice was just starting to form off Sand Point, so the ice is not safe yet. Catch rates for perch were still fair to good around Kipling. Try jigging minnows, wigglers or spikes in 5 to 17 feet of water. Check report on: www.bay-shore-resort.com/report.

This nice 'eye was taken on a Salmo lure.

At a Glance

What: Excellent walleye and perch fishing

Where: 17,000-acre Big and Little Bay de Noc

Why: Some of the best overall fishing anywhere

How: Jigging is most popular for walleyes

Regs: Has changed periodically. Check MI regulations

Information: Delta County Chamber of Commerce, (906) 786-2192, www.deltami.org.

Access: Anglers head out from Escanaba, Gladstone, Kipling and Rapid River. Access can be gained off US-2 near Bay Shore Resort, at Rapid River, Gladstone, and Escanaba and at Hunter's Point National Forest

Contacts/Guides: Captain Keith Wils, 10132 M-35, Gladstone 49837, (906) 428-1488, or 1-888-88FISH1, email: walleyeschoice@yahoo.com; **Hawg Heaven Guide Service,** Mark Peloza, 9121 Bay Shore Drive, Gladstone, 49837, (906) 428-3809, hawg-heaven@upmichigan.net; **Sall-Mar Resort, Captain Ken Lee,** Bay de Noc Charters 7989 US HWY 2, Rapid River, 49878, (906)-553-4850, info@sallmarresort.net

Bait & Tackle: Bay View Bait & Tackle, 7110 US Highway 2 41 M35, Gladstone, 49837. Located on Little Bay de Noc, (906) 786-1488, email: baitshop2@chartermi.net; **Bayshore Bait and Tackle,** (next to public boat launch), 1323 N. Lake Shore Drive, Gladstone, 49837, (906) 428-96-87

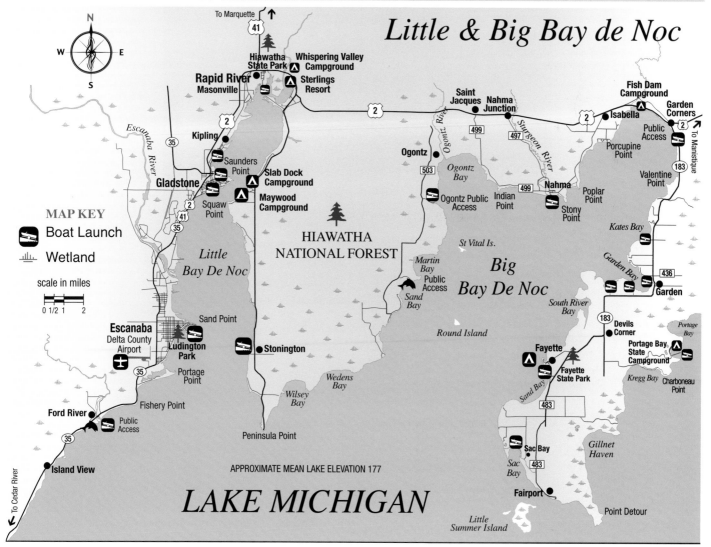

Ludington Mason County

Fishing is big business in Ludington. Numerous charter captains make Ludington their home port, and happily take people out on the lake to fish for salmon and trout. Here's a synopsis of what you can expect each month in the Ludington area:

Late April kicks off the walleye, northern pike, muskie and trout season. Brook, rainbow, and brown trout are ready for the catching in Pere Marquette River and along the Lake Michigan shoreline.

May and June are great for charter fishing as brown trout, lake trout and some salmon and steelhead are prevalent. Fly-fishing on the Pere Marquette River during this time of year is excellent. June is the time for perch fishing along the rocky waters off the Consumers Power Plant and on the inland lakes of Hamlin, Lincoln and Pere Marquette.

July and August are king salmon months and action is fast and furious. Charter boats often angle for salmon in the morning then move offshore to reel in a few steelhead to throw on the grill as well. Many charter captains and diehard fishermen flock to Ludington for the big fishing tournament in mid-July.

September is the month when thousands of mature salmon and steelhead mass off the river mouths for their annual migration upstream. On the inland lakes, crappie, bluegill and smallmouth bass fishing are excellent.

October brings steelhead catches on Pere Marquette River that empties into Lake Michigan. These jumpers are lively and, with minimal boat traffic at this time of year, the catches are even better for anglers. During the autumn steelhead and salmon runs, anglers line the banks of Big Sable River which courses through Ludington State Park. This mile-long stretch from Hamlin Lake is a favorite as the catches are definitely worth writing home about.

Captain Rich Laaksonen, who has chartered these waters since 1985, said that brown trout are netted here during April. He said fishing tight near the pier heads can land you some nice 4-12-pounders. As the water warms and baitfish move north, the kings follow up to Ludington. Mid July is the start of hot king fishing month. Laaksonen uses "old school" stuff, that is, Rapala J9s and 11s, mini discs with small spoons, and Dreamweaver WDs.

Anglers tend to fish in a circular motion inside the piers, whereby your outside boards will run shallow in a clockwise position and the inside rods will be in the deeper water. If the weather is pleasant, fish along the shoreline between the first and second sandbar in 4-8 feet of water. This fishing opportunity will taper off in May.

Photo courtesy of Free Style Charters, Ludington

Ludington is a popular Lake Michigan location for steelhead, salmon, and lakers.

At a Glance

What: King salmon fishing, along with lakers and steelies

Where: Ludington waters are some of the best anywhere for salmon

Information/Guides: Ludington Area Convention and Visitors Bureau, 5300 W. US 10, Ludington, 49431 (877) 420-6618; **Captain Richard & Tracy Laaksonen,** 2790 Jebavy Dr. Ludington, 49431, Home (231) 843-6634, (cells) (231) 425-0125, (231) 425-0288, email: info@finpowercharters.com, www.finpowercharters.com. **Fishing Report:** www.fish-ludington.com/fishingreport; www.visitludington.com; www.pureludington.com.

Landings: State dock on Loomis Street, one block south of the end of Ludington Avenue

Bait & Tackle: Captain Chuck's Bait & Tackle, 5770 W US10, Ludington, (231) 843-4458, captainchucks@hotmail.com, www.capt-chuck.com

Ludington

In May for salmon it pays to know the shelf or bank where the bottom drops like a ledge a short distance from the shoreline from 70 to 150 feet. This is a good reference point. The fish move off the bank and hang out in this area until they move up the rivers in later summer and fall. This bank is less than a mile off shore from Big Sable Point, which is the farthest point of land that juts out into Lake Michigan.

When using spoons, plugs, or flies, the spoons should be kept higher in the water column, with the flies deeper. Fishing with cut bait is the best bet when the fishing becomes slow and bites are few and far between. The advantage of using cut bait is the obvious stimulating of the olfactory sense in the fish. More and more anglers are using cut bait, especially in recent years.

When fishing early in the morning, particularly when the sun has not risen over the horizon yet, a glow plug or lure with glow tape is advisable. When the sun rises, greens, blues, and chartreuse colored lures seem to work well. But a lot of this use of color is also dependent on water clarity, and the level of natural (sun) light. So start with various colors and see what the fish are attracted to or, actually, what the fish can see based on the natural lighting available in the waters you are fishing.

Fishing mid-summer can be a great time to land some nice lakers or kings. Fish the bank, in 90-140 feet of water. You will find the lakers deeper in the water column, even on the bottom, and the kings higher. Kings are opportunistic fish. They will often leave their comfortable temperature zone to find baitfish. They do that more than any other fish I know. So don't be surprised if you have a hit by a king chasing baitfish up high.

Keep in mind that you may also pull in a traditional steelhead in this area. If you are lucky, maybe even a Skamania. Skamania are larger than traditional steelies, being 8-12 pounds versus 4-6 pounds for traditional steelhead. Skamania are also longer, have larger eyes, and the tail is usually beat-up due to the June run in the river to spawn. They are also a much stronger fish and can see better than traditional steelies.

Later in the summer, usually around September, as the 4-year-old salmon leave, the 3-year-old kings will now be the target. Coho come later, and lakers will most likely always be available. But older kings are indeed "top dog" of the waters when they are around. The Steelhead are now in the 200-400-foot depths.

In fall, move from the deep-water fishery to a more shallow depth. Lakers will be around the 100-foot depth, and steelies higher, with a few 3-year-old kings available.

Note: Keep in mind that after mid-October or so, Lake Michigan, and many of the Great Lakes, can be dangerous due to the increased winds and drop in water temperatures.

1. Barnhart's Marina
2. Laman's Landing
3. Sunset Bluff Resort
4. Lakeview Campsite
5. North Bayou Resort & Marina
6. Willow-By-The-Lake Resortmore
7. Ludington Area Visitors Guide
8. K's Edgewater Resort
9. Heaven On Hamlin
10. Waterside Resort & Boat Rentals

MAP KEY

Boat Launch

Wetland

Public Access

Lighthouse

scale in miles

0   1/2   1   2 miles

APPROXIMATE MEAN
LAKE ELEVATION 177

Saugatuck Allegan County

Saugatuck and Douglas are harbor villages that celebrate diversity—small-town America at its best! Here visitors can turn back the pages of time to enjoy a simpler life where no one hurries, and no one hurries you. Recently The National Trust for Historic Preservation selected Saugatuck/Douglas as one of the "Dozen Distinctive Destinations" in the U.S. and the writers and editors of *Midwest Living* Magazine ranked Saugatuck/Douglas fifth among the top 100 vacation destinations in the Midwest.

For anglers in this part of Lake Michigan a few browns can be landed in April, but the majority of spring action starts in May. Plenty of king salmon are caught in May in the 70-170-foot depths, depending, however, on the winds. There is plenty of action using lead core or downriggers in the 20-30-foot depths. Most anglers pursuing salmon this time of year use spoons, rather than flies.

King salmon will be in the area all of May then in June it gets tougher. Toward the end of June lakers are terrific. Lake trout are planted by Fish & Wildlife on the rocks located two miles south of the harbor. This rock bed consists of small rocks to boulders, and extends from the shoreline to about the 70-foot depth.

Dave Engel, who is a full-time charter captain in this area of Lake Michigan, says that when the alewives disappeared, the lakers seem to adapt to the gobies as a food source. You can catch some nice-sized 6-12-pound lakers in the 70-80-foot depths, but if you want the 20-plus-pounders, they are in the 400-foot depths, 20-30 miles offshore. As the season progresses in mid July, the king salmon fishing is fantastic. Kings averaging 15 pounds can be netted during this time of the summer, and some upwards of 20 pounds or more.

As a side note, the round goby is a small, bottom-dwelling fish that was first found in the Great Lakes region in 1990. Originally from the Black and Caspian seas of Eastern Europe, it is believed that this exotic species arrived in the ballast water of vessels coming into the Great Lakes. Since the first sighting in the St. Clair River, round gobies have spread to all of the Great Lakes and are working their way inland through the rivers and canal systems.

In spring brown trout also seem to feed on gobies in the deeper water.

In August, "it's lights out," says Engel. Limits of salmon and lakers in open-water trolling are common. Fish are generally found in the first 100 feet of water, trolling in a southerly manner. The fish use the strong current from the south, and if you troll in a northerly manner your success will diminish. Engel trolls down to Grand Haven, using green-and-blue flies, and Spin Doctors. Depending on the water temps, you generally will find the fish in the bottom 20 feet of water.

During the second week or so of September and right through the end of the month, there is a good run of kings. Forty five thousand are planted every year in the river, and, depending on the water temperatures once again, the kings move into the river system. Generally they are fished with single hook J-plugs. Consider the various Michigan made Dreamweaver products.

"The perch fishing is also quite productive in this area," say Engel. With all the rocks, the gobies eat up the perch eggs, so you will find the perch just off the rocks in the 35-70-foot depths. They eat the smaller gobies and shinners at these depths. I would edge out toward the 70-foot depth, although it is a bit of a challenge feeling the bite at this depth. Try drifting with minnows on a single gold hook. You can pick up some sizable 8-12-inch perch, or larger.

Note: Anglers can fish in the morning and enjoy their fresh catch at a local restaurant in the afternoon under a new program called Catch & Cook. The program brings together the best of a Michigan day—time on the water, and time at the table with family and friends—while supporting local economies and Michigan businesses.

At a Glance

What: Salmon, lakers and perch

Where: Easy access to most fishing in this area of Lake Michigan

Information/Guides: Saugatuck-Douglas Convention & Visitors Bureau, (269) 857-1701, www.saugatuck.com; **Best Chance Charters,** Dave Engel, 3041 Indian Pt. Road, Saugatuck, 49453, (616) 292-4812 or (616) 292-6098, email: bestchancetoo@hotmail.com

Landings: Spear St. Boat Landing at Water and Spear Streets is the deepest launch and will handle most any fishing boat. Fee involved. Call City Hall with any questions: (269) 857-2603

Bait & Tackle: Lakeshore Outfitters, 6398 Blue Star Hwy, Saugatuck, 49453 (269) 857-2248

Salmon anglers find excellent fishing in this area of Lake Michigan, with bonus browns and perch.

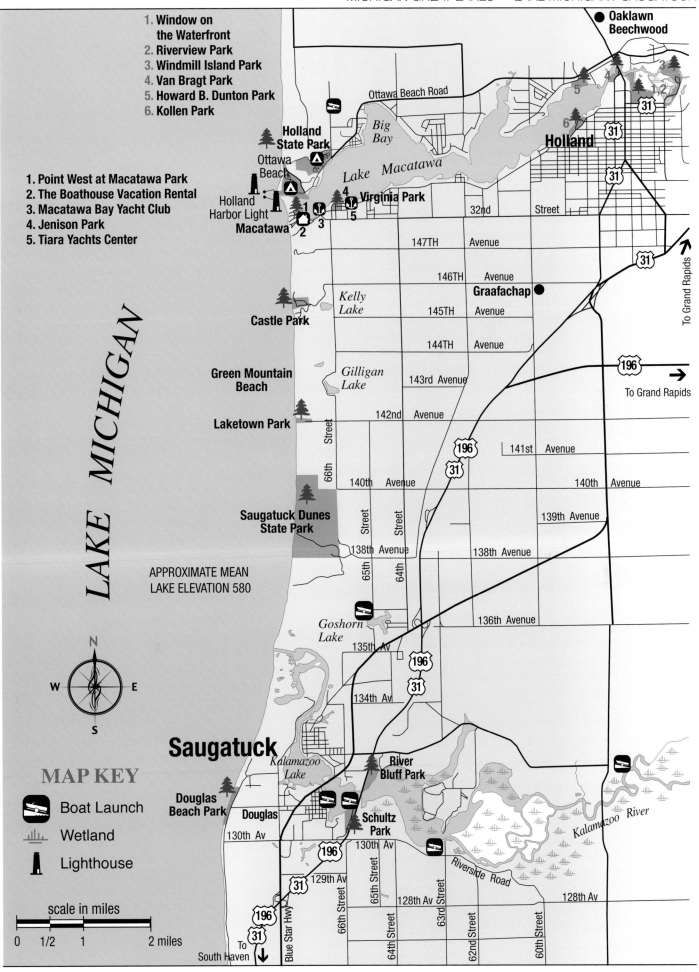

1. Window on
   the Waterfront
2. Riverview Park
3. Windmill Island Park
4. Van Bragt Park
5. Howard B. Dunton Park
6. Kollen Park

1. Point West at Macatawa Park
2. The Boathouse Vacation Rental
3. Macatawa Bay Yacht Club
4. Jenison Park
5. Tiara Yachts Center

Oaklawn
Beechwood

Holland State Park
Ottawa Beach
Holland Harbor Light
Macatawa

Big Bay
Lake Macatawa
Virginia Park
Holland

Ottawa Beach Road
32nd Street

147TH Avenue
146TH Avenue
Graafachap
145TH Avenue
144TH Avenue

Castle Park
Kelly Lake

Green Mountain Beach
Gilligan Lake
143rd Avenue

Laketown Park
142nd Avenue

141st Avenue

Saugatuck Dunes State Park
140th Avenue
140th Avenue
139th Avenue
138th Avenue
138th Avenue

136th Avenue

Goshorn Lake

To Grand Rapids
To Grand Rapids

LAKE MICHIGAN

APPROXIMATE MEAN
LAKE ELEVATION 580

N
W — E
S

Saugatuck

Kalamazoo Lake
River Bluff Park

Douglas Beach Park
Douglas
Schultz Park

130th Av
130th Av

Kalamazoo River

Riverside Road

MAP KEY

Boat Launch

Wetland

Lighthouse

scale in miles
0   1/2   1   2 miles

To
South Haven

Blue Star Hwy
129th Av
128th Av
128th Av

66th Street
65th Street
64th Street
63rd Street
62nd Street
60th Street

Grand Marais Alger County

Named by the French voyageurs in the 1600's, Grand Marais means the Great Pond, used as a Harbor of Refuge. Even today, Grand Marais is the only Harbor of Refuge between Marquette and Sault St. Marie.

Situated on the shore of Lake Superior, Grand Marais serves as the eastern entrance to the Pictured Rocks National Lakeshore. You can not only enjoy fishing here, but all the many other recreational activities offered by the Pictured Rocks. There are miles of pristine shoreline waiting to be explored as well as some of the largest and most rugged sand dunes in the country.

Grand Marais has a rich history as well. Established in the 1860's by the fishing and lumber industries, Grand Marais became a boom town. In 1910, the lumber industry declined and Grand Marais almost became a ghost town. It was saved by commercial fishing. This Harbor of Refuge has been served by the Coast Guard since 1899. Many shipping disasters have occurred at or near here. The anchor of the wrecked *Annie M. Peterson* rests near the town's Veteran's Memorial.

Lake Superior & West Bay

The town of Grand Marais is located on a harbor called West Bay, which is separated from Lake Michigan by a long peninsula. Access to the main lake is available at Woodland Park, just to the north. A long pier extends out into the lake at the mouth of the bay. Fishermen can catch whitefish from the pier, and spring and fall offer the chance to catch brown trout, steelhead and salmon. In summer, the fishing switches mainly to walleye, yellow perch and smallmouth bass. You can also launch a boat at any of several launch facilities located around the rim of the bay.

Rod Lowe has fished this area of Lake Superior since he was a kid, about 35 years ago. He knows the water and where the fish generally hang out. Listed below are the main species of game fish anglers pursue in this area of Lake Superior.

Lakers: Lake Superior is known as a lake trout fishery, and Grand Marais area, Rod Lowe starts his charters the first of June. "Earlier in the year," says Rod, "they are in the 200-plus-foot depth, and anywhere from 5-28 miles off shore. Look for reefs," he says, "where the water will go from around 400 feet up to 200 feet, then up to 150 feet or so. When you find a shelf, and fish located on it, they will probably be there tomorrow, the day after, and the day after that. "The fish don't move much," he says. Use area charts to give you some idea of where to go look for the reefs. Rod uses spoons, mostly in black and white. The lakers provide good action up until later in the summer and early fall. After October, the lake is hard to predict and not a good idea to venture far off shore. Remember the *Edmund Fitzgerald?*

One other area not too far from Grand Marais that anglers search for lake trout is the Big Reef that is about 12-14 miles offshore, approximately half way between Grand Marais and Munising. When you hit around the 70-foot depth, you will be right on top of the shelf where the lakers like to hang out.

Steelhead: As summer winds down, lakers give way to the popular and tasty steelhead that are fished in October and November off the river mouths with spawn bags. Lowe says that steelies average around five pounds, but some will be in the 7-8-pound category. Anglers fish for them wading from shore,

casting out in the lake, or in a boat close to shore. Occasionally you might also hook a nice coho since they run with the steelhead.

Whitefish: Whitefish are a popular angling experience off the pier. The best bait is a simple salmon egg on a #10 Aberdeen hook. Remember that whitefish have a small, exceedingly delicate mouth (another challenge for the angler) and it is therefore confined to dining on insects, freshwater shrimp, small fish and fish eggs, and bottom organisms. The best fishing is after a two-day-long northwest blow where foods from the lake are pushed in toward shore, and hence next to the pier, bringing the fish closer in.

Note: The lake trout is the largest trout native to the Great Lakes and other Michigan Lake waters. This fish strongly prefers a water temperature of 45-55 degrees F. Thus, while the lake trout may be found in shallow water only 10 to 15 feet deep in spring and fall, it follows these frigid water temperatures to depths of 100 to 200 feet in summer and winter. This restless denizen of the cold, deep waters is a true wanderer, often ranging many miles in search of prey. Relentless hunters, lake trout feed primarily on other fish. Although it seems to have a peculiar penchant for ciscoes, it also concentrates on alewives, smelt or sculpin (dead or alive), and sometimes takes crustaceans, insects, other fish, and even small mammals. (MDNR).

Many lake trout seem to return to the same spawning beds each fall, although some don't show this homing behavior. The eggs are deposited after dark, often on shoals. Young lake trout become sexually mature at 6 or 7 years of age. The average adult weighs in at 9-10 pounds but some individuals weigh up to 50 pounds (the Michigan record is 61 pounds 8 ounces). The life-span of the lake trout may exceed 25 years.

At a Glance

What: Lake trout

Where: Lake Superior off of Grand Marais

Why: A great historic area to fish for both lakers and whitefish.

Information/Guides: Grand Marais Chamber of Commerce, P.O. Box 139, Grand Marais, 49839, (906) 494-2447; www.grandmaraismichigan.com

Landings: Located at the very end of M-77. Harbor Master: (906) 494-2613. **The Burt Township Marina** offers a boat launch, transient dockage, gasoline and diesel fuel, electrical outlets, water hook-ups, and a pump-out station. The daily launch fee is $5. The annual launch permit is $45 and may be purchased at the township office. Township dredges the marina every spring and several times during the season to keep it open to boaters along a 90-mile stretch of Lake Superior's south shore, known as shipwreck coast; www.burttownship.com/Recreational/marina and for more information

Bait & Tackle: Grand Marais Outfitters, N 14277 Lake Ave., (906) 494-3333, www.grandmaraisoutfitters.net

When standing atop the Pictured Rocks landscape, you can often spot a large laker cruising the pristine waters below.

The shoreline along the Grand Marais plays host to water enthusiasts including anglers who seek out some sizable lakers.

Grand Marais

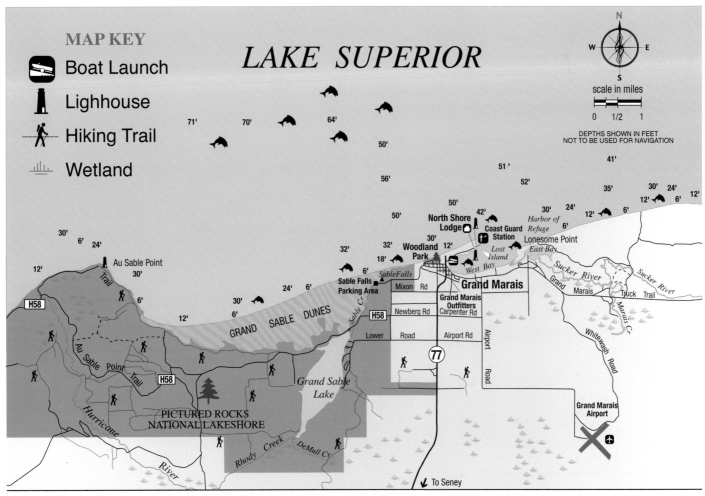

MAP KEY

Boat Launch

Lighhouse

Hiking Trail

Wetland

LAKE SUPERIOR

scale in miles

0   1/2   1

DEPTHS SHOWN IN FEET
NOT TO BE USED FOR NAVIGATION

Lake Erie Western Basin (Part 1)

Lake Erie is an awesome ice fishing destination for both perch and walleye if anglers can access the ice. Like Saginaw Bay, anglers have to be extremely cautious on Lake Erie. Make sure to check wind directions and do not go out if there is a strong west wind. Lake Erie does not lock in so you are taking your life into your hands with an offshore breeze. Most anglers fish in Brest Bay or around Erie Metropark. Airport Bay is also a hot spot but access is severely limited.

As for summer fishing, Captain Bruce Bronner has chartered the Lake Erie Western Basin for over 14 years. He has seen the ups and downs with fish populations, invasive species that have affected the fishing in this and many other areas, and knows where to go and how to fish walleye and perch. I would strongly suggest you pick up a chart of this area for locations of various structures and water depths (www.charts.noaa.gov).

Walleye: Bruce states that although walleye has not been quite as productive as some past years, you can still pick up some nice fish in the 3-4-pound category, and upwards of 6-8 pounds have been caught in these waters. "You have to search out the schools," he says, "and then stay on them." "In spring (April), the walleye move out of Maumee River in Ohio and move up to Michigan waters. This is when you will pick up some nice size fish closer to shore," he says.

Some productive areas to fish are the dumping grounds off Bolles Harbor. There are two of them, and the area between them is your best bet to land walleye. Also off the shipping channel that heads into the Maumee River is a site known as the "Sputnik" which is about 11 miles straight out from Raisin River. Much of this fishing is in 22-27 feet of water. Anywhere off Stony Point, and in front of the Monroe Fermi Nuclear Plant can be good walleye fishing as well. Some anglers target walleye up by the south island near Pt. Mouille. During the summer months, the sister islands, off Bolles Harbor, can provide some good action. The walleye tend to move in close to shore near Toledo Beach in spring.

Bruce mentions that you have a spring season where the fish can be sizable, then you move on to your early to mid-summer bite, followed by your hog walleye season in fall. The fall bite is an aggressive bite. It's all about preparing for the long winter months, and Lake Erie's walleyes will be stuffing themselves in order to build up their fat reserves. For those anglers who brave the north winds of late October and November, that is the time of the season to take stock of your crankbaits and be prepared with all your equipment. As for the cranks, consider Reef Runner 800, the Rapala and Storm lures such as Deep Husky Jerks, Taildancer TDD-11, Thundersticks, or the Bomber Deep Long A baits.

Avid angler and fishing guide, as well as a full-time airline pilot, Ryan Buddie of Lakewood, OH, displays a lunker walleye taken in Erie.

Tournament pros, Greg Yarbrough of Catawba Island, OH (left) and Gary Zart of Brunswick, OH (right) are no strangers to fishing this productive lake.

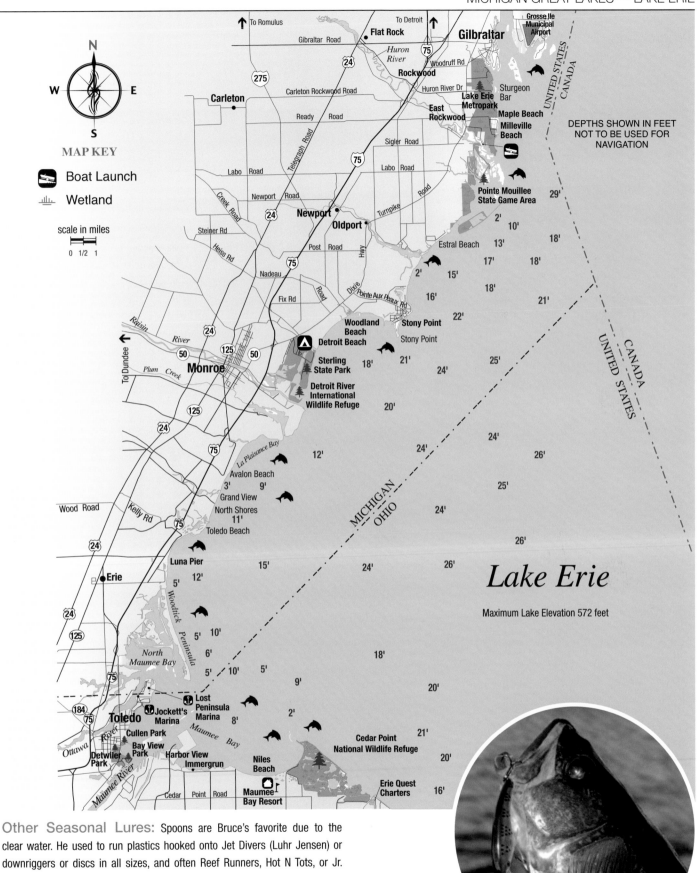

N
W E
S

MAP KEY

Boat Launch

Wetland

scale in miles

0   1/2   1

To Romulus

To Detroit

Flat Rock

Gibraltar Road

Gilbraltar

Grosse Ile Municipal Airport

Huron River

Woodruff Rd

Rockwood

Carleton Rockwood Road

Carleton

Huron River Dr

Sturgeon Bar

Lake Erie Metropark

East Rockwood

Maple Beach

Milleville Beach

Ready   Road

DEPTHS SHOWN IN FEET
NOT TO BE USED FOR
NAVIGATION

Sigler Road

Labo   Road

Pointe Mouillee State Game Area

29'

Labo   Road

Newport

Turnpike

2'

10'

Steiner Rd

Oldport

Estral Beach

13'

18'

Post Road

17'

18'

Nadeau

2'

15'

Pointe Aux Peaux Rd

Fix Rd

16'

18'

Raisin

River

22'

21'

Woodland Beach

Stony Point

Detroit Beach

Stony Point

Monroe

Sterling State Park

18'

21'

24'

25'

Detroit River International Wildlife Refuge

20'

La Plaisance Bay

24'

24'

Plum Creek

12'

24'

26'

Avalon Beach

3'   9'

25'

Grand View

North Shores

11'

Wood Road

24'

Kelly Rd

Toledo Beach

26'

MICHIGAN

OHIO

Luna Pier

15'

Lake Erie

Erie

5'   12'

24'

26'

Maximum Lake Elevation 572 feet

Woodtick Peninsula

10'

5'   10'

6'

North Maumee Bay

18'

5'   10'   5'

9'

20'

Lost Peninsula Marina

Jockett's Marina

Toledo

8'

2'

21'

Cullen Park

Maumee Bay

Cedar Point National Wildlife Refuge

20'

Bay View Park

Harbor View

Detwiler Park

Immergrun

Niles Beach

Ottawa

Erie Quest Charters

16'

Cedar Point Road

Maumee Bay Resort

Maumee River

Other Seasonal Lures: Spoons are Bruce's favorite due to the clear water. He used to run plastics hooked onto Jet Divers (Luhr Jensen) or downriggers or discs in all sizes, and often Reef Runners, Hot N Tots, or Jr. Thundersticks, but now only uses these methods when other offerings seem not to work. Some anglers drag crawlers on the bottom, or drift with them. In the spring when Bruce fishes the area just outside Maumee River, he will often drift using blade baits or purple-haired jigs tipped with a minnow.

Continued on page 190

Walleye lures are varied, with most of the popular ones productive in these waters.

Photo courtesy of Lindy Fishing Tackle

189

Lake Erie Western Basin (Part 2)

Walleye in this area of Lake Erie can range upwards of 3-6 pounds or more if you search them out.

Continued from page 189

Perch: Perch in the 7-10-inch size are common in this part of Lake Erie. In the early part of the year, before the walleye move in, you can catch perch in the more shallow waters. As the walleye move in, perch move to deeper water. In the early season try for perch out in the sailboat buoys off Bolles Harbor, by the Toledo Light marker that directs shipping traffic to the Maumee River, off shore from the Raison River, or by Stony Point. Typical perch rigs work best.

In fall, the sailboat buoys are still a good bet, along with the Toledo Light marker, Sputnik, or McDonalds which is a channel marker between the Toledo Light and Sputnik. There are many good areas for perch, so it is best to check with local bait and tackle shops before heading out.

Smallmouth bass fishing was great along the rock walls in Brest Bay and the shallow waters near the Raisin River.

Captain Rich Laaksonen, who fishes both Lake Michigan and the Western Basin of Lake Erie, says that he would often catch around 60 walleye in a 5-hour charter trip on Lake Erie, but not many were over 14 inches. Now he catches fewer fish, but many are in the 20-plus-inch size, making the total poundage of fish caught almost a draw from years ago compared to now.

He says the water being much cleaner with the zebra mussels results in the use of spoons and body baits. "Twenty years ago," says Laaksonen, "we would never think of trolling for walleye here, but today it is a standard method." He has fished for over 30 years in Lake Erie.

One of the problems when fishing Lake Erie, according to Captain Rich, is that when the wind is out of the east, the water easily becomes riled and subsequently dirty. You then have to move off shore, upwards of 15 miles or more. When the water is clear, you can fish from 3-15 miles from shore. As July approaches, the fish move deeper, and if the algae bloom hits in mid-summer, generally when the water temps hit the 80-degree mark, fishing becomes very difficult at best.

Laaksonen uses spoons (Dreamweaver) with small diving discs to fish the shallow waters in Lake Erie's Western Basin. He often fishes the dumping grounds where the structure is good and the phytoplankton hold the baitfish and thus the walleye as well as perch.

One of the most popular walleye fisheries in the Great Lakes, Erie constantly produces nice fish.

At a Glance

What: Hot spot for walleye, as well as good bass and perch on the rebound

Information/Guides: **www.walleyekid.com** (information on fishing this as well as other areas); **Captain Bruce Bronner,** *Kathy's Boyz 3* Docked behind the Erie Party Shoppe – Bolles Harbor, Michigan – Dock #20, 22140 Koths, Taylor, 48180, (313) 295-1533, (313) 415-6601 (cell); **CaptBruce@ KathysBoyz3.com; Captain Richard & Tracy Laaksonen,** 2790 Jebavy Dr. Ludington 49431, Home, (231) 843-6634; (cells) (231) 425-0125 or (231) 425-0288, email: info@finpowercharters.com, www.finpowercharters.com

Landings: Bolles Harbor DNR Boat Ramp, LaPlaisance Rd off I75 (Exit #11), Monroe, 48161; **Lake Erie Metro Park Boat Ramp,** 32481 Jefferson Ave., Rockwood, 48173, (734) 379-5020

Bait & Tackle:

• **Jeff's Bait & Tackle,** 1756 N. Dixie Hwy., Monroe, 48162, (734) 289-4901

• **jeffsbait.com.** Provides up-to date fishing reports on website

• **Erie Party Shoppe,** 6838 LaPlaisance Road, Monroe 48161, (734) 457-0006. Carries minnows, crawlers, sandwiches, soda, a good selection of local tackle favorites, as well as Michigan and Ohio fishing licenses. They can provide you with an up-to-date fishing report if you give them a call. They also offer fish-cleaning services. Park your boat on the road right in front of the store

• **Matthews Bait & Tackle,** 14011 LaPlaisance Rd., Monroe, 48161, (734) 241-4757. Offers a wide variety of services for people fishing out of the Bolles Harbor area. They have a fishing report online that is updated on a regular basis. They also offer fish-cleaning services, can hook you up with a guide, boat slip rentals

•**Bottomline Bait & Tackle,** 32660 Jefferson Ave., Rockwood, 48173, (734) 379-9762; Bottomline is located directly across from the Erie Metro Park entrance. Near the very southern end of the Detroit River and near Lake Erie. Selection of bait including minnows, crawlers, and a large selection of local and regional tackle. Minnows can be a problem in this area during the summer months as many of the bait shops catch their own supply – so call ahead

• **Bolles Harbor DNR Boat Ramp,** LaPlaisance Rd off I75 (Exit 11), Monroe, 48161

• **Lake Erie Metro Park Boat Ramp,** 32481 Jefferson Ave., Rockwood, 48173, (734) 379-5020